T0156035

Lecture Notes in Computer Science 14776

Founding Editors

Gerhard Goos
Juris Hartmanis

The series Lecture Notes in Computer Science (LNCS), including its subseries Lecture Notes in Artificial Intelligence (LNAI) and Lecture Notes in Bioinformatics (LNBI), has established itself as a medium for the publication of new developments in computer science and information technology research, teaching, and education.

LNCS enjoys close cooperation with the computer science R & D community, the series counts many renowned academics among its volume editors and paper authors, and collaborates with prestigious societies. Its mission is to serve this international community by providing an invaluable service, mainly focused on the publication of conference and workshop proceedings and postproceedings. LNCS commenced publication in 1973.

Da-Jung Cho · Jongmin Kim
Editors

Unconventional Computation and Natural Computation

21st International Conference, UCNC 2024
Pohang, South Korea, June 17–21, 2024
Proceedings

 Springer

Editors
Da-Jung Cho 🆔
Ajou University
Suwon, Korea (Republic of)

Jongmin Kim 🆔
Pohang University of Science and
Technology
Pohang, Korea (Republic of)

ISSN 0302-9743   ISSN 1611-3349 (electronic)
Lecture Notes in Computer Science
ISBN 978-3-031-63741-4   ISBN 978-3-031-63742-1 (eBook)
https://doi.org/10.1007/978-3-031-63742-1

This Springer imprint is published by the registered company Springer Nature Switzerland AG
The registered company address is: Gewerbestrasse 11, 6330 Cham, Switzerland

If disposing of this product, please recycle the paper.

Preface

The 21st International Conference on Unconventional Computation and Natural Computation (UCNC 2024) was held at the Pohang University of Science and Technology, Pohang, Gyeongsangbuk-do, Republic of Korea, on June 17–21, 2024.

This 21st edition of the conference series was dedicated to Professor Cristian Calude in recognition of his founding and further developing of this conference series. The first conference took place in Auckland, New Zealand in 1998, where he is currently Chair Professor of Computer Science at the University of Auckland. He was also UCNC Steering Committee Chair and Co-chair for a long time, during which time he contributed enormously to shaping and developing the conference series. The UCNC community is deeply grateful to Professor Calude for his guidance and influence through the years.

The UCNC series of international conferences is a forum bringing together scientists from many different backgrounds who are united in their interest in novel forms of computation, human-designed computation inspired by nature, and computational aspects of natural processes. The 21st conference of the series continued the tradition of focusing on current important theoretical and experimental results. Typical, but not exclusive, UCNC topics of interest include amorphous computing, cellular automata, chaos and dynamical systems-based computing, cellular, chemical, evolutionary, bacterial, molecular, neural and optical computing, collision-based computing, quantum computing, DNA computing, membrane computing, material computing and programmable matter, super-Turing computation, swarm intelligence, and other nature-inspired algorithms.

The G. Rozenberg Natural Computing Award was established in 2023 to recognize outstanding achievements in the field of natural computing. The award is named after Professor Grzegorz Rozenberg to acknowledge his distinguished scientific achievements in many areas of science, including natural computing, as well as his crucial role in developing the UCNC conference series. Professor Rozenberg also invented the name and defined the scope of the natural computing area and continues to serve as Chair Emeritus of the UCNC Steering Committee.

This annual award is presented at the Unconventional Computation and Natural Computation conference. The recipient of the award is invited to give the award lecture in the given year. The UCNC Awards Committee selected Professor Susan Stepney from the Department of Computer Science, the University of York, UK, to be the recipient of the award in 2024 (UCNC 2024). She was recognized for her contributions to Natural Computing and Unconventional Computing.

The program committee of UCNC 2024 reviewed 27 full paper submissions, of which 19 were selected for presentation at the conference and publication in these proceedings. In addition, the conference program included a poster session, and four invited plenary talks by Paola Flocchini (University of Ottawa, Canada), Nikola Kasabov (Auckland University of Technology, New Zealand), Sung Ha Park

(Sungkyunkwan University, Republic of Korea), and Friedrich Simmel (Technical University of Munich, Germany).

Co-located workshops are essential elements of UCNC conferences. This time there were two such workshops: The Fifth International Workshop on Theoretical and Experimental Material Computing (TEMC 2024), organized by Susan Stepney (University of York, UK), and The Workshop on Cellular Automata, organized by Enrico Formenti (Université Côte d'Azur, France), Jarkko Kari (University of Turku, Finland), and Katsunobu Imai (Fukuyama University, Japan).

We warmly thank the invited speakers and the workshop organizers, all the authors of the contributed papers and posters, as well as the organizers of the workshops. We are also grateful to the members of the program committee and the external reviewers for their invaluable help in reviewing the submissions and selecting the papers to be presented at the conference. We thank the organizing committee of UCNC 2024 for their tireless help in taking care of all the numerous details in organizing the event. The conference would not have happened without the active support of the Department of Life Sciences at Pohang University of Science and Technology; POSTECH conference program; and the Department of Software and Computer Engineering at Ajou University. Finally, we thank the EasyChair conference system, and the LNCS team at Springer for helping in the process of making these proceedings.

June 2024
Da-Jung Cho
Jongmin Kim

Organization

Steering Committee

Thomas Bäck	Leiden University, The Netherlands
Cristian S. Calude	University of Auckland, New Zealand
Enrico Formenti (Co-chair)	Université Côte d'Azur, France
Lov K. Grover	Bell Labs, USA
Mika Hirvensalo (Co-chair)	University of Turku, Finland
Natasha Jonoska	University of South Florida, USA
Jarkko Kari	University of Turku, Finland
Seth Lloyd	Massachusetts Institute of Technology, USA
Giancarlo Mauri	Università degli Studi di Milano-Bicocca, Italy
Gheorghe Paun	Institute of Mathematics of the Romanian Academy, Romania
Grzegorz Rozenberg (Emeritus Chair)	Leiden University, The Netherlands
Arto Salomaa	University of Turku, Finland
Shinnosuke Seki (Co-chair)	University of Electro-Communications, Japan
Tomasso Toffoli	Boston University, USA
Carme Torras	Institute of Robotics and Industrial Informatics, Spain
Jan van Leeuwen	Utrecht University, The Netherlands

Program Committee

Thomas Bäck	Leiden University, The Netherlands
Daniela Besozzi	Università degli Studi di Milano-Bicocca, Italy
Cristian S. Calude	University of Auckland, New Zealand
Ho-Lin Chen	National Taiwan University, Taiwan
Da-Jung Cho (Co-chair)	Ajou University, Republic of Korea
Benjamin Doerr	École Polytechnique, France
David Doty	University of California, Davis, USA
Jérôme Durand-Lose	LIFO, Université d'Orléans, France
Matthias Függer	CNRS & LMF, ENS Paris-Saclay, France
Cody Geary	Aarhus University, Denmark
Daniela Genova	University of North Florida, USA
Masami Hagiya	University of Tokyo, Japan
Yo-Sub Han	Yonsei University, Republic of Korea
Jarkko Kari	University of Turku, Finland
Lila Kari	University of Western Ontario, Canada
Jongmin Kim (Co-chair)	Pohang University of Science and Technology, Republic of Korea
Andreas Malcher	University of Giessen, Germany

Luca Mariot	University of Twente, The Netherlands
Ian McQuillan	University of Saskatchewan, Canada
Pekka Orponen	Aalto University, Finland
Matthew Patitz	University of Arkansas, USA
Zornitza Prodanoff	University of North Florida, USA
Christian Scheideler	University of Paderborn, Germany
Shinnosuke Seki	University of Electro-Communications, Japan
Susan Stepney	University of York, UK
Damien Woods	Maynooth University, Ireland
Abuzer Yakaryilmaz	University of Latvia, Latvia

Organizing Committee

Da-Jung Cho	Ajou University, Republic of Korea
Yunjeong Choi	Pohang University of Science and Technology, Republic of Korea
Seongho Hong	Pohang University of Science and Technology, Republic of Korea
Jongmin Kim	Pohang University of Science and Technology, Republic of Korea
Shinnosuke Seki	University of Electro-Communications, Japan

Additional Reviewers

Blanc, Manon	Dimitrijevs, Maksims
Formenti, Enrico	Glos, Adam
Hader, Daniel	Hagiya, Masami
Hertling, Peter	Kutrib, Martin
Lotfi, Ali	Moltmaker, Wout
Wendlandt, Matthias	Wood, Cai

Abstracts of Invited Talks

Moving and Computing in Continuous Spaces

Paola Flocchini

University of Ottawa, Canada
paola.flocchini@uottawa.ca

Moving and Computing refers to the study of systems of computational mobile entities operating in discrete environments or in continuous spaces. In the past two decades, there has been an extensive research focus within distributed computing on the computational and complexity issues arising in systems of entities (called *robots*) operating in the Euclidean plane. Capable of computations and mobility, the robots are autonomous (they have no external control), homogeneous (they have the same capabilities and behavior), and identical (they have no visibly distinguishing features). They operate in sequences of Look-Compute-Move (LCM) activity cycles: in each cycle, an entity perceives the position of the other entities within its local coordinate system (Look), executes a set of deterministic rules, the same for all entities, to compute a destination (Compute), and moves toward the computed destination (Move). The main research concern is on determining the minimal requirements allowing the robots to perform a required task, to solve a given problem, such as *gathering* and *convergence* [1–3, 9, 18], *pattern formation* [5, 8, 10, 13, 16–18], *scattering* [14], etc. See [7] and chapters therein for a recent account.

There are four basic models, each prescribing different robots capabilities. In the most common (and de-facto standard) model, OBLOT, the robots are *oblivious* (have no memory of their activities in the previous cycles) and *silent* (have no explicit means of communication). In the stronger LUMI model, each robot is provided with a constant-size persistent memory, called *light*, visible to all robots, providing a limited form of memory and communication. In between the first two models in terms of robot's capabilities are FSTA, where the robots have a constant-size persistent memory but are silent, and FCOM, where robots can communicate a constant number of bits but are oblivious.

In all models, a crucial factor is the level of synchronization of the robots (including their activation) and the duration of each operation in each LCM cycle. In the *synchronous* setting (SSYNC), time is divided in rounds and, in each round, a subset of the robots is activated and execute a LCM cycle simultaneously. In the *asynchronous* (ASYNC) setting, each robot follows its own cycle without time constraints and independently from the others. For any setting, when to activate a robot is decided by an adversarial scheduler. The computational power of the system depends, within a model, on the scheduler and on any additional assumption on the individual robot's capabilities (e.g., see [4, 6, 11, 12, 15]).

In this talk, I review algorithmic and computability issues arising in such systems of autonomous mobile robots, focusing on the impact that those factors have on the computational power of the swarm.

References

1. Agmon, N., Peleg, D.: Fault-tolerant gathering algorithms for autonomous mobile robots. SIAM J. Comput. **36**(1): 56–82 (2006)
2. Ando, H., Oasa, Y., Suzuki, I., Yamashita, M.: A distributed memoryless point convergence algorithm for mobile robots with limited visibility. IEEE Trans. Robot. Autom. **5**, 818–828 (1999)
3. Cieliebak, M., Flocchini, P., Prencipe, G., Santoro, N.: Distributed computing by mobile robots: gathering. SIAM J. Comput. **41**(4), 829–879 (2012)
4. Das, S., Flocchini, P., Prencipe, G., Santoro, N., Yamashita, M.: Autonomous mobile robots with lights. Theor. Comput. Sci. **609**, 171–184 (2016)
5. Das, S., Flocchini, P., Santoro, N., Yamashita, M.: Forming sequences of geometric patterns with oblivious mobile robots. Distrib. Comput. **28**(2), 131–145 (2015)
6. Di Luna, G.A., Flocchini, P., Santoro, N., Viglietta, G.: TuringMobile: a turing machine of oblivious mobile robots with limited visibility and its applications. Distrib. Comput. **35**(2), 105–122 (2022)
7. Flocchini, P., Prencipe, G., Santoro, N., (eds.) Distributed Computing By Mobile Entities: Current Research in Moving and Computing. LNCS. Springer, Cham (2019). https://doi.org/10.1007/978-3-030-11072-7
8. Flocchini, P., Prencipe, G., Santoro, N., Viglietta, G.: Distributed computing by mobile robots: uniform circle formation. Theor. Comput. Sci., **30**(6), 413–457 (2017)
9. Flocchini, P., Prencipe, G., Santoro, N., Widmayer, P.: Gathering of asynchronous robots with limited visibility. Theor. Comput. Sci. **337**(1–3), 147–168 (2005)
10. Flocchini, P., Prencipe, G., Santoro, N., Widmayer, P.: Arbitrary pattern formation by asynchronous, anonymous, oblivious robots. Theor. Comput. Sci. **407**(1–3), 412–447 (2008)
11. Flocchini, P., Santoro, N., Sudo, Y., Wada, K.: On asynchrony, memory, and communication: separations and landscapes. In: 27th International Conference on Principles of Distributed Systems (OPODIS), pp. 28:1–28:23 (2023)
12. Flocchini, P., Santoro, N., Viglietta, G., Yamashita, M.: Rendezvous with constant memory. Theor. Comput. Sci. **621**, 57–72 (2016)
13. Fujinaga, N., Yamauchi, Y., Ono, H., Kijima, S., Yamashita, M.: Pattern formation by oblivious asynchronous mobile robots. SIAM J. Comput. **44**(3), 740–785 (2016)
14. Izumi, T., Kaino, D., Gradinariu Potop-Butucaru, M., Tixeuil, S.: On time complexity for connectivity-preserving scattering of mobile robots. Theor. Comput. Sci. **738**, 42–52 (2018)
15. Kirkpatrick, D.G., Kostitsyna, I., Navarra, A., et al.: On the power of bounded asynchrony: convergence by autonomous robots with limited visibility. Distrib. Comput. (2024). https://doi.org/10.1007/s00446-024-00463-7

16. Suzuki, I., Yamashita, M.: Distributed anonymous mobile robots: formation of geometric patterns. SIAM J. Comput. **28**(4), 1347–1363 (1999)
17. Yamashita, M., Suzuki, I.: Characterizing geometric patterns formable by oblivious anonymous mobile robots. Theor. Comput. Sci. **411**(26–28), 2433–2453 (2010)
18. Yamauchi, Y., Uehara, T., Kijima, S., Yamashita, M.: Plane formation by synchronous mobile robots in the three dimensional Euclidean space. J. ACM **64**(3), 16:1–16:43 (2017)

Evolving Associative Memories in Bio-Neuro Systems and Intelligent Machines: This Is All We Need

Nikola K. Kasabov[1,2,3]

[1] Auckland University of Technology, Auckland, New Zealand
[2] Institute for Information and Communication Technologies, Bulgarian Academy of Sciences, Sofia, Bulgaria
[3]Computer Engineering Department, Dalian University, China
nkasabov@aut.ac.nz.
https://academics.aut.ac.nz/nkasabov

Evolving associative memory (EAM) is perhaps one of the most fundamental principle of evolution in nature and development of living organisms, the ultimate result being the human brain. Still this principle is not much explored in terms of intelligent computation. EAM are natural or artificial systems that associate and capture incrementally and continuously related items, objects, processes and can be recalled/triggered using partial information.

One class of EAM is the class of evolving spatio-temporal associative memories (ESTAM) [1]. An ESTAM is a machine learning model that is trained on a full set of spatio-temporal variables, but can be successfully recalled on only a subset of the variables measured in different time intervals. In addition, an ESTAM model can be further incrementally evolved on a new set of variables measured at different time windows. ESTAM are build with the use of *evolving spatio-temporal learning (ESTL)* methods, where existing spatial-, temporal- and other multimodal data are integrated to train the model. The model captures evolvable and explainable spatio/specro temporal patterns and can be further evolved on new data.

Inspired by the ability of the human brain to always create EAM, this paper develops a framework for building such ESTAM using brain-inspired spiking neural network architectures, exemplified by NeuCube [2, 3]. NeuCube, similar to the brain, processes information represented as spikes forming binary time sequences. It has a 3D structure that is initialised using a brain template for brain data applications, but in general it can be initialised in a different way, still accounting for similarity of input temporal variables [3].

An ESTAM can be created using the NeuCube SNN architecture following a procedure [1]. The association and generalization accuracy of such a model is evaluated. Such ESTAM are capable of incremental and life-long transfer learning [4].

A major advantage of building ESTAM with SNN is that once a model is trained on whole data sets, it can be recalled on smaller data sets in both space and time, allowing for efficient and early future event prediction. ESTAM opens the field of machine intelligence for the development of large-scale global models for spatio-temporal data *classification, prediction, pattern identification and pattern retrieval*, that can be recalled and used locally, within the available local spatio-temporal data.

The paper presents selected applications for ESTAM, such as: biological and brain signals [5]; audio-visual data; financial and economic data [6]; and other. Overall, the paper concludes that intelligence is based on EAM and intelligent machines should be also built on this principle.

A NeuCube software development system that allows for building ESTAM is available from: https://www.aut.ac.nz/neucube.

Acknowledgement. The work is sponsored by Knowledgeengineeing.ai.

References

1. Kasabov, N.: STAM-SNN: Spatio-Temporal Associative Memories in Brain-inspired Spiking Neural Networks: Concepts and Perspectives. TechRxiv. Preprint (2023). https://doi.org/10.36227/techrxiv.23723208.v1
2. Kasabov, N.: NeuCube: A Spiking Neural Network Architecture for Mapping, Learning and Understanding of Spatio-Temporal Brain Data, Neural Networks, vol. 52, pp. 62–76 (2014). Elsevier. https://doi.org/10.1016/j.neunet.2014.01.006
3. Kasabov, N., Time-Space, Spiking Neural Networks and Brain-Inspired Artificial Intelligence. Springer, Heidelberg (2019). https://doi.org/10.1007/978-3-662-57715-8
4. Kasabov, N., et al.: Transfer learning of fuzzy spatio-temporal rules in the neucube brain-inspired spiking neural network: a case study on EEG spatio-temporal data. IEEE Trans. Fuzzy Syst. **31**(12), 4542–4552 (2023). Print ISSN: 1063-6706, Online ISSN: 1941-0034. https://doi.org/10.1109/TFUZZ.2023.3292802
5. Kasabov, N., Bahrami, H., Doborjeh, M., Wang, A.: Brain inspired spatio-temporal associative memories for neuroimaging data: EEG and fMRI. Bioeng. MDPI **10** (12), 1341 (2023). https://doi.org/10.3390/bioengineering10121341, https://www.mdpi.com/journal/bioengineering
6. AbouHassan, I., Kasabov, N., Bankar, T., et al.: PAMeT-SNN: Predictive Associative Memory for Multiple Time Series based on Spiking Neural Networks with Case Studies in Economics and Finance. PrePrint, TechRxiv (2023)

Biological Data Storage Advances with DNA Lossy Compression

Seongjun Seo and Sung Ha Park

Department of Physics, Sungkyunkwan University, Suwon, 16419,
Republic of Korea
ssjun1207@gmail.com
sunghapark@skku.edu

Abstract. DNA data storage systems have made considerable progress in overcoming the constraints of conventional storage media [1]. Research in this area highlights the creative methods being applied to harness the biochemical properties of DNA for high-density, efficient, and dependable data storage [2]. Advances in complex encoding techniques have tackled key issues related to DNA data storage, such as error correction and the prevention of sequence loss.

This study introduces two innovative DNA lossy compression models, Model A and Model B, developed to encode grayscale images into DNA sequences. These models aim to enhance information density and enable high-fidelity image recovery. Model A processes pixels in overlapped domains using linear interpolation, whereas Model B employs non-overlapped domains with nearest-neighbor interpolation. Our comparative analysis with the traditional JPEG compression method demonstrates these models' superiority in terms of information density and image quality restoration.

Significantly, through the application of these models on the MNIST dataset, we validated their efficiency and the recognizability of decompressed images. The performance of convolutional neural networks in recognizing these images further corroborates their practical utility. Model B2, a specific iteration of Model B, excels in balancing high information density with preserved image quality, suggesting its potential for robust DNA-based data storage solutions.

This research not only presents a leap in the capabilities of DNA as a medium for high-density data storage but also opens new avenues for the future of biological data storage technologies. Our findings highlight the advantages of integrating DNA lossy compression into modern data storage systems, offering a promising direction for overcoming the limitations of conventional storage media. As we move forward, the scalability and sustainability of DNA data storage are set to redefine digital information storage, potentially revolutionizing how we manage data for generations to come.

Keywords: DNA data storage · Lossy compression · Information density · Image quality assessment · MNIST classification

References

1. Ceze, L., Nivala, J., Strauss, K. Molecular digital data storage using DNA. Nat. Rev. Genet. **20**(8), 456–466 (2019)
2. Church, G.M., Gao, Y., Kosuri, S.: Next-generation digital information storage in DNA. Science **337**(6102), 1628–1628 (2012)

Static and Dynamic Super-Assemblies of DNA Origami Building Blocks

Friedrich C. Simmel

School of Natural Sciences, Technical University of Munich, Germany
simmel@tum.de

Abstract. DNA origami allows the construction of almost arbitrarily shaped nanostructures with nanometer precision using around 100 individual oligonucleotides for objects around 100 nm in size, but this approach becomes impractical for much larger structures. Rather than making ever-larger origami objects, a better strategy is to use DNA origami structures as programmable building blocks for the self-assembly of super-structures. Recent years have seen various approaches to create such super-assemblies, seeking control through the shape of building blocks, precisely defined interactions, nucleation kinetics, or the accumulation of mechanical strain. Here, we discuss the formation of different structures using radially symmetric DNA origami building blocks with programmable nearest-neighbor interactions. These programmable blocks can self-assemble into giant flat membranes, closed containers of various sizes, and finite assemblies, depending on the designed interactions [1]. Furthermore, we explore making these origami blocks dynamic by attaching switchable molecular elements that can be manipulated with externally applied electric or magnetic fields. Such elements have recently enabled the realization of different molecular machines [2, 3]. By connecting these dynamic elements into extended arrays and allowing them to interact, we open up the possibility of creating dynamic cellular automata-like DNA origami assemblies, where each structure may exist in multiple states determined by its neighbors and an external field. This programmable self-assembly of static and dynamic DNA nanostructures from tailored building blocks offers a powerful bottom-up approach for constructing sophisticated nanoscale systems with potential applications in biomedical sensing and molecular computing.

Keywords: DNA origami · Self-assembly

References

1. Karfusehr, C., Eder, M., Simmel, F.C.: Self-assembled cell-scale containers made from DNA origami membranes. bioRxiv 2024.02.09.579479 (2024)
2. Vogt, M., Langecker, M., Gouder, M., et al.: Storage of mechanical energy in DNA nanorobotics using molecular torsion springs. Nat. Phys. **19**, 741–751 (2023). https://doi.org/10.1038/s41567-023-01938-3
3. Rothfischer, F., Vogt, M., Kopperger, E., Gerland, U., Simmel, F.C.: From brownian to deterministic motor movement in a DNA-based molecular rotor. Nano Lett. (2024). https://doi.org/10.1021/acs.nanolett.4c00675

Automata Chemistry Experiments with Replicators and Parasites

Susan Stepney (ID)

Department of Computer Science, University of York, UK
susan.stepney@york.ac.uk

The Stringmol automata chemistry is designed for studying *in silico* evolution [3], the evolution of evolution, and open-ended evolution [1, 6, 7, 9]. Strings of a specially-designed assembly language bind together, with one executing and the other providing data. Experiments start from an initial set of strings hand-designed to replicate, and evolve because the copy opcode copy has small probability of miscopying. Strings also have a low rate of decay, providing the evolutionary pressure: replicate or die.

A well-mixed (aspatial) system of Stringmol replicators undergoes evolution, exhibiting a series of emergent behaviours, such as mutant takeover, hypercycles, macromutations, and evolution of non-replicating parasites. Once parasites become dominant, the system rapidly goes extinct: parasites outcompete the replicators, then are unable to survive independently [4].

I will discuss experiments in an "RNA-world" like system, where strings designed to be replicators evolve in a spatial environment. Parasites still rapidly evolve, but the spatiality provides the distance and time for defences against those parasites to evolve; further parasites and further defences evolve in ever more complex scenarios [5]. The resulting complexity requires a move from defining 'parasites' in isolation to defining 'parasitic reaction networks' in the context of other strings [8].

I will also discuss experiments in a "DNA-world" like system, where an initial string is crafted to be an analogue of a von Neumann universal constructor, and show how this can evolve different behaviours without changing the string sequence; this 'semantic takeover' demonstrates that the meaning of the 'DNA' is contextual, depending on the other active strings in the system [2].

Acknowledgments. Some of this work was performed in the Plazzmid project (EPSRC grant EP/F031033/1) and some in the EvoEvo project (EU FET Proactive Grant ID 610427).

References

1. Banzhaf, W., et al.: Defining and simulating open-ended novelty: requirements, guidelines, and challenges. Theory Biosci. **135**(3), 131–161 (2016). https://doi.org/10.1007/s12064-016-0229-7

2. Clark, E.B., Hickinbotham, S.J., Stepney, S.: Semantic closure demonstrated by the evolution of a universal constructor architecture in an artificial chemistry. J. Roy. Soc. Interface **14**(130) (2017). https://doi.org/10.1098/rsif.2016.1033
3. Stepney, S., et al.: Maximising the adjacent possible in automata chemistries. Artif. Life **22**(1), 49–75 (2016). https://doi.org/10.1162/ARTL_a_00180
4. Hickinbotham, S., et al.: Diversity from a monoculture: effects of mutation-on-copy in a string-based artificial chemistry. In: ALife XII, pp. 386–393. MIT Press (2010)
5. Hickinbotham, S.J., Stepney, S., Hogeweg, P.: Nothing in evolution makes senseexcept in the light of parasitism: evolution of complex replication strategies. Roy. Soc. Open Sci. **8**(8), 210441 (2021). https://doi.org/10.1098/rsos.210441
6. Stepney, S.: Modelling and measuring open-endedness. In: OEE4 Workshop, at ALife 2021, Prague, Czech Republic (Online), July 2021 (2021). http://workshops.alife.org/oee4/
7. Stepney, S., Hickinbotham, S.: Innovation, variation, and emergence in an automatachemistry. In: ALife 2020, Montreal, Canada (Virtual), July 2020, pp. 753–760. MIT Press (2020). https://doi.org/10.1162/isal_a_00265
8. Stepney, S., Hickinbotham, S.: What is a Parasite? Defining reaction and networkproperties in an open ended automata chemistry. In: ALIFE 2021: The 2021 Conference on Artificial Life. MIT Press (2021). https://doi.org/10.1162/isal_a_00413
9. Stepney, S., Hickinbotham, S.: On the open-endedness of detecting open-endedness. Artif. Life **29** (2023). https://doi.org/10.1162/artl_a_00399

Contents

Bonding Grammars

Tikhon Pshenitsyn$^{(\boxtimes)}$ (ID)

Steklov Mathematical Institute of Russian Academy of Sciences, 8 Gubkina Street, Moscow 119991, Russian Federation
tpshenitsyn@mi-ras.ru

Abstract. We introduce bonding grammars, a graph grammar formalism developed to model DNA computation. It is a modification of fusion grammars introduced by Kreowski, Kuske and Lye in 2017. Bonding is a graph transformation that consists of merging two hyperedges into a single larger one. We show why bonding models DNA pairing better than fusion. Then, we investigate properties of bonding grammars. First, we study the relationship between bonding grammars and hyperedge replacement grammars proving that the classes of languages generated by them are incomparable. Secondly, we prove that bonding grammars naturally generalise regular sticker systems. Finally, we prove that the membership problem for bonding grammars is NP-complete.

Keywords: graph grammar · fusion grammar · sticker system · hyperedge replacement grammar · NP-complete · DNA computing

1 Introduction

There is a variety of formal apporaches developed to formalise DNA computation (see the overview of those in [8]). Since a nucleotide chain can be described as a string over the alphabet $\{A, T, C, G\}$, it is natural to model DNA computation as a series of transformations of string-based structures. A prominent example of such a string-based approach is sticker systems [10]. They deal with "incomplete molecules", structures defined as pairs of strings with certain properties, on which the sticking operation is defined. Thus, in general, most DNA-inspired formalisms belong to the language and automata theory for strings.

However, instead of simulating a DNA molecule by a generalised string, one could also represent it as a graph. This choice would allow one to describe the interactions occurring between molecules by means of graph transformations and thus to enter the vast field of graph transformation and graph grammars (see its overview in [12]). In 2017, such a novel kind of graph grammars was introduced by Kreowski, Kuske and Lye, which is called *fusion grammars* [4]. As the authors say, it is inspired by various fusion processes occurring in nature and abstract science, and, in particular, by fusion in DNA double strands according to the Watson-Crick complementarity. The thesis [7] is an extensive survey of fusion grammars. In the fusion grammar approach, molecules are modeled by hypergraphs (see the formal definition of a hypergraph in Sect. 2). Hypergraphs have labels on hyperedges; the label alphabet includes fusion labels, each fusion label A being accompanied with the complementary one $\overline{A}$. Hyperedges with complementary labels can be fused, which means that their corresponding incident vertices are identified, and the hyperedges themselves are removed. See an example of fusion below.

$$\tag{1}$$

In its simplest form, a fusion grammar is defined as a tuple $Z(1), \ldots, Z(k)$ consisting of connected hypergraphs $Z(i)$, which are informally interpreted as molecules. One can take arbitrary many exemplars of each "molecule" $Z(i)$ for $i = 1, \ldots, k$ and then apply fusions to the resulting collection of hypergraphs. Any connected component of the hypergraph obtained after fusions is said to be generated by the grammar. The definitions from [4] also involve a filtering procedure, which, however, we are not going to discuss in this paper.

Mathematically, fusion grammar is a nice formalism with interesting relations to other graph grammars [7]. However, it has two drawbacks. Firstly, one would expect that, in a graph-based approach modelling DNA pairing, one should represent a DNA strand as a path graph (at least as a first approximation). For example, one would anticipate that the strand defined by the sequence of nucleobases GAC should be represented by the graph $\overset{G\quad A\quad C}{\bullet\!\rightarrow\!\bullet\!\rightarrow\!\bullet\!\rightarrow\!\bullet}$. Then, one would expect that, in (1), if $\overline{A}$ stands for T, i.e. for the nucleobase complementary to A, then this fusion rule application should model forming a bond between the DNA strands GAC and CTG. However, the result of fusion presented in (1) does not look as two strands connected to each other. From the biological point of view, if an edge of a graph is interpreted as a nucleobase, then it is strange that fusion results in disappearance of the nucleobases participating in fusion. Instead, one would expect that fusion of two molecules binds them together, i.e. that fusion of two connected hypergraphs always results in a larger connected hypergraph. This is not the case in (1). Note that, in [5], the authors show how to adapt Adleman's experiment to fusion grammars; however, their adaptation does not directly represent biological structure of DNA molecules involved (see details in [5]) so one would like to seek for a more straightforward simulation using graph grammars.

Another drawback of fusion grammars is that no fast algorithms are known which check whether a hypergraph is generated by a fusion grammar; the recently claimed upper complexity bound is NEXPTIME [9]. Even decidability of this problem is hard to prove, which is again due to the fact that edges disappear after fusion without a trace. The question arises if the supposedly high algorithmic complexity of fusion grammars pays back; one might expect that the basic principles of DNA pairing could be described by a graph formalism of less complexity.

A natural and simple idea that solves all the abovementioned problems is to change the fusion operation in the following way. Instead of making two hyperedges disappear and their attachment vertices be identified, let us combine two hyperedges into a single larger hyperedge without identifying vertices. The fusion rule application (1) then turns into the following one:

$$
\begin{array}{c}
G \quad A \quad C \\
\bullet\!\!\to\!\bullet\!\!\to\!\bullet\!\!\to\!\bullet \\
\bullet\!\!\to\!\bullet\!\!\to\!\bullet\!\!\to\!\bullet \\
C \quad T \quad G
\end{array}
\;\Rightarrow\;
\begin{array}{c}
G \quad 1 \qquad 2 \quad C \\
\bullet\!\!\to\!\bullet\; \boxed{A \otimes T} \;\bullet\!\!\to\!\bullet \\
\bullet\!\!\to\!\bullet\; {}_{3} \qquad {}_{4} \;\bullet\!\!\to\!\bullet \\
C \qquad\qquad\qquad G
\end{array}
\qquad (2)
$$

Here $A \otimes T$ is the label of the resulting hyperedge, which stands for the combination of A and T. We call such an operation of combining two hyperedges into a single one *bonding* because it models the situation where two nucleobases are paired with each other via a hydrogen bond thus forming a base pair. If the edges with the labels A and T from (2) are interpreted as nucleobases, then the hyperedge with the label $A \otimes T$, which is obtained after bonding, should be interpreted as a base pair[1].

On the basis of bonding, in Sect. 3, we define the notion of *bonding grammar* analogous to the notion of fusion grammar. In Sect. 3.1, we study properties of this new kind of graph grammars, in particular, its relation to hypergraph context-free grammars (also known as hyperedge replacement grammars [12]). We show that either of the two formalisms is able to generate a language the other one cannot generate. In Sect. 3.2, we prove that bonding grammars form a subclass of fusion grammars. In Sect. 3.3, we show that bonding grammars naturally extend regular sticker systems. In Sect. 3.4, we prove that the membership problem for bonding grammars is NP-complete, which is better than the known NEXPTIME algorithm for fusion grammars. This shows that bonding grammars have reasonable level of complexity, many problems from the graph theory being NP-complete. To prove NP-hardness we use the problem of partitioning a graph into triangles for graphs of bounded degree [11].

2   Preliminaries

By $[k]$ we denote the set $\{1, \ldots, k\}$. In this work, elements of A^k are treated either as strings (words), as tuples or as multisets with a fixed linear order. If $w \in A^k$, then its i-th component is denoted by $w(i)$ (for $i \in [k]$). If $w \in A^k$, then $|w| = k$ is the length of w as a string. A^* is the union of A^k for $k \in \mathbb{N}$, and $A^0 = \{\lambda\}$ consists of the empty word. The notation $a \in w$ for $w \in A^k$ stands for $a \in \{w(1), \ldots, w(k)\}$.

---

[1] The notation $\otimes$ refers to the multiplicative conjunction of linear logic. Linear logic is usually considered as a logic of resources, and the formula $A \otimes B$ of linear logic stands for a combination of a resource of type A and a resource of type B. This interpretation is similar to the one from this work. It is interesting to study whether bonding and other operations on DNA molecules can be described using linear logic.

Hypergraphs. Our definition of a hypergraph is similar to that from [4] where hypergraphs are directed and have labels on hyperedges. This way of defining hypergraph is common in the literature on hyperedge replacement grammars [2].

A *typed set* M is the set M along with a fixed type function $type : M \to \mathbb{N}$.

Definition 1. *Given a typed set Σ called the label alphabet, a hypergraph H over Σ is a tuple $H = (V, E, att, lab)$ where V is a finite set of vertices, E is a finite set of hyperedges, $att : E \to V^*$ is an attachment (a function that assigns a string consisting of vertices to each hyperedge; these vertices are called attachment vertices), and $lab : E \to \Sigma$ is a labeling such that $type(lab(e)) = |att(e)|$ for any $e \in E_H$. The components of H are denoted by V_H, E_H, att_H and lab_H. The set of hypergraphs over Σ is denoted by $\mathcal{H}(\Sigma)$.*

In drawings of hypergraphs, small circles represent vertices, labeled rectangles represent hyperedges with their labels, and attachment is represented by numbered lines. If a hyperedge has exactly two attachment vertices, then it is depicted by a labeled arrow that goes from the first attachment vertex to the second one.

Example 1. The hypergraph (V, E, att, lab) where $V = \{v_1, v_2, v_3\}$, $E = \{e_1, e_2, e_3\}$, $att(e_1) = v_1$, $att(e_2) = v_1v_2v_3$, $att(e_3) = v_2v_2$, $lab(e_1) = X$, $lab(e_2) = Y$, $lab(e_3) = Z$ looks as follows: .

The function $type : E_H \to \mathbb{N}$ returns the number of attachment vertices of a hyperedge in the hypergraph H: $type(e) := |att_H(e)|$.

Given a hypergraph H, a sequence $(i_1, e_1, o_1), \ldots, (i_n, e_n, o_n) \in (\mathbb{N} \times E_H \times \mathbb{N})^*$ is a *path between* $v \in V_H$ *and* $v' \in V_H$ if $att_H(e_1)(i_1) = v$, $att_H(e_n)(o_n) = v'$, and $att_H(e_k)(o_k) = att_H(e_{k+1})(i_{k+1})$ for $k = 1, \ldots, n-1$. A hypergraph is *connected* if there is a path between any two vertices.

The notion of an isomorphism of hypergraphs is standard. As is usually done in the literature on graph grammars (see discussion in [12]), we often identify isomorphic hypergraphs because we are interested in their structure rather than in what objects their vertices and hyperedges are.

Below we define several operations on hypergraphs.

1. The *disjoint union* $H_1 + H_2$ of hypergraphs H_1, H_2 is the hypergraph $(V_{H_1} \sqcup V_{H_2}, E_{H_1} \sqcup E_{H_2}, att, lab)$ such that $att|_{H_i} = att_{H_i}$, $lab|_{H_i} = lab_{H_i}$ $(i = 1, 2)$. That is, we just put the hypergraphs H_1 and H_2 together. Let $k \cdot H$ be the disjoint union of k isomorphic copies of H. Let $0 \cdot H$ be the hypergraph with no vertices and no hyperedges.
2. Given a vector $m = (m(1), \ldots, m(k)) \in \mathbb{N}^k$ and a tuple of hypergraphs $H = (H(1), \ldots, H(k))$, let $m \cdot H$ denote $m(1) \cdot H(1) + \ldots + m(k) \cdot H(k)$.
3. Let H be a hypergraph and let $E \subseteq E_H$. Then $H - E$ is the hypergraph $(V_H, E_H \setminus E, att_H \upharpoonright_{E_H \setminus E}, lab_H \upharpoonright_{E_H \setminus E})$; i.e. we simply remove hyperedges that belong to E from H.
4. Let H be a hypergraph and let $\equiv$ be an equivalence relation on V_H. Then $H/\equiv$ is the hypergraph with the set $\{[v]_\equiv \mid v \in V_H\}$ of vertices, the set E_H

of hyperedges, the same labeling lab_H and with the new attachment defined as follows: $att_{H/\equiv}(e) = [att_H(e)(1)]_\equiv [att_H(e)(2)]_\equiv \ldots [att_H(e)(type(e))]_\equiv$.

Sets of hypergraphs are called *hypergraph languages*. The "canonical" formalism for generating hypergraph languages is *hyperedge replacement grammar* (HR-grammar), also known as hypergraph context-free grammar. It naturally generalises context-free grammars for strings and, in particular, enjoys many similar properties, such as the pumping lemma, the Parikh theorem etc. We shall compare generative capacity of bonding grammars with that of HR-grammars. However, we are not going to provide the formal definition of the latter because we do not need it for reasonings. We refer the reader to [2, 12] for the definitions.

Fusion Grammar. Fusion grammar was introduced in [4]. After that, its definition has undergone slight modifications, its most recent version is presented in [7]. There, the notion of fusion grammars is based on the fusion operation along with additional procedures such as filtering the hypergraphs using markers and removing hyperedges labeled by connector labels. In this paper, we are not concerned with these operations. The formalism we are going to introduce is called *fusion grammar without markers* in [4]; we, however, call it simply *fusion grammar* for the sake of brevity. Let T and F be two disjoint finite typed alphabets called the *terminal alphabet* and the *fusion alphabet* resp. Let $\overline{F} = \{\overline{A} \mid A \in F\}$ be the alphabet of complementary fusion labels.

Definition 2. *A* fusion grammar *is a triple* $FG = (Z, F, T)$ *where* $Z = (Z(1), \ldots, Z(k))$ *is a tuple of connected hypergraphs* $Z(i) \in \mathcal{H}(T \cup F \cup \overline{F})$.

Definition 3. *Let* H *be a hypergraph with two hyperedges* $e, \overline{e} \in E_H$ *such that* $lab_H(e) = A \in F$ *and* $lab_H(\overline{e}) = \overline{A} \in \overline{F}$. *Let* $X = H - \{e, \overline{e}\}$ *and let* $H' = X/\equiv$ *where* $\equiv$ *is the smallest equivalence relation on* V_H *such that* $att_H(e)(i) \equiv att_H(\overline{e})(i)$ *for all* $i = 1, \ldots, type(A)$. *In other words,* H' *is obtained from* X *by identifying corresponding attachment vertices of* e *and* $\overline{e}$. *Then we say that* H' *is obtained from* H *by* fusion *and denote this as* $H \Rightarrow_{fs} H'$.

Definition 4. *A fusion grammar* $FG = (Z, F, T)$ *such that* $|Z| = k$ *generates a hypergraph* H *if there exist* $m \in \mathbb{N}^k$ *and* G *such that* $m \cdot Z \Rightarrow_{fs}^* G$, *and* H *is a connected component of* G.

Example 2. Let (Z, F, T) be the fusion grammar where $Z = (Z(1), Z(2))$ consists of the hypergraphs $Z(1) = \overset{\overline{C}\ \ A\ \ C}{\bullet\!\!\rightarrow\!\!\bullet\!\!\rightarrow\!\!\bullet\!\!\rightarrow\!\!\bullet}$ and $Z(2) = \overset{C\ \ \overline{A}\ \ \overline{C}}{\bullet\!\!\rightarrow\!\!\bullet\!\!\rightarrow\!\!\bullet\!\!\rightarrow\!\!\bullet}$. This grammar generates the hypergraph $H_0 = \overset{\overline{C}\ \ \ C}{\bullet\!\!\rightarrow\!\!\bullet\!\!\leftarrow\!\!\bullet}$, as (1) shows. Indeed, $Z(1) + Z(2) \Rightarrow_{fs} H$ where H contains H_0 as a connected component (assuming that $G = \overline{C}$ and $T = \overline{A}$).

Sticker Systems. An overview of sticker systems can be found in [8, 10]. We are going to use the definitions from [6]. In the original definition, sticker systems generate double strands (pairs of strings) such that symbols in the upper strand are in the complementarity relation with those in the lower strand. However, for the sake of simplifying presentation, following [6], we consider only sticker systems with the identity complementarity relation.

Let Σ be a finite alphabet. The set $D_{\overline{\Sigma}}^{=}$ consists of complete double strands of the form $\begin{bmatrix} w \\ w \end{bmatrix}$ for $w \in \Sigma^*$, $w \neq \lambda$. The set E_Σ of sticky ends consists of pairs of strings of the form $\begin{pmatrix} v \\ \lambda \end{pmatrix}$ and $\begin{pmatrix} \lambda \\ v \end{pmatrix}$ where $v \in \Sigma^*$; if $v = \lambda$, then the corresponding sticky end is denoted by λ. Let $LR_\Sigma = E_\Sigma \cdot D_{\overline{\Sigma}}^{=} \cdot E_\Sigma$ and let $R_\Sigma = D_{\overline{\Sigma}}^{=} \cdot E_\Sigma$; here the product stands for juxtaposition (and λ is the unit of this product). Finally, the set D_Σ of *dominoes* (called *incomplete molecules* in [8]) equals $E_\Sigma \cup LR_\Sigma$. Below, we present several examples of dominoes along with another way of their representation, which we call *domino representation*.

$$\begin{pmatrix} ab \\ \lambda \end{pmatrix} \begin{bmatrix} cd \\ cd \end{bmatrix} \begin{pmatrix} \lambda \\ e \end{pmatrix} = \boxed{\begin{smallmatrix} a\ b\ c\ d \\ \ \ \ c\ d\ e \end{smallmatrix}}\ ; \qquad \begin{bmatrix} aa \\ aa \end{bmatrix} \begin{pmatrix} e \\ \lambda \end{pmatrix} = \boxed{\begin{smallmatrix} a\ a\ e \\ a\ a \end{smallmatrix}}\ ; \qquad \begin{pmatrix} \lambda \\ abc \end{pmatrix} = \boxed{\ \underset{a\ b\ c}{}\ }.$$

Given $x \in LR_\Sigma$ and $y \in D_\Sigma$, one can define the sticking operation $x \cdot y$ and $y \cdot x$. Informally, sticking $x \cdot y$ of x and y consists of placing y to the right from x and then assembling them into a single domino if the right sticky end of x matches the left sticky end of y. For example:

$$\begin{pmatrix} ab \\ \lambda \end{pmatrix} \begin{bmatrix} cd \\ cd \end{bmatrix} \begin{pmatrix} \lambda \\ e \end{pmatrix} \cdot \begin{pmatrix} e \\ \lambda \end{pmatrix} \begin{bmatrix} aab \\ aab \end{bmatrix} = \begin{pmatrix} ab \\ \lambda \end{pmatrix} \begin{bmatrix} cdeaab \\ cdeaab \end{bmatrix} = \boxed{\begin{smallmatrix} a\ b\ c\ d\ e\ a\ a\ b \\ \ \ \ c\ d\ e\ a\ a\ b \end{smallmatrix}}$$

The formal definition of sticking can be found in [8]. A *sticking rule* is a pair of dominoes $r = (d_1, d_2) \in D_\Sigma^2$ (at least one domino in r must be non-empty). An application of r to $u \in LR_\Sigma$ consists of sticking d_1 to the left from u and d_2 to the right from u resulting in $u' = d_1 \cdot u \cdot d_2$. This is denoted by $u \Rightarrow_{st} u'$. A *sticker system* is a triple $SS = (\Sigma, A, D)$ where $A \subseteq LR_\Sigma$ is a finite set of axioms and D is a finite set of sticking rules. We say that a sticker system *generates* $d \in LR_\Sigma$ if $a \Rightarrow_{st}^* d$ for some $a \in A$. A sticker system (Σ, A, D) is *regular* if each rule in D is of the form (λ, d) and if $A \subseteq R_\Sigma$. Note that, if a domino d is generated by a regular sticker system, then $d \in R_\Sigma$.

3   Bonding Grammar

Our goal is to modify fusion grammars in order to develop a graph grammar approach better representing pairing of DNA molecules. We adhere to the following principle: a hyperedge of a hypergraph must either represent a nucleotide or a bond between nucleotides. Fusion grammars do not meet this requirement because, if two hyperedges e_1 and e_2 are fused, then they disappear, which is strange from the biological point of view (how can two compounds vanish after being connected?). During annealing of two single DNA strands, hydrogen bonds arise, and pairs of bonded nucleobases form new units called *base pairs*. This leads us to the following natural idea: if e_1 and e_2 are two hyperedges representing two complementary nucleobases, then the process of fusing them should be modeled by a graph transformation where these hyperedges merge into a single hyperedge. This idea is formalised in the following definitions.

Definition 5. *A* bonding grammar *is a tuple* $(Z, N, T, \otimes)$ *where*

1. *N and T are disjoint finite typed sets;*
2. *$Z = (Z(1), \ldots, Z(k))$ is a tuple of connected hypergraphs $Z(i) \in \mathcal{H}(N \cup T)$;*
3. *$\otimes : N \times N \to T$ is a partial injective function called the* bond function *such that, if $A_1 \otimes A_2$ is defined, then $type(A_1 \otimes A_2) = type(A_1) + type(A_2)$.*

The set N (nonterminal alphabet) consists of nucleobases. The bond function takes two labels corresponding to nucleobases and returns a label that denotes the resulting base pair. E.g. if $C, G \in N$, then $C \otimes G$ denotes the base pair of cytosine and guanine. We consider the label $C \otimes G$ to be terminal. The domain of the bond function is interpreted as the complementarity relation on N, which describes between which pairs from $N \times N$ bonds can arise.

It is natural to assume that the bond function is injective because, if a nucleobase A_1 is paired with a nucleobase A_2 and B_1 is paired with B_2 for $(A_1, A_2) \neq (B_1, B_2)$, then the resulting base pairs are also different, so $A_1 \otimes A_2 \neq B_1 \otimes B_2$. Of course, one could define bonding grammars without the requirement on $\otimes$ being injective. However, this restriction simplifies technical arguments; moreover, bond functions are indeed injective in all the bonding grammars considered in this paper. Thus we decide to include injectivity of $\otimes$ in the definition.

Definition 6. *Let $BG = (Z, N, T, \otimes)$ be a bonding grammar and let H be a hypergraph with two distinct hyperedges $e_1, e_2 \in E_H$ such that $lab_H(e_i) = A_i \in N$. Assume that $A_1 \otimes A_2$ is defined. Let us define the hypergraph H' as follows.*

- *$V_{H'} = V_H$;$\quad$ $E_{H'} = (E_H \setminus \{e_1, e_2\}) \cup \{e'\}$ where e' is a new hyperedge;*
- *$att_{H'}(e) = att_H(e)$ and $lab_{H'}(e) = lab_H(e)$ for $e \neq e'$;*
- *$att_{H'}(e') = att_H(e_1)att_H(e_2)$ and $lab_{H'}(e') = A_1 \otimes A_2$.*

We say that H' is obtained from H by bonding *and denote this by $H \Rightarrow_{BG} H'$ or by $H \Rightarrow_{bn} H'$ (if the grammar is clear from the context).*

Example 3. Using bonding, the process of pairing two single DNA strands, say, GAC and CTG, is represented as follows (for $C \otimes G$ and $A \otimes T$ being defined):

8   T. Pshenitsyn

Definition 7. *A* bonding grammar *$BG = (Z, N, T, \otimes)$ such that $|Z| = k$ generates a hypergraph $H \in \mathcal{H}(N \cup T)$ if there exists $m \in \mathbb{N}^k$ such that $m \cdot Z \Rightarrow_{BG}^* H$. The* language *$L(BG)$ consists of hypergraphs from $\mathcal{H}(T)$ generated by BG.*

Example 4. The following example is inspired by [4, Example 2]. Consider the bonding grammar $PsT = (Z, N, T, \otimes)$ with $N = \{A, B, C, D\}$ (all the labels are of type 1) and $T = \{a, b\}$ (all the labels are of type 2). Let $\otimes$ be defined as follows:

$A \otimes C = a$, $B \otimes D = b$. Let Z consist of the hypergraph $Z(1) = \boxed{C}\!-\!\bullet\!-\!\boxed{A}$ (with $\boxed{B}$ above and $\boxed{D}$ below). Below,

an example of a derivation starting with the hypergraph $2 \cdot Z(1)$ is presented.

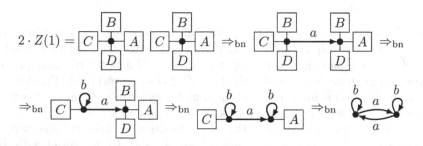

More generally, the bonding grammar PsT is able to generate grids with a-labeled and b-labeled hyperedges and with borders marked by hyperedges of type 1, as shown on the below left figure:

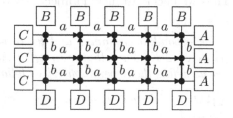 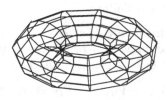

Clearly, if one also applies bonding to the remaining nonterminal hyperedges in this grid, they can obtain a toroidal graph. The shape of a toroidal graph is illustrated by the above right figure (the labels and directions of hyperedges are omitted). Therefore, the language $L(PsT)$ generated by the grammar of interest contains all toroidal graphs. However, obviously, there are many ways of bonding A-labeled and C-labeled hyperedges in a grid as well as B-labeled and D-labeled ones resulting in many different graphs. In [4], they are called *pseudotori* because they include tori but also Klein bottles and other shapes.

In Example 4, the hypergraph $Z(1)$ consists of several hyperedges of type 1 attached to the same vertex. We shall use hypergraphs of such a form later so let us introduce a more general definition.

Definition 8. Let $S = (S(1), \ldots, S(k))$ be a string of labels of type 1. Then $\&(S)$ is the hypergraph G defined as follows: $V_G = \{v\}$; $E_G = [k]$; $att_G(i) = v$, $lab_G(i) = S(i)$ for $i \in [k]$.

Here are two more examples of languages generated by bonding grammars.

Proposition 1. For each fixed $k \in \mathbb{N}$, the following languages are generated by bonding grammars:

- the set of connected k-regular (all vertices have degree k) directed graphs;
- the set of connected directed graphs of maximum degree $\leq k$.

Proof. Let $N = \{I, O\}$ where I, O are labels of type 1 and let $T = \{b\}$. Let $O \otimes I = b$. We define the hypergraph $Z_j^{(i)}$ for $0 \leq j \leq i$ as $\&(I^j, O^{i-j})$. Here I^j means $I, \ldots, I$ repeated j times. Then, to generate k-regular graphs, take the bonding grammar $BG_{reg}^{(k)} = \left(Z_{reg}^{(k)}, N, T, \otimes \right)$ where $Z_{reg}^{(k)} = \left(Z_0^{(k)}, \ldots, Z_k^{(k)} \right)$. Indeed, if $m \cdot Z_{reg}^{(k)} \Rightarrow_{bn}^* H$ for a connected hypergraph H, then, before bonding, there are exactly k hyperedges attached to each vertex (labeled by either O or I). After bonding, this results in each vertex having the degree exactly k; more precisely, if there are j I-labeled hyperedges and $(k-j)$ O-labeled hyperedges attached to a vertex v before bonding, then, after bonding, the in-degree of v equals j and the out-degree of v equals $(k-j)$.

To generate graphs of maximum degree at most k, take the bonding grammar $BG_{deg}^{(k)} = \left(Z_{deg}^{(k)}, N, T, \otimes \right)$ where the tuple $Z_{deg}^{(k)}$ is the concatenation of the tuples $Z_{reg}^{(0)}, \ldots, Z_{reg}^{(k)}$. $\qquad\square$

Example 5. Below, the hypergraphs $Z_j^{(i)}$ are presented for $0 \leq j \leq i \leq 2$.

$$Z_0^{(0)} = \bullet \qquad Z_0^{(1)} = \bullet\!-\!\boxed{O} \qquad Z_1^{(1)} = \bullet\!-\!\boxed{I}$$

$$Z_0^{(2)} = \boxed{O}\!-\!\bullet\!-\!\boxed{O} \qquad Z_1^{(2)} = \boxed{I}\!-\!\bullet\!-\!\boxed{O} \qquad Z_2^{(2)} = \boxed{I}\!-\!\bullet\!-\!\boxed{I}$$

To generate the hypergraph $\bullet \xrightarrow{b} \bullet \xrightarrow{b} \bullet$ using $BG_{deg}^{(2)}$, take the hypergraphs $Z_0^{(1)}$, $Z_1^{(1)}$, and $Z_1^{(2)}$ and apply bonding as follows:

$$\bullet\!-\!\boxed{O}\,\boxed{I}\!-\!\bullet\!-\!\boxed{O}\,\boxed{I}\!-\!\bullet \;\Rightarrow_{bn}\; \bullet \xrightarrow{b} \bullet\!-\!\boxed{O}\;\boxed{I}\!-\!\bullet \;\Rightarrow_{bn}\; \bullet \xrightarrow{b} \bullet \xrightarrow{b} \bullet$$

The language of pseudotori from Example 4 as well as the language of connected k-regular graphs and that of connected graphs of maximum degree k (for $k > 3$) have unbounded treewidth. Indeed, all of them contain toroidal graphs, and it is proved in [3] that the toroidal graph obtained from the $n \times n$ grid by wrapping around edges between the topmost row and the bottom-most row and between the leftmost column and the rightmost column has treewidth $\geq 2n - 2$. As noted in [4], it is proved in [1, Proposition 4.7] that any language generated by an HR-grammar has bounded treewidth, and thus none of the abovementioned languages is generated by an HR-grammar.

3.1   Properties of Bonding Grammars

Let us discuss basic properties of bonding grammars. We start with the following simple observations that will be used later.

1. If $H \Rightarrow^*_{bn} H'$, then H and H' have the same set of vertices.
2. If $H \Rightarrow^*_{bn} H'$ and there is a path in H between two vertices $v_1, v_2 \in V_H$, then there also is a path between them in H'.

The reader might have noticed that, in Definition 7, the notion of a bonding grammar generating a hypergraph H is defined as the fact that $m \cdot Z \Rightarrow^*_{BG} H$ for some m, which is not the same as the corresponding definition for fusion grammars (Definition 4). To recall, a fusion grammar generates a hypergraph H if $m \cdot Z \Rightarrow^*_{fs} G$ for some G such that H is its connected component. We shall prove that these two definitions are equivalent for bonding grammars.

Proposition 2. *Let $BG = (Z, N, T, \otimes)$ be a bonding grammar. If $m \cdot Z \Rightarrow^*_{BG} G$ and H is a connected component of G, then $m' \cdot Z \Rightarrow^*_{BG} H$ for some m'.*

Proof. Let $Y = m \cdot Z$. Bonding does not change the set of vertices in a hypergraph, so $V_Y = V_G \supseteq V_H$. Consider the subhypergraph Y' of Y induced by the vertices from V_H. We claim that $Y' = m' \cdot Z$. Indeed, let Y consist of connected components $Y_1, \dots, Y_n$ (each of them is isomorphic to $Z(i)$ for some i). If $v_1 \in V_{Y_i} \cap V_H$ and $v_2 \in V_{Y_i}$, then v_2 must also belong to V_H, because, since v_1 and v_2 are connected by a path in Y, they are also connected by a path in G, so they belong to the same connected component of G, i.e. to H. Thus, Y' is the disjoint union of some connected components $Y_{i_1}, \dots, Y_{i_l}$ as desired. $\square$

There is an operation converse to bonding, which we call *breaking a bond*.

Definition 9. *Let H' be a hypergraph with a hyperedge e' such that $lab_{H'}(e') = A_1 \otimes A_2$. Let $type(A_i) = t_i$ for $i = 1, 2$. Let H be obtained from H' by removing e' and adding new hyperedges e_1, e_2 such that $att_H(e_1)(i) = att_{H'}(e')(i)$ for $i = 1, \dots, t_1$ and $att_H(e_2)(i) = att_{H'}(e')(t_1 + i)$ for $i = 1, \dots, t_2$. Let $lab_H(e_i) = A_i$ for $i = 1, 2$. Then we say that H is obtained from H' by* breaking the bond e'.

Clearly, H is obtained from H' by breaking a bond if and only if H' is obtained from H by bonding. Note that, for any $e' \in E_{H'}$, there is at most one pair of labels A_1 and A_2 such that $A_1 \otimes A_2 = lab_{H'}(e')$ due to injectivity of $\otimes$.

Definition 10. *Given a bonding grammar $BG = (Z, N, T, \otimes)$ and a hypergraph $H \in \mathcal{H}(N \cup T)$, a bond set for H is a set $\mathcal{B} \subseteq E_H$ such that the hypergraph obtained from H by breaking the bond e for each $e \in \mathcal{B}$ is of the form $m \cdot Z$.*

Clearly, H is generated by BG if and only if there is a bond set for H.

Remark 1. The following non-deterministic polynomial-time algorithm enables one to check if a hypergraph H can be generated by a bonding grammar BG:

1. Non-deterministically choose a set $\mathcal{B} \subseteq E_H$;
2. Break the bond e for each $e \in \mathcal{B}$ if possible (this is done deterministically);

3. Non-deterministically check if each connected component of the resulting hypergraph is isomorphic to $Z(j)$ for some j. If so, then H is generated by BG, otherwise it is not.

Therefore, the membership problem for bonding grammars lies in NP. Contrast this with the membership problem for fusion grammars, which is decidable but proving this is rather hard; the known deciding algorithm is in NEXPTIME [9]. In Sect. 3.4, we shall prove that bonding grammars are able to generate an NP-complete hypergraph language, so the membership problem for bonding grammars is intrinsically NP-complete. For graph grammars, the NP complexity level is acceptable because many problems from the graph theory are NP-complete. In particular, HR-grammars, also known as hypergraph context-free grammars, are able to generate an NP-complete graph language [12].

   Example 4 and Proposition 1 show that bonding grammars can generate languages of unbounded treewidth, which HR-grammars cannot generate. Conversely, HR-grammars can generate languages that bonding grammars cannot generate. To show this, let us define the notions of degree and degree set.

Definition 11. *For a hypergraph H, the degree of a vertex $v \in V_H$ is the cardinality of the set $\{(e, i) \mid e \in E_H, i \in [type(e)], and\ att_H(e)(i) = v\}$. The degree set of H is the set of degrees of its vertices.*

Proposition 3. *Let $BG = (Z, N, T, \otimes)$ be a bonding grammar where $|Z| = k$ and $M(i)$ is the degree set of $Z(i)$ for $i = 1, \ldots, k$. If BG generates a hypergraph H, then the degree set of H is contained in $M(1) \cup \ldots \cup M(k)$.*

This proposition follows from the trivial observation that bonding does not change degrees of vertices. Consequently, for any bonding grammar BG, the language $L(BG)$ has bounded degree. In what follows, bonding grammars cannot generate e.g. the language of star graphs, which can be generated by a HR-grammar [2]. Therefore, we have proved.

Theorem 1. *The class of languages generated by HR-grammars neither contains nor is contained in the class of languages generated by bonding grammars.*

3.2 Bonding Grammars and Fusion Grammars

Although bonding is defined differently from fusion, the former can be simulated using the latter. E.g., let $(Z, N, T, \otimes)$ be a bonding grammar and let $A_1, A_2 \in N$. If, for example, $type(A_1) = type(A_2) = 2$, then bonding looks as follows:

Let us introduce the fusion grammar (Z', N, T) where Z' is obtained from Z by adding, for each $A_1, A_2 \in N$ with $type(A_i) = t_i$, the hypergraph H to it such that: $V_H = [t_1 + t_2]$; $E_H = \{e_1, e_2, e'\}$; $att_H(e')(i) = i$ for $i \in [t_1 + t_2]$;

$att_H(e_1)(i) = i$ for $i \in [t_1]$; $att_H(e_2)(i) = t_1 + i$ for $i \in [t_2]$; $lab_H(e') = A_1 \otimes A_2$; $lab_H(e_i) = \overline{A_i}$ for $i = 1, 2$. For example, if $t_1 = t_2 = 2$, then

$$H = \overline{A_1} \begin{array}{c} 2 \\ \uparrow \end{array} \boxed{A_1 \otimes A_2} \begin{array}{c} 4 \\ \uparrow \end{array} \overline{A_2}$$

Then, one can easily prove that the language generated by this fusion grammar equals the language generated by the original bonding grammar. Thus bonding grammars actually represent a fragment of fusion grammars. Nevertheless, we claim that this is an important fragment because it is more feasible in terms of complexity than fusion grammars yet quite expressive, as we shall see.

3.3   Bonding Grammars and Sticker Systems

Bonding grammars are designed to model sticking of DNA molecules. Nicely, it turns out that they are able to simulate regular sticker systems. Below, we present an embedding of the latter in the former (compare it with Example 3).

Let $S = (\Sigma, A, D)$ be a regular sticker system. We define the bonding grammar $BG(S) = (Z_S, N, T, \otimes)$ as follows. The set N equals $\Sigma \cup \overline{\Sigma} \cup \{\alpha, \beta\}$ where $\overline{\Sigma} = \{\overline{a} \mid a \in \Sigma\}$ consists of new labels of the form $\overline{a}$, and α, β are also new labels. The set T equals $\widetilde{\Sigma} \cup \{\varphi\}$ where $\widetilde{\Sigma} = \{\widetilde{a} \mid a \in \Sigma\}$ also consists of new labels corresponding to those from Σ. Let $type(a) = type(\overline{a}) = 2$ and $type(\widetilde{a}) = 4$ for $a \in \Sigma$; let $type(\alpha) = type(\beta) = 1$; let $type(\varphi) = 2$. The bond function is defined as follows: $a \otimes \overline{a} = \widetilde{a}$ (for $a \in \Sigma$); $\alpha \otimes \beta = \varphi$. Clearly, it is injective.

Now, our goal is to present the function $\tau_D : D_\Sigma \setminus \{\lambda\} \to \mathcal{H}(N \cup T)$ that transforms dominoes into hypergraphs such that sticking of two dominoes is modeled by bonding of corresponding hypergraphs. Defining this function formally would be extremely tedious, so instead we start with illustrative examples.

Generally, if $d = \begin{bmatrix} a_1 \ldots a_n \\ a_1 \ldots a_n \end{bmatrix}$, then $\tau_D(d)$ has a sequence of hyperedges of type 4 with labels $\tilde{a}_1, \ldots, \tilde{a}_n$ consecutively connected by φ-labeled edges; there also are two α-labeled and two β-labeled hyperedges at the corners of this hypergraph. If a domino $d = d_1 d_2 d_3$ with $d_2 \in D_{\overline{\Sigma}}$ has the sticky end $d_1 = \begin{pmatrix} b_1 \ldots b_n \\ \lambda \end{pmatrix}$, then the sequence of edges with the labels $b_1, \ldots, b_n$ consecutively connected by φ-labeled edges replaces the northwestern β-labeled hyperedge of $\tau_D(d_2)$. Other kinds of sticky ends are treated similarly.

Each part of this translation is biologically grounded. Edges labeled by symbols from Σ and $\overline{\Sigma}$ model nucleobases; hyperedges with the labels α and β model 3′ and 5′ ends of a DNA strand; hyperedges with labels from $\tilde{\Sigma}$ model base pairs; φ-labeled edges represent phosphodiester bonds between nucleobases.

Let us also define the function $\tau_R : R_\Sigma \to \mathcal{H}(N \cup T)$. For $d \in R_\Sigma$, $\tau_R(d)$ is the hypergraph obtained from $\tau_D(d)$ by removing the northwestern β-labeled hyperedge and the southwestern α-labeled one. Now, we are ready to define Z_S:

Definition 12. *For a regular sticker system $S = (\Sigma, A, D)$, Z_S is the tuple composed of the hypergraphs from the set $\{\tau_R(a) \mid a \in A\} \cup \{\tau_D(d) \mid (\lambda, d) \in D\}$.*

Theorem 2. *A sticker system $S = (\Sigma, A, D)$ generates a domino $r \in R_\Sigma$ if and only if the bonding grammar $\mathrm{BG}(S)$ generates $\tau_R(r)$.*

Proof. To prove the "only if" direction it suffices to notice that, if sticking $x \cdot y$ of $x \in R_\Sigma$ and $y \in D_\Sigma$ is defined, then one can apply several bondings to $\tau_R(x)$ and $\tau_D(y)$ in such a way that the result is $\tau_R(x \cdot y)$ (see Example 6). Then the proof is by induction on the length of a derivation in S. Conversely, suppose that $H = \tau_R(r)$ is generated by $\mathrm{BG}(S)$. Assume that $r = \begin{array}{|ccc ccc|} \hline a_1 & \ldots & a_m \\ a_1 & \ldots & a_m & a_{m+1} & \ldots & a_M \\ \hline \end{array}$ for $m \leq M$ (other cases are treated similarly). Then

Let $e_1^1, \ldots, e_{m-1}^1$ be the upper φ-labeled edges in H and let $e_1^2, \ldots, e_{M-1}^2$ be the lower φ-labeled edges in H (named from left to right). Let also $e_1^0, \ldots, e_m^0$ be the hyperedges of type 4 such that e_i^0 is labeled by $\tilde{a}_i$. Let us denote the vertex $att_H(e_1^0)(1)$ by nw and the vertex $att_H(e_1^0)(4)$ by sw.

Fix some bond set $\mathcal{B}$ for H and do the following with the domino representation of r. If $e_i^1 \in \mathcal{B}$, then draw a vertical line between a_i and a_{i+1} in the upper strand of r. If $e_i^2 \in \mathcal{B}$, then draw a vertical line between a_i and a_{i+1} in the lower strand of r. If $e_i^0 \in \mathcal{B}$, then draw a horizontal line between a_i in the upper strand and a_i in the lower strand of r. These lines divide r into several pieces $r_1, \ldots, r_t$. Now, let us break the bond e for each $e \in \mathcal{B}$; let us denote the resulting hypergraph by F. Clearly, breaking a bond $e_i^j \in \mathcal{B}$ in H corresponds to drawing a line in r according to the procedure described above. Thus, there is a one-one correspondence between the pieces $r_1, \ldots, r_t$ and the connected components of F. Let F_i be the connected component of F corresponding to r_i (for $i = 1, \ldots, t$). Since $\mathcal{B}$ is the bond set, $F_i \in Z_S$, so either $F_i = \tau_R(d)$ or $F_i = \tau_D(d)$ for some d.

Note that $e_1^0 \notin \mathcal{B}$ because if this was the case, then F would look like

$$\xrightarrow{a_1}\bullet \cdots$$
$$\xleftarrow{\overline{a_1}}\bullet \cdots$$

, so some F_i would contain the a_1-labeled edge to which first attachment vertex no other hyperedge is attached. This, however, cannot be the case. Indeed, F_i either equals $\tau_D(d)$ or $\tau_R(d)$ for some d, and the definitions of τ_D and τ_R imply that either a φ-labeled or a β-labeled hyperedge must be attached to the first attachment vertex of the a_1-labeled edge in F_i. Therefore, e_1^0 belongs to E_F, so it belongs to one of its connected components, say, to F_1. Clearly, $F_1 = \tau_R(r_1)$ because, if $F_1 = \tau_D(r_1)$, then a β-labeled hyperedge would be attached to nw.

For each $v \in V_H \setminus \{nw, sw\}$, a hyperedge with one of the labels α, β or φ is attached to v in H. Breaking the bonds from $\mathcal{B}$ preserves this property because, if $e \in \mathcal{B}$ and $lab_H(e) = \varphi$, then, after breaking the bond e, an α-labeled hyperedge and a β-labeled one appear instead of e. Thus $F_i = \tau_D(r_i)$ for $i = 2, \ldots, t$; indeed, if F_i equaled $\tau_R(r_i)$, then there would exist a vertex in V_{F_i} to which no hyperedge with a label α, β, or φ is attached in F. Concluding, r is obtained from the pieces $r_1, \ldots, r_t$ by means of sticking where the leftmost domino r_1 is from A and, for $i = 2, \ldots, t$, $(\lambda, r_i) \in D$. Thus r is generated by S. □

Example 6. Let $a_0 = \boxed{\begin{matrix} a \\ a\,b \end{matrix}}$, $d_1 = \boxed{\begin{matrix} b\,c \\ c\,b \end{matrix}}$, $d_2 = \boxed{b\,d}$, and $r = \boxed{\begin{matrix} a\,b\,c\,b\,d \\ a\,b\,c\,b \end{matrix}}$. Let $\Sigma = \{a, b, c, d\}$, let $A = \{a_0\}$, and let $D = \{(\lambda, d_1), (\lambda, d_2)\}$. Clearly, the regular sticker system $S = (\Sigma, A, D)$ generates r. The hypergraph $\tau_R(r)$ can be obtained from $\tau_R(a_0)$, $\tau_D(d_1)$ and $\tau_D(d_2)$ by bonding as shown below.

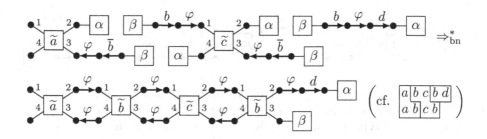

3.4   Membership Problem for Bonding Grammars

In Remark 1, we have already discussed that the membership problem for bonding grammars is in NP. Now, we are going to prove its NP-hardness even in the case when a bonding grammar is defined by only one connected hypergraph.

Theorem 3. *There is a bonding grammar $(Z, N, T, \otimes)$ with $|Z| = 1$ that generates an NP-complete language.*

Proof. In [11], it is proved that the problem of partitioning an undirected graph of maximum degree 4 into triangles is NP-complete. The input of this problem is an undirected simple graph $G = (V, E)$ with $3q$ vertices such that the degree of each vertex is at most 4; the question is whether V can be partitioned into 3-element sets $V_1, \ldots, V_q$ such that, for each i, any two vertices in V_i are adjacent. Moreover, it is shown in [11, Lemma 3] that this problem can be reduced to the same problem for *4-regular* graphs in linear time.

Let us introduce a similar problem involving *connected* 5-regular graphs.

Problem 5RCON-PIT
Input: undirected connected 5-regular graph (V, E, inc) with $|V| = 3q$.
Question: can V be partitioned into 3-element sets $V_1, \ldots, V_q$ such that, for each i, any two vertices in V_i are adjacent?

Here E in the input graph is a finite set and inc is a function from E to 2-element subsets of V. The former problem can be reduced to 5RCON-PIT in polynomial time. Indeed, if $G = (V, E)$ is a 4-regular simple graph consisting of connected components $G_1, \ldots, G_l$, then, for each $i \in [l]$, choose two distinct vertices v_i^1 and v_i^2 in G_i and add the edge $\{v_i^2, v_{i+1}^1\}$ to G for each $i \in [l-1]$. The resulting graph G' is connected; the degree of each its vertex is either 4 or 5. Finally, for each vertex v in G' of degree 4, let us append the following graph to it:

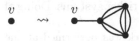

The resulting graph G'' is 5-regular (although not simple). Clearly, G'' can be partitioned into triangles if and only if so can be G.

Let us fix a terminal label b; then, let us represent an undirected graph $G = (V, E, inc)$ by the hypergraph $\ulcorner G \urcorner = (V, E \times \{1, 2\}, att, lab)$ where $att(e, 1) = v_1 v_2$ and $att(e, 2) = v_2 v_1$ for $\{v_1, v_2\} = inc(e)$ and where $lab(e, 1) = lab(e, 2) = b$. In other words, each undirected edge is represented by the pair of hyperedges

$\bullet\!\!\overset{b}{\underset{b}{\rightleftarrows}}\!\!\bullet$, which we shall depict as $\bullet\!\!\leftarrow\!\!\rightarrow\!\!\bullet$.

Now, let us define the bonding grammar $\mathcal{T} = (Z, N, T, \otimes)$ where $N = \{I, O\}$ with $type(I) = type(O) = 1$; $T = \{b\}$; $I \otimes O = b$ (as in the proof of Proposition 1). Let Z consist of the following hypergraph $Z(1)$.

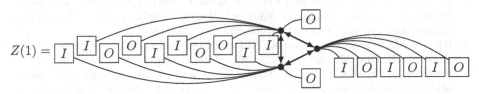

We claim that, given an input $G = (V, E, inc)$, the answer to 5RCON-PiT is YES if and only if $\ulcorner G \urcorner$ is generated by $\mathcal{T}$. First, assume that the answer to the question of 5RCON-PiT is YES, i.e. that V is the disjoint union of 3-element sets $V_1, \ldots, V_q$ such that the vertices $\{v_j^1, v_j^2, v_j^3\}$ in V_j are pairwise adjacent. For each $1 \le j \le q, 1 \le x < y \le 3$, choose one hyperedge e such that $inc(e) = \{v_j^x, v_j^y\}$; let E' consist of these hyperedges. Let $\mathcal{B} = E_{\ulcorner G \urcorner} \setminus E'$. We claim that $\mathcal{B}$ is a bond set for $\ulcorner G \urcorner$. Indeed, after breaking all the bonds from $\mathcal{B}$, the subhypergraph of the resulting hypergraph induced by V_j has the shape of the triangle with three I-labeled hyperedges and three O-labeled ones attached to each vertex; hence it is isomorphic to $Z(1)$. Secondly, assume that $\ulcorner G \urcorner$ is generated by $\mathcal{T}$, i.e. that $m \cdot Z \Rightarrow^*_{\mathrm{bn}} \ulcorner G \urcorner$ for some m. The hypergraph $m \cdot Z$ consists of q connected components $Y_1, \ldots, Y_q$, each one being isomorphic to $Z(1)$. In what follows, the vertices in V_{Y_i} are pairwise adjacent in $m \cdot Z$ and thus in $\ulcorner G \urcorner$ as well.   □

Let us conclude. Bonding grammars, a modification of fusion grammars, are NP-complete and enjoy a simple algorithm for checking membership (Remark 1). Still, they generate a number of interesting languages, e.g. the language of pseudotori, the language of k-regular graphs, an NP-complete language. Even more importantly, bonding grammars generalise regular sticker systems in a biologically meaningful way, which additionally supports their motivation and even allows one to name them *hypergraph regular sticker systems*.

Apart from bonding, it would be interesting to represent other operations from the field of DNA computing as graph transformations. Besides, it seems promising to combine bonding grammars with HR-grammars, which would result in a formalism extending all sticker systems. Doing this remains an open problem.

Acknowledgments. This work was performed at the Steklov International Mathematical Center and supported by the Ministry of Science and Higher Education of the Russian Federation (agreement no. 075-15-2022-265).

Disclosure of Interests. The author has no competing interests to declare that are relevant to the content of this article.

References

1. Courcelle, B., Engelfriet, J.: Graph Structure and Monadic Second-Order Logic. A Language-Theoretic Approach. Encyclopedia of Mathematics and Its Applications, vol. 138, Cambridge University Press, Cambridge (2012)
2. Engelfriet, J.: Context-free graph grammars. In: Rozenberg, G., Salomaa, A. (eds.) Handbook of Formal Languages, Volume 3: Beyond Words, pp. 125–213. Springer, Cham (1997). https://doi.org/10.1007/978-3-642-59126-6_3
3. Kiyomi, M., Okamoto, Y., Otachi, Y.: On the treewidth of toroidal grids. Discret. Appl. Math. **198**, 303–306 (2016). https://doi.org/10.1016/j.dam.2015.06.027
4. Kreowski, H., Kuske, S., Lye, A.: Fusion grammars: a novel approach to the generation of graph languages. In: de Lara, J., Plump, D. (eds.) Graph Transformation - 10th International Conference, ICGT 2017, Held as Part of STAF 2017, Marburg,

Germany, July 18-19, 2017, Proceedings. LNCS, vol. 10373, pp. 90–105. Springer, Cham (2017). https://doi.org/10.1007/978-3-319-61470-0_6

5. Kreowski, H.-J., Kuske, S., Lye, A.: Relating DNA computing and splitting/fusion grammars. In: Guerra, E., Orejas, F. (eds.) ICGT 2019. LNCS, vol. 11629, pp. 159–174. Springer, Cham (2019). https://doi.org/10.1007/978-3-030-23611-3_10

6. Kutrib, M., Wendlandt, M.: String assembling systems: comparison to sticker systems and decidability. In: Kostitsyna, I., Orponen, P. (eds.) Unconventional Computation and Natural Computation, pp. 101–115. Springer, Cham (2021). https://doi.org/10.1007/978-3-030-87993-8_7

7. Lye, A.: Generalization of natural computing models: variants of fusion grammars and reaction systems over categories, August 2022

8. Păun, G., Rozenberg, G., Salomaa, A.: DNA Computing: New Computing Paradigms. Springer, Cham (1998). https://doi.org/10.1007/978-3-662-03563-4

9. Pshenitsyn, T.: On decidability and expressive power of fusion grammars (2023). https://doi.org/10.48550/arxiv.2309.00954

10. Păun, G., Rozenberg, G.: Sticker systems. Theoret. Comput. Sci. **204**(1), 183–203 (1998). https://doi.org/10.1016/S0304-3975(98)00039-5

11. Rooij, J.M.M.V., van Kooten Niekerk, M.E., Bodlaender, H.L.: Partition into triangles on bounded degree graphs. Theory Comput. Syst. **52**, 687–718 (2013). https://doi.org/10.1007/s00224-012-9412-5

12. Rozenberg, G.: Handbook of Graph Grammars and Computing by Graph Transformation. World Scientific, Singapore (1997). https://doi.org/10.1142/3303

Card-Based Overwriting Protocol
for Equality Function and Applications

Suthee Ruangwises[1]([✉]) [iD], Tomoki Ono[1], Yoshiki Abe[1,2], Kyosuke Hatsugai[1], and Mitsugu Iwamoto[1] [iD]

[1] The University of Electro-Communications, Tokyo, Japan
{ruangwises,onotom,yoshiki,hatsugai,mitsugu}@uec.ac.jp
[2] National Institute of Advanced Industrial Science and Technology, Tokyo, Japan

Abstract. Research in the area of secure multi-party computation with an unconventional method of using a physical deck of playing cards began in 1989 when den Boer proposed a protocol to compute the logical AND function using five cards. Since then, the area has gained interest from many researchers and several card-based protocols to compute various functions have been developed. In this paper, we propose a card-based protocol called the *overwriting protocol* that can securely compute the k-candidate n-variable *equality function* $f : \{0, 1, \ldots, k-1\}^n \to \{0, 1\}$. We also apply the technique used in this protocol to compute other similar functions.

Keywords: card-based cryptography · secure multi-party computation · equality function

1 Introduction

During a presidential election with k candidates, a group of n friends decide that they will talk about politics only if all of them support the same candidate. However, each person does not want to reveal his/her preference to the group (unless it is known that everyone supports the same candidate). They need a way to find out whether their preferences all coincide without leaking information about any individual's preference (not even probabilistic information).

Theoretically, this is equivalent to each i-th person having an integer $a_i \in \{0, 1, \ldots, k-1\}$, indicating the candidate he/she prefers. Define an *equality function* $E(a_1, a_2, \ldots, a_n) := 1$ if $a_1 = a_2 = \cdots = a_n$, and $E(a_1, a_2, \ldots, a_n) := 0$ otherwise. Our goal is to develop a protocol that can compute the value of $E(a_1, a_2, \ldots, a_n)$ without leaking any other information.

This situation is an example of secure multi-party computation, one of the most actively studied areas in cryptography, which studies how multiple parties can compare their private information without revealing it. In contrast to digital protocols, unconventional protocols using physical objects such as coins [8] and combination locks [10] have also been studied, but the most used object is a deck of playing cards. Thus, this research area is often called card-based cryptography.

D.-J. Cho and J. Kim (Eds.): UCNC 2024, LNCS 14776, pp. 18–27, 2024.
https://doi.org/10.1007/978-3-031-63742-1_2

Card-based protocols have benefits that they do not require computers, and also allow external observers to verify that all parties truthfully execute the protocol (which is often a challenging task for digital protocols). They also have a great didactic value and thus can be used to teach the concept of secure multi-party computation to non-experts.

1.1 Related Work

Research in card-based cryptography began in 1989 when den Boer [3] proposed a protocol called the *five-card trick* to compute the logical AND function of two players' bits using five cards. After that, other AND function protocols [1,2,6,7,11,12,14,19,24] were also developed. These subsequent protocols either reduced the number of required cards or shuffles, or improved properties of the protocol involving output format, type of shuffles, etc.

Apart from the AND function protocols, protocols to compute other functions have been developed as well, including XOR function protocols [2,12,13], *majority function* protocols [16,25] (deciding whether there are more 1s than 0s in the input bits), a copy protocol [12] (duplicating the input), and a voting protocol [9] (adding input bits and storing the sum in binary representation). Nishida et al. [15] proved that any n-variable Boolean function can be computed using $2n + 6$ cards, and any such function that is symmetric can be computed using $2n + 2$ cards. In fact, many classes of such symmetric functions can be optimally computed using $2n$ cards [17].

While almost all of the existing card-based protocols were designed to compute Boolean functions, a few results also focused on computing functions in $\mathbb{Z}/k\mathbb{Z}$ for $k > 2$, such as [18,21,23].

Equality Function Protocols. Several previous results have been focused on computing the equality function. For the Boolean equality function (where $k = 2$), a protocol for a special case $n = 3$ has been independently proposed by Heather et al. [4] and by Shinagawa and Mizuki [22]. Later, Ruangwises and Itoh [20] developed two protocols to compute the Boolean equality function for any n. Their work can also be generalized to compute the k-candidate n-variable equality function $f : \{0, 1, \ldots, k - 1\}^n \rightarrow \{0, 1\}$ for any k and n by converting each input into binary representation.

1.2 Our Contribution

In this paper, we propose a new card-based protocol called the *overwriting protocol*, which can securely compute the k-candidate n-variable equality function $f : \{0, 1, \ldots, k - 1\}^n \rightarrow \{0, 1\}$ using kn cards and n shuffles.

Comparing to the existing protocol of Ruangwises and Itoh [20] which uses $2\lceil \lg k \rceil n$ cards and $\lceil \lg k \rceil n - 1$ shuffles, our protocol uses fewer cards when $k = 3$ or 5 (and uses equal number of cards when $k = 2$, 4, or 6), and also uses fewer shuffles for every $k \geq 3$. See Table 1 for comparison. In addition, our protocol is simpler and more intuitive, as it does not require each player to convert an integer into binary representation.

We also apply the overwriting technique used in our protocol to compute two other functions: the *set function* and the *set size function* (where the definitions are given in Sect. 5). See Table 2 for comparison.

Table 1. Number of required cards and shuffles for each equality function protocol

Protocol	Equality Function	#Cards	#Shuffles
Heather et al. [4]	$E : \{0,1\}^3 \to \{0,1\}$	6	1
Shinagawa-Mizuki [22]		6	1
Ruangwises-Itoh [20]	$E : \{0,1\}^n \to \{0,1\}$	$2n$	$n-1$
Ruangwises-Itoh [20]	$E : \{0,1,\ldots,k-1\}^n \to \{0,1\}$	$2\lceil \lg k \rceil n$	$\lceil \lg k \rceil n - 1$
Ours (Sect. 3)		kn	n

Table 2. Number of required cards and shuffles for each of our three protocols

Protocol	Function	#Cards	#Shuffles
Equality (Sect. 3)	$E : \{0,1,\ldots,k-1\}^n \to \{0,1\}$	kn	n
Set Size (Sect. 5.1)	$SS : \{0,1,\ldots,k-1\}^n \to \{0,1,\ldots,k\}$	kn	n
Set (Sect. 5.2)	$S : \{0,1,\ldots,k-1\}^n \to \mathcal{P}(\{0,1,\ldots,k-1\})$	$k(n+1)$	n

2   Preliminaries

2.1   Equality Function

Define an equality function $E : \{0,1,\ldots,k-1\}^n \to \{0,1\}$ as

$$E(a_1, a_2, \ldots, a_n) := \begin{cases} 1, & \text{if } a_1 = a_2 = \cdots = a_n; \\ 0, & \text{otherwise.} \end{cases}$$

2.2   Cards

Each card used in our protocol has either a ♣ or a ♡ on the front side. All cards have indistinguishable back sides.

An integer $i \in \{0,1,\ldots,k-1\}$ is encoded by a sequence of k consecutive cards, all of them being ♡s except the $(i+1)$-th leftmost card being a ♣. Such a sequence is called $E_k(i)$, e.g. $E_4(1)$ is ♡♣♡♡ .

2.3   Pile-Scramble Shuffle

A *pile-scramble shuffle* [5] rearranges the columns of an $n \times k$ matrix of cards by a uniformly random permutation unknown to all parties, i.e. moves each Column i to Column p_i for a uniformly random permutation $p = (p_1, p_2, \ldots, p_k)$ of $(1, 2, \ldots, k)$. See Fig. 1.

It can be implemented in real world by putting all cards in each column into an envelope, and scrambling all envelopes together completely randomly on a table.

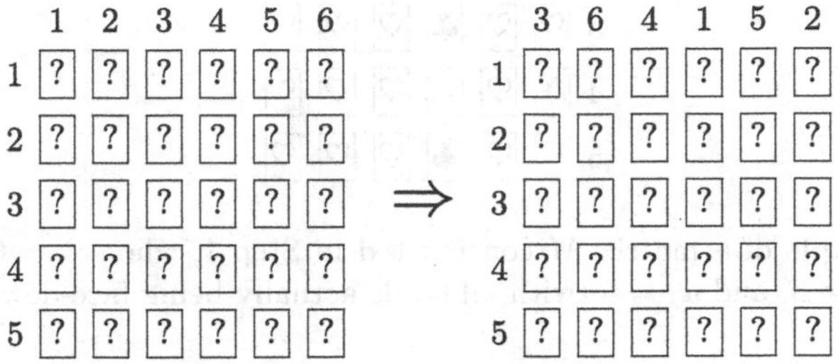

```
     1  2  3  4  5  6              3  6  4  1  5  2
  1 [?][?][?][?][?][?]          1 [?][?][?][?][?][?]
  2 [?][?][?][?][?][?]          2 [?][?][?][?][?][?]
  3 [?][?][?][?][?][?]    ⟹     3 [?][?][?][?][?][?]
  4 [?][?][?][?][?][?]          4 [?][?][?][?][?][?]
  5 [?][?][?][?][?][?]          5 [?][?][?][?][?][?]
```

Fig. 1. An example of a pile-scramble shuffle on a 5×6 matrix

2.4   Pile-Shifting Shuffle

A *pile-shifting shuffle* [23] rearranges the columns of an $n \times k$ matrix of cards by a random cyclic shift unknown to all parties, i.e. moves each Column i to Column $i + r$ for a uniformly random $r \in \{0, 1, \ldots, k - 1\}$ (where Column j means Column $j - k$ for $j \geq k$). See Fig. 2.

It can be implemented in real world by putting the cards in each column into an envelope, and taking turns to apply *Hindu cuts* (taking several envelopes from the bottom and putting them on the top), to the pile of envelopes [26].

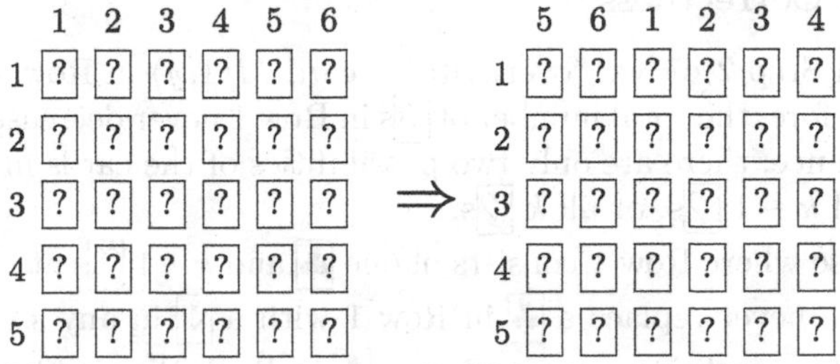

```
     1  2  3  4  5  6              5  6  1  2  3  4
  1 [?][?][?][?][?][?]          1 [?][?][?][?][?][?]
  2 [?][?][?][?][?][?]          2 [?][?][?][?][?][?]
  3 [?][?][?][?][?][?]    ⟹     3 [?][?][?][?][?][?]
  4 [?][?][?][?][?][?]          4 [?][?][?][?][?][?]
  5 [?][?][?][?][?][?]          5 [?][?][?][?][?][?]
```

Fig. 2. An example of a pile-shifting shuffle on a 5×6 matrix

3   Protocol for Equality Function

Each player is given k cards: one ♣ and $k-1$ ♡s. Each i-th player secretly arranges the given cards as a face-down sequence $E_k(a_i)$, encoding the value of a_i. Then, all players together perform the following steps.

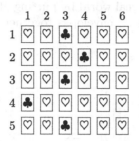

Fig. 3. An example of a matrix M constructed in Step 1, where $k = 6$, $n = 5$, $a_1 = a_3 = a_5 = 2$, $a_2 = 3$, and $a_4 = 0$ (with all cards actually being face-down)

1. Construct an $n \times k$ matrix M by putting a sequence $E_k(a_i)$ in Row i of M for each $i = 1, 2, \ldots, n$. See an example in Fig. 3. Let $M(x, y)$ denotes a card at Row x and Column y of M (the indices start at 1, not 0).
2. Perform the following steps for $i = 2, 3, \ldots, n$.
   (a) Apply the pile-scramble shuffle to M.
   (b) Turn over all cards in Row i of M.
   (c) For each $j = 1, 2, \ldots, k$, if $M(i, j)$ is a ♡, swap $M(i, j)$ and $M(1, j)$.
   (d) Turn over all face-up cards.
3. Apply the pile-scramble shuffle to M.
4. Turn over all cards in Row 1 of M. If the cards consist of one ♣ and $k-1$ ♡s, output 1; otherwise, output 0.

4   Proofs of Correctness and Security

4.1   Proof of Correctness

Observe that in Step 2(c), we "overwrite" a card $M(1, j)$ in Row 1, replacing it with a ♡. Therefore, the total number of ♡s in Row 1 never decreases throughout the protocol. Hence, there are only two possibilities of the cards in Row 1 at the end: one ♣ and $k-1$ ♡s, or all k ♡s.

The only case where Row 1 consists of one ♣ and $k-1$ ♡s at the end occurs if and only if we never replace a ♣ in Row 1 with a ♡ in any step throughout the protocol. This condition occurs when a ♣ in Row i lies in the same column as a ♣ in Row 1 for every $i = 2, 3, \ldots, n$, i.e. $a_1 = a_2 = \ldots = a_n$, which is exactly the condition where the equality function outputs 1. Hence, our protocol is always correct.

4.2 Proof of Security

It is sufficient to show that any step that reveals face-up cards does not leak any information about the inputs.

Consider Step 2(b). The cards in Row i have never been swapped with cards from other row before, so they consist of one ♣ and $k-1$ ♡s. Moreover, due to the pile-scramble shuffle in Step 2(a), the only ♣ has an equal probability of $1/k$ to be in each column no matter what a_i is. Therefore, this step does not leak information about the inputs.

Consider Step 4. As proved in Sect. 4.1, Row 1 either consists of all k ♡s, or one ♣ and $k-1$ ♡s. In the latter case, due to the pile-scramble shuffle in Step 3, the only ♣ has an equal probability of $1/k$ to be in each column. Therefore, this step only reveals the value of $E(a_1, a_2, \ldots, a_n)$ without leaking other information about the inputs.

5 Applications to Set and Set Size Functions

Suppose during a job recruitment, a total of k candidates have applied for the position. Each of the n referees secretly selects a candidate he/she prefers. Candidate(s) that are selected by at least one referee will advance to the final round interview. The referees need a method to find out which candidate(s) will advance to the final round without leaking the preference of any individual referee.

This situation is similar to that of the equality function where each i-th referee has an integer $a_i \in \{0, 1, \ldots, k-1\}$ indicating the candidate he/she prefers, but we instead want to find a set of integers that are equal to at least one input value. Define a *set function* $S : \{0, 1, \ldots, k-1\}^n \to \mathcal{P}(\{0, 1, \ldots, k-1\})$ as

$$S(a_1, a_2, \ldots, a_n) := \{j | \exists i, a_i = j\},$$

where $\mathcal{P}$ denotes the power set. For example, $S(3, 2, 3, 0, 5, 0) = \{0, 2, 3, 5\}$. Our goal is to develop a protocol to securely compute the set function between n players.

A closely related problem is when we want to find only the number of candidates that will advance to the final round (e.g. for the purpose of venue preparation), but not *which* candidate(s). In this case, define a *set size function* $SS : \{0, 1, \ldots, k-1\}^n \to \{0, 1, \ldots, k\}$ as

$$SS(a_1, a_2, \ldots, a_n) := |S(a_1, a_2, \ldots, a_n)|$$
$$= |\{j | \exists i, a_i = j\}|.$$

For example, $SS(3, 2, 3, 0, 5, 0) = |\{0, 2, 3, 5\}| = 4$. Note that $SS(a_1, a_2, \ldots, a_n) = 1$ if and only if $E(a_1, a_2, \ldots, a_n) = 1$. We also want to develop a protocol for the set size function between n players.

It turns out that a protocol for the set size function is very similar to the one for the equality function, so we will introduce it first. Then, we will introduce a protocol for the set function.

5.1   Protocol for Set Size Function

Luckily, we can slightly modify the equality function protocol in Sect. 3 to compute the set size function. The setup phase is the same, with each i-th player having a sequence $E_k(a_i)$. In the modified protocol, all players together perform the following steps.

1. Construct an $n \times k$ matrix M by putting a sequence $E_k(a_i)$ in Row i of M for each $i = 1, 2, \ldots, n$.
2. Perform the following steps for $i = 2, 3, \ldots, n$.
   (a) Apply the pile-scramble shuffle to M.
   (b) Turn over all cards in Row i of M.
   (c) For each $j = 1, 2, \ldots, k$, if $M(i, j)$ is a ♣, swap $M(i, j)$ and $M(1, j)$.
   (d) Turn over all face-up cards.
3. Apply the pile-scramble shuffle to M.
4. Turn over all cards in Row 1 of M. Output the total number of ♣s in Row 1.

The only differences from the equality function protocol are that in Step 2(c), we replace a card $M(1, j)$ by a ♣ instead of a ♡, and that in Step 4, we output the total number of ♣s in Row 1.

Proof of Correctness. Observe that in Step 2(c), we "overwrite" a card $M(1, j)$ in Row 1, replacing it with a ♣. Therefore, once a card in Row 1 becomes a ♣, it will always stay a ♣ throughout the protocol.

Consider a card $M(1, j)$ at the beginning of the protocol (we consider this exact card no matter which column it later moves to). If it is a ♣ at the beginning, i.e. $a_1 = j - 1$, it will stay a ♣ at the end. On the other hand, if it is a ♡ at the beginning, it will become a ♣ at the end if and only if it has been replaced by a ♣ from Row $i \geq 2$ at some step during the protocol, which occurs when $a_i = j - 1$.

Therefore, we can conclude that a card $M(1, j)$ at the beginning becomes a ♣ at the end if and only if there is an index $i \in \{1, 2, \ldots, n\}$ such that $a_i = j - 1$. This means the number of ♣s in Row 1 at the end is equal to the number of such indices j, which is exactly the output of the set size function. Hence, our protocol is always correct.

Proof of Security. It is sufficient to show that any step that reveals face-up cards does not leak any information about the inputs.

Consider Step 2(b). The cards in Row i have never been swapped with cards from other row before, so they consist of one ♣ and $k - 1$ ♡s. Moreover, due to the pile-scramble shuffle in Step 2(a), the only ♣ has an equal probability of $1/k$ to be in each column no matter what a_i is. Therefore, this step does not leak information about the inputs.

Consider Step 4. Suppose Row 1 consists of ℓ ♣s and $k - \ell$ ♡s. Due to the pile-scramble shuffle in Step 3, the ℓ ♣s have an equal probability to be in each of the $\binom{k}{\ell}$ combinations of columns. Therefore, this step only reveals the value $\ell = SS(a_1, a_2, \ldots, a_n)$ without leaking other information about the inputs.

5.2 Protocol for Set Function

We modify the set size function protocol in Sect. 5.1 to compute the set function. The setup phase is the same, with each i-th player having a sequence $E_k(a_i)$. All players together perform the following steps.

1. Construct an $(n+1) \times k$ matrix M by putting a sequence $E_k(a_i)$ in Row i of M for each $i = 1, 2, \ldots, n$ and putting a sequence $E_k(0)$ in Row $n+1$.
2. Perform the following steps for $i = 2, 3, \ldots, n$.
   (a) Apply the pile-shifting shuffle to M.
   (b) Turn over all cards in Row i of M.
   (c) For each $j = 1, 2, \ldots, k$, if $M(i, j)$ is a ♣, swap $M(i, j)$ and $M(1, j)$.
   (d) Turn over all face-up cards.
3. Apply the pile-shifting shuffle to M.
4. Turn over all cards in Row $n+1$ of M. Shift the columns of M cyclically such that the only ♣ in Row $n+1$ moves to Column 1.
5. Turn over all cards in Row 1 of M. Output the set $\{j \mid M(1, j+1)$ is a ♣$\}$.

Note that in this protocol, we apply the pile-shifting shuffle instead of the pile-scramble shuffle in Steps 2(a) and 3. The purpose of Row $n+1$ and Step 4 is to revert the matrix M to its original position before any pile-shifting shuffle.

Proof of Correctness. By the same reasons as the proof of correctness in Sect. 5.1, a card $M(1, j)$ at the beginning becomes a ♣ at the end if and only if there is an index $i \in \{1, 2, \ldots, n\}$ such that $a_i = j - 1$.

In this protocol, we only apply pile-shifting shuffles without pile-scramble shuffles, so the columns of M only move cyclically throughout the protocol. Thus, in Step 4 where the ♣ in Row $n+1$ returns to its original position in Column 1, the columns of M must also return to their original order at the beginning of the protocol. This means the set outputted in Step 5 is exactly the set $\{j \mid \exists i, a_i = j\}$. Hence, our protocol is always correct.

Proof of Security. It is sufficient to show that any step that reveals face-up cards does not leak any information about the inputs.

Consider Step 2(b). The cards in Row i have never been swapped with cards from other row before, so they consist of one ♣ and $k - 1$ ♡s. Moreover, due to the pile-shifting shuffle in Step 2(a), the only ♣ has an equal probability of $1/k$ to be in each column no matter what a_i is. Therefore, this step does not leak information about the inputs.

Consider Step 4. The cards in Row $n+1$ have never been swapped with cards from other row before, so they consist of one ♣ and $k - 1$ ♡s. Moreover, due to the pile-shifting shuffle in Step 3, the only ♣ has an equal probability of $1/k$

to be in each column. Therefore, this step does not leak information about the inputs.

Consider Step 5. The positions of all ♣s in Row 1 only reveal the set $\{j|\exists i, a_i = j\}$, which is exactly the output of the set function. Therefore, this step does not leak information about the inputs.

6   Future Work

We developed three protocols to compute the equality, set, and set size functions. Possible future work includes reducing the number of required cards and shuffles in these protocols, or proving the lower bounds of them. Also, as all results so far have been focusing on using two types of cards, it is an interesting question that whether we can reduce the number of cards if three or more types of cards are used. Other challenging work includes developing protocols to compute other functions in $\mathbb{Z}/k\mathbb{Z}$ for $k > 2$.

References

1. Abe, Y., Hayashi, Y., Mizuki, T., Sone, H.: Five-Card AND computations in committed format using only uniform cyclic shuffles. N. Gener. Comput. **39**(1), 97–114 (2021)
2. Crépeau, C., Kilian, J.: Discreet solitary games. In: Stinson, D.R. (ed.) CRYPTO 1993. LNCS, vol. 773, pp. 319–330. Springer, Heidelberg (1994). https://doi.org/10.1007/3-540-48329-2_27
3. den Boer, B.: More efficient match-making and satisfiability *The Five Card Trick*. In: Quisquater, J.-J., Vandewalle, J. (eds.) EUROCRYPT 1989. LNCS, vol. 434, pp. 208–217. Springer, Heidelberg (1990). https://doi.org/10.1007/3-540-46885-4_23
4. Heather, J., Schneider, S., Teague, V.: Cryptographic protocols with everyday objects. Formal Aspects Comput. **26**(1), 37–62 (2014)
5. Ishikawa, R., Chida, E., Mizuki, T.: Efficient card-based protocols for generating a hidden random permutation without fixed points. In: Calude, C.S., Dinneen, M.J. (eds.) UCNC 2015. LNCS, vol. 9252, pp. 215–226. Springer, Cham (2015). https://doi.org/10.1007/978-3-319-21819-9_16
6. Koch, A.: The landscape of optimal card-based protocols. Math. Cryptol. **1**(2), 115–131 (2021)
7. Koch, A., Walzer, S., Härtel, K.: Card-based cryptographic protocols using a minimal number of cards. In: Iwata, T., Cheon, J.H. (eds.) ASIACRYPT 2015. LNCS, vol. 9452, pp. 783–807. Springer, Heidelberg (2015). https://doi.org/10.1007/978-3-662-48797-6_32
8. Komano, Y., Mizuki, T.: Coin-based secure computations. Int. J. Inf. Secur. **21**(4), 833–846 (2022)
9. Mizuki, T., Asiedu, I.K., Sone, H.: Voting with a logarithmic number of cards. In: Proceedings of the 12th International Conference on Unconventional Computation and Natural Computation (UCNC), pp. 162–173 (2013)
10. Mizuki, T., Kugimoto, Y., Sone, H.: Secure multiparty computations using a dial lock. In: Proceedings of the 4th Annual Conference on Theory and Applications of Models of Computation (TAMC), pp. 499–510 (2007)

11. Mizuki, T., Kumamoto, M., Sone, H.: The five-card trick can be done with four cards. In: Wang, X., Sako, K. (eds.) ASIACRYPT 2012. LNCS, vol. 7658, pp. 598–606. Springer, Heidelberg (2012). https://doi.org/10.1007/978-3-642-34961-4_36

12. Mizuki, T., Sone, H.: Six-card secure AND and four-card secure XOR. In: Deng, X., Hopcroft, J.E., Xue, J. (eds.) FAW 2009. LNCS, vol. 5598, pp. 358–369. Springer, Heidelberg (2009). https://doi.org/10.1007/978-3-642-02270-8_36

13. Mizuki, T., Uchiike, F., Sone, H.: Securely computing XOR with 10 cards. Australas. J. Combin. **36**, 279–293 (2006)

14. Niemi, V., Renvall, A.: Secure multiparty computations without computers. Theoret. Comput. Sci. **191**, 173–183 (1998)

15. Nishida, T., Hayashi, Y., Mizuki, T., Sone, H.: Card-based protocols for any boolean function. In: Jain, R., Jain, S., Stephan, F. (eds.) TAMC 2015. LNCS, vol. 9076, pp. 110–121. Springer, Cham (2015). https://doi.org/10.1007/978-3-319-17142-5_11

16. Nishida, T., Mizuki, T., Sone, H.: Securely computing the three-input majority function with eight cards. In: Dediu, A.-H., Martín-Vide, C., Truthe, B., Vega-Rodríguez, M.A. (eds.) TPNC 2013. LNCS, vol. 8273, pp. 193–204. Springer, Heidelberg (2013). https://doi.org/10.1007/978-3-642-45008-2_16

17. Ruangwises, S.: The landscape of computing symmetric n-variable functions with $2n$ cards. In: Proceedings of the 20th International Colloquium on Theoretical Aspects of Computing (ICTAC), pp. 74–82 (2023)

18. Ruangwises, S.: Using five cards to encode each integer in $\mathbb{Z}/6\mathbb{Z}$. In: Ryan, P.Y., Toma, C. (eds.) Proceedings of the 14th International Conference on Security for Information Technology and Communications (SecITC), pp. 165–177. Springer, Cham (2022). https://doi.org/10.1007/978-3-031-17510-7_12

19. Ruangwises, S., Itoh, T.: AND protocols using only uniform shuffles. In: van Bevern, R., Kucherov, G. (eds.) CSR 2019. LNCS, vol. 11532, pp. 349–358. Springer, Cham (2019). https://doi.org/10.1007/978-3-030-19955-5_30

20. Ruangwises, S., Itoh, T.: Securely computing the n-variable equality function with $2n$ cards. Theoret. Comput. Sci. **887**, 99–110 (2021)

21. Shinagawa, K., Mizuki, T.: Card-based protocols using triangle cards. In: Proceedings of the 9th International Conference on Fun with Algorithms (FUN), pp. 31:1–31:13 (2018)

22. Shinagawa, K., Mizuki, T.: The six-card trick: secure computation of three-input equality. In: Lee, K. (ed.) ICISC 2018. LNCS, vol. 11396, pp. 123–131. Springer, Cham (2019). https://doi.org/10.1007/978-3-030-12146-4_8

23. Shinagawa, K., et al.: Card-based protocols using regular polygon cards. IEICE Trans. Fundamentals **100.A**(9), 1900–1909 (2017)

24. Stiglic, A.: Computations with a deck of cards. Theoret. Comput. Sci. **259**, 671–678 (2001)

25. Toyoda, K., Miyahara, D., Mizuki, T.: Another use of the five-card trick: card-minimal secure three-input majority function evaluation. In: Adhikari, A., Küsters, R., Preneel, B. (eds.) INDOCRYPT 2021. LNCS, vol. 13143, pp. 536–555. Springer, Cham (2021). https://doi.org/10.1007/978-3-030-92518-5_24

26. Ueda, I., Miyahara, D., Nishimura, A., Hayashi, Y., Mizuki, T., Sone, H.: Secure implementations of a random bisection cut. Int. J. Inf. Secur. **19**(4), 445–452 (2020)

A Methodology for Comparing and Benchmarking Quantum Devices

Jessica Park[1,2(✉)], Susan Stepney[1] ⓘ, and Irene D'Amico[2]

[1] Department of Computer Science, University of York, York, UK
{jlp567,susan.stepney}@york.ac.uk
[2] School of Physics, Engineering and Technology, University of York, York, UK
irene.damico@york.ac.uk

Abstract. Quantum Computing (QC) is undergoing a high rate of development, investment and research devoted to its improvement. However, there is little consensus in the industry and wider literature as to what improvement might consist of beyond ambiguous statements of "more qubits" and "fewer errors". Before one can decide how to improve something, it is first necessary to define the criteria for success: what are the metrics or statistics that are relevant to the problem? The lack of clarity surrounding this question has led to a rapidly developing capability with little consistency or standards present across the board. This paper lays out a framework by which any user, developer or researcher can define, articulate and justify the success criteria and associated benchmarks that have been used to solve their problem or make their claim.

1 Introduction and Motivations

The theory of quantum mechanics and its potential use in computing having been under research for over 100 years. Quantum computing hardware is still in relative infancy, however, with limitations in both size (qubit number) and capability (error rates). The current state of play is often referred to as the Noisy Intermediate Scale Quantum (NISQ) era.

Noisy refers to the fact that there are unprogrammed interactions present both between qubits in the device, and between qubits and their environment; these interactions may cause the device to perform in a non-ideal way, and be a source of errors. A description of the causes and effects of errors in quantum devices is presented in Sect. 2.1.

Intermediate Scale refers both to the limited number of qubits in these devices, and to the limited connectivity between them. Desired (non-noisy) interactions between qubits require direct connection; limited connectivity limits the circuits that can be implemented natively on the device. SWAP gates can be used to implement indirect connections, but at the expense of potentially more errors and longer circuit times.

Being able to characterise both the scale and noise of a quantum device is crucial both for monitoring the development of the field and for determining if a particular device is fit for a particular purpose. There are a number of ways

D.-J. Cho and J. Kim (Eds.): UCNC 2024, LNCS 14776, pp. 28–42, 2024.
https://doi.org/10.1007/978-3-031-63742-1_3

that quantum devices are being characterised at present, but there are no standard measures for comparing devices across manufacturers, qubit realisations or computational models. This is discussed further in Sect. 2.3.

After discussing these issues (Sect. 2), we propose a methodology for designing and performing characterisation experiments on quantum computers (Sect. 3), and illustrate its use through an example of the design of a benchmarking experiment where the relevant choices are documented and justified (Sect. 4).

2 Background

2.1 Errors in Quantum Computing

Any effects or interactions unaccounted for in one's model of the ideal hardware are equivalent to unknown terms in the actual Hamiltonian that is encoded and enacted on the device. When the enacted Hamiltonian is not equal to the desired Hamiltonian, the energy landscape that it describes is also different. If the discrepancy is severe enough, or the landscape is particularly rugged, the two Hamiltonians may have different ground states. The ground state determines the solution of the problem, so different ground states means that the optimal solution cannot be found.

When the mathematical form of the unintended interactions can be estimated, they can be included in the Hamiltonian to model their effects on the quantum solver. Example effects include random noise, onsite energies, next-nearest neighbour interactions and inter-excitation interactions. For example, the effects of these on perfect state transfer in spin chains have been modelled [35]. By understanding the relative effects of each type of phenomenon on the fidelity of state transfer, one can then focus on the elements of the hardware or software that may need to be optimised.

D-Wave, who manufacture and sell quantum annealers, include in their documentation details on Integrated Control Errors (ICE), which limit the dynamic range of the user defined h and J values, the programmable values that encode the problem to be solved [12]. The five main sources they identify are:

1. Background Susceptibility: Next-nearest neighbour interactions and applied bias (h value) leakage between neighbouring qubits
2. Flux Noise of the Qubits: Noise that varies with time and logical qubit size (chain lengths)
3. DAC Quantisation: Precision effects between digital and analogue controls
4. I/O System Effect: Parameter control depending on aspects such as annealing schedule
5. Distribution of h and J Scale Across Qubits: Fabrication imperfections that give qubits slightly different properties. This is also a time-varying error

A number of other errors sources are also mentioned in brief, such as temperature, photon flux and readout fidelity. The challenges that these effects present in real use cases for the D-Wave machines are well documented [10,24,32].

Error modelling and estimation can be used to investigate the effect of noise and errors on a device and its results, and aid decisions when selecting or using a device. For example, algorithms such as EQUAL inject perturbations in the quantum Hamiltonian to mitigate the estimated systematic error in the D-Wave quantum annealer [5].

It is important to understand how the errors in the hardware affect the probability of success (defined as finding a state with lower energy than the known excited states of the intended problem) and how this scales with problem size. Albash et al. [3] study this in both simulated quantum annealers and the D-Wave 2000Q. The study considers the quantum computing chip to have one overall error and does not attempt to attribute it to any particular effect.

Zaborniak and de Sousa [39] begin to characterise the noise seen in both D-Wave2000Q chip and the newer 5000 qubit Advantage System. Their results show that in the 2000Q system, the noise is frequency dependent according to $1/f^{0.7}$, and in the Advantage system, the noise amplitude is 2–3 times larger whilst also being affected by further noise sources at short annealing times. The mathematical description and numerical results for the 2000Q system fit with the errors described by the D-Wave documentation when explaining the ICE.2-Flux Noise [12]. This presents evidence that on-chip measurements can be directly related to theoretical sources of error, and that the newer, larger device is subject to larger errors. Further research on this is likely to shape the future development and usage of quantum annealing chips.

Quantum computing architectures have further parameters involved in the running of the solver that affect the quality of the solutions. D-Wave parameters are user controlled in the accompanying software [12] and include spin reversal (to mitigate the effect of spin bath polarization) and anneal offsets (changing the qubit freeze-out rate). Barbosa et al. [7] show that these parameters can be optimised for entire classes of problems, removing the need for computationally expensive optimisation for each individual problem. A fixed problem embedding is used when considering multiple problems from the same class. This allows for easier attribution of the optimisation, but at the cost of potentially not fully optimising the device or preventing the optimisation from generalising. Each parameter is optimised independently; the authors state that simultaneous optimisation would likely yield better results.

Most of the error measurement schemes discussed in the literature involve either running specialised benchmarking algorithms [39], or consider outputs of large numbers of runs [3]. The first method is generally computationally expensive and the second ignores any time dynamics to the noise. A continuous monitoring scheme that does not involve any additional algorithms [40] has been tested on both emulated and real quantum hardware and on both single- and two-qubit gates. Drawbacks include the limitation to small circuit sizes and inherent assumptions on the noise model; these are areas of future research.

Pelofske et al. [31] suggest another approach to continuously monitor performance of a quantum annealer. The basic principle is to embed a second QUBO, the Performance Indicator (PI), onto the quantum annealer using unused qubits that remain after the problem QUBO has been embedded. The set-up phase involves running multiple anneals and subsequent readouts of the PI and problem QUBO, and creating a time series of the moving averages. Since the PI has comparable trends in performance to the problem QUBO, the PI performance can be used to predict the quality of the result from the problem QUBO.

In addition to whole-chip measurements, one can consider computing fidelity at the single qubit level. Nelson et al. [25] have developed Quantum Annealing Single-qubit Assessment (QASA) to characterise individual qubits within a quantum annealer. Each qubit is repeatedly sampled through a range of input fields, and four parameter values are extracted: effective temperature, noise, transverse field gain, and bias. The authors are clear that, although their model and associated parameters appear to fit the results of the measurements, it does not account for the physical origins of the behaviours. The QASA protocol is performed for all the qubits within a chip in parallel, and the variations and correlations across the chip analysed. There are spatial variations across the chip, and there is a difference in behaviour between the horizontally and vertically oriented qubits. Their results show clear heterogeneity at the very lowest level of hardware. Although the QASA protocol is aimed at the single qubit level, the authors have also considered how changes in other layers of the model may affect their results by repeating the experiment with different annealing schedules. They show that bias and transverse field gain are largely robust to a change in anneal schedule, but effective temperature increases logarithmically with anneal time. Hence, when optimising or correcting for effective temperature, the anneal time needs to be taken into account. Their results show the importance of full stack considerations, from detailed hardware to abstract algorithms, when developing a quantum computing pipeline.

2.2   Error Correction and Mitigation

Because of the high levels of noise and errors in NISQ devices, quantum error correction and mitigation methods are needed to make best use of these machines. Extensive research into the theory and measurements of errors in these devices has lead to increasingly effective error correction schemes. We overview a selection of these methods, chosen to highlight their range.

The quantum fault-tolerance theorem states that, given uncorrelated noise and a sufficiently low gate fail rate, a quantum computer can give arbitrarily accurate solutions to computations of any length [29]. In quantum gate model computers, error correcting protocols can be used to achieve the desired accuracy with some qubit and gate overhead [1,17]. One theory of quantum error correcting codes, by Knill and Laflamme [16], is based on the idea of "encoding states into larger Hilbert spaces subject to known interactions". The larger Hilbert space is made of ancilla qubits, and the exact encoding is designed such that any gate fault preserves the quantum information in the state. There are a number of different quantum error correction algorithms that are based on encoding one logical qubit in anywhere between 5 and 9 physical qubits. Quantum error correction codes work well in theory with gate model computers, and give the potential for universal quantum computation. However, they reduce the number of logical qubits achievable with a given device.

Quantum error correction codes are typically discrete in nature, using unitary gates to flip states to recover lost information. In practice these are difficult to implement in a number of qubit types including SQUIDs [15] and trapped ions [14]. Ahn et al. [2] proposed a scheme of continuous measurements in situations where discrete error correction is not applicable; Hamiltonian operators filter out the noisy signals. Borah et al. [9] have implemented this scheme, and shown it provides fidelity improvement over uncorrected states. The parameter that controls the feedback strength is important in preserving state fidelity: feedback and detailed knowledge of one's system is required for optimisation.

Developing error-correction protocols for quantum annealers is an area of active research. It is as yet unproven whether a noisy quantum annealer could accurately replicate an ideal device for arbitrarily large problems. However, there are proposed methods for error correction in annealing qubits. Inspired by circuit model error correction, Pudenz et al. [34] use ancilla qubits to create repetition; this imposes an energy penalty to stabilise the bit flip operations across the ancilla qubits of the same logical qubit. They demonstrate 344 physical qubits emulating antiferromagnetic chains of lengths between 0 and 90 spins, and find improved performance over both classical and uncorrected quantum methods. These results are promising; however, the parameters that define the energy penalty have to be tuned to the specific problem, which requires some advance knowledge of the correct solution. Further work is needed to use this protocol more universally. According to the methodology proposed below, energy penalty parameters form part of the formulation stage in the information processing pipeline, and could therefore be included in the overall optimisation algorithm.

Classical post-processing is often used for error mitigation schemes. There are a number of different schemes, ranging from bit-flip hill climbing (that ignores spin interactions) to randomised multi-qubit correction (RMQC) in which shuffled groups of quits are flipped in such a way that tunnels through to lower energy states of the whole system [6]. A benefit of the RMQC approach is that it is deterministic (unlike most post-processing methods) and does not require hyperparameter tuning, so there are fewer variables to optimise.

2.3   Device Characterisation and Benchmarking

Measuring the errors in a quantum device is a way of characterising that device. This provides useful information for manufacturers and researchers, but it is not simple for users to discern how errors might affect performance when applied to their real world problem. It is not always clear in benchmarking literature whether error mitigation schemes have been used, and if so, how that has affected not only the results of the benchmark but also the complexity in number of qubits and circuit depth. If the error mitigation happens by default when using a particular device, we have to rely on the provider to complete these steps successfully and reliably. When manufacturers change their default processes over time, these need to be communicated to users, so that they can be taken into account when comparing past results.

The majority of the leading quantum device companies produce gate model devices; key exceptions are D-Wave (annealers) and a handful of photonic specialists (PsiQuantum, Xanadu and ORCA). It can be difficult to compare performance between different hardware architectures and qubit types. Even properties that can be attributed both to circuit model devices and to annealers, such as number of qubits, cannot be compared easily: they affect the operation very differently. Including photonic and topological devices makes any comparison harder still. A particular challenge when comparing commercial quantum solvers is lack of consistency in reporting fidelity or error measurements. As this is a new field, there is no precedent for what measures users need, understand or care about when choosing a device. What measures are important depends on specific use cases and algorithms. In many cases, users access the devices indirectly through cloud software, and it is infeasible for users to measure the relevant values, due to high calculation costs and the amount of device control required. With more discerning users with more pressing problems, providers will need to conform to a standard set of performance measures; but which ones?

Suau et al. [36] have measured some operational parameters such as qubit response, bias and saturation in both major hardware architectures. The authors recognise that there are more thorough qubit analyses that can be done in either circuit model or annealers, but state that the benefit of their approach is its applicability to a variety of hardware types. Their work raises an important issue: in order to compare approaches, it is necessary to have some comparison measures. This issue gets increasingly fraught as hardware setups include different architectures and qubit types at various granularities within the same device.

Quantum Volume [23] is one candidate measure. It is defined as $\tilde{V}_Q = min[N, d(N)]^2$, where N is the number of qubits, and d is the circuit depth, the maximum number of steps (unitary operations) executed in one run of the device. Different connectivities and error rates limit how many steps can be completed. Variants consider the largest square circuit ($N = d$) that a quantum computer can implement [11].

Pelofske et al. [30] compare the quantum volume of 24 NISQ devices available to users in 2022. The quantum volumes are determined in-house, using the same approach, rather than taking values determined by the manufacturers or previous investigations. The particular transpilation/compilation methods used by each device have an effect on the maximum circuit size that can be executed, and therefore on the resulting quantum volume. So users need to consider how a device is to be used, and its compatibility with the desired problem(s), when choosing a suitable device.

Quantum volume appears to be a useful measure for comparing circuit model quantum computers. It is unclear how this might translate to either annealing or topological quantum computing architectures, however, where N has different implications and d is not always well-defined. Some attempts have been made to quantify the Quantum Volume of D-Wave quantum annealers by using equivalent problems that it can solve [37]; since quantum annealers are not thought to be universal solvers, the applicability of this approach is not clear.

There are a number of quantum computing benchmarks focused on performance against particular problems. These are advertised as more useful measures for the user than system parameters such as coherence time or gate fidelity, and can provide a more direct comparison between fundamentally different qubit and architecture types [21]. Benchmarking tasks can typically be applied to a range of devices or parameter scenarios, to provide information that can be generalised to performance on problems of interest to the user. Atos (a digital transformation company) have developed a Q Score [22], a single number measure of the largest number of variables in a 'Max Cut' problem that a device can optimise. There are other similar application-driven measures developed by a number of companies [18].

How the performance of a benchmark task translates to the real world problems that a user is interested in determines the utility of this kind of measure. It may not be practical or useful to compare quantum hardware in isolation from the specific problem set of interest. It might be that, for each problem complexity and class, different quantum computers should be compared only on the quality of- and time to- solution, themselves complex functions of qubit number, error rate, connectivity etc. Linke et al. [20] compare two 5 qubit systems with different qubit realisations and connectivities, finding that the architecture that most closely matches the desired circuit tends to perform better.

These kinds of results, albeit on a small scale, suggest that different quantum processors should be chosen for different tasks or even subtasks within a processing pipeline; but how to choose?

3   Proposed Methodology

There are a great number of choices that have to be made when characterising and comparing quantum devices. Even for users of the devices, who may not be making these choices themselves, it is crucial that the decisions that have been made are well communicated and justified for the measure to be useful.

We propose the following methodology for deciding on and executing any type of characterisation and benchmarking, designed to provoke a deep consideration of the desired and unintended consequence of all the choices being made at each step. The steps are:(1) Purpose (2) Success Measure (3) Generalisability (4) Robustness (5) Expressivity (6) Limitations, discussed below.

3.1   Purpose and Success Measure

Q1: What is the main purpose of the intended measure?

(a) to compare architectures and implementations of quantum computers
(b) to compare fabrications/alternative chips of the same architecture
(c) to compare the relative difficulty of particular problems

(d) to monitor the effect of error correction/mitigation and calibration methods
(e) to measure the improvements and developments between iterations of quantum devices
(f) other

When answering Q1, there is unlikely to be a single option that covers the purpose, but it is important to prioritise the different purposes, and to keep the decision in mind when answering Q2.

Q2: How do you define "success" when considering a quantum computer?

(a) has the best of a desired hardware measure (eg. number of qubits)
(b) executes the process it was programmed to do
(c) produces a quantum state that matches that from an ideal exact simulation
(d) produces a probability distribution that matches that from an ideal exact simulation
(e) provides a "useful" result to a problem that is challenging to solve by other means (either due to solution quality or time to solution)
(f) other

Objective Function. The answers to these two questions give a purpose and definition for success. These now need to be translated into an *objective function* that gives a number or set of numbers that can be used to directly answer the question of purpose. The development of objective functions has been considered in length in the field of genetic algorithms (see Pare et al. [28] for an image processing example). Obtaining a useful objective function is key in ensuring the benchmark provides as much relevant information as possible. Choosing an objective function is likely to be a trade-off between simplicity, interpretability, and multifaceted complexity.

3.2 Generalisability, Robustness, Expressivity

Given the answers to Q1 and Q2, and an objective function, there should now be a developing idea of a potential benchmark. Related to the options above, some appropriate choices might be:(a) read off the device specification or get recent calibration data; (b) Quantum Process Tomography to give process fidelity or Direct Characterisation of Quantum Dynamics; (c) Quantum State Tomography to calculate trace distance between states;(d) Total Variance Distance to calculate the similarity between distributions [26]; (e) compare result to an existing solution given by best available alternative device. Although this is a small subset of the tools that could be used to benchmark, discussing them further highlights the importance of methodology considerations (3)–(5). Generalisability, robustness and expressivity are criteria by which the designer can consider whether the proposed benchmark is fit for (their specific) purpose. These criteria also provide a framework by which any documentation of the benchmark can justify the choices made.

Generalisability. Option (e) is the most overtly problem specific, yet any method chosen at this stage leads to further choices, and these affect the generalisability of the benchmark. This is mentioned briefly in Sect. 2, where particular embeddings are used to optimise a different area of the process. In all options, one choice is the actual task to be given to the quantum device. This typically means designing a circuit to complete a quantum process, prepare a quantum state, or provide a probability distribution. In the most general case, random circuits composed from the device's basis gates can be generated [8,11]; if enough circuits are run, we may assume the results to be maximally general. From this, we here define *generalisablity* as the ability for a quantum computer to complete a large range of tasks to a set standard. Despite being maximally general in theory, Proctor et al. [33] show that randomised circuits are often limited to small numbers of qubits. By choosing a particular class of circuit (in that case, randomised mirror circuits), generalisability can be preserved whilst providing more opportunity to scale. Additionally, because those circuits have some structure, they are more similar to algorithmic circuits; this should make them more predictive of the device's performance on real world problems.

Robustness. We define *robustness* to be the stability of the performance to changes in the choices made during the benchmarking. In any quantum device, there are many operational parameters that affect performance; when benchmarking, one must understand how these are used. Once a circuit has been designed, it needs to be embedded onto the hardware, taking into account the limited connectivity of the qubits. Most hardware manufacturers provide a tool that does this automatically for their devices in an efficient way, typically to minimise the number of additional SWAP gates. Different providers, as well as having different connectivities, may have different algorithms that perform this step. How do the benchmarking results change if the choice of embedding algorithm is changed?

Another operational parameter choice is the use of error correction or mitigation strategies in the benchmark task. If the top priority answer to Q1 is to measure the effects of these strategies, then this becomes the independent variable in the benchmark experiment. In other cases, the use of error reduction strategies should be considered and justified based on the purpose of the measure. One device may exhibit better native performance; another device may be more receptive to error correction and therefore display overall better performance when these strategies are applied. Traditionally, benchmarks are considered useful for comparing so-called like-for-like performance; however, if the definition of a successful quantum computer is one that provides the most accurate result to a problem, then it might be more beneficial to compare best-for-best performance. Conversely, if the definition of a successful quantum computer also includes the time to solution, how these factors are balanced will influence any decision on the best benchmarking methodology.

Expressivity. Another factor to consider when deciding on a benchmark is its ability to show significant difference between the results of different tests. When comparing quantum devices, one would like to be able to distinguish between potentially incremental improvements. We define *expressivity* as this range of results, complementing generalisability, which considers a range of tasks. For example, if the problem is too easy, all quantum devices may give a performance above 95% (in some particular measure); it can seem as if the devices perform very similarly. However, when applied to a harder problem, these devices could show a great range in results. An example of this is the MNIST dataset of hand-written digits, often used to benchmark machine learning classification algorithms, which has been heavily criticised for its simplicity and lack of variability [13], with the PaperWithCode.com leaderboard (as of 28/04/2023) showing 63 algorithms with an error rate below 1% [27].

Martiel et al. [22], when benchmarking quantum processors, define a β^* function that defines how demanding a problem is; $\beta^* = 0$ means the problem can be solved via a coin toss, and $\beta^* = 1$ requires an exact solver. Their objective function for the benchmark then computes a score which can be compared to this threshold value for each problem.

3.3 Practical Limitations

It might not be possible to execute the full benchmark suggested by the methodology at this point. First is the matter of cost: executing a benchmark requires time, access to the device, computational power, and money. These costs might make full benchmark execution too expensive. Second, where ideal simulation results are required, this limits the size of the benchmark problems; quantum simulation on classical devices is currently limited to 10 s of qubits for most tasks.

When faced with these limitations, the user needs to justify any reductions made to the ideal benchmarking experiment, and document how these limit the conclusions.

3.4 Justificiation and Documentation of Choices

In order to make any benchmarking operation as informative and useful as possible, it is crucial that all the choices made in the process are documented and where possible, justified in way that relates back to the answers of the two key questions. In this documentation, any potential consequences of the choices made should also be discussed. Benchmarking studies are most useful when they are as transparent as possible in their execution and consistency is upheld wherever possible despite the heterogeneity in the range of quantum architectures, qubit realisations and potential algorithms.

4 Example Workflow

To demonstrate how the methodology proposed here might be put into practice, we provide an example here.

Scenario: You are developing a quantum algorithm to perform image classification for medical screening purposes, initially on current NISQ devices, but more importantly for larger, upcoming models. You have tested one quantum device, but before progressing further you would like to determine which device might give the best performance for your algorithm. You know that you require a gate model device, but have no other restrictions on access, qubit realisation etc. What can you do in order to determine which quantum device to use for your application?

Q1: Purpose. From the scenario, your purpose is to compare different architectures and implementations of quantum computers (option (a) as listed above). Thinking a little deeper, a secondary purpose might be to compare alternative chips of the same architecture (option (b)) as it would be useful to know results are portable between chips of the same design.

Q2: Success Measure. In this scenario, success is most closely defined as option (e); providing a "useful" result to a problem. For this use case, you are more concerned with solution quality than time to solution. In image classification, performance is typically measured by properties like precision and recall, so it is likely that these will be factors in the objective function. An additional consideration here is option (b), that it executes the process it was programmed to do. Medical imaging is a high stakes problem, and you would like some assurance that on a gate level, the device is performing as expected.

From these answers to Q1 and Q2, it is now possible to define an objective function. In this case, you choose to define a simple objective function with a single parameter. You use the F1 score, the harmonic mean of precision and recall for the 'true' class [4]. It is typically used in cases where there is an imbalance in the number of true and false cases. This is likely to be the case in a medical screening of a large population for a relatively rare condition.

You could also choose a more complex two-dimensional objective function where the first dimension is the F1 score, and second dimension is a measure of how well the device in question can perform single-qubit rotation gates: $R_{x,y,z}(\theta)$. These gates are integral to running quantum neural networks, with the θ parameter updated in the learning process [19]. Having some assurance that these gates can be executed effectively provides confidence in the overall algorithm.

The next step is to choose the benchmarking task. In this scenario, the task is the algorithm that you have already developed. Due to the focused task and use case, you already have a training and test set of labelled data. If this were not the case, or if the images in the data set are too large for the currently available quantum devices, you would have to choose a surrogate data set to use in the benchmarking.

Generalisability. You are not concerned with how well your dataset and subsequent results generalise to other problems. Generalisability in this case refers to choosing a dataset that represents your eventual (but currently unavailable) problem set. To do this, you need to consider the salient features of your dataset. Assume that the relevant medical images are typically in 8-bit greyscale with 2000 × 2000 pixels, and approximately 1 in 10 are labelled as true. The real images are too large so a dataset with smaller images should be considered. Aside from this factor, you should try to find a dataset with 8-bit greyscale pixels in a square arrangement whereby the false case is present approximately 9 times more often than the true. To ensure generalisability, if time permits, you could even find multiple datasets that fit the criteria.

Robustness. To consider robustness, you need to think closely about both the algorithm and the surrounding software used to access the quantum device. The algorithm requires embedding on to the quantum device, and the current process has been tuned to your existing quantum device. Because you want to test the devices and not the algorithm, you decide to use each manufacturer's recommended embedding tool for each device. In this way, you are comparing the best case (or at least the best-known) scenario for each device.

There are other choices and predefined parameters that are used in the algorithm, such as the learning rate for the neural network and the method for entangling the qubits. In this case, you decide to use the best known values from the initial work, and keep these constant across all the tested devices. You have determined that these are unlikely to affect the comparative performance of the devices at this stage, and leave further refinement for latter stages.

Expressivity. The difficulty of an image classification task can be increased by adding variation in the training set, such as by introducing edge cases, or adding artificial noise to existing images. Larger images are likely to provide a harder problem, due to a higher potential for natural variation, as well as requiring more qubits to be operational, increasing the need for more SWAP gates and also likelihood of gate errors from crosstalk. Where datasets are available publicly or have been used in previous studies, an impression of their potential expressivity can be gained, otherwise a good approach may be to have multiple benchmarks of different estimated difficulties.

Chosen Benchmark. From considering these three factors, you are now able to choose an appropriate benchmarking task that is likely to achieve the aims set out in the answers to questions 1 and 2. In the scenario presented here, you choose 8-bit greyscale images that are 100–200 pixels in each dimension. You require two classes, where one class is 9 times more prevalent than the other; this could be achieved by down-selecting from a larger dataset. An example that fits these criteria is the publicly available "30K Cats and Dogs", which has images that are in 8-bit greyscale and 150 × 150 pixels in size [38]. The full dataset contains around 15,000 of each class so for this experiment, I use 1,500 cats and 13,500 dogs.

Limitations. Due to the size of current NISQ devices, you have chosen a surrogate dataset for the benchmarking task. Although you have tried to ensure that it representative, there may sill be performance differences from the real case. The effects of this could be further limited by repeating the benchmark with a different dataset (with similar characteristics) and looking at how performance varies. Another limitation that will affect your benchmarking are access to the quantum compute time and the wall-clock time you have available to complete the benchmark.

One of the main benefits of using this methodology to determine a benchmarking strategy is that it encourages an awareness of all the intended and unintended consequences of the choices made. When one has this awareness, it is much easier to ensure that any literature written on the benchmarking task has adequate documentation and justification. Transparent benchmarking is important both within a development team and in sharing results with the wider community.

5   Summary and Conclusion

We propose a methodology for designing, running and documenting benchmarking tasks. The aim is to ensure that tasks are chosen based on their intended purpose, rather than the alternative approach of completing 'standard' benchmarking tasks and then attempting to determine what useful information can be gleaned from the results.

The methodology begins by asking the user two questions to clarify their purpose, and their definition of success. Starting with these two focused questions, the user is then lead to develop an objective function to quantitatively measure the success as defined by the answers. After this step, the user has to determine a task that provides the data fed into the objective function. We offer suggestions of what these tasks might look like depending on the objective function. When determining the benchmarking task, the methodology suggests three key considerations: generalisability, robustness and expressivity. These factors have to be balanced depending on priorities brought to focus by the initial questions.

As well as being a practical guide to determining the benchmarking task, the methodology also aids in the documentation and justification of the choices made, and leads the user to think more deeply about the consequences of these choices. This represents a step towards transparency and coherency in a relatively young and rapidly developing field.

Acknowledgements. The authors acknowledge Defence Science Technical Laboratory (Dstl) who are funding this research. Content includes material subject to ©Crown copyright (2024), Dstl. This material is licensed under the terms of the Open Government Licence except where otherwise stated. To view this licence, visit http://www.nationalarchives.gov.uk/doc/open-government-licence/version/3, or write to the Information Policy Team, The National Archives, Kew, London TW9 4DU, or email: psi@nationalarchives.gov.uk.

References

1. Aharonov, D., Ben-Or, M.: Fault-tolerant quantum computation with constant error rate. SIAM J. Comput. **38**(4), 1207–1282 (2008)
2. Ahn, C., Doherty, A.C., Landahl, A.J.: Continuous quantum error correction via quantum feedback control. Phys. Rev. A **65**(4), 042301 (2002)
3. Albash, T., Martin-Mayor, V., Hen, I.: Analog errors in Ising machines. Quantum Sci. Technol. **4**(2), 02LT03 (2019)
4. Allwright, S.: What is a good F1 score and how do I interpret it? (2022). https://stephenallwright.com/good-f1-score/. Accessed 5 Feb 2024
5. Ayanzadeh, R., Das, P., Tannu, S.S., Qureshi, M.: EQUAL: improving the fidelity of quantum annealers by injecting controlled perturbations. arXiv: 2108.10964 [quant-ph] (2021)
6. Ayanzadeh, R., Dorband, J., Halem, M., Finin, T.: Multi-qubit correction for quantum annealers. Sci. Rep. **11**(1), 16119 (2021)
7. Barbosa, A., Pelofske, E., Hahn, G., Djidjev, H.N.: Optimizing embedding-related quantum annealing parameters for reducing hardware bias. In: Ning, L., Chau, V., Lau, F. (eds.) PAAP 2020. CCIS, vol. 1362, pp. 162–173. Springer, Singapore (2021). https://doi.org/10.1007/978-981-16-0010-4_15
8. Boixo, S., et al.: Characterizing quantum supremacy in near-term devices. Nat. Phys. **14**(6), 595–600 (2018)
9. Borah, S., Sarma, B., Kewming, M., Quijandria, F., Milburn, G.J., Twamley, J.: Measurement-based estimator scheme for continuous quantum error correction. Phys. Rev. Res. **4**(3), 033207 (2022)
10. Chancellor, N., et al.: Error measurements for a quantum annealer using the one-dimensional Ising model with twisted boundaries. NPJ Quantum Inf. **8**(1), 1–8 (2022)
11. Cross, A.W., Bishop, L.S., Sheldon, S., Nation, P.D., Gambetta, J.M.: Validating quantum computers using randomized model circuits. Phys. Rev. A **100**(3), 032328 (2019)
12. D-Wave Systems: D-Wave system documentation. https://docs.dwavesys.com/docs/latest. Accessed 16 May 2022
13. Hargreaves, T.: Is it time to ditch the MNIST dataset? (2020). https://www.ttested.com/ditch-mnist/. Accessed 28 Apr 2023
14. Hennrich, M., et al.: Experimental repetitive quantum error correction with trapped ions. In: CLEO: 2011 - Laser Science to Photonic Applications (2011)
15. Kelly, J., et al.: State preservation by repetitive error detection in a superconducting quantum circuit. Nature **519**(7541), 66–69 (2015)
16. Knill, E., Laflamme, R.: Theory of quantum error-correcting codes. Phys. Rev. A **55**(2), 900–911 (1997)
17. Knill, E., Laflamme, R., Zurek, W.H.: Resilient quantum computation. Science **279**(5349), 342–345 (1998)
18. Langione, M., Bobier, J.F., Krayer, L., Park, H., Kumar, A.: The race to quantum advantage depends on benchmarking (2022). https://www.bcg.com/publications/2022/value-of-quantum-computing-benchmarks. Accessed 26 Oct 2022
19. Li, W., Lu, Z.D., Deng, D.L.: Quantum neural network classifiers: a tutorial. SciPost Phys. Lect. Notes **61** (2022)
20. Linke, N.M., et al.: Experimental comparison of two quantum computing architectures. PNAS **114**(13), 3305–3310 (2017)

21. Lubinski, T., et al.: Application-oriented performance benchmarks for quantum computing. arXiv: 2110.03137 [quant-ph] (2021)
22. Martiel, S., Ayral, T., Allouche, C.: Benchmarking quantum coprocessors in an Application-Centric, Hardware-Agnostic, and scalable way. IEEE Trans. Quantum Eng. **2**, 1–11 (2021)
23. Moll, N., et al.: Quantum optimization using variational algorithms on near-term quantum devices. Quantum Sci. Technol. **3**(3), 030503 (2018)
24. Nelson, J., Vuffray, M., Lokhov, A.Y., Albash, T., Coffrin, C.: High-quality thermal Gibbs sampling with quantum annealing hardware. Phys. Rev. Applied **17**(4), 044046 (2022)
25. Nelson, J., Vuffray, M., Lokhov, A.Y., Coffrin, C.: Single-qubit fidelity assessment of quantum annealing hardware. IEEE Trans. Quantum Eng. **2**, 1–10 (2021)
26. Paltenghi, M.: Cross-platform testing of quantum computing platforms. In: 2022 IEEE/ACM 44th International Conference on Software Engineering: Companion Proceedings (ICSE-Companion), pp. 269–271 (2022)
27. Papers with Code: Image classification on MNIST. https://paperswithcode.com/sota/image-classification-on-mnist. Accessed 28 Apr 2023
28. Pare, S., Bhandari, A.K., Kumar, A., Singh, G.K., Khare, S.: Satellite image segmentation based on different objective functions using genetic algorithm: a comparative study. In: 2015 IEEE International Conference on Digital Signal Processing (DSP), pp. 730–734 (2015)
29. Pearson, A., Mishra, A., Hen, I., Lidar, D.A.: Analog errors in quantum annealing: doom and hope. NPJ Quantum Inf. **5**(1), 1–9 (2019)
30. Pelofske, E., Bärtschi, A., Eidenbenz, S.: Quantum volume in practice: what users can expect from NISQ devices. IEEE Trans. Quantum Eng. **3**, 1–19 (2022)
31. Pelofske, E., Hahn, G., Djidjev, H.N.: Noise dynamics of quantum annealers: estimating the effective noise using idle qubits. Quantum Sci. Technol. **8**(3), 035005 (2023)
32. Pochart, T., Jacquot, P., Mikael, J.: On the challenges of using D-Wave computers to sample Boltzmann random variables. In: 2022 IEEE 19th International Conference on Software Architecture Companion (ICSA-C), pp. 137–140 (2022)
33. Proctor, T., Seritan, S., Rudinger, K., Nielsen, E., Blume-Kohout, R., Young, K.: Scalable randomized benchmarking of quantum computers using mirror circuits. Phys. Rev. Lett. **129**(15), 150502 (2022)
34. Pudenz, K.L., Albash, T., Lidar, D.A.: Error-corrected quantum annealing with hundreds of qubits. Nat. Commun. **5**, 3243 (2014)
35. Ronke, R., Spiller, T.P., D'Amico, I.: Effect of perturbations on information transfer in spin chains. Phys. Rev. A **83**(1), 012325 (2011)
36. Suau, A., Nelson, J., Vuffray, M., Lokhov, A.Y., Cincio, L., Coffrin, C.: Single-qubit cross platform comparison of quantum computing hardware. arXiv: 2108.11334 [quant-ph] (2021)
37. Tiziano, M.: Estimating quantum volume for advantage (2020). https://support.dwavesys.com/hc/en-us/community/posts/360051945133-Estimating-Quantum-Volume-for-Advantage. Accessed 10 June 2022
38. Unmoved: 30k cats and dogs 150 × 150 greyscale (2023). https://www.kaggle.com/datasets/unmoved/30k-cats-and-dogs-150x150-greyscale
39. Zaborniak, T., de Sousa, R.: Benchmarking Hamiltonian noise in the D-Wave quantum annealer. IEEE Trans. Quantum Eng. **2**, 1–6 (2021)
40. Zolotarev, Y.F., Luchnikov, I.A., López-Saldivar, J.A., Fedorov, A.K., Kiktenko, E.O.: Continuous monitoring for noisy intermediate-scale quantum processors. arXiv: 2205.06191 [quant-ph] (2022)

Benchmarking the D-Wave Quantum Annealer as a Sparse Boltzmann Machine: Recognition and Timing Performances

Jess Park[1,5], Nick Chancellor[2,3], David Griffin[1], Viv Kendon[4], and Susan Stepney[1(✉)]

[1] Department of Computer Science, University of York, York, UK
susan.stepney@york.ac.uk
[2] Quantum Chancellor, Durham, UK
[3] School of Computing, Newcastle University, Newcastle upon Tyne, UK
[4] Department of Physics, University of Strathclyde, Glasgow, UK
[5] Dstl, Salisbury, UK

Abstract. We investigate the effectiveness of using a 'sparse' Boltzmann Machine (SBM) fitted natively to the D-Wave quantum annealer architecture, for image classification, and the benefits in terms of execution time over using a classical annealer. We design a series of SBM networks, and run a series of image classification experiments, measuring both the accuracy of the trained networks, and the training times running both on the D-Wave QPU and simulated on a CPU. We find poor recognition accuracy. This may be due to sparsity, or to using default D-Wave parameter settings. We find that the sampling step is faster on the D-Wave QPU than simulated on a classical CPU, and the benefit increases with network size (larger problems). Overheads, from Internet and queuing latencies and from input bottlenecks, mean that this advantage is not seen on the full problem until an unrealistically high number of reads per anneal. On a dedicated local machine with no queuing, however, this number reduces significantly, such that the QPU is more efficient than the CPU on the full problem.

1 Introduction

Quantum computing promises benefits in terms of processing speed. The D-Wave quantum annealer can solve a particular subset of problems; the sampling used in annealing is faster when done natively than when simulated classically, offering speed advantages. However, quantum devices have severe limitations when I/O latencies and sizes are considered.

Here we investigate the use of the D-Wave Advantage 4.1 QPU with Pegasus qubit interconnection topology [13] to implement a 'sparse' Boltzmann Machine, a different application than typically used, and measure its performance on an image classification tasks in terms of both accuracy and timing, as a function of input image size.

© The Author(s), under exclusive license to Springer Nature Switzerland AG 2024
D.-J. Cho and J. Kim (Eds.): UCNC 2024, LNCS 14776, pp. 43–57, 2024.
https://doi.org/10.1007/978-3-031-63742-1_4

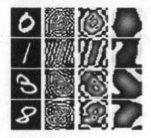 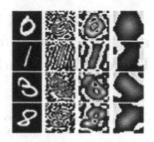

Fig. 1. Effect of DCT Truncation Compression on MNIST images of the digits used in this study (0,1,3,8) with compressions values (running left to right) of U,16,8,4. U is the original uncompressed 28×28 greyscale image. Compression value n is a 28×28 image transformed by a Type-II DCT, compressed (truncated) to $n \times n$ pixels, then expanded back to the original 28×28 size using the type-III DCT. (left) full 32-bit values per pixel in the compressed form; (right) quantised to 5-bit values per pixel, showing only minor differences.

The structure of this paper is as follows: Sect. 2 discusses the front end image compression used; Sect. 3 describes the D-Wave experiments; Sect. 4 describes the comparison classical experiments; Sect. 5 compares results across the D-Wave and CPU platforms; Sect. 6 concludes and suggests future work.

2   Front End Compression

Image Dataset. Our dataset is derived from the MNIST handwritten digit images, comprising 28×28 pixels $\times$ 256 greyscale images, with 60,000 training and 10,000 testing images. We reduce the size of the dataset, to make the task feasible on the D-Wave. We choose four digits: 0, 1, 3, and 8. We also subsample the dataset to 50 samples per digit from the training data. Neural networks can achieve good results on MNIST with even smaller datasets [14].

Image Compression. The D-Wave has limited I/O capabilities, making the presentation of multiple images as needed for image classification slow. Image compression reduces the amount of data that needs to be input.

We use a Type-II Discrete Cosine Transform (DCT) [2], then compress by truncating the series, which maintains spatial information. The DCT-Truncation algorithm is scale invariant: any size of input can be provided, and the DCT-Truncation will provide an output of the requested size. A sample of original and compressed images is shown in Fig. 1. High compression values are noisy and only the black background of the image is reconstructed, whereas lower values are primarily reconstructing the major details of the shape of the digit.

Table 1. The number and sizes of hidden layers in the benchmark NNs, and the D-Wave networks with a comparable number of hidden nodes.

name	hidden layer sizes	comparable D-Wave
small	12	4×4, Fig. 3
medium	$64, 32, 16$	8×8, Fig. 4
huge	$1024, 512, 256, 128, 64$	28×28, Fig. 6

D-Wave Quantisation. Images are supplied to the D-Wave as input weights, supplied as 8-bit values. Our understanding is that in practice only about 5-bits of precision are actually realised. The values from the DCT-Truncated representation are 32-bit floats. We further compress the DCT output to 8-bits of precision. Figure 1(right) show a visual representation of the images after the DCT-Truncated representation is quantised to the realised 5 bits. As can be seen, the effect is relatively minor.

Classical Neural Network Baseline. The reduced data set has been subsampled from ten to four digits, and from 60,000 to 50 samples per digit, compressed by DCT truncation, and quantised from 32 to effectively 5-bit values. To check that this reduced data set can still be successfully classified, we tested using off the shelf classical neural networks with comparable numbers of nodes to the D-Wave networks used later (Sect. 3).

Different sizes of classical neural networks are used to classify at each level of compression n (U,16,8,4). For each network size, the input layer is size n^2 (the compressed image size), the number and sizes of hidden layers are as in Table 1, and the output layer is the number of possible labels for inputs: 4.

The results of these tests show the following. Our subsampled MNIST dataset can be correctly classified with accuracy of 70% for uncompressed images and medium-sized networks. Small networks are too small to classify well; huge networks appear to overfit, and also perform poorly. The compressed images are classified at least as well as uncompressed images. Using 32 bit or 5 bit quantisation has little effect on the results at compression values used here.

Thus we conclude that our reduced, compressed, quantised dataset is suitable training data for the main D-Wave experiments.

3   D-Wave Training and Classification Experiments

3.1   Boltzmann Machine Variants

The D-Wave Advantage Pegasus qubit interconnection topology has a maximum of 15 connections per qubit. If more connectivity is needed, then embedding can be used [6,7], where strongly coupled physical qubits represent one logical qubit, which benefits from the connectivity of all the physical qubits. This comes at the expense of qubits, which limits the network size that can be used.

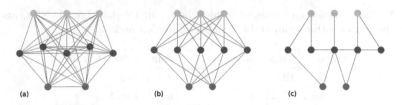

Fig. 2. Schematic view of different network layouts, illustrating the connectivities of the different variants of Boltzmann Machines. Input nodes are yellow, hidden nodes are blue, output nodes are red. (a) Boltzmann Machine: fully connected graph. (b) Restricted Boltzmann Machine: fully connected between layers; no connections within layers. (c) Sparse Boltzmann Machine: sparsely connected (that is, less than fully connected) both between and within layers, with all input nodes nevertheless having a path to all output nodes. (Color figure online)

Table 2. The total number of nodes N in the designed D-Wave networks, comprising n^2 inputs, approximately n^2 hidden nodes (see design method for how the actual number is determined) and 4 output nodes. The maximum number of connections possible in the designed D-Wave networks using native connectivity is $15N/2$; the number in a fully connected Boltzmann Machine is $N(N-1)/2$. Sparsity is the maximum number of native connections divided by the number of BM connections.

image	inputs	hidden	outputs	N	native	BM	sparsity %	figure
4×4	16	12	4	32	240	496	48	Fig. 3
8×8	64	460	4	528	3,960	139,128	2.9	Fig. 4
16×16	256	460	4	720	5,400	258,840	2.1	Fig. 5
28×28	784	1210	4	1998	14,985	1,995,003	0.75	Fig. 6

Standard quantum Boltzmann Machines [3] (BMs) are fully connected (Fig. 2a), Restricted quantum Boltzmann Machines [1] (RBMs) have fully connected layers (Fig. 2b); neither of these are possible to implement on the D-Wave Pegasus without considerable embedding overhead, and then only for small networks. Indeed, any network with more than 15 inputs would need to use embedding.

Instead, we design what we term 'sparse' BM networks (Fig. 2c) that use only the D-Wave Pegasus native connectivity, a sparse quasi-planar graph. These sparse networks have some connectivity between hidden layers nodes, unlike an RBM. They also have a path from all input nodes to all output nodes, to ensure that all input information can have an effect on the output.

In Table 2 we show the effect of using a quasi-planar graph with 15 connections per node (and hence a maximum number of $15N/2$ connections available for an N node graph), versus the number of connections in a fully connected BM graph, $N(N-1)/2$ connections, for the network sizes we use.

3.2   Network Layouts

We have designed specific networks for each image size investigated: see Table 2 and Figs. 3, 4, 5 and 6. Each network has one input node for each pixel in the relevant image. The greyscale value of that pixel is input as the bias value on that node. This is supplied as a quantised 8-bit value, but we assume that the precision on the physical hardware is limited to approximately 5 bits.

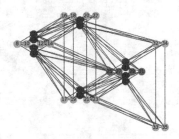

Fig. 3. 4 × 4 network: 16 input (yellow), 12 hidden (blue), 4 output (red) node network (32 nodes in total). Connections used in the network are shown in green; the remaining available connections are in grey. (Color figure online)

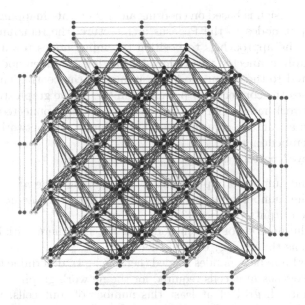

Fig. 4. 8 × 8 network: 64 input (yellow), 460 hidden (blue), 4 output (red) node network (528 nodes in total). Connections used in the network are shown in green; the remaining available connections are in grey. (Color figure online)

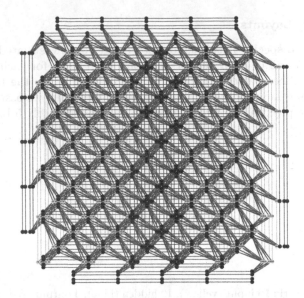

Fig. 5. 16 × 16 network: 256 input (yellow), 460 hidden (blue), 4 output (red) node network (720 nodes in total). Connections used in the network are shown in green; the remaining available connections are in grey. (Color figure online)

Our network design is based on choosing an appropriate mapping of the input nodes and output nodes to the Pegasus architecture: the remaining nodes are hidden nodes. The approach is to position the input nodes towards the outer edges of the graph, connected to a tighter-knit region of hidden nodes, which are in turn connected to the output nodes positioned in the centre. This "bullseye" design maximises the connectivity permitted in the native graph structure. This produces a network much sparser than traditional fully-connected BMs. However, it has the advantage of using one physical qubit per network node; there is no need for embedding.

The "bullseye" pattern is designed as follows:

– determine the number of input nodes, here the image size n^2
– determine the number of output nodes, here 4 from the one-hot encoding of four possible outputs (see Sect. 3.3)
– determine the number of hidden nodes for the BM, here initially chosen to be the same as the number of input nodes, n^2
– from the total number of nodes needed (here $2n^2+4$), determine the minimum number of Pegasus unit cells required for the network graph
– choose a squarish grid of at least this number of unit cells, which give a specific number of nodes that fit this choice
– place the network, taking into account 'dead' (non-functional) qubits: there are physically non-functional qubits in a specific D-Wave device, so extract a list of "live" qubits, which are then the only ones available for assignment to the network. Smaller networks can typically be placed as designed to avoid

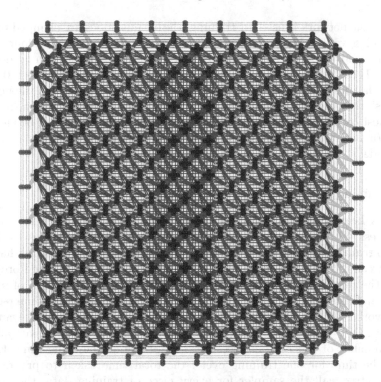

Fig. 6. 28×28 network: 784 input (yellow), 1210 hidden (blue), 4 output (red) node network (1998 nodes in total). Connections used in the network are shown in green; the remaining available connections are in grey. (Color figure online)

dead qubits; larger network design may need to take dead qubits into account in their resulting number of nodes

- partition the input nodes into two groups, and allocate each group to nodes at the far left and far right of the graph (this arrangement is for case of implementation, given the D-Wave qubit numbering system)
- allocate the output nodes to nodes close together towards the centre of the graph
- assign all other nodes in the graph as hidden nodes (this may be a slightly different number from n^2, depending on the number of unit cells assigned, and the number of dead qubits to be avoided).
- include in the network all the native connections between all included nodes

3.3 Output Encoding

The number of output nodes depends on the number of output classes needed, and how the output classes are encoded. Here we use 'one-hot' encoding, with one output node per class in the data. The four classes used here are encoded as: $(0) \rightarrow [1, 0, 0, 0]$; $(1) \rightarrow [0, 1, 0, 0]$; $(3) \rightarrow [0, 0, 1, 0]$; $(8) \rightarrow [0, 0, 0, 1]$.

When the network is used for training, the output nodes are clamped to their relevant class values. When the network is used for classification, all four output nodes are read out, and each has a value of either 0 or 1 for each read of the sampler. These are averaged over all the reads to give a value between 0 and 1 for that class node. This value represents the confidence with which the network "believes" that the given input belongs to that class. Typically, and in this case, the highest confidence value is taken as the result, and is marked as being either correct or incorrect, regardless of the confidence value placed on that or any other node.

3.4   Training Timings on D-Wave

D-Wave's Leap dashboard provides timing information for different stages of the process [8, Sect. "Operation and Timing"]. The key measures used here are: **Programming time** [from dashboard]: An initialisation step that happens once per call to the QPU. Here, this takes the network of weights and programs it onto the real device. **Sample time** [from dashboard]: The sum of anneal, readout and delay times, over n reads. **Service time**: The sum of time required by the worker before and after QPU access, which includes the I/O, wait time in queues, QPU access time and post-processing times. This is in part affected by the number of other users accessing the service at the same time. **Epoch time**: The time for one training cycle: the total time taken to program the weight matrix, call the sampler for every piece of training data, then on the CPU calculate the gradient and update the weight matrix. This scales with the amount of training data used and encompasses the scaling present in the other timing metrics. It includes internet latency and device access queueing latency. **Local epoch time**: A derived measure: the epoch time as it would be on a dedicated machine, with no internet latency or device access queueing latency. See Sect. 5.

Figure 7 shows how these measures are related to the BM training algorithm. Given T training images, $T + 1$ calls to the D-Wave are required every training epoch: T calls for sampling the 'clamped' weight matrix for each training image, and one call for a comparison 'unclamped' sample. Each sample is accomplished with n reads. The number of training epochs that are required is problem- (and desired solution quality) dependent, discussed Sect. 3.5.

Training Timing Results. Getting a good sample in order to train weights requires multiple reads. Here we investigate how various times scale with number of reads per sample. How the various stages of the BM training algorithm scale with the number of reads and with the size of the input data are given in Figs. 8 and 9. Data points are taken over a single run of each input size, averaged over a number of examples within that single run.

Programming time, Fig. 8a. From the results no clear dependence is evident between the programming time and the number of reads or the size of the input

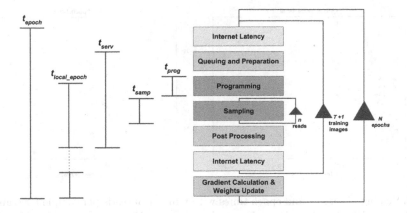

Fig. 7. Breakdown of the training algorithm with the key timing metrics indicated. The loops show how many times each step is repeated. The green boxes execute on the D-Wave servers (but not on the QPU itself), the blue boxes execute on the QPU, and the red box execute on the local classical machine. (Color figure online)

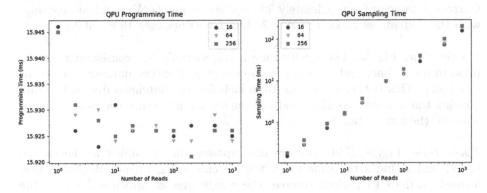

Fig. 8. Scaling of programming and sampling times with number of reads per sample, for training on D-Wave QPU, for three input image sizes 4×4, 8×8, 16×16. (Note the logarithmic y axis in the sampling time plot.)

data. This is as expected: the programming step is done only once per call to the sampler, regardless of the number of reads, and it requires the whole chip to be programmed regardless of the number of non-zero nodes and edges. Note from the scale that the programming time is largely consistent across all the data points; compared to the time taken in the sampling stage, it is unlikely to be the source of a bottleneck.

Sampling time, Fig. 8b. The sampling time scales linearly with the number of reads, but is unaffected by the size of the input data. This is as expected: the sampling is run on the entire chip, regardless of how many nodes and edges are non-zero. The only limit to increasing the size of the input data, in terms of

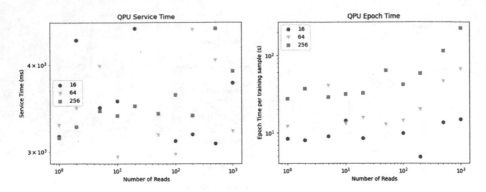

Fig. 9. Scaling of service and epoch times with number of reads per sample for training on D-Wave QPU, for three input image sizes $4 \times 4 = 16$, $8 \times 8 = 64$, $16 \times 16 = 256$. (Note the logarithmic y axis in the sampling time plot.)

the sampling time, is the maximum size of the network that can fit on one chip. Currently, there are approximately 5000 qubits on one D-Wave Advantage chip; with the current networks, the 28×28 image network uses 1998 qubits.

Service time, Fig. 9a. The service time is considerably less consistent than the programming time, and does not scale clearly with either number of reads or input size. This is because service time includes long latencies due to I/O and queuing times (note the millisecond scale on the sampling time versus the seconds scale on the service time).

Epoch time, Fig. 9b. This measure encompasses the variability in the service times, and includes the time taken for the classical gradient calculation performed on the CPU, which involves the weight matrix, which scales with the number of nodes in the network. This explains the longer epoch times for larger input sizes. Even when the sampling is performed on the QPU, the CPU calculations in the rest of the algorithm can be a limiting factor.

3.5　Classification Evaluation

Training and Classification Parameter Values. To train BMs to perform classification, there are a number of algorithm parameters that need to be set, such as learning rate, number of reads, and effective temperature. Here we choose values based on related literature or default parameters, rather than performing a parameter sweep.

For the D-Wave annealer we used the default parameters. The number of reads used in the classification experiment is 100. This is a value used by [9], and is expected to show enough expressivity in the sampler.

When a weight matrix is passed to the annealer, it is usually automatically rescaled to use the whole range of values available on the chip, which sets the temperature of the anneal. For better control of the process, we disable autoscaling. To force the annealer to operate at the higher temperature thought to be required for the BM, the values in the weight matrix are constrained to 50% of their full range (reducing the range increases the effective temperature) [5].

Classification Experiments and Results. Classification evaluations are run over a test set that includes 5 examples of each class (20 samples in total) taken from the training set. Hence the network will have seen these examples during training. This was done here to determine a best case limit.

Due to the parameter-choice constraints (including sparse connectivity, number of epochs), the results are not expected to be comparable with classical NN classification. However, considering the literature [9] on D-Wave implemented RBMs, we would expect to see some evidence of training in the limited dataset we have produced. This is not the case. We would expect the number of incorrectly classified data points to reduce as the number of training epochs increases. However, the number of incorrectly classified points fluctuates around 15 (an accuracy of 25%), which is the same as random guessing.

There are some possible explanations for the poor classification results that we are seeing here that encompass the parameter selection and the graph design. These are discussed in Sect. 6.

4   Classical Annealing Simulator Comparison Experiments

D-Wave provide a 'simulated annealer' module that takes the same inputs as the quantum processing sampler. This runs identical experiments on a classical CPU (where the only difference is classical simulated sampling rather than D-Wave thermal sampling, and all other parameters have the same values) just by changing a 'sampler' flag in the code. We repeat the D-Wave experiments using the simulated annealer; these like-for-like experiments allow us to provide a cross-platform comparison of D-Wave and CPU performance (Sect. 5). We use an Intel i7 2.6 GHz CPU with 64 GB RAM for these experiments.

Training Timing Results. The results for sampling and epoch times are shown in Fig. 10. Unlike on the D-Wave, there is no programming time broken out in the simulated annealer, and sampling time and service time are equivalent as there is no I/O or queuing time required.

In the case of the simulated annealer, both the sampling time and the epoch timescale scale with both number of reads and the problem input size. The sampling time scales approximately linearly for each input size, which is to be expected as the same process simply repeats for each read.

Classification Results. The classification tests on the network trained on the simulated annealer perform equally badly as on the D-Wave trained network. This implies that there are factors beyond the sampler that are preventing the networks from training.

5   Comparison of Timing Results Across Platforms

Sampling Time Comparison. Figure 11 shows the sampling timing data for the D-Wave quantum annealer and simulated annealer for different input sizes.

Independent of input size, the sampling process is faster on the QPU than on the simulated annealer. This speed-up is more noticeable in the larger network, because the sampling time does not scale with input size on the QPU, unlike on the CPU (compare Figs. 8, 9 and 10). This suggests that it becomes more advantageous to use the quantum annealer when moving from "toy problems" to more realistic scenarios (ignoring the limitation on current chip size).

Epoch Time Comparison. Figure 12 shows that for the networks tested here, the QPU requires significantly more time per epoch than does the CPU, due to access overheads. However, the scaling with the number of reads is slower, and suggests that in cases where the required number of reads is high (higher than tested here), there would be grounds (purely based on timings) to use the QPU over the CPU. In the cases with 16 input nodes, this crossover point is estimated to be approximately 10,000 reads.

The use of the QPU involves significant internet latency and waiting in queues on the D-Wave servers for preprocessing and hardware availability. If a dedicated

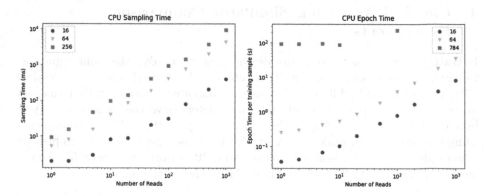

Fig. 10. Timing Graphs for training on D-Wave provided simulated annealer running on a CPU. Definitions of the different timing metrics are given in the appendix.

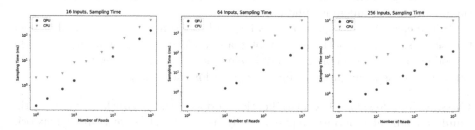

Fig. 11. Sampling time on the QPU and CPU for different size inputs

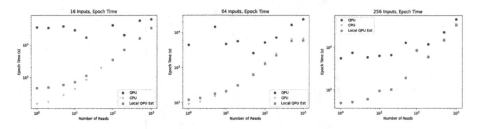

Fig. 12. Epoch time on the QPU and CPU for different input sizes. "Local QPU Est" is the estimated time an epoch would take on a dedicated QPU, Eq. 1. As the number of reads and number of inputs increases, it becomes beneficial to use the QPU over the CPU simulated annealer: beneficial for 16 inputs at 10 reads, 64 inputs at 5 reads; for 256 inputs, always beneficial.

and local quantum annealer were available, these latencies would not apply. To estimate what the epoch time might be for such a local device, we define 'local epoch time':

$$t_{local\_epoch} = t_{prog} + (t_{samp}(T + 1)) + t_{grad} \qquad (1)$$

where t_{prog} is the programming time, t_{samp} is the sampling time, T is the number of images in the training set, and t_{grad} is the CPU time taken to calculate the gradient and update the weights matrix. The value for t_{grad} is taken from timings measured on the local CPU used to run the training. This measure does not include the physical device's I/O times required to load the weights or to read out the values on the output nodes, and therefore represents a lower bound on the time an epoch would take on a local dedicated QPU.

This estimate for epoch time (Fig. 12, green squares) shows when it is beneficial to use the QPU over the CPU simulated annealer. For the 16 input node network, this is at 10 reads, for the 64 input node network, at approximately 5 reads, for the 256 input node network, it is always beneficial. The scaling with number of reads is also much slower, so the benefit in using the QPU grows with the number of reads required to achieve a good sample estimate.

This conclusion does assume that we have optimally chosen the annealing time in these experiments. This optimal time is generally not known, and needs to be established on an application-by-application basis. This quantity and how it scales involves the detailed physics of the device. Furthermore, the scaling of this quantity is difficult to predict; it could potentially be very long, if the device enters a spin glass regime, where relevant timescales span many orders of magnitude [4]. Increasing the annealing time increases the time per read.

Epoch time combines both the quantum and classical elements of the training algorithm; we show how this scales with input size in Fig. 13. For the sizes tested here, the QPU takes longer, but it may scale more beneficially than the purely CPU process, because bottlenecks in the QPU processes (such as I/O issues) do not scale with input size. Therefore, for problems with input sizes large enough, the QPU annealing will provide a faster epoch time than the CPU version,

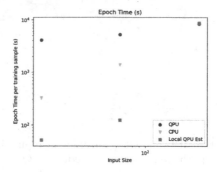

Fig. 13. Epoch time in relation to the size of the input problem. Green squares indicate local epoch time. (Color figure online)

provided the network is still small enough to fit on the chip. The local epoch time (green squares), however, is significantly lower than the CPU time.

6   Conclusions and Future Work

The results from the timing study indicate that the QPU may be beneficial at larger problem sizes (both in terms of network size and number of reads), in terms of training time, especially if a dedicated local machine is available.

The size of the BM network, and hence of the input image, is limited by the physical number of qubits in the hardware chip. There is research into techniques that can split larger problems into sub-graphs that can be run sequentially on a single chip or potentially in parallel on multiple chips (e.g., [15]).

D-Wave classification performance, even after what should be sufficient training, is poor. This poor performance may be due to the D-Wave parameter settings used, to the sparsity of the BM used, or to the quasi-planar nature of the D-Wave connectivity graph [10].

Due to D-Wave access time constraints in producing the analysis documented here, many parameters used to set the annealing schedule could not be fully investigated. In this work, default annealing schedule parameter values were used, as these provide good performance for a large variety of optimisation problems. However, using the D-Wave annealer in a different mode, here as a BM instead, may well require different parameter values. In optimisation the aim is to reach the ground state of the given network; in a BM mode of operation, we aim instead to sample from the whole distribution, which may require longer sampling times.

We use the default annealing schedule, a standard 'forward anneal' temperature reduction, as used in optimisation. Other more complex annealing schedules might be more appropriate for a BM [12].

We have used a sparse BM, tailored to the D-Wave's native graph, with the connectivity limited by the couplers between the qubits. For large networks this leads to very low connectivity in the BM. The performance consequence of this effect should be considered further: it might be that such sparse networks are not sufficiently capable recognisers.

Even after optimising parameter settings and investigating sparseness, it might transpire that the BM is not an appropriate application for the D-Wave hardware. A major issue is that training requires much input, as many training samples each need to be presented many times; the relatively slow input is a bottleneck. Other machine learning models might be adapted to overcome the I/O bottleneck, and should be investigated.

Acknowledgements. The authors wish to acknowledge Defence Science Technical Laboratory (Dstl) who have funded this research [11]. Content includes material subject to © Crown copyright (2024), Dstl. This material is licensed under the terms of the Open Government Licence, except where otherwise stated. To view this licence, visit http://www.nationalarchives.gov.uk/doc/open-government-licence/version/3.

References

1. Adachi, S.H., Henderson, M.P.: Application of quantum annealing to training of deep neural networks. arXiv:1510.06356 [quant-ph] (2015)
2. Ahmed, N., Natarajan, T., Rao, K.R.: Discrete cosine transform. IEEE Trans. Comput. **100**(1), 90–93 (1974)
3. Amin, M.H., Andriyash, E., Rolfe, J., Kulchytskyy, B., Melko, R.: Quantum Boltzmann machine. Phys. Rev. X **8**(2), 021050 (2018)
4. Berthier, L., Reichman, D.R.: Modern computational studies of the glass transition. Nat. Rev. Phys. **5**(2), 102–116 (2023)
5. Chancellor, N., Szoke, S., Vinci, W., Aeppli, G., Warburton, P.A.: Maximum-entropy inference with a programmable annealer. Sci. Rep. **6**(1), 22318 (2016)
6. Choi, V.: Minor-embedding in adiabatic quantum computation: I. The parameter setting problem. Quantum Inf. Process. **7**(5), 193–209 (2008)
7. Choi, V.: Minor-embedding in adiabatic quantum computation: II. Minor-universal graph design. Quantum Inf. Process. **10**(3), 343–353 (2011)
8. D-Wave: QPU solver datasheet (2022). https://docs.dwavesys.com/docs/latest/doc_qpu.html
9. Higham, C.F., Bedford, A.: Quantum deep learning: sampling neural nets with a quantum annealer. arXiv:2107.08710 [quant-ph] (2021)
10. Katzgraber, H.G., Novotny, M.A.: How small-world interactions can lead to improved quantum annealer designs. Phys. Rev. Appl. **10**(5), 054004 (2018)
11. Madahar, B.K., Park, J., Till, S.: Engineering QUantum Enabled Information Processing (EQUIP)—A Journey So Far! In: Quantum Technology for Defence and Security STO-MP-IST-SET-198. NATO STO (2023)
12. Marshall, J., Venturelli, D., Hen, I., Rieffel, E.G.: Power of pausing: advancing understanding of thermalization in experimental quantum annealers. Phys. Rev. Appl. **11**(4), 044083 (2019)
13. McGeoch, C., Farré, P.: The advantage system: performance update. Technical report 14-1054A-A, D-Wave (2021). https://www.dwavesys.com/media/kjtlcemb/14-1054a-a_advantage_system_performance_update.pdf
14. Nielsen, M.: Reduced MNIST: how well can machines learn from small data? (2017). https://cognitivemedium.com/rmnist
15. Pelofske, E., Hahn, G., Djidjev, H.N.: Solving larger maximum clique problems using parallel quantum annealing. arXiv:2205.12165 [quant-ph] (2022)

Software Testing in Computable Analysis

Klaus Meer[1(✉)] and Martin Ziegler[2]

[1] BTU Cottbus-Senftenberg, 03046 Cottbus, Germany
meer@b-tu.de
[2] KAIST School of Computing, Daejeon, Republic of Korea
ziegler@kaist.ac.kr

Abstract. We initiate research on software testing in the realm of computable analysis over the real numbers and general topological spaces. The goal is to develop a general framework and to show some first results of testing algorithms for checking probabilistically whether a Type-2 machine approximately performs the task it is supposed to. We give a testing algorithm for Type-2 programs supposed to compute the exponential function. As main result, we design a test whether a program approximately computes a univariate polynomial of given degree. Its analysis reveals close relations to computational learning theory.

1 Introduction

Software testing and verification has been established as an important field in many areas of Computer Science. This holds also in Theoretical Computer Science. As one field of applications, studying questions about verification leads to the study of methods in (finite) model theory, see as general reference [2]. A second application is provided by the huge field of problems in property testing, an area which has emerged from fundamental work on probabilistically checkable proofs, see [4]. It seems fair to say that this research so far mainly has been carried out in the framework of discrete computations over finite words using the classical Turing machine as model.

The purpose of the present work is to initiate research on testing problems in the realm of computable analysis over the real numbers and general topological spaces. In this framework, computations over the real numbers are performed on finite approximations of reals. This is formalized by so-called Type-2 machines, Turing machines which compute better and better approximations of the true result the more accurate a (name of a) real argument is provided, see [9]. Then the general task is to verify in a suitable sense, whether a given Type-2 program computes what is it supposed to. We shall first work out what this precisely should mean. Given the underlying machine model and its approximate nature, it is obvious that a task can only be performed allowing for errors up to a certain degree. Whereas Type-2 machines in principle can perform longer and longer computations, our verification algorithms after a finite number of steps should come to the conclusion whether the given program is accepted or rejected.

D.-J. Cho and J. Kim (Eds.): UCNC 2024, LNCS 14776, pp. 58–73, 2024.
https://doi.org/10.1007/978-3-031-63742-1_5

Therefore, verification algorithms in what follows will be randomized Turing machines. Judging the quality of a verification will be related to measures defined on the used naming system for reals. After the general framework of verification has been set up in the next subsection, we study basically two problems. As first appetizer, we give two verification algorithms for a Type-2 program to compute the exponential function on $[0, 1]$. Then, our main result will verify, whether such a program computes a univariate polynomial of bounded degree on the unit interval. The analysis that the verifier works correctly will make heavy use of a result about approximate interpolation from computational learning theory.

Since we believe the description of the entire framework to be of substantial importance, the proofs of all results are postponed to the full version.

1.1   The Setting

Our goal is as follows: We are given a program computing a function P. For outlining our ideas we suppose P to be a univariate real-valued function on the unit interval: $P : [0, 1] \mapsto \mathbb{R}$. Since our framework is computable analysis, P is given via typical program in this setting, i.e., a Type-2 Turing machine M_P that computes P along the requirements of computable analysis [9].

Depending on the verification task to handle, we expect P and M_P, respectively, to have certain properties. In our first scenario, a function $f : [0, 1] \mapsto \mathbb{R}$ is fixed beforehand. The software checking task then is to verify whether the given program M_P computes in a reasonable sense (to be specified) function f. Here, we consider the exponential function for f. In this setting it is assumed that in principle all information about f is available, for example, there is a Type-2 machine M_f computing f in the sense of computable analysis. As our second and main example, we want to check whether the function computed by a given M_P has a certain property, i.e., is close to a family $\mathcal{F}$ of functions. We study this question for univariate polynomials on $[0, 1]$ having a bounded degree.

To make the above tasks interesting we have to specify in which sense the checking procedure V has to work in order to be successful. This refers foremost to the conditions according to which M_P is considered to (approximately) compute f or an element from $\mathcal{F}$ in a reasonable way, and also to the resources it needs. Concerning the latter it is obvious that they should be considerably less than what is needed, say, for a pointwise approximate comparison of P and f in all points of a suitably narrow grid. As consequence V will work in a randomized manner and thus may err with certain probability when judging whether M_P is doing well. The expected result of V is an 'accept' or a 'reject'; thus, in contrast to Type-2 machines for general real valued functions, V should give a 0-1-answer after a finite amount of time. We choose V as a normal randomized Turing machine having access to the program M_P, and also to M_f if applicable.

Next, we have to make precise in which sense V qualifies M_P to be a good program for f; the considerations for approximating an element from a set $\mathcal{F}$ are similar, with the difference that in this case V has no concrete element available but in addition must check whether one exists. Both M_P and M_f get as inputs not exact real arguments $y \in [0, 1] \subset \mathbb{R}$, but initial segments of so-called names representing y. More precisely, a name for y is an infinite sequence of symbols over a suitable finite alphabet Σ, such that its initial segments provide approximations of y with increasing precision. Similarly, the output of a program approximates its real number result, see [9]. Now, if V is working in a randomized fashion and if we want to judge its performance under a probabilistic point of view, we first have to define a reasonable measure on the set of names and its initial segments. If, for example, $\Sigma = \{0,1\}$ and $\alpha :\subseteq \Sigma^\omega \to X := [0,1]$ is a representation in the above sense, then usually the domain $dom(\alpha)$ has measure 0 with respect to the coin-flipping process and its related measure on $\{0,1\}^\omega$, thus preventing a reasonable approach of formalizing the measure of inputs for which M_P works fine or badly, respectively. Therefore, we first have to choose a reasonable measure for the domain of the representation map. Such distributions have been introduced in quite a general form resulting from 'probabilistic processes' on Σ^ω in [7]. For explaining our ideas, we fix as one such distribution one resulting from the signed-digit representation.

Let us assume for the moment that we have already chosen a representation $\alpha :\subseteq \Sigma^\omega \to [0,1]$ for a suitable finite alphabet Σ as well as a distribution $\hat{\pi}$ on $dom(\alpha)$ of α. For a parameter $\delta > 0$ define $\Delta(P,f,\delta) := \{w \in dom(\alpha)| \ |P(\alpha(w)) - f(\alpha(w))| > \delta\}$ as set of inputs on which the function P computed by program M_P is more than δ-far away from the correct values of f. The following definition makes more precise how well a function P given via program M_P approximates f as well as in which sense a verifier checks this. The precise definition of the representation we use and the measure it induces will be given in the next subsection. The definition is closely related to similar notions studied in the Turing machine model for approximating functions on finite domains. The survey by Kiwi et al. [5] gives a historic account on such results.

Definition 1. *Let Σ be a finite alphabet, $\alpha :\subseteq \Sigma^\omega \to [0,1]$ be a representation of $[0,1]$ and $\hat{\pi}$ a measure on Σ^ω resulting from a probabilistic process π and generating a probabilistic name for α (see below). Let $P, f : [0,1] \mapsto \mathbb{R}$ be computable functions with corresponding Type-2 machines M_P, M_f. a) For $\delta > 0$ define $\Delta(P,f,\delta) := \{w \in dom(\alpha)| \ |P(\alpha(w)) - f(\alpha(w))| > \delta\}$. We call $\hat{\pi}(\Delta(P,f,\delta))$ the δ-distance of f and P with respect to π and α (and usually omit π, α if clear from the context).*

b) Let $0 \leq \epsilon_1 < \epsilon_2 \leq 1, 0 < \delta_1 < \delta_2$ be parameters and let $\beta \in (0,1)$ be a confidence parameter. A randomized Turing machine V (called verifier) is an $(\epsilon_1, \delta_1, \epsilon_2, \delta_2)$-approximate tester for f (with respect to π, α) if the following holds: Verifier V has access to M_P and M_f to compute (in the Type-2 sense) approximations of P and f in certain points. At the end of its computation V either accepts or rejects M_P as program computing a suitable approximation P of f. More precisely:

– for all M_P s.t. the δ_2-distance of P and f is $\geq \epsilon_2$ it is the case that $Pr(V$ rejects $M_P) \geq 1 - \beta$ and
– for all M_P s.t. the δ_1-distance of P and f is $\leq \epsilon_1$ it is the case that $Pr(V$ accepts $M_P) \geq 1 - \beta$.

Since parameters $\epsilon_i, \delta_i, \beta$ will occur in our verification algorithms they should be computable and therefore assumed to be rational. The probabilistic part of our verification algorithms will basically consist of picking random elements of certain length from Σ^*. Since any probabilistic process used to define a measure on $dom(\alpha)$ canonically generates a discrete distribution on each Σ^k, it then seems appropriate that V picks elements from some Σ^k according to this distribution.

Note that above we do not restrict the resources of V. Though it works similarly to an oracle machine having access to evaluation of both P and f, it is reasonable later on to take into account as well the resources M_P needs and compare it with the resources of a good program M_f for f (which is supposed to be available). Thus, f and M_f are assumed to be fixed, whereas good approximating programs M_P and related P should not deviate too much from M_f as well with respect to the complexity. However, in our setting it seems not clear how to test this randomly. We comment on this point below.

Another most important aspect is the question, which precision M_P requires in order to evaluate P with a given accuracy at a point x. In the Type-2 model this is formalized using the modulus of continuity of P. Given an $n \in \mathbb{N}, M_P$ as part of its computation determines the precision $\mu_P(n)$ being necessary for input $w \in \Sigma^\omega$ to compute $P(\alpha(w))$ within accuracy 2^{-n}, i.e., for every v such that $|\alpha(w) - \alpha(v)| \leq 2^{-\mu_P(n)}$ it is $|P(\alpha(w)) - P(\alpha(v))| \leq 2^{-n}$. Below, this is a fundamental step for all verifiers we consider and a verifier can only judge the program M_P with respect to its quality approximating f or a class of functions if it has *knowledge about the modulus of continuity of M_P*. Since in general already the problem of deciding whether a Turing machine is a Type-2 machine is undecidable, the testing scenario must assume this information to be given in the spirit of a *promise problem*, see [3]. We therefore throughout the paper assume the following

Proviso: In all studied verification problems, when a verifier has to deal with a program M_P it is promised that M_P indeed is a Type-2 machine and that its modulus of continuity μ_P is available to V. It is not necessarily required here, that the modulus is the minimal possible, instead the verifier tests the given program with respect to the promised information. One way to realize this, for example, is a promise on the running time of M_P, since the complexity allows a direct estimate for the modulus, see [9]. For sake of simplicity we present our results under the assumption of knowing the modulus. It would be no problem to derive them, for example, from a promised running time.

1.2   Formal Definitions and Basic Technical Results

The way to deal with real number functions in computable analysis is by using continuous representations of real numbers. The latter are obtained by mapping infinite words over a finite alphabet Σ to reals via a map $\alpha \subseteq \Sigma^\omega \to \mathbb{R}$ such that, among other properties, longer and longer initial segments of an infinite word give better and better approximations of the represented real. We consider Σ^ω as a topological space equipped with the Cantor topology defined by the family of open sets $\mathcal{O}(\Sigma^\omega) := \{W\Sigma^\omega | W \subseteq \Sigma^*\}$, where $W\Sigma^\omega := \{w\Sigma^\omega | w \in W\}$. On (subsets of) the reals we consider the (induced) Euclidean topology.

There are many such continuous representations suitable for use in computable analysis, see [9]. We outline our ideas using one particular such representation for computing real functions from $[0,1] \to \mathbb{R}$, the so called signed digit representation ρ_{sd}. In order to then quantify how successful a probabilistic algorithm works on inputs from $dom(\rho_{sd})$ (in the sense of: what measure has the set of inputs on which the algorithm performs well in view of precise criteria), we need to introduce a measure on $dom(\rho_{sd})$. We follow the approach in [7].

Firstly, we analyse certain basic open sets A_x in the above Cantor topology on Σ^ω with respect to their measures and the structure of $\rho_{sd}(A_x)$ in $[0,1]$.

Definition 2. *Let* $\Sigma := \{0, 1, \bar{1}\}$ *and* $\bar{\Sigma} := \{0, 1, \bar{1}, .\}$. *The signed digit presentation* ρ_{sd} *maps the elements from the set* $dom(\rho_{sd}) := 0.0^*1\Sigma^\omega \cup 1.0^*\bar{1}\Sigma^\omega \subset \bar{\Sigma}^\omega$ *to* $[0,1] \subset \mathbb{R}$ *via* $\rho_{sd}(x_0.x_1x_2\ldots) = \sum_{n\in\mathbb{N}} x_n 2^{-n}$, *where on the right hand side the symbol* $\bar{1}$ *is interpreted as* -1. *We denote by* $A := \{x \in \bar{\Sigma}^* | x\bar{\Sigma}^\omega \cap \rho_{sd}^{-1}[0,1] \neq \emptyset\}$ *all initial segments of* ρ_{sd}-*names for points in the unit interval.*

The signed digit representation is continuous with respect to the Cantor topology on its domain and the Euclidean topology on $Y := [0,1]$. We now want to define a probability measure on Y which fits to the representation given by ρ_{sd} in a specific sense. The concept of probabilistic processes on Γ^ω, Γ a finite alphabet, which was introduced in [7], provides a general framework for doing so for continuous representations. In our framework such a process π_{sd} is a specific mapping from $\bar{\Sigma}^* \to [0,1]$ which generates a measure on $dom(\rho_{sd})$.

Definition 3 *([7]).* *Let* Γ *be a finite alphabet,* $\lambda \in \Gamma^*$ *the empty word, and* Y *a topological space. a) A probabilistic process on* Γ^ω *is a map* $\pi : \Gamma^* \to [0,1]$ *satisfying* $\pi(\lambda) = 1$ *and for all* $w \in \Gamma^* :$ $\pi(w) = \sum_{b\in\Gamma} \pi(wb)$.

b) Let $\alpha :\subseteq \Gamma^\omega \to Y$ *be a continuous representation of* Y *(with respect to the Cantor topology on* Γ^ω*). A probabilistic name for* α *is a probabilistic process* π *on* Γ^ω *such that for all open* $U \subseteq Y$ *and open* $V_1, V_2 \subseteq \Gamma^\omega$ *with* $V_1 \cap dom(\alpha) = V_2 \cap dom(\alpha) = \alpha^{-1}(U)$ *it holds that* $\hat{\pi}(V_1) = \hat{\pi}(V_2)$. *Here,* $\hat{\pi}$ *denotes the outer regular Borel measure on the Cantor space* Γ^ω*, defined by* $\hat{\pi}(W\Gamma^\omega) := \sum_{w\in W} \pi(w)$ *for all prefix-free* $W \subseteq \Gamma^*$.

For a probabilistic process on Γ^ω and fixed k it is $\sum_{w\in\Gamma^k} \pi(w) = 1$, yielding a discrete distribution on Γ^k. Below, verifiers pick random elements according to this distribution.

An example of a probabilistic process yielding a probabilistic name for the signed-digit representation is the following. It will be the process used below.

Definition 4 *Let* $\bar{\Sigma}, \rho_{sd}$ *be as above,* $m, n \in \mathbb{N}$. *Define* $\pi_{sd} : \bar{\Sigma}^* \to [0,1]$ *as follows:*

$\pi_{sd}(\lambda) = 1, \pi_{sd}(0) = \pi_{sd}(1) = \pi_{sd}(0.) = \pi_{sd}(1.) = \frac{1}{2}$

$\pi_{sd}(0.0^n) = \pi_{sd}(1.0^n) = 2^{-n-1}$

$\pi_{sd}(0.0^n 1) = \pi_{sd}(1.0^n \bar{1}) = 2^{-n-2}$

$\pi_{sd}(0.0^n 1 \bar{\Sigma}^m) = \pi_{sd}(1.0^n \bar{1} \bar{\Sigma}^m) = 2^{-n-2} \cdot 3^{-m}$

$\pi_{sd}(w) = 0$ *for all other* $w \in \bar{\Sigma}^*$ (*i.e., all* $w \in \bar{\Sigma}^* \setminus A$, *A as in Definition* 2).

It is easy to check that π_{sd} is a probabilistic process on $\bar{\Sigma}^\omega$ and that it is a probabilistic name for ρ_{sd}. According to Theorem 8 in [7] it induces a Borel measure on $[0,1]$. In what follows our probabilistic verification algorithms frequently pick random points from some fixed $\bar{\Sigma}^k$ and evaluate the program that shall be tested in these points. It seems reasonable then to take $\pi_{sd}|_{\bar{\Sigma}^k}$ as distribution for the verifier. In this context, the following objects occur frequently. Recall from Definition 2 that $A = \{x \in \bar{\Sigma}^* | x \bar{\Sigma}^\omega \cap \rho_{sd}^{-1}[0,1] \neq \emptyset\}$.

Definition 5 *For* $x \in A$ *we denote by* $A_x := x \bar{\Sigma}^\omega$ *the basic open set with initial segment* x. *For* $k \in \mathbb{N}$ *let* $B_k := \{x \in A | x = x_0.x_1 \ldots x_k\}$ *be the set of all initial segments of* ρ_{sd}-*names with precisely* k *components following the binary dot. We denote by* $\hat{\pi}_{sd}$ *the outer Borel measure on* $\bar{\Sigma}^\omega$ *generated by* π_{sd} *as above.*

Proposition 1 *Let* $k \in \mathbb{N}$ *fixed,* $x, \tilde{x} \in B_k$ *with* $x \neq \tilde{x}$.

a) *It is* $\left(\frac{1}{3}\right)^{k+1} \leq \hat{\pi}_{sd}(A_x) \leq \left(\frac{1}{2}\right)^{k+1}$

b) *The set* $\rho_{sd}(x\bar{\Sigma}^\omega)$ *is contained in an interval of (Euclidean) length* 2^{-k+1} *in* $[0,1]$. *The Euclidean distance of* $\rho_{sd}(x0^\omega)$ *and* $\rho_{sd}(\tilde{x}0^\omega)$ *is at least* 2^{-k}.

c) *Let* $\epsilon > 0$ *and* $k^* := \lceil \log \frac{1}{2\epsilon^2} \rceil$. *Let* $w \in A$ *be such that* $\hat{\pi}_{sd}(A_w) \geq \epsilon^2$. *Then,* A_w *contains a point* $x0^\omega$ *such that* $x \in B_{k^*}$ *and* $A_x \subseteq A_w$.

Moreover, for k^* *it holds* $\left(\frac{1}{3}\right)^{k^*+1} > \frac{1}{9}\sqrt{8}\epsilon^4$.

2   Software Testing for Continuous Functions on $[0,1]$

We are now ready to give first verification algorithms that check whether a Type-2 program M_P computes a function $P : [0,1] \to \mathbb{R}$ which approximates a computable $f : [0,1] \to \mathbb{R}$. More precisely, we design two $(\epsilon_1, \delta_1, \epsilon_2, \delta_2)$-approximate testers for f for various parameter values. For sake of simplicity when explaining the ideas we take f as the exponential function. It will be straightforward to obtain similar results for any computable function on a computable compact set in some $\mathbb{R}^d$.

2.1   Approximate Tester for *exp*

Suppose positive (rational) parameters ϵ, δ, β to be given. Below, we assume $\epsilon^2 < \delta/10e$ and comment on other choices later on. Let $f(x) := exp(x) : [0,1] \to \mathbb{R}$ be computable via a Type-2 machine M_f. Let $P : [0,1] \to \mathbb{R}$ be computable via a Type-2 machine M_P. We use the signed digit representation ρ_{sd} for reals in the unit interval as well as the probabilistic process π_{sd} and the measure $\widehat{\pi}_{sd}$ as defined above. The randomized verifier below has access to these two programs. Recall the Proviso from Sect. 1.1.

Test Algorithm 1: Let $\beta \in (0,1), \epsilon, \delta > 0$, $\epsilon^2 < \delta/10e < 1$, and $k^* := \lceil \log \frac{1}{2\epsilon^2} \rceil$.

Step 1. Verifier V randomly picks a point $x \in B_{k^*}$ according to the distribution generated by π_{sd}, i.e., with probability $\widehat{\pi}_{sd}(x\bar{\Sigma}^\omega)$. V then evaluates $P(\rho_{sd}(x0^\omega))$ and $exp(\rho_{sd}(x0^\omega))$ with accuracy $\delta/200$. Let $\tilde{P}(x)$ and $\widetilde{exp}(x)$ denote the approximations computed.

If $|\tilde{P}(x) - \widetilde{exp}(x)| \geq (\frac{1}{2} + \frac{1}{100}) \cdot \delta$, then V rejects, otherwise goto Step 2.

Step 2. Define $n^* := \lceil - \log \frac{\delta}{4} \rceil$.

V requests the number $\mu_P(n^*)$ of symbols from $x0^\omega$ necessary for computing $P(\rho_{sd}(x0^\omega))$ within an accuracy 2^{-n^*} (see Proviso). If $\mu_P(n^*) > k^*$ it rejects.

Step 3. V repeats Steps 1 and 2 independently $t^* := \lceil \frac{\log 1 - \beta}{\log (1 - \sqrt{8}\epsilon^4/9)} \rceil$ times. If at least once a reject occurs, then V rejects altogether, otherwise it accepts M_P.

Theorem 1 *Given parameters ϵ, δ, β as above, verifier V from Test Algorithm 1 is a $(0, \delta/100, \epsilon, \delta)$-approximate tester for exp on $[0,1]$ using ρ_{sd} as representation and π_{sd} as probabilistic process, respectively.* □

Remark 1 a) If in the setting of the theorem program M_P overestimates the modulus of continuity of the function P it computes, i.e., returns too a high accuracy needed, then V might reject programs M_P even if the $\delta/100$-distance of P and exp is 0. This seems unavoidable for verifiers which in one or the other way make decisions depending on the modulus of continuity. If we do not want to rely on M_P in this way, one can change the statement making success depending on how good the estimate given by M_P is. In such a situation the parameters for accepted functions might become worse. Below we give another test algorithm where a bound on the modulus of continuity witnessed by M_P again comes into play quite naturally.
b) One could tune the parameters in many ways to get (slightly) different statements that perhaps fit better to the intended outcome in a particular situation. Above, we assumed a situation where the threshold value ϵ of the bad set of points is not too large, expressed in relation to $\sqrt{\delta}$. This seems reasonable since in the end one would hope for checking only programs M_P which work reasonably well. If, however, ϵ becomes much larger, one could perform a corresponding analysis of a verifier working with a choice for k^* depending on δ instead of ϵ.
c) In Theorem 1 the verifier accepts with probability 1 programs for P with $\widehat{\pi}_{sd}(\Delta(P, exp, \frac{\delta}{100})) = 0$, if they are not rejected in Step 2 because of an overestimated modulus of continuity. One can as well obtain acceptance by

the same V of programs P allowing a positive measure $\widehat{\pi}_{sd}(\Delta(P, exp, \delta_1)) \leq \epsilon_1$ for small enough positive ϵ_1, δ_1 if we assume more on the modulus of continuity of P, for example relating it to that of exp.

d) Analogues of Theorem 1 clearly hold in a broader sense both with respect to the functions f considered, the domain of f and the used probabilistic process. For such variants, the structure of Test Algorithm 1 can be used, but calculations of course have to be adapted.

2.2   Another Testing Algorithm

As it is formalized in the general Definition 1 of a tester it might be reasonable to also allow small errors for programs that should be accepted. Another aspect is that if the verifier is a randomized Turing machine running within a certain time bound, then it necessarily can only perform approximate function evaluations on randomly chosen points from a fixed finite set. So any function P which behaves well on those points but, due to a large modulus of continuity, satisfies $\widehat{\pi}_{sd}(\Delta(P, exp, \delta_1)) > \epsilon_1$ will be accepted by the verifier. Avoiding such a behaviour necessarily requires some knowledge about the modulus of continuity of P. This can be realized by putting a restriction on the modulus, compare Remark 1, part c) above. A natural way to achieve such a restriction is incorporating a corresponding check into the verifier's computation. In our second test algorithm below we thus include a test which guarantees, if satisfied, an inequality of the form $|P(r) - P(s)| \leq ce|r - s|$ for sufficiently close r, s in the range of ρ_{sd} and an arbitrarily chosen constant $c > 1$. Note that such an inequality relates the modulus of P to that of exp because $|exp(r) - exp(s)| \leq e|r - s|$ on $[0, 1]$. Below we (again) take $c = 3$.

Let M_P again be a Type-2 machine computing a $P : dom(\rho_{sd}) \to \mathbb{R}$. We first explain the general idea of the test and its analysis. Actually, it is a small variation of Test 1. Verifier V again works on a 'grid' B_{k^*} of points in $\bar{\Sigma}^*$ being fine enough using a suitable value $k^* \in \mathbb{N}$. It first checks the modulus of continuity of P for pairs close enough to a grid point. Then, V picks randomly points $x \in B_{k^*}$. The main test once more is checking the inequality $|\tilde{P}(x) - \widetilde{exp}(x)| \geq \frac{51}{100}\delta$. If for a 'bad' program M_P the verifier does not realize an error working with x, then the choices of the parameters will guarantee that no point in A_x will contribute to the set $\Delta(P, exp, \delta)$ of bad points. Similarly, if a program M_P is 'good' with respect to another pair of parameters ϵ_1, δ_1, we show that if an x leads to an error in the test, then all points in A_x are bad with respect to parameter δ_1. Repeating this sufficiently many times and using Chernoff's bounds will lead to the result. To make the analysis work it will be central to make the grid B_{k^*} fine enough so that, due to the modulus of continuity, points in relevant A_x all behave the same. Recall the Proviso from Sect. 1.1.

Test Algorithm 2: Let $\epsilon, \beta \in (0, 1), \delta > 0$, and $t, t_1, t_2 \in \mathbb{N}$ be such that $t_1 < t_2 \leq t$. Concrete values are specified below. Let $n^* := \lceil - \log(6e\epsilon^2)\rceil, k^* := \lceil \log \frac{1}{2\epsilon^2} \rceil$.

Step 1) V requests the number $\mu_P(n^*)$ of symbols from an $x0^\omega$ necessary for any $x \in B_{k^*}$ to compute $P(\rho_{sd}(x0^\omega))$ with accuracy 2^{-n^*}. If $\mu_P(n^*) > \lceil -\log 2\epsilon^2 \rceil$, then V rejects.

For t many rounds V repeats the following two steps:

Step 2) V picks randomly according to the restriction of π_{sd} to B_{k^*} an $x \in B_{k^*}$ and evaluates $P(\rho_{sd}(x0^\omega))$ and $exp(\rho_{sd}(x0^\omega))$ with accuracy $\delta/200$. Let $\tilde{P}(x)$ and $\widetilde{exp}(x)$ denote the approximations computed.

Step 3) V checks whether $|\tilde{P}(x) - \widetilde{exp}(x)| \geq (\frac{1}{2} + \frac{1}{100}) \cdot \delta$ holds.

If in at most t_1 rounds the inequality holds, then V accepts M_P; if in at least t_2 rounds the inequality holds, then V rejects M_P. For any M_P not satisfying one of the two conditions V makes an arbitrary decision.

Theorem 2 *Let $\epsilon, \beta \in (0,1), \delta > 0$ be rationals such that $\epsilon^2 < \frac{\delta}{20e}$, let $t \geq \frac{3}{\epsilon^2} \log (1/\beta), t_1 := 2\epsilon^2 t, t_2 := \frac{1}{2}\epsilon t$. Finally, let $\delta_1 := \frac{\delta}{10}$. Then verifier V from Test Algorithm 2 has the following properties: It rejects all programs M_P which do not satisfy $|P(\rho_{sd}(z)) - P(\rho_{sd}(y))| \leq 6e\epsilon^2$ for all $|\rho_{sd}(z) - \rho_{sd}(y)| \leq 2\epsilon^2$. For other programs, V is an $(\epsilon^2, \delta_1, \epsilon, \delta)$-approximate tester for exp on $[0,1]$.* □

3 Testing Univariate Polynomials

We next turn to a more general (and more difficult) question than the ones treated so far. Now instead of testing whether a program computes a function that is close to a fixed function like exp we want to verify whether it approximates a function from an entire class. We take as example in this section the class $\mathcal{F}_d(M)$ of univariate real polynomials of degree bounded by a $d \in \mathbb{N}$. The approach works similarly in a multivariate setting, see remarks below.

Before presenting the details, some remarks are necessary on what kind of result we can expect at all in our setting. First, it does not make sense to consider a class which is a dense set (with respect to the maximum norm) in the set of continuous functions. For example, since every Type-2 program computes a continuous function, without degree restriction there is always a univariate polynomial f approximating a given program P on a compact domain such that $\Delta(P, f, \delta) = \emptyset$ in the sense of Sect. 2. Secondly, and more importantly, we need to somehow control or know, respectively, the modulus of continuity not only of the given program M_P for function P, but also for the members of the class it should approximate. Since the verifier is a normal Turing machine working on finite strings of some alphabet, evaluating M_P and a potential function it approximates at finitely many points only will not allow us to draw any conclusion on the quality of the approximation with respect to a probability measure on $dom(\rho_{sd})$ unless we have additional information about the modulus. Therefore, below we shall restrict the class $\mathcal{F}_d$ a bit further in a natural way, others are certainly reasonable as well.

We shall now design a verification algorithm testing such univariate polynomials in a suitable way. Let us first extend Definition 1.

Definition 6 *a) For $d \in \mathbb{N}$ denote by $\mathcal{F}_d$ the set of univariate real polynomials defined on the domain of a representation of $[0,1]$ and of degree at most d with rational coefficients.*
If, in addition, we require the coefficients of such a polynomial to be bounded in absolute value by some rational constant $M > 0$, the resulting set of polynomials is denoted by $\mathcal{F}_d(M)$.

b) Let Σ be a finite alphabet, $\alpha :\subseteq \Sigma^\omega \to [0,1]$ be a representation of $[0,1]$ and $\hat{\pi}$ a measure on Σ^ω resulting from a probabilistic process π and generating a probabilistic name for α. Let $P : [0,1] \mapsto \mathbb{R}$ be a computable function with corresponding Type-2 machine M_P. Consider fixed parameters $0 \leq \epsilon_1 < \epsilon_2 \leq 1, 0 < \delta_1 < \delta_2$ and $\beta \in (0,1)$. A randomized Turing machine V that has access to M_P to compute (in the Type-2 sense) approximations of P is an $(\epsilon_1, \delta_1, \epsilon_2, \delta_2)$-approximate tester for $\mathcal{F}_d(M)$ (with respect to π, α) if:

  – for all M_P such that the δ_2-distance of P and every $f \in \mathcal{F}_d(M)$ is at least ϵ_2, it is $Pr(V$ rejects $M_P) \geq 1 - \beta$ and
  – for all M_P for which there exists an $f \in \mathcal{F}_d(M)$ such that the δ_1-distance of P and f is at most ϵ_1, it is $Pr(V$ accepts $M_P) \geq 1 - \beta$.

For sake of simplicity in the description below we again take the signed digit representation and the probabilistic process π_{sd} from Sect. 2, Definitions 2 and 4 defined on $\bar{\Sigma}^\omega$. Note, however, that though the above requirements on V in principle might depend on a specific probability measure, our algorithm works kind of uniformly for a larger set of probability distributions on the set of continuous names, as long as certain upper and lower bounds on the measure of intervals are available (compare with the above Remark 1,d)). This will be a consequence of results from computational learning theory that are used in the analysis. We comment on this below.

Before presenting the test algorithm V and its analysis formally let us briefly give an outline. Given a Type-2 program M_P for a function $P : dom(\rho_{sd}) \to \mathbb{R}$, verifier V generates a suitable number m of random points $\{x_i | 1 \leq i \leq m\}$ in $\bar{\Sigma}^*$ and computes an approximation $\tilde{P}(\rho_{sd}(x_i 0^\omega))$ of P in those points. The number m depends on the chosen parameters for accuracy and success probability. Next, V computes a solution of the discrete Chebyshev approximation problem for the data set $\{(\rho_{sd}(x_i 0^\omega), \tilde{P}(\rho_{sd}(x_i 0^\omega)))\}_i$ and the approximating set $\mathcal{F}_d(M)$. This means that V finds the best degree-d polynomial $\tilde{f}$ with bounded coefficients with respect to minimizing the maximal distance between the values of $\tilde{P}$ and $\tilde{f}$ on the discrete data set. Finally, V rejects if this maximal distance is too large. In the precise analysis, the main point is to find a criterion guaranteeing that if for given parameters the solution $\tilde{f}$ of the Chebyshev problem is too bad, then V has to reject. Such a criterion will be provided by results about approximate interpolation from computational learning theory given in [1].

3.1 Discrete Chebyshev Approximation; Learning from Approximate Interpolation

In this subsection, two known results necessary for the later analysis are collected. As one step of the verifier's computation a discrete approximation prob-

lem with respect to minimizing a maximum norm is solved. We briefly overview
the well known corresponding computational results with respect to this discrete
Chebyshev approximation. Next, in order to qualify this solution as good enough
or not for the verifier to accept a program, a result from learning functions from
approximate interpolations is crucial. The corresponding main theorem from [1]
is described and adopted to our setting.

Definition 7 *Let $m, d \in \mathbb{N}, M > 0$ a constant and data points $(z_i, y_i) \in \mathbb{R}^2, 1 \leq i \leq m$ be given. The* discrete Chebyshev approximation problem *with respect to space $\mathcal{F}_d(M)$ is to compute a degree-d polynomial $f \in \mathcal{F}_d(M)$ such that f minimizes the maximal distance to the data in the given points, i.e.*

$$\max_{1 \leq i \leq m} |f(z_i) - y_i| \leq \min_{g \in \mathcal{F}_d(M)} \max_{1 \leq i \leq m} |g(z_i) - y_i| .$$

The following is folklore from approximation and complexity theory

Theorem 3 *Given $m, d \in \mathbb{N}, M \in \mathbb{Q}^+$ and rational data $(z_i, y_i) \in \mathbb{Q}^2, 1 \leq i \leq m$ as above, a solution $f \in \mathcal{F}_d(M)$ of the Chebyshev problem exists and can be computed in polynomial time (in the Turing model) in the size of the input.* □

The verifier we are going to construct computes the solution of the above
Chebyshev approximation problem for approximate values of the given program
computed in sufficiently many randomly generated points. If the computed function P in a certain sense is close enough to $\mathcal{F}_d(M)$, then the best Chebyshev
approximation computed in the discrete point set will not be worse than a degree-
d polynomial being close to P, and thus the maximum distance between the
former and the approximate values of P in the chosen discrete point set will be
relatively small. The verifier will then accept such M_P. More difficult, suppose
a given P is not close to such a degree-d polynomial, but the computed solution
of the Chebyshev problem in the chosen points gives a relative small distance
to the values of P. This means that the produced finite data set allows a good
interpolation by a degree-d polynomial in $\mathcal{F}_d(M)$, though the entire function P
does not. Such a situation might lead the verifier to accept instances it should
reject. In order to show that such a situation only can happen with small probability, we now summarize the necessary prerequisites for stating a result from
computational learning theory in [1]. In our situation it basically implies that
there can only be a good interpolation from $\mathcal{F}_d(M)$ to P on a large enough finite
point set when the entire function is approximated reasonably well.

Let us first compile the corresponding notions and the main result from
[1]. The domain X is throughout supposed to bear a probability measure on a
suitable σ-algebra of subsets of X.

Definition 8 [1]. *Let $m \in \mathbb{N}, \epsilon, \beta \in (0, 1), \delta > 0$.[1] For an arbitrary set X we consider sets $\mathcal{C}$ and $\mathcal{H}$ of functions from X to $\mathbb{R}$, called* concepts *and* hypotheses, *respectively.*

---

[1] The use and meaning of parameters in [1] is slightly different from ours. The parameters η, ϵ, δ in [1] correspond to our δ, ϵ, β, respectively.

a) *For a set of points* $\mathbf{x} := \{x_i \in X | 1 \leq i \leq m\}$ *an* $h \in \mathcal{H}$ *is called* δ-approximate interpolant *of a* $c \in \mathcal{C}$ *on* $\mathbf{x}$, *iff* $\forall i : |h(x_i) - c(x_i)| < \delta$.

b) *For a probability distribution* $\mathcal{P}$ *on* X *a sample* $\mathbf{x}$ *is called* $(\mathcal{P}, \mathcal{H}, \epsilon, \delta)$-reliable *for a concept* $c \in \mathcal{C}$ *iff every* δ-approximate interpolant $h \in \mathcal{H}$ *of* c *on* $\mathbf{x}$ *satisfies* $\mathcal{P}(\{x \in X \mid |h(x) - c(x)| \geq \delta\} < \epsilon$.

c) *A sample length* m *is said to* suffice *for valid* $(\delta, \epsilon, \beta)$-generalization *of* $\mathcal{C}$ *by* $\mathcal{H}$ *from* δ-approximate interpolation *if for any concept* $c \in \mathcal{C}$ *and any distribution* $\mathcal{P}$ *on* X *the following holds: With* $\mathcal{P}^m$-*probability at least* $1 - \beta$, *a sample* $\mathbf{x} \in X^m$ *is* $(\mathcal{P}, \mathcal{H}, \epsilon, \delta)$-reliable *for* c.

d) *The hypothesis class* $\mathcal{H}$ validly generalizes $\mathcal{C}$ *from approximate interpolation, iff for any* $\delta > 0, \epsilon, \beta \in (0, 1)$ *there exists an integer* $m_0 = m_0(\delta, \epsilon, \beta)$ *such that, for all distributions* $\mathcal{P}$ *on* X *and all concepts* $c \in \mathcal{C}$ *a sample of length at least* m_0 *is* $(\mathcal{P}, \mathcal{H}, \epsilon, \delta)$-reliable *with probability at least* $1 - \beta$.

Roughly said, if $\mathcal{H}$ validly generalizes $\mathcal{C}$ from approximate interpolation, then for a large enough sample with high probability any hypothesis that interpolates a concept well on the discrete point set given by the sample already interpolates it well on the entire set X. This is precisely what is used below for proving that our verifier works correctly. Of course, before we can use the approach, conditions must be identified under which classes $\mathcal{H}, \mathcal{C}$ have this property. A parameter that characterizes this is the so-called band-dimension of $\mathcal{H}$.

Definition 9 [1]. *Let* $X, \mathcal{H}$ *be as above,* $s \in \mathbb{N}, \gamma > 0$.

a) *A finite set* $T := \{(x_1, y_1), \ldots, (x_s, y_s)\} \subset X \times \mathbb{R}$ *is* γ-band-shattered *by* $\mathcal{H}$ *if for every* $\mathbf{b} := (b_1, \ldots, b_s) \in \{0, 1\}^s$ *there exists a function* $h_{\mathbf{b}} \in \mathcal{H}$ *such that*

$$|h_{\mathbf{b}}(x_i) - y_i| \begin{cases} < \gamma \ \textit{if} \ b_i = 1 \\ \geq \gamma \ \textit{if} \ b_i = 0 \end{cases}$$

b) *The* γ-band-dimension $Bdim_{\mathcal{H}}(\gamma)$ *of* $\mathcal{H}$ *is the cardinality of the largest set* γ-band-shattered *by* $\mathcal{H}$, *and* ∞ *if finite sets of each arbitrary cardinality are shattered. This way, a function* $Bdim_{\mathcal{H}} : (0, 1) \rightarrow \mathbb{N} \cup \{\infty\}$ *is defined.*

In [1], the band-dimension and further similar parameters are used to characterize the ability of $\mathcal{H}$ to validly generalise from approximate interpolation in particular the set $\mathcal{C}$ of all real valued functions from X to $\mathbb{R}$. For our purposes, we consider this set $\mathcal{C}$ as a concept class with the (continuous) functions P computed by given Type-2 programs M_P as particular subset, and as hypothesis class $\mathcal{H} := \mathcal{F}_d$, where now univariate polynomials formally are defined on $X := dom(\rho_{sd})$ and have rational (i.e., computable) coefficients. Below, as hypotheses, we only use functions from $\mathcal{F}_d(M)$, but apply the learning results for the entire $\mathcal{F}_d$. The following theorem is an amalgam of several results in [1], suitably combined for our concrete situation. More precisely, Theorem 3 of [1] gives a characterization of valid generalizability for a class $\mathcal{H}$ of $[0, 1]$-valued functions with domain an arbitrary set X in terms of finiteness of $Bdim(\gamma)$ for all $\gamma \in (0, 1)$, together with a bound on the necessary sample length m_0 depending on the band-dimension. Then, Proposition 18 extends this result to arbitrary real valued functions from X to $\mathbb{R}$ in case $\mathcal{H}$ is a linear space, and relates $Bdim(\gamma)$ with the linear dimension of $\mathcal{H}$. Below, X will be the set of initial segments of ρ_{sd}-names of a certain length k, i.e. $X := B_k$, compare Definition 5. On such a set, the verifier will compute a hypotheses which is a degree-d polynomial on $[0, 1]$. Thus, $\mathcal{H} := \mathcal{F}_d$ with linear dimension $d + 1$. This leads to

Theorem 4 ([1], **Adapted to Present Situation**)**.** *Let* $d \in \mathbb{N}, \delta > 0, \epsilon, \beta \in (0, 1)$. *Let* $k \in \mathbb{N}$ *be fixed. Consider the set* B_k *of initial segments of* (ρ_{sd})-*names of length* k *after the dot (see Definition 5) and let* $\mathcal{H} := \mathcal{F}_d$ *denote the set of univariate real polynomials on* $[0, 1]$ *with degree at most* d *and rational coefficients. Then* $\mathcal{H}$ *validly generalises the set* $\mathcal{C}$ *of all functions from* B_k *to* $\mathbb{R}$ *from approximate interpolation. Moreover, a suitable sample size is given by*

$$m_0(\delta, \epsilon, \beta) := \frac{1}{\epsilon(1 - \sqrt{\epsilon})} \left(30(d + 1) \ln(\frac{6}{\epsilon}) + \ln(\frac{2}{\beta}) \right).$$

If $\beta \le 1/6$ *and* $d \ge 3$, *then* $m_0(\delta, \epsilon, \beta) \ge \max\{\frac{1-\epsilon}{\epsilon} \log(1/\beta), \frac{d-1}{24\epsilon}\}$.[2]   □

Note that just as with many results in the area of computational learning the above result is independent from the underlying distribution, which also might be unknown. This is basically caused by the fact that both the sample and the a posteriori measuring of the error are done with respect to the same distribution. However, below we shall use the fixed distribution which π_{sd} generates on B_k for the randomization of the verifier and $\hat{\pi}_{sd}$ for measuring the quality of P. Nevertheless, independence of the above result on the distribution implies that our verification algorithm similarly works for a larger set of distributions as long as certain technical conditions (mainly upper and lower bounds for the measure of the pre-images of intervals) remain valid.

3.2   Testing Degree-d Polynomials

We now present an algorithm for testing degree-d polynomials in $\mathcal{F}_d(M)$ for fixed $M > 0$ according to Definition 6. The algorithm is using parameters $\delta > 0, \epsilon, \beta \in (0, 1)$. In terms of Definition 6, ϵ, δ play the role of ϵ_2, δ_2, i.e., are the parameters determining input programs M_P for which V will likely reject. Parameters ϵ_1, δ_1 for acceptance will be specified below.

One additional technical remark: As explained above, in the algorithm, the verifier needs to work with the modulus of continuity μ_P of involved functions like P. This means that for achieving an accuracy $|P(y) - P(z)| \le 2^{-n}$ for $y, z \in [0, 1]$ it is sufficient to require $|y - z| \le 2^{-\mu_P(n)}$. For the signed digit presentation over alphabet $\bar{\Sigma} = \{0, 1, \bar{1}, .\}$ it is easy to see that this accuracy is guaranteed if ρ_{sd}-names for y, z are specified with $k := \mu_P(n) + 1$ symbols

---

[2] Note that a dependence of m_0 on δ or $Bdim(\delta)$, respectively, is hidden by the fact that $Bdim(\delta)$ in our specific situation is bounded from above by $15(d + 1)$ and from below by $d + 1$, see Propositions 3.1 and 6.1 in [1].

following the dot, i.e., choosing an $x = x_0.x_1 \ldots x_k$ from set B_k, see Definitions 2 and 5. This follows from the easy observation, that in the worst cases the symbols following the position x_k either all are 1's or $\bar{1}$'s. In the former case, the numerical value is $\rho_{sd}(x0^\omega) + (\frac{1}{2})^k$, in the latter $\rho_{sd}(x0^\omega) - (\frac{1}{2})^k$. This observation explains an additional '+1' below in the value of k^*. Recall the Proviso from Sect. 1.1.

ALGORITHM TESTING DEGREE-d-POLYNOMIALS: Let $d \in \mathbb{N}, M > 0$ be constants. Let $\delta > 0, \epsilon, \beta \in (0,1)$ be given. Consider as input a Type-2 program M_P computing a function $P : dom(\rho_{sd}) \to \mathbb{R}$ with μ_P being its modulus of continuity.

Step 1: Define $k^* := \max\{\lceil \log(4/\delta) + \log(Md^2) \rceil + 1, \mu_P(\log(10/\delta)) + 2\}, \delta^* := \frac{3}{10}\delta$, and choose $\epsilon^* > 0$ such that $\epsilon^* \leq \epsilon \cdot (\frac{2}{3})^{k^*+1}$.

Step 2: Let $m := m_0(\delta^*, \epsilon^*, \beta/2)$ for the function m_0 as given in Theorem 4. Choose randomly m points in the set B_{k^*} according to the distribution π_{sd} yields on B_{k^*}. Let $\mathbf{x} = (x_1, \ldots, x_m) \in B_{k^*}^m$ denote the drawn sample.

Step 3: For every $x_i, 1 \leq i \leq m$ compute an approximation $\tilde{P}(\rho_{sd}(x_i 0^\omega))$ of $P(\rho_{sd}(x_i 0^\omega))$ with accuracy $\leq \delta/10$ using the given program M_P.

Step 4: Solve the discrete Chebyshev approximation problem (Theorem 3) for a degree-d polynomial $f(z) = \sum\limits_{j=0}^{d} f_j z^j$ for points $(\rho_{sd}(x_i 0^\omega), \tilde{P}(\rho_{sd}(x_i 0^\omega))) \in [0,1] \times \mathbb{R}, 1 \leq i \leq m$ and such that $|f_j| \leq M \ \forall 0 \leq j \leq d$. Let $\tilde{f} \in \mathcal{F}_d(M)$ denote the solution.

Step 5: For all $1 \leq i \leq m$ check whether

$$|\tilde{f}(\rho_{sd}(x_i 0^\omega)) - \tilde{P}(\rho_{sd}(x_i 0^\omega))| < \delta^* := \frac{3}{10}\delta. \tag{1}$$

If this holds for all drawn points, then V accepts, otherwise it rejects.

Theorem 5. *For given parameters $M, d, \epsilon, \delta, \beta$ as above the verifier from the algorithm* TESTING DEGREE-d-POLYNOMIALS *is a $(0, \delta/10, \epsilon, \delta)$-approximate tester for the set $\mathcal{F}_d(M)$ of univariate degree-d polynomials on $[0,1]$ with coefficients bounded by M in absolute value. This refers to $\hat{\pi}_{sd}$ as distribution and ρ_{sd} as continuous name used.* □

3.3 Complexity Considerations and Conclusion

A useful verification algorithm should work efficiently. Above, we restrained from defining precisely what dependence on which parameters is allowed in order to call the verification efficient. It seems reasonable to first derive more results of the kind presented here before a general such definition is given. Nevertheless, let us outline which parameters influence the verification algorithm for univariate polynomials and in how far the respective dependence seems unavoidable.

Clearly, the first aspect influencing V's running time is the complexity of computing approximations of the desired quality for values of P using the given program M_P. This, of course, is not avoidable since M_P is the program that should be tested. As consequence, the coding size of the approximate data generated by M_P, i.e., of the values of $\tilde{P}$ in the chosen points, should be one parameter in which the subsequent running time is measured. The latter basically will be the k^* chosen in the algorithm. Then, two additional parameters influencing the performance of V are the number m of points in which according to Theorem 4 the interpolation has to be performed, and the complexity of solving the related Chebyshev approximation. The latter is polynomial in the coding size of the linear inequality system, which again depends on the number m of points, the coding size of the data $x \in B_{k^*}$ and $\tilde{P}(\rho_{sd}(x0^\omega))$, the degree d of the approximating polynomials and the bit-size of the (kind of arbitrary) bound M for the coefficients. Finally, concerning the size m of a sample, the used results from learning theory give a polynomial dependence of V's running time on the parameters $1/\epsilon, \log 1/\beta$ and the degree d. Note once again that in the sample size statements the vector space dimension $d+1$ of $\mathcal{F}_d$ is absorbing the dependence on δ. Of course, k^* depends on $\log 1/\delta$ since it influences the required accuracy.

Beside the questions on complexity and on improving dependence on the parameters, one immediate question is that of improving the parameters in the approximate tester, and here in particular ϵ_1. In Theorem 5, its value is 0 meaning that V accepts programs for which not a single value is approximated badly by a hypothesis from $\mathcal{F}_d(M)$. Is it possible to set up a test which allows at least for a few bad approximation results? The problem with our above test seems to be that then for the Chebyshev problem we have to detect outliers.

Extensions of our results seem possible both with respect to other distributions and to a multivariate setting. Concerning further distributions at least similar results can be obtained when the technical demands for doing the calculations in the proof are satisfied; this has been commented already in Remark 1, d). The same holds for testing multivariate polynomials of a bounded degree. Here, it is important that Theorem 4 also holds in a multivariate setting.

Then of course a more general question for future work is: Which reasonable properties of functions computed by Type-2 machines can be tested as well?

Acknowledgment. Thanks go to the anonymous referees for careful reading and several helpful remarks.

References

1. Anthony, M., Bartlett, P., Ishai, Y., Shawe-Taylor, J.: Valid generalization from approximate interpolation. Comb. Probab. Comput. **5**(3), 191–214 (1996)
2. Clarke, E.M., Henziger, T.A., Veith, H., Bloem, R. (eds.): Handbook of Model Checking. Springer (2018)
3. Goldreich, O.: On promise problems (a survey). In: Theoretical Computer Science: Essays in memory of Shimon Even. LNCS, vol. 3895, pp. 254–290. Springer (2006)
4. Goldreich, O.: Introduction to Property Testing. Cambridge University Press (2017)
5. Kiwi, M.A., Magniez, F., Santha, M.: Exact and approximate testing/correcting of algebraic functions: a survey. In: Theoretical Aspects of Computer Science, pp. 30–83 (2000)

6. Ko, K.: Complexity theory of real functions. In: Progress in Theoretical Computer Science. Birkhäuser, Boston (1991)
7. Schröder, M., Simpson, A.: Representing probability measures using probabilistic processes. J. Complex. **22**(6), 768–782 (2006)
8. Schröder, M., Steinberg, F., Ziegler, M.: Average-case bit-complexity theory of real functions. In: Kotsireas, I.S., et al. (eds.) Proceedings of the MACIS 2015. LNCS, vol. 9582, pp. 505–519. Springer (2016)
9. Weihrauch, K.: Computable Analysis: An Introduction. Springer (2000)

Card-Based Cryptography Meets 3D Printer

Yuki Ito$^{(\boxtimes)}$ [ID], Hayato Shikata [ID], Takuo Suganuma [ID], and Takaaki Mizuki$^{(\boxtimes)}$ [ID]

Tohoku University, Sendai, Japan
yuki.ito.q7@dc.tohoku.ac.jp , mizuki+lncs@tohoku.ac.jp

Abstract. Card-based protocols perform cryptographic functionalities, such as secure computations, using a deck of cards. Basically, these protocols are supposed to be implemented by humans' manipulating physical cards. This paper is the first attempt to make use of a 3D printer for better physical implementations of card-based protocols: we have designed and fabricated a couple of physical devices using a 3D printer that are useful for humans to implement protocols. The first device we created is the "five-card-trick turner," which can turn over five cards simultaneously in an amusing manner; this operation appears in the final step of the five-card trick, which is the most famous card-based protocol. The second device we created is a special card box for storing a pile of cards, whose concept was proposed in 2015 but the device had not been created in reality thus far. The special boxes can be used for implementing complex shuffles that seem difficult to implement only by hand. Furthermore, we propose another use of these special boxes so that we can efficiently perform secure computations of symmetric functions.

Keywords: Card-based cryptography · 3D printer · Secure computation · Symmetric function

1 Introduction

The development of *card-based cryptography*, which performs cryptographic functionalities such as secure computations using a deck of cards, has continued in recent years (e.g. [7,8]). Card-based cryptography is a very unconventional type of computation.

Numerous card-based cryptographic protocols have been developed (cf. [3,10,16]), and many of them are simple enough to be easily implemented by non-experts, including high school students. Such protocols are implemented by humans' manipulating a physical deck of cards (along with a table on which the cards are placed). This paper begins with a description of the five-card trick [1] as a concrete example of a practical card-based protocol.

1.1 The Five-Card Trick

The five-card trick [1] is the first card-based protocol in history; it performs a secure two-input AND computation using five cards.

Suppose that Alice and Bob want to perform a secure AND computation. That is, Alice and Bob holding private bits $a \in \{0, 1\}$ and $b \in \{0, 1\}$, respectively, want to know

D.-J. Cho and J. Kim (Eds.): UCNC 2024, LNCS 14776, pp. 74–88, 2024.
https://doi.org/10.1007/978-3-031-63742-1_6

only the AND value $a \wedge b$. Using two cards ♣ ♥ of different colors, whose backs are both ?, Alice secretly creates a *commitment* to her private bit $a \in \{0, 1\}$

$$\underbrace{?\,?}_{a},$$

which follows the following encoding rule:

$$\boxed{♣}\,\boxed{♥} = 0, \qquad \boxed{♥}\,\boxed{♣} = 1. \tag{1}$$

That is, the pair of face-down cards is a commitment to a, and its order is ♣ ♥ when $a = 0$ and ♥ ♣ when $a = 1$. Bob creates a commitment to $b \in \{0, 1\}$ in the same way, and another red card ♥ is placed in the middle:

$$\underbrace{?\,?}_{a}\,♥\,\underbrace{?\,?}_{b}.$$

Given such a sequence of five cards as input[1], the five-card trick proceeds as follows.

1. The leftmost two cards are swapped so that the commitment to a is converted to its negation $\bar{a}$:

$$\underbrace{?\,?}\,♥\,\underbrace{?\,?}$$
$$\underbrace{?\,?}_{\bar{a}}\,♥\,\underbrace{?\,?}_{b}.$$

2. Turn over the center ♥ card:

$$\underbrace{?\,?}_{\bar{a}}\,♥\,\underbrace{?\,?}_{b} \quad \rightarrow \quad \underbrace{?\,?}_{\bar{a}}\,\underbrace{?\,?}\,\underbrace{?\,?}_{b}.$$

   Note that $a \wedge b = 1$ if and only if the three cards in the middle are ♥ ♥ ♥.

3. Apply a *random cut* (denoted by the symbol $\langle \cdot \rangle$):

$$\left\langle\, ?\,?\,?\,?\,? \,\right\rangle.$$

   A random cut is a cyclic shuffling operation, where the sequence of cards is shifted by a random number. A random cut can be easily implemented in the real world by the so-called *Hindu cut* [20].

4. Turn over all the five cards and obtain the value of $a \wedge b$ as follows:

♣ ♥ ♥ ♥ ♣		♥ ♣ ♥ ♣ ♥
♥ ♥ ♥ ♣ ♣		♣ ♥ ♣ ♥ ♥
♥ ♥ ♣ ♣ ♥	or	♥ ♣ ♥ ♥ ♣
♥ ♣ ♣ ♥ ♥		♣ ♥ ♥ ♣ ♥
♣ ♣ ♥ ♥ ♥		♥ ♥ ♣ ♥ ♣
$a \wedge b = 1$		$a \wedge b = 0$.

---

[1] The original paper [1] used ♠ instead of ♣, and put ♠ in the middle. We place ♥ in the middle because three heart suits ♥ ♥ ♥ may be more convincing when announcing $a \wedge b = 1$.

This AND protocol is very simple and can be easily implemented with five physical cards by human hand, as shown in the picture in Fig. 1.

Fig. 1. An implementation of the final step of the five-card trick

In this paper, we use a 3D printer to create a device, called the "five-card-trick turner," that turns over five cards at once in the final step, as mentioned later.

1.2 Special Boxes for Implementing Complex Shuffles

In the computational model of card-based protocols [9], a "shuffle" is mathematically defined, and the model includes "complex" shuffles which seem difficult for humans to implement only by hand. On the other hand, somewhat interestingly, it is known that making use of such complex shuffles leads to protocols having a smaller number of cards or shuffles (e.g. [6,13,19]). Furthermore, it was pointed out that some of such complex shuffles could be implemented (in the real world) by using special card boxes illustrated in Fig. 2a [12–14].

The main feature of this box is that several boxes can be stacked and piles of cards stored in boxes can be combined into a single pile, as shown in Fig. 2b.

(a) Special box whose lid and bottom can be slid.   (b) Stack boxes and combine piles of cards.

Fig. 2. The special card boxes

To the best of our knowledge, such a special card box had never been made in the real world. Thus, we created such physical boxes using a 3D printer for the first time.

1.3   Contribution of This Paper

As mentioned in Sects. 1.1 and 1.2, this paper reports that, using a 3D printer, we designed and created two physical devices useful for implementing card-based protocols: the *five-card-trick turner* and the *special card boxes* for storing and combining piles.

(a) Flipping five face-down cards   (b) Revealed five cards

Fig. 3. The five-card-trick turner

Five-Card-Trick Turner

We created a device for flipping five cards simultaneously in an amusing manner in the final step of the five-card trick; we name it the five-card-trick turner, and our actually created one is shown in Fig. 3. Due to the page limitation, we omit the details in this paper. As mentioned above, the five-card trick is very simple, and it has attracted many lay-people such as high school students; thus, we expect that this new device will further increase the appeal of the five-card trick.

Special Card Boxes

As mentioned in Sect. 1.2, the special card boxes illustrated in Fig. 2 were considered to potentially implement complex shuffles (some of which could theoretically reduce the numbers of required cards or shuffles), but we had not seen any real implementation. We then actually created special card boxes using a 3D printer, as shown in Fig. 4.

As a demonstration, using the created boxes, we have actually executed the existing five-copy protocol [13], which requires a complex shuffle, and confirmed that the protocol can be executed securely and reliably.

In addition, we propose a novel use of these special card boxes: we show that they can be used for securely computing any symmetric function efficiently. Specifically, in terms of the number of times we make a pile of cards, the existing method [15] requires $n^2/2 + 3n/2 - 2$ times, whereas our method uses only $2n - 2$ times. This result is very interesting from both theoretical and practical perspectives.

Let us emphasize that the main scientific contribution of this paper lies in revealing how new physical devices can enable a novel and efficient protocol.

Fig. 4. Created special card boxes for complex shuffles

1.4 Organization of This Paper

The rest of this paper is organized as follows. In Sect. 2, to be familiar with the computational model of card-based protocols, we show a pseudo-code for the five-card trick. Next, in Sect. 3, we report on the creation of the special card boxes on a 3D printer and the actual execution of the five-card copy protocol. Next, in Sect. 4, we show that the special card boxes provide "sorting functionality," (whereby we will construct an efficient protocol for any symmetric function in Sect. 6). Next, in Sect. 5, we introduce the existing protocol for symmetric functions. Then, in Sect. 6, we present our protocol for symmetric functions based on the special card boxes. Finally, we conclude in Sect. 7.

2   Pseudo-Code for the Five-Card Trick

In this section, we give a formal description of the five-card trick introduced in Sect. 1.1 using a pseudo-code as shown in Pseudo-code 1. Remember that this protocol uses five cards ♥ ♥ ♥ ♣ ♣ and each input commitment is placed using two cards ♣ ♥ according to the encoding rule (1).

Here, $(\mathsf{perm}, (1\,2))$ means an action permuting a sequence of cards based on the cyclic permutation $(1\,2)$, and $(\mathsf{turn}, \{3\})$ means to turn over the third card. The next action

$$(\mathsf{shuf}, \{\mathsf{id}, (1\,2\,3\,4\,5), (1\,2\,3\,4\,5)^2, (1\,2\,3\,4\,5)^3, (1\,2\,3\,4\,5)^4\})$$

indicates a random cut: one of the five permutations is chosen uniformly at random and applied, where $(1\,2\,3\,4\,5)$ is a cyclic permutation and id denotes the identity. The next action $(\mathsf{turn}, \{1, 2, 3, 4, 5\})$ means that all five cards are turned over.

3   Special Card Boxes for Complex Shuffles

In card-based cryptography, complex shuffles have sometimes been used in protocol construction, especially when designing protocols with extremely small numbers of cards or shuffles. In this section, we report that, using a 3D printer, we actually created special card boxes for implementing such complex shuffles.

Pseudo-code 1. Five-card trick	**Pseudo-code 2.** Five-card copy
Input: $\boxed{?}\boxed{?}\boxed{\heartsuit}\boxed{?}\boxed{?}$	Input: $\boxed{?}\boxed{?}\boxed{\clubsuit}\boxed{\clubsuit}\boxed{\heartsuit}$

<table>
<tr>
<td>

Input: $\underbrace{\boxed{?}\,\boxed{?}}_{a}\,\boxed{\heartsuit}\,\underbrace{\boxed{?}\,\boxed{?}}_{b}$

(perm, $(1\,2)$)
(turn, $\{3\}$)
(shuf, $\{\mathrm{id}, (1\,2\,3\,4\,5), (1\,2\,3\,4\,5)^2,$
$\qquad\qquad (1\,2\,3\,4\,5)^3, (1\,2\,3\,4\,5)^4\})$
(turn, $\{1,2,3,4,5\}$)
if $\heartsuit\heartsuit\heartsuit$ appears **then**
(result, "$a \wedge b = 1$")
else
(result, "$a \wedge b = 0$")
endif

</td>
<td>

Input: $\boxed{?}\,\boxed{?}\,\underbrace{\boxed{\clubsuit}\,\boxed{\clubsuit}}\,\boxed{\heartsuit}$
$\qquad\qquad\;\; a$

(perm, $(1\,2\,4\,5\,3)$)
(shuf, $\{\mathrm{id}, (1\,4\,2\,5\,3)\}$)
(perm, $(2\,5\,3)$)
(turn, $\{5\}$)
if $\clubsuit$ appears **then**
(result, $(1,2), (3,4)$)
else
(perm, $(1\,2)$)
(turn, $\{5\}$)
return to the beginning
endif

</td>
</tr>
</table>

3.1 Complex Shuffles by Special Card Boxes

A card-based protocol is formulated by an abstract machine [9]. Specifically, as seen in the pseudo-code of the five-card trick shown in Sect. 2, a protocol consists mainly of a combination of three actions perm, turn, and shuf. Of these, shuf is said to be the most important action, and a shuffle is formulated as (shuf, $\Pi, \mathcal{F}$) using a set of permutations Π and a probability distribution $\mathcal{F}$ on it. That is, a permutation $\pi \in \Pi$ is chosen according to the distribution $\mathcal{F}$, and π is applied to the sequence of cards.

Thus, Π and $\mathcal{F}$ in a shuffle (shuf, $\Pi, \mathcal{F}$) in the computational model of card-based protocols can be arbitrary. If $\mathcal{F}$ is a uniform distribution, the shuffle is said to be *uniform* and is sometimes written as (shuf, Π) for short. If the set of permutations Π is closed, i.e., a subgroup of permutations, we say that the shuffle is *closed*.

A non-uniform or non-closed shuffle is often called a *complex* shuffle and is difficult for humans to implement. The first concrete complex shuffle in the history of card-based cryptography is (shuf, $\{\mathrm{id}, (1\,4\,2\,5\,3)\}$). This is a shuffle in which the left two cards and the remaining three cards in a sequence of five cards are considered as piles, and the two piles are swapped with a probability of $1/2$:

$$
\begin{array}{ccccc}
1 & 2 & 3 & 4 & 5 \\
\boxed{?} & \boxed{?} & \boxed{?} & \boxed{?} & \boxed{?}
\end{array}
\rightarrow
\left\{
\begin{array}{ccccc}
1 & 2 & 3 & 4 & 5 \\
\boxed{?} & \boxed{?} & \boxed{?} & \boxed{?} & \boxed{?} \\
3 & 4 & 5 & 1 & 2 \\
\boxed{?} & \boxed{?} & \boxed{?} & \boxed{?} & \boxed{?}
\end{array}
\right. .
$$

This shuffle is uniform but not closed (because $(1\,4\,2\,5\,3)^2 \neq \mathrm{id}$), and is difficult to implement with human hands (e.g., if you make a pile of two cards and a pile of three cards by fixing them with rubber bands and stir them together, the difference in the number of cards will tell you whether the two piles have been switched or not). This shuffle was presented by Eddie Cheung, Christa Hawthorne, and Patrick Lee, students in D. R. Stinson's class CS 758: Cryptography/Network Security (Fall Semester, 2013) project at the University of Waterloo.

Later in 2015, this shuffle was used to construct a five-card copy protocol [13], which makes two copied commitments from a given commitment (before this protocol, the copy protocol using the fewest cards required six cards [11]). A pseudo-code of the five-card copy protocol is shown in Pseudo-code 2, where (result, $(1, 2), (3, 4)$) indicates that the first and second cards are a commitment to a, and so are the third and fourth.

The first mention of how to physically implement the shuffle (shuf, {id, $(1\ 4\ 2\ 5\ 3)$}) was made in the paper [13], and it was expected that it could actually be implemented using two special card boxes like Fig. 2a in Sect. 1. Specifically, a pile of two cards and a pile of three cards are each placed in a box and switch them randomly:

Then, slide the top and bottom of the boxes to merge the two piles into a single pile, as shown in Fig. 2b in Sect. 1. Although how to implement is shown in this way, to the best of our knowledge, such a card box has never been physically created and implemented in the real world.

In the paper [12], the conditions on special card boxes that must be satisfied are listed on p. 1498. The following is a quote from that part, where this special box-shaped equipment is referred to as a 'case.'

"..., we assume physical cases that satisfy the following properties.
1. It is possible to store a pile of cards in a case without changing its order.
2. It is possible to take out a pile of cards from a case without changing its order.
3. It is possible to take out multiple piles without changing their orders by opening multiple cases at the same time. No information leak will be caused by this action.
4. A number of cases that possibly contain piles of cards are indistinguishable from one another, and we cannot obtain any information about the cards inside.

Based on the above, we have designed a special card box, as will be described in Sect. 3.2.

3.2   Design and Creation of Special Boxes

Basically, the special box was designed to meet the requirements described in Sect. 3.1. In addition, design innovations were added to ease protocol execution. Specifically, notches are included at the top and bottom of the stacked boxes to prevent dislodging during operation. In addition, when sliding the bottom or lid of the stacked boxes, the other slides in tandem with it. The productions are shown in Fig. 4 in Sect. 1.

We added another useful feature: the ejector shown in Fig. 5, which helps securely eject a pile of cards from boxes. If we flip the card box to eject a pile of cards, then it may lead to a partial view of the cards and protocol failure. Instead, by using the ejector, cards can be securely ejected without the need to flip the box. The process of ejecting piles of cards using these devices is shown in Fig. 6.

Fig. 5. Ejector device and support equipment

Fig. 6. Removing cards using the ejector

3.3   Real Implementation of the Five-Card Copy Protocol

Figure 7 shows an actual implementation of the complex shuffle (shuf, {id, (1 4 2 5 3)}). Based on this, we have actually implemented the five-card copy protocol described in Sect. 3.1. We think that this was the first secure physical implementation of the five-card copy protocol in history.

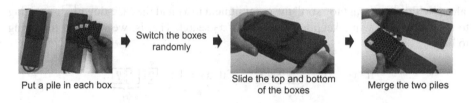

Put a pile in each box   Slide the top and bottom   Merge the two piles
                                   of the boxes

Fig. 7. Implementation of the complex shuffle with special boxes

4   Sorting Piles Secretly with Special Boxes

In this section, we consider another use of the special card box: we introduce a new mechanism for storing a card on top of each box whereby we can sort a sequence of piles secretly according to the order of some face-down cards.

4.1   Attaching Card on Top of Box

We consider attaching a face-down card to a special card box, as shown in Fig. 8. The attached card could be fixed with the box using a rubber band or something, but, using a 3D printer, we introduced a new feature to realize this more easily.

Specifically, we have created a card box with a mechanism for storing a card in the top of the box, as shown in Fig. 9. The card storage mechanism is attached to the top lid of the box, allowing a single card to be inserted. This structure improves preventing card removal and other protocol errors when shuffling card boxes.

Fig. 8. Attach a card to the top of the box

Fig. 9. Card housing mechanism

4.2 Example of Box Use

Here, we give a concrete example of making use of the feature of the special box explained in Sect. 4.1.

Given commitments to $x_1, x_2 \in \{0, 1\}$

$$\boxed{?}\boxed{?}\; \boxed{?}\boxed{?}$$
$$\underbrace{}_{x_1}\; \underbrace{}_{x_2}$$

along with $\boxed{\heartsuit}$, we want to "sort" the commitment to x_1 and the face-down $\boxed{\heartsuit}$ according to the value of x_2 while keeping the value of x_2 secret. That is, we want the following to be:

$$\text{if } x_2 = 0: \underbrace{\boxed{?}\boxed{?}}_{x_1}\overset{\heartsuit}{\boxed{?}}, \quad \text{if } x_2 = 1: \overset{\heartsuit}{\boxed{?}}\underbrace{\boxed{?}\boxed{?}}_{x_1}.$$

This can be done as follows.

1. Open the tops of two special card boxes, insert the commitment to x_1 and the face-down $\heartsuit$ card, and close the tops:

$$\underbrace{\boxed{?}\boxed{?}}_{x_1}\overset{\heartsuit}{\boxed{?}} \;\rightarrow\; \boxed{\;\boxed{?}\boxed{?}\;}\;\; \boxed{\;\boxed{?}\;}.$$

2. Place the left card of the commitment to x_2 on top of the left box (by the storage mechanism) and the right card to the top of the right box:

3. Shuffle the two special boxes until they are no longer clear which is which:

$$\left\langle \boxed{?} \Big| \boxed{?} \right\rangle.$$

4. Take out the cards at the tops of the boxes and turn them over; then, one is ♣ and the other ♥. Stack the two boxes so that the ♥ box is under the ♣ box, and pull out the middle dividers to merge the two piles inside the boxes into a single pile.

   This procedure accomplishes the above.

4.3 General Description

Here, we generalize the method mentioned in Sect. 4.2. That is, we now demonstrate that we can sort k piles (of possibly different sizes) based on face-down numbered cards ranging from 1 to k.

Assume that there are k piles of arbitrary sizes, and that we have k face-down numbered cards arranged by the numbers from 1 to k in a specific order.

1. Place each pile in a special box:

   $$\boxed{?\,?\cdots?}\quad\boxed{?\,?\cdots?}\quad\cdots\quad\boxed{?\,?\cdots?}\ .$$

2. Place the face-down numbered card on top of each special box (without changing the order):

   $$\boxed{?}\qquad\boxed{?}\qquad\boxed{?}$$
   $$\boxed{?\,?\cdots?}\quad\boxed{?\,?\cdots?}\quad\cdots\quad\boxed{?\,?\cdots?}\ .$$

3. Shuffle the k special boxes, take out the numbered cards, turn them over, and sort the boxes in ascending order based on the revealed numbered cards:

   $$\boxed{1}\qquad\boxed{2}\qquad\boxed{k}$$
   $$\boxed{?\,?\cdots?}\quad\boxed{?\,?\cdots?}\quad\cdots\quad\boxed{?\,?\cdots?}\ .$$

4. All the special boxes are concatenated and the partitions are pulled out to obtain a sorted sequence of cards:

   $$\boxed{?\,?\,?\,?\cdots?}\ .$$

   For piles of the same size, the sort sub-protocol proposed in [5] can be used, but for piles of irregular sizes, the method described in this paper is effective.

   As seen later, our method above will provide an efficient addition of commitments, by which we can construct an efficient protocol for any symmetric function. To compare our protocol with the existing one, we first introduce the existing protocol in Sect. 5, followed by our protocol presented in Sect. 6.

5 Secure Computation of Symmetric Function: Existing Method

Ruangwises and Itoh [15] proposed a generic protocol for any symmetric function $f : \{0, 1\}^n \to R$ such that its range R can be an arbitrary set. In this section, we introduce this existing protocol. Note that a function is said to be *symmetric* if it is invariant under permutations of its variables.

5.1 Preliminaries

We first introduce the *pile-shifting shuffle* [12, 18]. Suppose that there are k piles B_1, $\cdots$, B_k of the same size. Applying a pile-shifting shuffle to this results in

$$\left\langle \underbrace{\boxed{?}\boxed{?}\cdots\boxed{?}}_{B_1} \middle| \cdots \middle| \underbrace{\boxed{?}\boxed{?}\cdots\boxed{?}}_{B_k} \right\rangle \rightarrow \underbrace{\boxed{?}\boxed{?}\cdots\boxed{?}}_{B_{1+r}} \cdots \underbrace{\boxed{?}\boxed{?}\cdots\boxed{?}}_{B_{k+r}},$$

where $r \in \{0, 1, \cdots, k-1\}$ is random and if the subscript exceeds k, the value shall return to 1. The pile-shifting shuffle can be implemented by fixing piles with envelopes, rubber bands, or sleeves and applying the Hindu cut to them.

We next explain how to express a non-negative integer as a sequence of cards [15]. Let $k \geq 2$; then, using $k-1$ ♣ cards and a ♥ card, we represent an integer i, $0 \leq i \leq k-1$, by placing $\boxed{♥}$ at the $(i+1)$-th position:

$$\underbrace{\boxed{♣}}_{1}\underbrace{\boxed{♣}}_{2}\cdots\underbrace{\boxed{♥}}_{i+1}\cdots\underbrace{\boxed{♣}}_{k}.$$

Hereinafter, such a sequence of face-down cards is denoted by $E_k^♥(i)$. If we reverse the colors, we denote the resulting sequence by $E_k^♣(i)$.

5.2 Addition of Non-Negative Integers

Ruangwises and Itoh [15] proposed a method for performing addition, given two face-down sequences representing non-negative integers. (This method is based on the idea of Shinagawa et al. [17].)

1. Given $E_k^♣(a)$ and $E_k^♥(b)$ representing two non-negative integers a, b, for the sake of explanation, we name each card in each sequence as follows:

$$E_k^♣(a): \underset{x_0}{\boxed{?}}\,\underset{x_1}{\boxed{?}}\cdots\underset{x_{k-1}}{\boxed{?}}\,, \quad E_k^♥(b): \underset{y_0}{\boxed{?}}\,\underset{y_1}{\boxed{?}}\cdots\underset{y_{k-1}}{\boxed{?}}\,.$$

2. Rearrange the cards as follows:

$$\overset{y_{k-1}}{\boxed{?}}\underset{x_0}{\boxed{?}}\;\overset{y_{k-2}}{\boxed{?}}\underset{x_1}{\boxed{?}}\cdots\overset{y_0}{\boxed{?}}\underset{x_{k-1}}{\boxed{?}}.$$

3. Apply a pile-shifting shuffle, where r is a random number:

$$\left[\overset{y_{k-1}}{\boxed{?}}\underset{x_0}{\boxed{?}}\middle|\overset{y_{k-2}}{\boxed{?}}\underset{x_1}{\boxed{?}}\right\cdots\left|\overset{y_0}{\boxed{?}}\underset{x_{k-1}}{\boxed{?}}\right] \rightarrow \overset{y_{k-1-r}}{\boxed{?}}\underset{x_{0+r}}{\boxed{?}}\;\overset{y_{k-2-r}}{\boxed{?}}\underset{x_{1+r}}{\boxed{?}}\cdots\overset{y_{0-r}}{\boxed{?}}\underset{x_{k-1+r}}{\boxed{?}}.$$

4. Rearrange the cards as in the original:

$$E_k^♣(a-r): \underset{x_{0+r}}{\boxed{?}}\,\underset{x_{1+r}}{\boxed{?}}\cdots\underset{x_{k-1+r}}{\boxed{?}}\,, \quad E_k^♥(b+r): \underset{y_{0-r}}{\boxed{?}}\,\underset{y_{1-r}}{\boxed{?}}\cdots\underset{y_{k-1-r}}{\boxed{?}}\,.$$

Here, the random value r is subtracted from a and r is added to b.

5. Turn over the cards in $E_k^\heartsuit(b + r)$, and the sequence of $E_k^\clubsuit(a - r)$ is cyclically shifted to the right by the revealed number $s = b + r$:

$$E_k^\clubsuit(a - r): \boxed{?}\ \boxed{?}\ \cdots\ \boxed{?} \quad \rightarrow \quad E_k^\clubsuit(a + b): \boxed{?}\ \boxed{?}\ \cdots\ \boxed{?}\ .$$
$$\quad\quad\quad\quad\quad x_{0+r}\ x_{1+r}\quad\ x_{k-1+r}\quad\quad\quad\quad\quad x_{0+r-s}\ x_{1+r-s}\quad x_{k-1+r-s}$$

This allows a secure computation of $(a - r) + (b + r) = a + b$ without leaking the values of a and b. That is, $E_k^\clubsuit(a + b)$ is obtained.

Although the addition method has been explained for $E_k^\clubsuit(a)$ and $E_k^\heartsuit(b)$, it can also be performed for other color combinations such as $E_k^\heartsuit(a)$ and $E_k^\clubsuit(b)$.

5.3 Secure Computation of Symmetric Function

Let $f : \{0, 1\}^n \rightarrow R$ be a symmetric function. We want to construct a protocol that outputs only the value of $f(x_1, \ldots, x_n)$, given n commitments to $x_1, \ldots, x_n$:

$$\underbrace{\boxed{?}\,\boxed{?}}_{x_1}\ \underbrace{\boxed{?}\,\boxed{?}}_{x_2}\ \cdots\ \underbrace{\boxed{?}\,\boxed{?}}_{x_n}\quad \rightarrow\quad \cdots\quad \rightarrow\quad f(x_1, \ldots, x_n),$$

where each commitment follows the encoding rule (1).

Since f is symmetric, it is well known that the output value of $f(x_1, \ldots, x_n)$ depends only on the sum $\sum_{i=1}^n x_i$. That is, there exists a function $g : \{0, 1, \ldots, n\} \rightarrow \{0, 1\}$ such that $f(x_1, \ldots, x_n) = g\left(\sum_{i=1}^n x_i\right)$. Therefore, if we want to calculate the symmetric function f, we only need to find the sum $\sum_{i=1}^n x_i$.

Thus, it suffices to obtain a sequence $E_{n+1}^\clubsuit(x_1 + \cdots + x_n)$ or $E_{n+1}^\heartsuit(x_1 + \cdots + x_n)$ from the input commitments. Using the addition of non-negative integers described in Sect. 5.2, we can generate $E_{n+1}^\heartsuit(x_1 + \cdots + x_n)$ with two additional cards [15]. Although the details are omitted, the value of $f(x_1, \ldots, x_n)$ can be obtained by dividing, shuffling, and turning over cards, based on the above function g [15].

Remember that when applying a pile-shifting shuffle, we have to make a pile of cards using an envelope or something. During an execution of the existing protocol, the number of times making piles is $n^2/2 + 3n/2 - 2$. In practice, making a pile, i.e., fixing a number of cards using an envelope, is a time-consuming operation, and hence, we want to reduce this repetition. To this end, the special card boxes will be used for reducing the number of times making piles in our proposed protocol presented in the next section.

6 Secure Computation of Symmetric Function: Our Method

In this section, making use of the special card boxes described in Sect. 4, we propose a generic protocol for any symmetric function $f : \{0, 1\}^n \rightarrow R$. Our protocol uses only one additional card and two special boxes; the number of piles made is $2n - 2$.

6.1 Adding Commitments with Special Boxes

As explained in Sect. 5.3, to securely compute a symmetric function, it suffices to obtain $E_{n+1}^\clubsuit(x_1 + \cdots + x_n)$ or $E_{n+1}^\heartsuit(x_1 + \cdots + x_n)$. Therefore, we give only a procedure for generating the sum $E_{n+1}^\clubsuit(x_1 + \cdots + x_n)$ from input commitments.

Note that a commitment to x_1 can be regarded as $E_2^{\clubsuit}(x_1)$:

$$\underbrace{\boxed{?}\,\boxed{?}}_{x_1} = \underbrace{\boxed{?}\,\boxed{?}}_{E_2^{\clubsuit}(x_1)} .$$

Note furthermore that placing a face-down ♥ card to the right of it results in $E_3^{\clubsuit}(x_1)$:

$$\underbrace{\boxed{?}\,\boxed{?}}_{x_1} \boxed{♥} \rightarrow \underbrace{\boxed{?}\,\boxed{?}\,\boxed{?}}_{E_3^{\clubsuit}(x_1)},$$

and placing a face-down ♥ card to the left results in $E_3^{\clubsuit}(x_1 + 1)$:

$$\boxed{♥}\underbrace{\boxed{?}\,\boxed{?}}_{x_1} \rightarrow \underbrace{\boxed{?}\,\boxed{?}\,\boxed{?}}_{E_3^{\clubsuit}(x_1+1)} .$$

Therefore, notice that the example described in Sect. 4.2 is actually a procedure which produces $E_3^{\clubsuit}(x_1 + x_2)$:

$$\underbrace{\boxed{?}\,\boxed{?}}_{x_1}\underbrace{\boxed{?}\,\boxed{?}}_{x_2}\boxed{♥} \rightarrow \cdots \rightarrow \underbrace{\boxed{?}\,\boxed{?}\,\boxed{?}}_{E_3^{\clubsuit}(x_1+x_2)} .$$

We extend this idea; given n commitments along with one additional card, using two special boxes, we obtain $E_{n+1}^{\clubsuit}(x_1 + \cdots + x_n)$ as follows.

1. Add two commitments to x_1 and x_2 using the method described in Sect. 4.2, and obtain $E_3^{\clubsuit}(x_1 + x_2)$:

$$\underbrace{\boxed{?}\,\boxed{?}}_{x_1}\underbrace{\boxed{?}\,\boxed{?}}_{x_2}\boxed{♥} \rightarrow \underbrace{\boxed{?}\,\boxed{?}\,\boxed{?}}_{E_3^{\clubsuit}(x_1+x_2)}\boxed{♣}\,\boxed{♥} .$$

2. Place $E_3^{\clubsuit}(x_1 + x_2)$ obtained in Step 1 in the left box and the ♥ card in the right box, place the commitment to x_3 on tops of the boxes, and apply the addition in a similar way:

$$\begin{array}{cc}\boxed{?} & \boxed{?}\\ \boxed{?}\,\boxed{?}\,\boxed{?} & \boxed{?}\end{array}\boxed{♣} \rightarrow \cdots \rightarrow \underbrace{\boxed{?}\,\boxed{?}\,\boxed{?}\,\boxed{?}}_{E_4^{\clubsuit}(x_1+x_2+x_3)}\boxed{♣}\,\boxed{♣}\,\boxed{♥} .$$

3. Repeat such an operation until x_n is reached:

$$\underbrace{\boxed{?}\,\boxed{?}\,\boxed{?}\,\boxed{?}}_{E_4^{\clubsuit}(x_1+x_2+x_3)}\boxed{♣}\,\boxed{♣}\,\boxed{♥} \rightarrow \underbrace{\boxed{?}\,\boxed{?}\,\boxed{?}\,\boxed{?}\,\boxed{?}}_{E_5^{\clubsuit}(x_1+x_2+x_3+x_4)}\boxed{♣}\,\boxed{♣}\,\boxed{♣}\,\boxed{♥}$$

$$\rightarrow \cdots \rightarrow \underbrace{\boxed{?}\,\boxed{?}\cdots\boxed{?}}_{E_{n+1}^{\clubsuit}(x_1+x_2+\cdots+x_n)}\underbrace{\boxed{♣}\,\boxed{♣}\cdots\boxed{♣}\,\boxed{♥}}_{n-1 \text{ cards}} .$$

This is our protocol.

The existing protocol [15] requires two additional cards, while our protocol uses only one additional card, i.e., it reduces the number of cards by one by using two special boxes.

Also, the number of times to make piles (namely, the number of times a pile is placed in a sleeve or envelope) is $n^2/2 + 3n/2 - 2$ times in the existing protocol [15], while the number of times to make piles (namely, the number of times we place cards in a special box) is $2n - 2$ times. In terms of this, our protocol is very efficient[2].

Table 1 summarizes their performances.

Table 1. The existing protocol and our protocol for symmetric functions

	# of cards	# of making a pile
Ruangwises–Itoh [15]	$2n + 2$	$n^2/2 + 3n/2 - 2$
Ours	$2n + 1$	$2n - 2$

7 Conclusion

In this paper, we reported that, using a 3D printer, we created the five-card-trick turner and the special card boxes useful for implementing card-based protocols. We also proposed another use of the special card boxes so that we can efficiently perform secure computations of symmetric functions. Specifically, our protocol needs only $2n - 2$ times for making piles while the existing protocol needs $n^2/2 + 3n/2 - 2$ times.

In order for secure computations or other cryptographic technologies to be widely used in society, it is necessary for a wide range of stakeholders to understand the meaning and significance of these cryptographic functionalities [2]. We hope that card-based cryptography and its implementation will help in this regard.

Acknowledgements. We thank the anonymous referees, whose comments have helped us improve the presentation of the paper. This work was supported in part by JSPS KAKENHI Grant Numbers JP24K02938 and JP23H00479.

References

1. Boer, B.D.: More efficient match-making and satisfiability the five card trick. In: EURO-CRYPT 1989. LNCS, vol. 434, pp. 208–217. Springer, Heidelberg (1990)
2. Hanaoka, G.: Towards user-friendly cryptography. In: Paradigms in Cryptology–Mycrypt 2016. Malicious and Exploratory Cryptology. LNCS, vol. 10311, pp. 481–484. Springer, Cham (2017)

---

[2] Although making piles when applying a pile-shifting shuffle is a reasonable implementation, it should be noted that this metric depends on implementations in a sense (cf. [4]).

3. Koch, A.: Cryptographic Protocols from Physical Assumptions. Ph.D. thesis, Karlsruhe Institute of Technology (2019)
4. Koch, A., Walzer, S.: Foundations for actively secure card-based cryptography. In: Fun with Algorithms. LIPIcs, vol. 157, pp. 17:1–17:23. Schloss Dagstuhl, Dagstuhl, Germany (2020)
5. Koch, A., Walzer, S.: Private function evaluation with cards. New Gener. Comput. **40**, 115–147 (2022)
6. Koch, A., Walzer, S., Härtel, K.: Card-based cryptographic protocols using a minimal number of cards. In: Advances in Cryptology—ASIACRYPT 2015. LNCS, vol. 9452, pp. 783–807. Springer, Heidelberg (2015)
7. Mizuki, T.: Preface: Special issue on card-based cryptography. New Gener. Comput. **39**, 1–2 (2021)
8. Mizuki, T.: Preface: Special issue on card-based cryptography 2. New Gener. Comput. **40**, 47–48 (2022)
9. Mizuki, T., Shizuya, H.: A formalization of card-based cryptographic protocols via abstract machine. Int. J. Inf. Secur. **13**(1), 15–23 (2014)
10. Mizuki, T., Shizuya, H.: Computational model of card-based cryptographic protocols and its applications. IEICE Trans. Fundam. **E100.A**(1), 3–11 (2017)
11. Mizuki, T., Sone, H.: Six-card secure AND and four-card secure XOR. In: Frontiers in Algorithmics. LNCS, vol. 5598, pp. 358–369. Springer, Berlin, Heidelberg (2009)
12. Nishimura, A., Hayashi, Y., Mizuki, T., Sone, H.: Pile-shifting scramble for card-based protocols. IEICE Trans. Fundam. **101**(9), 1494–1502 (2018)
13. Nishimura, A., Nishida, T., Hayashi, Y., Mizuki, T., Sone, H.: Five-card secure computations using unequal division shuffle. In: Theory and Practice of Natural Computing. LNCS, vol. 9477, pp. 109–120. Springer, Cham (2015)
14. Nishimura, A., Nishida, T., Hayashi, Y., Mizuki, T., Sone, H.: Card-based protocols using unequal division shuffles. Soft. Comput. **22**, 361–371 (2018)
15. Ruangwises, S., Itoh, T.: Securely computing the n-variable equality function with 2n cards. Theor. Comput. Sci. **887**, 99–110 (2021)
16. Shinagawa, K.: On the Construction of Easy to Perform Card-Based Protocols. Ph.D. thesis, Tokyo Institute of Technology (2020)
17. Shinagawa, K., et al.: Multi-party computation with small shuffle complexity using regular polygon cards. In: Provable Security. LNCS, vol. 9451, pp. 127–146. Springer, Cham (2015)
18. Shinagawa, K., et al.: Card-based protocols using regular polygon cards. IEICE Trans. Fundam. **E100.A**(9), 1900–1909 (2017)
19. Shinagawa, K., Nuida, K.: A single shuffle is enough for secure card-based computation of any Boolean circuit. Discret. Appl. Math. **289**, 248–261 (2021)
20. Ueda, I., Nishimura, A., Hayashi, Y., Mizuki, T., Sone, H.: How to implement a random bisection cut. In: Theory and Practice of Natural Computing. LNCS, vol. 10071, pp. 58–69. Springer, Cham (2016)

Self-assembly of Patterns in the Abstract Tile Assembly Model

Phillip Drake[1], Matthew J. Patitz[1(✉)], Scott M. Summers[2], and Tyler Tracy[1]

[1] University of Arkansas, Fayetteville, AR 72701, USA
{padrake,patitz,tgtracy}@uark.edu
[2] University of Wisconsin-Oshkosh, Oshkosh, WI 54901, USA
summerss@uwosh.edu

Abstract. In the abstract Tile Assembly Model, self-assembling systems consisting of tiles of different colors can form structures on which colored patterns are "painted." We explore the complexity, in terms of the numbers of unique tile types required, of assembling various patterns. We first demonstrate how to efficiently self-assemble a set of simple patterns, then show tight bounds on the tile type complexity of self-assembling 2-colored patterns on the surfaces of square assemblies. Finally, we demonstrate an exponential gap in tile type complexity of self-assembling an infinite series of patterns between systems restricted to one plane versus those allowed two planes.

1 Introduction

During the process of self-assembly, a disorganized collection of components experiencing only random motion and local interactions combine to form structures. Examples of self-assembly abound in nature, from crystals to cellular components, and these systems have inspired researchers to study them to better understand the underlying principles governing them as well as to engineer systems that mimic them. Along the spectrum of both natural and artificial self-assembling systems are those which (1) use very small numbers of component types and form simple, unbounded, repeating patterns, (2) use a large number of component types, on the order of the entire sizes of the structures created, to form structures with highly-specified, asymmetric designs, and (3) those which use very small numbers of components to make arbitrarily large, bounded or unbounded, symmetric or asymmetric structures whose growth is directed algorithmically.

Systems in category (2), so-called *fully-addressed* or *hard-coded* have the benefit of being able to uniquely define each "pixel" of the structure and therefore to "paint" arbitrary pictures, which we'll refer to as *patterns*, on their surfaces [14,18,20]. Although it is easy to see that in models of tile-based self-assembly such as the abstract Tile Assembly Model (aTAM) [19] any finite structure or pattern can self-assemble from a hard-coded system, it has previously been

S. M. Summers—This author was supported in part by University of Wisconsin Oshkosh Research Sabbatical (S581) Fall 2023.

shown that there exist infinite structures and patterns that cannot self-assemble in the aTAM [9,10]. The benefits of the *algorithmic self-assembly* [6,15,21] of category (3) include precise formation of shapes using exponentially fewer types of components [16,17], thus reducing the cost, reducing the effort to fabricate and implement, and increasing the speed of growth of these systems [3]. However, the drastic reduction in the number of component types means a corresponding increase in their reuse. This results in copies of the same component type appearing in many locations throughout the resulting target structure, thus removing the ability to uniquely address each pixel when forming patterns. This generally results in a reduction in the number of patterns that are producible.

In this paper we study the trade-off between the numbers of unique components, or *tile types*, needed to self-assemble designed patterns and the complexities of the patterns that can self-assemble. Past lines of work have dealt with the self-assembly of patterns in the aTAM from the perspective of the computational complexity of designing minimal tile sets to self-assemble given patterns (the so-called "PATS" problem) [2,8,11,12] and others have shown the possibilities and impossibilities of assembling some classes of infinite patterns [9,13]. In contrast, our first results present constructions for making tile sets that self-assemble a series of relatively simple patterns to demonstrate how efficiently they can be built algorithmically. These consist of patterns of white and black pixels on the surfaces of squares, and include (1) a pattern with a single black pixel, (2) a pattern with some number k of black pixels, and (3) grids of alternating black and white stripes. All of these are shown to have exponential reductions in tile type requirements, a.k.a. *tile complexity*, over fully-addressed systems.

Our next pair of results combine to show a tight bound on the tile complexity of self-assembling arbitrary patterns of two colors on the surfaces of $n \times n$ squares for almost all patterns. Using an information theoretic argument we prove a lower bound, namely that for almost all patterns on $n \times n$ squares, such patterns have tile complexity $\Omega\left(\frac{n^2}{\log n}\right)$. We then provide a construction that, when given an arbitrary $n \times n$ pattern of black and white pixels, generates a tile set of $O\left(\frac{n^2}{\log n}\right)$ tile types that self-assemble an $n \times n$ square with black and white tiles that form that pattern. Although this is not a significant improvement over the n^2 tile types required to naively implement a fully-addressed set of tile types, the lower bound proves that for almost all patterns this is the best possible tile complexity.

Although the prior result showed that any $n \times n$ pattern can self-assemble using $O\left(\frac{n^2}{\log n}\right)$ tile types, our next result shows that, if given two planes in which tiles can self-assemble (one on top of the other) then it is possible for some patterns to self-assemble using exponentially fewer tile types than when systems are restricted to a single plane. (In fact, this result can be modified for arbitrary separation in tile complexity.) The proof of this result uses a novel application of diagonalization to tile-based self-assembly. Namely, one system simulates every system of a given tile complexity class for a bounded number of steps, sequentially and within a square of one plane, in order to algorithmically generate a pattern that is guaranteed not to be made by any of those systems, and then prints that generated pattern on the square of the second plane above the assembly that performed the simulations. We also show how to extend these square patterns infinitely to cover the plane, while maintaining the same tile complexity argument.

Overall, our results demonstrate boundaries on tile complexities of algorithmic self-assembling systems when forming patterns, and help to demonstrate their benefits over fully-addressed systems. To make some of our results easier to understand, we have created a set of programs and tile sets that can be used to view examples. These can be found online: Pattern Self-Assembly Software [5]. Due to space limitations, proofs are omitted in this version but a full version can be found online [4].

2 Preliminary Definitions and Models

In this section we define the terminology and model used throughout the paper.

2.1 The Abstract Tile-Assembly Model

We work within the abstract Tile-Assembly Model [19] in 2 and 3 dimensions. We will use the abbreviation *aTAM* to refer to the 2D model, *3DaTAM* for the 3D model, and *barely-3DaTAM* to refer to the 3D model when restricted to the use of only 2 planes of the third dimension (a.k.a. the "just barely 3D aTAM"), meaning that tiles can only be placed in locations with z coordinates equal to 0 or 1 (use of the other two dimensions is unbounded). These definitions are borrowed from [7] and we note that [10,16] are good introductions to the model for unfamiliar readers.

Let $\mathbb{N}$ be the set of nonnegative integers, and for $n \in \mathbb{N}$, let $[n] = \{0, 1, ..., n - 2, n - 1\}$. Fix $d \in \{2, 3\}$ to be the number of dimensions and Σ to be some alphabet with Σ^* its finite strings. A *glue* $g \in \Sigma^* \times \mathbb{N}$ consists of a finite string *label* and non-negative integer *strength*. There is a single glue of strength 0, referred to as the *null* glue. A *tile type* is a tuple $t \in (\Sigma^* \times \mathbb{N})^{2d}$, thought of as a unit square or cube with a glue on each side. A *tile set* is a finite set of tile types. We always assume a finite set of tile types, but allow an infinite number of copies of each tile type to occupy locations in the $\mathbb{Z}^d$ lattice, each called a *tile*.

Given a tile set T, a *configuration* is an arrangement (possibly empty) of tiles in the lattice $\mathbb{Z}^d$, i.e. a partial function $\alpha : \mathbb{Z}^d \dashrightarrow T$. Two adjacent tiles in a configuration *interact*, or are *bound* or *attached*, if the glues on their abutting sides are equal (in both label and strength) and have positive strength. Each configuration α induces a *binding graph* B_α whose vertices are those points occupied by tiles, with an edge of weight s between two vertices if the corresponding tiles interact with strength s. An *assembly* is a configuration whose domain (as a graph) is connected and non-empty. The *shape* $S_\alpha \subseteq \mathbb{Z}^d$ of assembly α is the domain of α. For some $\tau \in \mathbb{Z}^+$, an assembly α is τ-*stable* if every cut of B_α has weight at least τ, i.e. a τ-stable assembly cannot be split into two pieces without separating bound tiles whose shared glues have cumulative strength τ.

Given two assemblies α, β, we say α is a *subassembly* of β (denoted $\alpha \sqsubseteq \beta$) if $S_\alpha \subseteq S_\beta$ and for all $p \in S_\alpha$, $\alpha(p) = \beta(p)$ (i.e., they have tiles of the same types in all locations of α).

A *tile-assembly system* (TAS) is a triple $\mathcal{T} = (T, \sigma, \tau)$, where T is a tile set, σ is a finite τ-stable assembly called the *seed assembly*, and $\tau \in \mathbb{Z}^+$ is called the *binding threshold* (a.k.a. *temperature*). If the seed σ consists of a single tile, i.e. $|\sigma| = 1$, we say $\mathcal{T}$ is *singly-seeded*. Given a TAS $\mathcal{T} = (T, \sigma, \tau)$ and two τ-stable assemblies α and β, we say that α $\mathcal{T}$-*produces* β *in one step* (written $\alpha \rightarrow_1^\mathcal{T} \beta$) if $\alpha \sqsubseteq \beta$ and $|S_\beta \setminus S_\alpha| = 1$. That is, $\alpha \rightarrow_1^\mathcal{T} \beta$ if β differs from α by the addition of a single tile. The $\mathcal{T}$-*frontier* is the set $\partial^\mathcal{T} \alpha = \bigcup_{\alpha \rightarrow_1^\mathcal{T} \beta} S_\beta \setminus S_\alpha$ of locations in which a tile could τ-stably attach to α. When $\mathcal{T}$ is clear from context we simply refer to these as the *frontier* locations.

We use $\mathcal{A}^T$ to denote the set of all assemblies of tiles in tile set T. Given a TAS $\mathcal{T} = (T, \sigma, \tau)$, a sequence of $k \in \mathbb{Z}^+ \cup \{\infty\}$ assemblies $\alpha_0, \alpha_1, \dots$ over $\mathcal{A}^T$ is called a $\mathcal{T}$-*assembly sequence* if, for all $1 \leq i < k$, $\alpha_{i-1} \rightarrow_1^\mathcal{T} \alpha_i$. The *result* of an assembly sequence is the unique limiting assembly of the sequence. For finite assembly sequences, this is the final assembly; whereas for infinite assembly sequences, this is the assembly consisting of all tiles from any assembly in the sequence. We say that α $\mathcal{T}$-*produces* β (denoted $\alpha \rightarrow^\mathcal{T} \beta$) if there is a $\mathcal{T}$-assembly sequence starting with α whose result is β. We say α is $\mathcal{T}$-*producible* if $\sigma \rightarrow^\mathcal{T} \alpha$ and write $\mathcal{A}[\mathcal{T}]$ to denote the set of $\mathcal{T}$-producible assemblies. We say α is $\mathcal{T}$-*terminal* if α is τ-stable and there exists no assembly that is $\mathcal{T}$-producible from α. We denote the set of $\mathcal{T}$-producible and $\mathcal{T}$-terminal assemblies by $\mathcal{A}_\square[\mathcal{T}]$. If $|\mathcal{A}_\square[\mathcal{T}]| = 1$, i.e., there is exactly one terminal assembly, we say that $\mathcal{T}$ is *directed*. When $\mathcal{T}$ is clear from context, we may omit $\mathcal{T}$ from notation.

2.2   Patterns

Let C be a set of colors and let $P \subseteq (\mathbb{Z}^d \times C)$. We say that P is a d-*dimensional pattern*, i.e., a set of locations and corresponding colors. Let dom P be the set of locations that are assigned a color. A pattern is k-*colored* when the number of unique colors used is k. Let $\texttt{Color}(P, l)$ be a function that takes a pattern and a location l and returns the color of the pattern at that location. (and is undefined if $l \notin \text{dom}(P)$).

Given a TAS $\mathcal{T} = (T, \sigma, \tau)$, we allow each tile type to be assigned exactly one *color* from some set of colors C. Let $C_P \subseteq C$ be a subset of those colors, and $T_{C_P} \subseteq T$ be the subset of tiles of T whose colors are in C_P. Given an assembly $\alpha \in \mathcal{A}[\mathcal{T}]$, we use dom (α) to denote the set of all locations with tiles in α and dom $_{C_p}(\alpha)$ to denote the set of all locations of tiles in α with colors in C_P. Given a location $l \in \mathbb{Z}^d$, let $\texttt{Color}(\alpha, l)$ define a function that takes as input an assembly and a location and returns the color of the tile at that location (and is undefined if $l \notin \text{dom}(\alpha)$). We say $\mathcal{T}$ *weakly self-assembles pattern* P iff for all $\alpha \in \mathcal{A}_\square[\mathcal{T}]$, dom $_{C_P}(\alpha) = P$ and $\forall (l, c) \in P, c = \texttt{Color}(\alpha, l)$. We say $\mathcal{T}$ *strictly self-assembles pattern* P iff $T_{C_P} = T$, i.e. all tiles of T are colored from C_P, and $\mathcal{T}$ weakly self-assembles P (i.e. all locations receiving tiles are within P).

Let the set of all patterns be $\mathbb{P}$, the set of all c-colored patterns be $\mathbb{P}_c$, and $\mathtt{SQPATS}_{c,n} \subset \mathbb{P}_c$ be the set of all c-colored patterns that are on the surfaces of $n \times n$ squares. Let $\mathtt{SQPATS}_c = \bigcup_{n \in \mathbb{Z}^+} \mathtt{SQPATS}_{c,n}$, i.e., the set of all c-colored patterns that are on the surfaces of squares. A *pattern class* is an infinite set of patterns parameterized by some set of values X, and can be represented as a function $PC : X \to \mathbb{P}$ that maps parameters X to some pattern $P \in \mathbb{P}$. Let $\mathbb{T}$ be the set of all aTAM systems. A *construction for pattern class PC* is a function $C_{PC} : \mathbb{P} \to \mathbb{T}$ that takes a pattern $P \in \mathbb{P}$ and outputs an aTAM system $\mathcal{T} \in \mathbb{T}$ such that $\mathcal{T}$ weakly self-assembles P.

3 Simple Patterns

In this section, we define several relatively simple pattern classes and present constructions that can build them efficiently.

First we define a pattern class whose patterns each consist of a 2-colored $n \times n$ square that is completely white except for a single black pixel.

Definition 1 (Single-Pixel Pattern Class). *Given $n, i, j \in \mathbb{N}$, where $i, j < n$, define $SinglePixel(n, i, j) \to P$ such that (1) $P \in SQPATS_{2,n}$, (2) $\forall l \in dom(P) - \{(i,j)\}$, $Color(P, l) = White$, and (3) $Color(P, (i,j)) = Black$.*

Theorem 1. *For all $n, i, j \in \mathbb{N}$ such that $n \geq i, j$, there exists an aTAM system $\mathcal{T} = (T, \sigma, 2)$ such that $|\sigma| = 1$, $|T| = O(\log(n))$, and $\mathcal{T}$ weakly self-assembles $SinglePixel(n, i, j)$.*

Proof. We present a construction that, given an $n, i, j \in \mathbb{N}$ such that $i, j < n$, creates a TAS $\mathcal{T}$ with tile complexity of $O(\log n)$ that weakly self-assembles $P = \mathtt{SinglePixel}(n, i, j)$. Figure 1 shows a high-level depiction of how we build the assembly.

The assembly starts by growing a hard-coded rectangle with an empty interior called a *counter box*. Each side of the box has glues for a counter to attach. The side lengths are $s = \lceil \log n \rceil$, as this is the maximum length needed to encode the bits required for a binary counter to count a full dimension of the entire square (which is the maximum that could be necessary). Thus, the counter box uses $O(\log n)$ tiles types.

Each side of the counter box has a number encoded in the outward-facing glues. These numbers are pre-computed so that binary counter tiles (i.e. sets of tiles that operate as standard binary counters) grow outward from them to form a cross-like structure that extends to each boundary of the $n \times n$ square. A constant-sized set of tile types (independent of i, j, and n) is used for each of the four counters. To complete the $n \times n$ square, a constant-sized set of filler tiles fill in between the counters and inside the counter box.

The seed tile is a single black tile, from which the counter box grows, while all other tile types are white. If the black tile is within $\log n$ of the side of the square, then the counter box grows away from the edge, meaning the counter box always has room to grow inside of the $n \times n$ square.

We have shown that the tile complexity of this assembly is $O(\log n)$ and that it weakly self-assembles P. Thus, the Theorem 1 is proved.

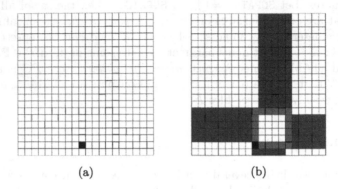

(a)   (b)

Fig. 1. (a) An example of a single-pixel pattern. The black pixel is located at $(10, 2)$. (b) The same single-pixel pattern but with the counter box and counter tiles colored for demonstration. The counter box is colored red. The counters are colored blue. The white locations are filled by generic filler tiles. (Color figure online)

Next, we define a pattern class whose patterns each consist of a 2-colored $n \times n$ square that is completely white except for a set of (separated and individual) black pixels.

Definition 2 (Multi-pixel Pattern Class). *Given $n \in \mathbb{N}$ and a set of locations $L \subseteq [0, n-1]^2$ such that $\forall (x, y), (x', y') \in L, |x - x'| \geq \lceil \log n \rceil \vee |y - y'| \geq \lceil \log n \rceil$, define $\texttt{MultiPixel}(n, L) \rightarrow P$ such that (1) $P \in SQPATS_{2,n}$, and (2) $\forall v \in dom(P), Color(P, v) = Black$ if $v \in L$ else White.*

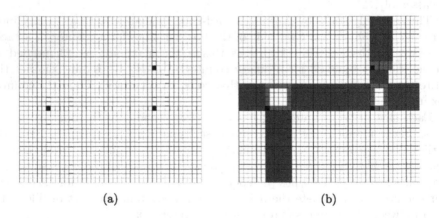

(a)   (b)

Fig. 2. (a) An example of a multi-pixel pattern with three black pixels. (b) A tree of counters is constructed to grow to each pixel and the edges of the square. The counter boxes are colored red. The counters are colored blue. The white locations are filled by generic filler tiles. (Color figure online)

Theorem 2. *For all $n \in \mathbb{N}$ and sets of locations $L \subseteq [0, n-1]^2$ such that $\forall (x, y), (x', y') \in L$, $|x - x'| \geq \lceil \log n \rceil \vee |y - y'| \geq \lceil \log n \rceil$, there exists an aTAM system $T = (T, \sigma, 2)$ such that $|\sigma| = 1$, $|T| = O(|L| \log n)$, and T weakly self-assembles* MultiPixel(n, L).

The proof of Theorem 2 uses a construction that is an extension of that used in the proof of Theorem 1, and essentially uses a series of counters to build a path connecting all pixels and filler tiles for the remaining portion of the square. A high-level depiction is shown in Fig. 2, and full details can be found in [4].

The final (relatively) simple pattern class that we define contains patterns that each consist of a 2-colored $n \times n$ square with a set of repeating black horizontal rows and a set of repeating black vertical columns.

Definition 3 (Stripes Pattern Class). *Given $n, i, j \in \mathbb{N}$, where $i, j < n$, define* Stripes$(n, i, j) \rightarrow P$ *such that (1) $P \in SQPATS_{2,n}$, and (2) $\forall x, y \in [0, n-1]$, Color$(P, (x, y)) = Black$ if $x \mod i = 0$ or $y \mod j = 0$, else White.*

Theorem 3. *For all $n, i, j \in \mathbb{N}$, where $i, j < n$, there exists an aTAM system $T = (T, \sigma, 2)$ such that $|\sigma| = 1$, $|T| = O(\log(n))$ and T weakly self-assembles* Stripes(n, i, j).

The proof of Theorem 3 can be found in [4]. It is done by construction, where the construction has counters that grow vertically to count to, and mark, the locations of horizontal strips, and counters that grow horizontally to count to, and mark, the locations of vertical stripes. Counters also keep track of the distance to the boundaries of the square to ensure growth stops at the correct locations. An overview can be seen in Fig. 3.

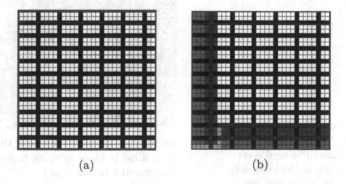

(a)   (b)

Fig. 3. (a) An example of a stripes pattern. (b) The blue tiles count to the next stripe, while the red tiles count the number of stripes. Green tiles represent the starting rows for the counters (with the seed tile being at the corner where the green row and column intersect). Dark grey tiles represent counter tiles that are colored black (Color figure online)

4   Tight Bounds for Patterns on $n \times n$ Squares

In this section, we prove tight bounds on the tile complexity of self-assembling 2-colored patterns on the surfaces of $n \times n$ squares for almost all such patterns.

Theorem 4. *For almost all positive integers n and $P \in SQPATS_{2,n}$, the tile complexity of weakly self-assembling P by a singly-seeded system in the aTAM is $\Theta \left(\frac{n^2}{\log n} \right)$.*

We prove Theorem 4 by separately proving the lower and upper bounds, as Lemma 1 and Lemma 2, respectively.

Lemma 1. *For almost all patterns $P \in SQPATS_2$, the tile complexity of weakly self-assembling P by a singly-seeded system in the aTAM is $\Omega \left(\frac{n^2}{\log n} \right)$.*

The proof of Lemma 1 is a straight-forward information-theoretic argument and can be found in [4].

To prove the upper bound for Theorem 4, we prove the following, which is a stronger result that applies to all positive integers n.

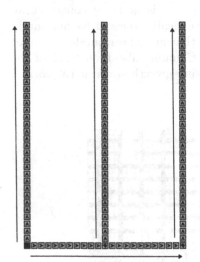

(a) The skeleton. The seed is represented in green in the lower left and the arrows show the directions of growth.

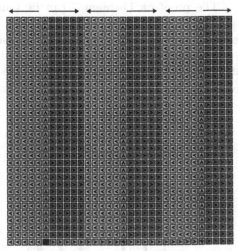

(b) The square once the ribs of the skeleton have filled in (blue growing to the left, yellow growing to the right).

Fig. 4. A schematic example of the construction of the proof of Lemma 2. Instead of showing the black and white colors corresponding to the pattern, we color the tiles to show the pieces of the construction to which they belong.

Lemma 2. *For all positive integers n and $P \in \text{SQPATS}_{2,n}$, there exists an aTAM system $\mathcal{T} = (T, \sigma, 1)$ such that $|\sigma| = 1$, $|T| = O\left(\frac{n^2}{\log n}\right)$ and $\mathcal{T}$ weakly self-assembles P.*

Proof. We proceed by construction. Let $n \in \mathbb{Z}^+$ be the dimensions of the square and P be the $n \times n$ pattern of black and white pixels to weakly self-assemble on the square. Our construction will yield a system $\mathcal{T} = (T, \sigma, 1)$ that self-assembles an $n \times n$ square on which P is formed by the black and white tiles of T. The tile set T will be composed of two subsets, T_s whose tiles form the *skeleton*, and T_r whose tiles form the *ribs*. We first explain the formation of the skeleton, then that of the ribs. Figure 4 shows a high-level depiction.

Skeleton. The seed is part of the skeleton and is placed at location $(\lfloor \log n \rfloor, 0)$ and is given the color $\texttt{Color}(P, (\lfloor \log n \rfloor, 0))$. Since a vertical column of the skeleton has width one, and the ribs growing off of each side have length $\lfloor \log n \rfloor$, the width of a pair of ribs and its skeleton column (which we will call a *rib-pair*) is $2\lfloor \log n \rfloor + 1$. Dividing the full width n by the width of a rib-pair, and taking the floor, gives the number of full rib-pairs that will fit. Let $f = \lfloor \frac{n}{2\log n + 1} \rfloor$ be this number. Let $r = n \bmod (2\lfloor \log n \rfloor + 1)$ be the remaining width after the last full rib-pair. If $r < \lfloor \log n \rfloor + 1$, then a column of the skeleton grows up immediately to the right of the last full rib-pair, and its ribs are of length $r - 1$ and grow to the right. If $r \geq \lfloor \log n \rfloor + 1$, then the last skeleton column grows upward $\lfloor \log n \rfloor$ positions to the right of the last full rib-pair and has full-length ribs (i.e., $\lfloor \log n \rfloor$) that grow to its left and ribs of length $r - (\lfloor \log n \rfloor + 1)$ grow to its right. In the first case, the row of the skeleton that forms the bottom row of the square extends from the seed to x-coordinate $f(2\lfloor \log n \rfloor + 1) + 1$. In the second case, that row extends from the seed to x-coordinate $f(2\lfloor \log n \rfloor + 1) + \lfloor \log n \rfloor + 1$. The tiles of that row are hard-coded and there are $O(n)$ of them. Starting with the seed and then occurring at every $2\lfloor \log n \rfloor + 1$ locations of the bottom row, a hard-coded set of tiles grows a column of height $n - 1$. This row and set of columns are the full skeleton. The number of tile types is $O(n)$ for the row and $O(n)$ for each of the $O\left(\frac{n}{\log n}\right)$ columns, for a total of $O(n) + O\left(\frac{n^2}{\log n}\right) = O\left(\frac{n^2}{\log n}\right)$ tile types. Note that each skeleton tile type is given the color of the corresponding location in the pattern P.

Ribs. From the east and west sides of each location on the columns of the skeleton, ribs grow. Each rib is composed of $\lfloor \log n \rfloor$ tiles (except the ribs growing from the easternmost column, which may be shorter). Since there are two possible colors for each of the $\lfloor \log n \rfloor$ locations of a rib, there are a maximum of $2^{\lfloor \log n \rfloor} \leq n$ possible color patterns for any rib to match the corresponding locations in P. (Note that we will discuss the construction of the tiles for ribs that grow to the east, and for ribs that grow to the west the directions are simply reversed.) For any given rib r, let the portion of P corresponding to the locations of r be represented by the binary string of length $\lfloor \log n \rfloor$ where each black location is represented by a 0, and each white by a 1. For example, for a rib r of length 5 growing eastward from a column, if the corresponding locations of P are "black,

black, white, black, white", then the binary string will be "00101". For each possible binary string b of length $\lfloor \log n \rfloor$, i.e. $b \in \{0,1\}^{\lfloor \log n \rfloor}$, a unique tile type, t_b, is made. with the glue b on its west side and the glue $b[1:]$ (i.e. b with its left bit truncated) on its east side. This tile type is given the color corresponding to the first bit of b. Additionally, for each skeleton column tile from which a rib should grow to the east with pattern b, the glue b will be on its east side, allowing t_b to attach. This results in the creation of a maximum of n unique tile types (and there will be another n for the first tiles of each westward growing rib). Recall that the tile types for the skeleton were already accounted for and each is hard-coded so that the placement of these glues does not require any new tile types for the skeleton.

Now, the process is repeated for each binary string from length $b-1$ to 1, with the color of each tile being set to the value of the first remaining bit. Each iteration requires half as many tile types to be created as the previous, i.e. $2^{\lfloor \log n \rfloor - 1}$, then $2^{\lfloor \log n \rfloor - 2}$, ..., 2. Intuitively, each rib position has glues that encode their bit value in the pattern and the portion of the pattern that must be extended outward from them, away from the skeleton. Therefore, for the last position on the tip of each rib, there are exactly 2 choices, white or black, and so all ribs share from a set of two tile types made specially for the ends of ribs. For the tile types of ribs that grow to the east, the total summation is $\sum_{x=0}^{\log n - 1} 2^{\log n - x} = 2n - 2 = O(n)$. Accounting for the additional tile types needed for westward growing ribs, the full tile complexity of the ribs is $O(n)$.

Thus, the total tile complexity for the tile types of the skeleton plus those of the ribs is $O\left(\frac{n^2}{\log n}\right) + O(n) = O\left(\frac{n^2}{\log n}\right)$.

Correctness of Construction. The system T designed to weakly self-assemble P, as discussed, has a seed of a single tile, and since all tile attachments require forming a bond with a single neighbor, the temperature of the system can be $\tau = 1$. Our prior analysis shows that the tile complexity is correct at $O\left(\frac{n^2}{\log n}\right)$, and showing that T weakly self-assembles P is trivial since (1) the tiles of the skeleton are specifically hard-coded to be colored for their corresponding locations in P, and (2) for each possible pattern corresponding to a rib there is a hard-coded set of rib tiles that match that pattern and grow from the skeleton into those locations. Thus, P is formed and Lemma 2 is proved, and with both Lemmas 1 and 2, Theorem 4 is proved. (Example aTAM systems for this construction, as well as software capable of generating other systems for patterns derived from image files, and for simulating them, can be found online [5].)

5   Repeated Patterns

In this section, we discuss patterns consisting of repeated, arbitrary square sub-patterns, and that efficient systems exist that weakly self-assemble them (Fig. 5).

Definition 4 (Grid Repeat Pattern Class). *Given $n, m \in \mathbb{Z}^+$ and $P \in$ SQPATS$_{2,n}$, define* GridRepeat$(P, m) \rightarrow P'$ *such that $P' \in$ SQPATS$_{2,nm}$ is an*

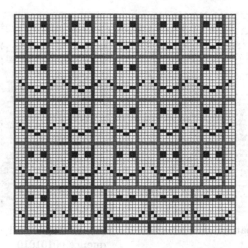

Fig. 5. An example of an assembly that repeats a pattern $m = 5$ times horizontally and vertically. Each spine is colored solely for clarity of presentation, and in the actual construction, the colors of the tiles on the spines would match the pixels of the pattern. Red spines represent a 1, and blue spines represent a 0. The spines count upwards until the counter is finished (Color figure online)

$nm \times nm$ *square consisting of an* $m \times m$ *square composed of an* $n \times n$ *grid of copies of the pattern* P.

Theorem 5 (Repeated Pattern Tile Complexity). *For all* $n, m \in \mathbb{N}$, *and* $P \in SQPATS_{2,n}$ *there exists an aTAM system* $\mathcal{T} = (T, \sigma, 2)$ *such that* $|\sigma| = 1$, $|T| = O(\frac{n^2}{\log n} + \log mn)$ *and* $\mathcal{T}$ *weakly self-assembles* $GridRepeat(P, m)$.

The proof of Theorem 5 can be found in [4]. It makes use of an extension of the construction for the proof of Lemma 2 and embeds a counter into the skeleton and ribs so that the copies of the sub-pattern are correctly counted.

6 Barely-3DaTAM Patterns

In this section, we show that there exist patterns, both finite and infinite, that can be weakly self-assembled using exponentially fewer tile types by barely-3DaTAM systems than by any regular, 2D aTAM systems. (We also note that the exponential separation can be increased arbitrarily.)

Theorem 6. *For all* $n \in \mathbb{Z}^+$, *for some* $m \in \mathbb{Z}^+$ *there exists a 7-colored* $m \times m$ *pattern,* p_n, *such that (1) no aTAM system* $\mathcal{T}_{\leq n} = (T, \sigma, \tau)$ *exists where* $|T| \leq n$, $|\sigma| = 1$, *and* $\mathcal{T}_{\leq n}$ *weakly self-assembles* p_n, *but (2) a barely-3DaTAM system* $\mathcal{T}_{p_n} = (T_{p_n}, \sigma_{p_n}, 2)$ *exists where* $|T_{p_n}| = O(\log n / \log \log n)$, $|\sigma_{p_n}| = 1$, *and* $\mathcal{T}_{p_n}$ *weakly self-assembles* p_n.

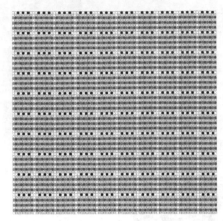 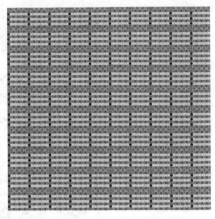

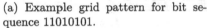

(a) Example grid pattern for bit sequence 11010101.

(b) Example grid pattern for bit sequence 00101010.

Fig. 6. Example p_n patterns created by the construction in the proof of Theorem 6. The (repeatedly copied) binary sequence derived from the results of the simulations of aTAM systems starts at the top, with the two colors of that row, and all subsequent boundary rows, being determined by the first bit of that pattern. During the downward growth from that row, during which the full $m \times m$ square is formed, the repeating grid formed by the copies of that pattern is copied both downward and to both sides. The boundary columns also have two colors determined by the first bit of the sequence (one of them the same as in the boundary rows) for a total of 3 boundary colors. The interiors always use the same 4 colors.

Proof Sketch. (Here we give a sketch of the full proof of Theorem 6. The full proof can be found in [4].) We prove Theorem 6 by giving the details of such a pattern p_n that consists of a repeating "grid" of 7-colored lines on the surface of an $m \times m$ square, for $m \in \mathbb{Z}^+$ to be defined, and a barely 3D aTAM system $\mathcal{T}_{p_n} = (T_{p_n}, \sigma, 2)$ that weakly self-assembles p_n, with the tiles in $z = 1$ colored in the pattern of p_n, and $|T_{p_n}| = O(\log n / \log \log n)$ tile types. We show that every 2D aTAM system $\mathcal{T}_{\leq n}$ with $\leq n$ tile types fails to weakly self-assemble p_n by constructing p_n so that it differs, in at least one location in each "cell" of a repeating grid of cells, from an assembly producible in each $\mathcal{T}_{\leq n}$. Two different examples of such patterns can be seen in Fig. 6. Each pattern p_n consists of an $m \times m$ square that is covered in a repeating grid of square "cells." Each cell is a $c \times c$ square (for $c \in \mathbb{Z}^+$, to be defined) where the north row and west column of each is considered "boundary," and the rest of each cell is considered "interior." The easternmost column and the southernmost row of cells may consist of truncated cells depending on the values of m and c (i.e., if $m \mod c \neq 0$). Since each cell contributes a north and west boundary, each cell interior is completely surrounded by boundaries (except, perhaps, the easternmost column and southernmost row). Depending on a bit sequence specific to each p_n (to be discussed), the set of colors of the boundaries will be either {White, Green, Black} or {Red, Green, Black}. The set of colors of the interiors will be {Aqua, Blue, Yellow, Fuchsia}. Thus, each pattern p_n will be composed of 7 colors.

The bit sequence that determines the colors used by the boundaries, and the ordering of the colors on the boundaries and in the interiors, is determined via simulations of a series of aTAM systems. Intuitively, our proof utilizes a construction that performs a diagonalization against all possible aTAM systems with $\leq n$ tile types by simulating each for a bounded number of steps, and for each keeping track of the color of tile it places in a location specific to the index of that system so that it can ultimately generate the colored pattern p_n that differs in at least one location from every simulated system (Fig. 7).

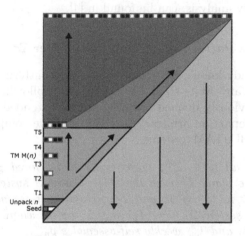

Fig. 7. Schematic overview of the portion of the construction for the proof of Theorem 6 that grows in plane $z = 0$. Modules are not shown to scale. (Green) The seed tile, (Fuchsia) the base conversion module that unpacks the binary representation of n, (Aqua) the module that simulates the Turing machine M on input n, which itself simulates each aTAM system with $\leq n$ tile types in sequence and saves a result bit (Black or White) for each, (Yellow and Grey) the pattern of result bits is copied repetitively to the right until it covers the entire top row. (Light Grey) A "filler" tile causes the assembly to form a complete square.

The dimensions of each $c \times c$ cell are $c = \mathrm{SF}(n)$, where $\mathrm{SF}(n)$ is a function that takes a number of tile types and returns an upper bound on the number of all possible singly-seeded aTAM systems with $\leq n$ tile types and ≤ 8 colors. (Note that $\mathrm{SF}(n)$ is actually greater than the number of such systems, and details of $\mathrm{SF}(n)$ can be found in [4].) The colors of the rows and columns encode the bit sequence generated by the simulations, with the same bit sequence encoded in both the rows and the columns via an assignment of colors. There is a unique color assigned for each intersection of two bits (i.e. 00, 01, 10, and 11), with 4 colors reserved for boundaries of grid cells and 4 separate colors reserved for the interior locations of the grid cells. Therefore, the colored pattern of every cell differs from the assemblies produced by all aTAM systems with $\leq n$ tile types.

It forms on the top layer of a two-layered $m \times m$ square where $m = O(n^{21n})$, and the barely-3DaTAM system that forms it uses $O(\log n / \log \log n)$ tiles since the tiles types for all modules are constant except those that encode n using optimal encoding [1]. (Note that the value of m could be smaller, $O(n^{4n}n^8)$, if it wasn't desired that both planes be the same size. Additionally, by having M simulate systems with larger tile sets, the value of m would increase but the difference in tile complexity between the barely-3DaTAM system and the systems incapable of making its patterns could be increased beyond the current exponential bound.) Additional technical details, including pseudocode for the algorithms of the Turing machine M and its simulations of all systems with $\leq n$ tile types, the layout of data structures used during the simulation of a system, and time complexity analysis, can be found in [4].

6.1   Extending a Pattern p_n to Infinitely Cover $\mathbb{Z}^2$

Although it is already known that there are infinite patterns that can't weakly self-assemble from any finite-sized tile set [9], the following corollary simply shows how the previously defined patterns can be extended to infinitely cover the plane, while keeping an arbitrary spread in the tile complexity required by aTAM and barely-3DaTAM systems.

Corollary 1. *For all $n \in \mathbb{Z}^+$, there exists a 7-colored pattern, p_{n_∞}, that infinitely covers the plane $\mathbb{Z}^2$ such that (1) no aTAM system $\mathcal{T}_{\leq n} = (T, \sigma, \tau)$ exists where $|T| \leq n$, $|\sigma| = 1$, and $\mathcal{T}_{\leq n}$ weakly self-assembles p_{n_∞}, but (2) a barely-3DaTAM system $\mathcal{T}_{p_n} = (T_{p_n}, \sigma_{p_n}, 2)$ exists where $|T_{p_n}| = O(\log n / \log \log n)$, $|\sigma_{p_n}| = 1$, and $\mathcal{T}_{p_n}$ weakly self-assembles p_{n_∞}.*

To prove Corollary 1, we extend the construction from the proof of Theorem 6 so that every pattern p_n from the proof of Theorem 6 is extended to infinitely cover the $\mathbb{Z}^2$ plane, becoming p_{n_∞}, by usage of "grid-reconstruction," i.e., a method of copying the square grid infinitely to each side. This requires $O(1)$ unique tile types in addition to those used in the previous construction. Due to the symmetry exhibited by all $m \times m$ squares of p_n patterns along their northeast $\rightarrow$ southwest diagonal, copies of the same pattern may be copied along these diagonals infinitely. Details of the construction can be found in [4].

References

1. Adleman, L., Cheng, Q., Goel, A., Huang, M.D.: Running time and program size for self-assembled squares. In: Proceedings of the 33rd Annual ACM Symposium on Theory of Computing, pp. 740–748. Hersonissos, Greece (2001)
2. Czeizler, E., Popa, A.: Synthesizing minimal tile sets for complex patterns in the framework of patterned DNA self-assembly. In: Stefanovic, D., Turberfield, A. (eds.) DNA Computing and Molecular Programming. LNCS, vol. 7433, pp. 58–72. Springer, Heidelberg (2012)

3. Doty, D., Fleming, H., Hader, D., Patitz, M.J., Vaughan, L.A.: Accelerating self-assembly of crisscross slat systems. In: 29th International Conference on DNA Computing and Molecular Programming (DNA 29). Leibniz International Proceedings in Informatics (LIPIcs), vol. 276, pp. 7:1–7:23. Schloss Dagstuhl – Leibniz-Zentrum für Informatik, Dagstuhl (2023)

4. Drake, P., Patitz, M.J., Summers, S.M., Tracy, T.: Self-assembly of patterns in the abstract tile assembly model. Tech. Rep. arXiv preprint arXiv:2402.16284 (2024)

5. Drake, P., Patitz, M.J., Tracy, T.: Pattern self-assembly software (2024). http://self-assembly.net/wiki/index.php/Pattern_Self-Assembly

6. Evans, C.G.: Crystals that count! Physical principles and experimental investigations of DNA tile self-assembly. Ph.D. thesis, California Institute of Technology (2014)

7. Hader, D., Koch, A., Patitz, M.J., Sharp, M.: The impacts of dimensionality, diffusion, and directedness on intrinsic universality in the abstract tile assembly model. In: Chawla, S. (ed.) Proceedings of the 2020 ACM-SIAM Symposium on Discrete Algorithms, SODA 2020, Salt Lake City, 5–8 January 2020, pp. 2607–2624. SIAM (2020)

8. Kari, L., Kopecki, S., Meunier, P., Patitz, M.J., Seki, S.: Binary pattern tile set synthesis is np-hard. Algorithmica **78**(1), 1–46 (2017)

9. Lathrop, J.I., Lutz, J.H., Patitz, M.J., Summers, S.M.: Computability and complexity in self-assembly. Theory Comput. Syst. **48**(3), 617–647 (2011)

10. Lathrop, J.I., Lutz, J.H., Summers, S.M.: Strict self-assembly of discrete Sierpinski triangles. Theoret. Comput. Sci. **410**, 384–405 (2009)

11. Lempiäinen, T., Czeizler, E., Orponen, P.: Synthesizing small and reliable tile sets for patterned DNA self-assembly. In: Proceedings of the 17th International Conference on DNA Computing and Molecular Programming (DNA 2011), pp. 145–159. Springer, Heidelberg (2011). http://dl.acm.org/citation.cfm?id=2042033.2042048

12. Ma, X., Lombardi, F.: Synthesis of tile sets for DNA self-assembly. IEEE Trans. CAD Integrat. Circuits Syst. **27**(5), 963–967 (2008)

13. Patitz, M.J., Summers, S.M.: Self-assembly of decidable sets. Nat. Comput. **10**(2), 853–877 (2011)

14. Rothemund, P.W.K.: Folding DNA to create nanoscale shapes and patterns. Nature **440**(7082), 297–302 (2006)

15. Rothemund, P.W.K., Papadakis, N., Winfree, E.: Algorithmic self-assembly of DNA Sierpinski triangles. PLoS Biol. **2**(12), e424 (2004)

16. Rothemund, P.W.K., Winfree, E.: The program-size complexity of self-assembled squares (extended abstract). In: Proceedings of the thirty-second annual ACM Symposium on Theory of Computing (STOC 2000), pp. 459–468. ACM, Portland (2000)

17. Soloveichik, D., Winfree, E.: Complexity of self-assembled shapes. SIAM J. Comput. **36**(6), 1544–1569 (2007)

18. Tikhomirov, G., Petersen, P., Qian, L.: Fractal assembly of micrometre-scale DNA origami arrays with arbitrary patterns. Nature **552**(7683), 67–71 (2017)

19. Winfree, E.: Algorithmic Self-Assembly of DNA. Ph.D. thesis, California Institute of Technology (1998)

20. Wintersinger, C.M., et al.: Multi-micron crisscross structures grown from DNA-origami slats. Nat. Nanotechnol. 1–9 (2022)

21. Woods, D., et al.: Diverse and robust molecular algorithms using reprogrammable DNA self-assembly. Nature **567**(7748), 366–372 (2019)

Rate-Independent Continuous Inhibitory Chemical Reaction Networks Are Turing-Universal

Kim Calabrese$^{(\boxtimes)}$ and David Doty$^{(\boxtimes)}$

University of California, Davis, USA
{ebcalabrese,doty}@ucdavis.edu

Abstract. We study the model of continuous chemical reaction networks (CRNs), consisting of reactions such as $A + B \rightarrow C + D$ that can transform some continuous, nonnegative real-valued quantity (called a *concentration*) of chemical species A and B into equal concentrations of C and D. Such a reaction can occur from any state in which both reactants A and B are present, i.e., have positive concentration. We modify the model to allow *inhibitors*, for instance, reaction $A + B \xrightarrow{I} C + D$ can occur only if the reactants A and B are present and the inhibitor I is absent.

The computational power of non-inhibitory CRNs has been studied. For instance, the reaction $X_1 + X_2 \rightarrow Y$ can be thought to compute the function $f(x_1, x_2) = \min(x_1, x_2)$. Under an "adversarial" model in which reaction rates can vary arbitrarily over time, it was found that exactly the continuous, piecewise linear functions can be computed, ruling out even simple functions such as $f(x) = x^2$. In contrast, in this paper we show that inhibitory CRNs can compute any computable function $f : \mathbb{N} \rightarrow \mathbb{N}$.

Keywords: Chemical Reaction Networks · Mass-Action · Analog Computation · Turing Universal

1 Introduction

The model of continuous chemical reaction networks (CRNs) consists of reactions such as $A + B \rightarrow C + D$ that can transform some continuous, nonnegative real-valued quantity (called a *concentration*) of chemical species A and B (the *reactants*) into equal concentrations of C and D (the *products*). This model has long held an important role in modeling naturally occurring chemical systems and predicting their evolution over time. Recently, the model has been investigated, not as a modeling language, but as a *programming* language for describing desired behavior of engineered chemicals. For example, the reaction $X_1 + X_2 \rightarrow Y$ can be thought to compute the function $f(x_1, x_2) = \min(x_1, x_2)$, in the sense that if we start in configuration $\{x_1 X_1, x_2 X_2\}$, i.e., concentration x_1 of species X_1 and concentration x_2 of species X_2, as long as the reaction keeps happening, it will eventually produce concentration $\min(x_1, x_2)$ of species Y.

D.-J. Cho and J. Kim (Eds.): UCNC 2024, LNCS 14776, pp. 104–118, 2024.
https://doi.org/10.1007/978-3-031-63742-1_8

The computational power depends greatly on how reaction rates are defined. The most common rate model is *mass-action*, which says that the rate of a reaction like $A + B \xrightarrow{k} C + D$, with positive *rate constant* $k > 0$, proceeds at rate $k \cdot [A] \cdot [B]$, where $[S]$ represents the concentration of species S. The rates of all reactions affecting a species S determines its derivative $\frac{d[S]}{dt}$ (adding rates of reactions where S is a product, and subtracting rates where it is a reactant), so the concentrations evolve according to a system of polynomial ODEs. It was recently shown that mass-action CRNs are capable of Turing universal computation [5], a very complex construction resulting from a long and deep line of research that culminated in showing the surprising computational power of polynomial ODEs [2].

What if reaction rates are not so predictable over time? One could imagine a solution does not remain well-mixed, so that some reactions go faster in a certain part of the volume where some species are more concentrated. It is also the case that it is difficult experimentally to engineer precise rate constants [8]. To address these issues, Chen, Doty, Reeves, and Soloveichik [3] defined a model of *adversarial* reaction rates and asked what functions can be computed when the rates can vary arbitrarily over time. They found that this model, called *stable computation*, is much more computationally limited than with mass-action rates: exactly the continuous, piecewise linear functions $f : \mathbb{R}^d \to \mathbb{R}$ can be stably computed.[1] An open question from [3] concerns a natural modification of the CRN model, inspired by similar models of gene regulatory networks, in which the presence of a species can *inhibit* a reaction from occurring. For example, the reaction $A + B \xrightarrow{I} C + D$ can occur only if its reactants are present ($[A], [B] > 0$) and its inhibitor is absent ($[I] = 0$). We call such a network an *inhibitory chemical reaction network* (iCRN).[2]

The negative results of [3], showing computation is limited to continuous piecewise linear functions, heavily use the fact that the reachability relation $\leadsto$ (defined in Sect. 2) on CRN configurations is *additive*: if $\mathbf{x} \leadsto \mathbf{y}$ for configurations $\mathbf{x}, \mathbf{y}$ (nonnegative vectors representing concentrations of each species), then for all nonnegative $\mathbf{c}$, we have $\mathbf{x} + \mathbf{c} \leadsto \mathbf{y} + \mathbf{c}$; in other words the presence of extra molecules (represented by $\mathbf{c}$) cannot *prevent* reactions from occurring. However,

---

[1] Technically this is using the so-called *dual-rail* encoding, which represents a single real value x as the difference of *two* species concentrations $[X^+] - [X^-]$. If one encodes inputs and output directly as nonnegative concentrations, then some discontinuities can occur, but only when some input x_i goes from 0 to positive.

[2] Note that our notation $A + B \xrightarrow{I} C + D$ puts inhibitors above the reaction arrow where a rate constant would normally be written, but since we consider rate-independent computation, we will have no rate constants. We also note that in gene regulatory networks, typically a species (called *transcription factor* in that literature) inhibits another *species*, which is assumed to be produced at some otherwise constant rate by a single reaction, whereas our model is more general in allowing inhibitors of arbitrary reactions (so I could inhibit production of C via one reaction $A \xrightarrow{I} C$ but not via another reaction $B \to C$.).

with inhibitors reachability is no longer additive (if c contains inhibitors that are absent in x), so it is natural to wonder if inhibitors increase the computational power of the model.

It is well-known "folklore" that in the *discrete* model of iCRNs, where the amount of a species is modeled as a nonnegative integer *count*, in which reactions discretely increment or decrement species counts, then inhibitors give the model Turing-universal power. It is worth seeing why this is true, to understand the novel contribution of this paper (and why it is not trivially solved in the continuous model by the discrete iCRN we describe next). It is well-known that register machines—finite-state machines equipped with a fixed number of nonnegative integer *registers*, each of which can be incremented, decremented, or tested for 0—are Turing universal [6]. An example register machine is:

```
1   dec r1,5
2   inc r2
3   inc r2
4   goto 1
5   halt
```

Line (a.k.a., *state*) 1 has the interpretation: decrement register r_1 and then go to line 2, unless r_1 is 0, in which case go to line 5. Increment instructions always increment the specified register and go to the next line. The `goto 1` statement on line 4 is syntactic sugar for `dec r3,1` for some register r_3 that is always 0. The above register machine, interpreted as taking an input x in register r_1 and halting with an output value in register r_2, computes the function $f(x) = 2x$.

For a register machine consisting of such increment and decrement instructions, the following is a straightforward transformation of the instruction for line/state i to iCRN reactions:

inc r_j	$L_i \to L_{i+1} + R_j$
dec r_j,k	$L_i + R_j \to L_{i+1}$
	$L_i \xrightarrow{\;\;R_j\perp\;\;} L_k$

It is clear that at any time exactly one reaction is applicable, and it simulates the next instruction of the register machine. In particular, when on a decrement instruction, the power of inhibition is used to ensure that if R_j has positive count, then only the first of the two decrement reactions is applicable (and as in the non-inhibitory CRN model, when R_j is absent, only the second decrement reaction is applicable). Note that a `halt` instruction on line i is not explicitly implemented as any reaction; the simple lack of any reaction with L_i as a reactant means that the CRN will terminate when the register machine does.

Our main construction in Sect. 3 follows this basic strategy of simulating register machines, using inhibition to detect when a register is 0. However, our main novel contribution is a way to "discretize" the behavior of the continuous CRN, so that the discrete steps of the register machine can be simulated faithfully. This is primarily done by introducing a *stable oscillator*, shown in Sect. 3.1.

2   Preliminaries

These definitions largely follow those of [3], the only exception being the definition of *applicable reaction*, which is modified to account for inhibitors.

For any set A, let $\mathcal{P}(A)$ denote the power set of A (set of all subsets of A). Let $\mathbb{N}$ denote the nonnegative integers and $\mathbb{R}$ denote the real numbers. Given a finite set F and a set S, let S^F denote the set of functions $\mathbf{c} : F \to S$. In the case of $S = \mathbb{R}$ (resp. $\mathbb{N}$), we view $\mathbf{c}$ equivalently as a real-valued (resp. integer-valued) vector indexed by elements of F. Given $x \in F$, we write $\mathbf{c}(x)$, to denote the real number indexed by x. The notation $\mathbb{R}^F_{\geq 0}$ is defined similarly for nonnegative real vectors. Throughout this paper, let Λ be a finite set of chemical *species*. Given $S \in \Lambda$ and $\mathbf{c} \in \mathbb{R}^\Lambda_{\geq 0}$, we refer to $\mathbf{c}(S)$ as the *concentration of S in* $\mathbf{c}$. When the configuration $\mathbf{c}$ is understood from context, we write $[S]$ to denote $\mathbf{c}(S)$. For any $\mathbf{c} \in \mathbb{R}^\Lambda_{\geq 0}$, let $[\mathbf{c}] = \{S \in \Lambda \mid \mathbf{c}(S) > 0\}$, the set of species *present* in $\mathbf{c}$ (a.k.a., the *support* of $\mathbf{c}$). We write $\mathbf{c} \leq \mathbf{c}'$ to denote that $\mathbf{c}(S) \leq \mathbf{c}'(S)$ for all $S \in \Lambda$. Given $\mathbf{c}, \mathbf{c}' \in \mathbb{R}^\Lambda_{\geq 0}$, we define the vector component-wise operations of addition $\mathbf{c} + \mathbf{c}'$, subtraction $\mathbf{c} - \mathbf{c}'$, and scalar multiplication $x\mathbf{c}$ for $x \in \mathbb{R}$.

A *reaction* over Λ is a triple $\alpha = (\mathbf{r}, \Delta, \mathbf{p}) \in \mathbb{N}^\Lambda \times \mathcal{P}(\Lambda) \times \mathbb{N}^\Lambda$, such that $\mathbf{r} \neq \mathbf{p}$, specifying the stoichiometry of the reactants, products, as well as the inhibitors of the reaction respectively.[3] We say a reaction α is *inhibited* by species I if $I \in \Delta$. For instance, given $\Lambda = \{A, B, C, I\}$, the reaction $A + 2B \xrightarrow{I} A + 3C$ is the triple $((1, 2, 0), \{I\}, (1, 0, 3))$.

An *inhibitory chemical reaction network (iCRN)* is a pair $\mathcal{C} = (\Lambda, R)$, where Λ is a finite set of chemical *species*, and R is a finite set of reactions over Λ. A *configuration* of a iCRN $\mathcal{C} = (\Lambda, R)$ is a vector $\mathbf{c} \in \mathbb{R}^\Lambda_{\geq 0}$. Given a configuration $\mathbf{c}$ and reaction $\alpha = (\mathbf{r}, \Delta, \mathbf{p})$, we say that α is *applicable* in $\mathbf{c}$ if $[\mathbf{r}] \subseteq [\mathbf{c}]$ (i.e., $\mathbf{c}$ contains positive concentration of all of the reactants) and $[\mathbf{c}] \cap \Delta = \emptyset$ (no inhibitor is present in $\mathbf{c}$). If no reaction is applicable in configuration $\mathbf{c}$, we say $\mathbf{c}$ is *static*.

Fix an iCRN $\mathcal{C} = (\Lambda, R)$. We define the $|\Lambda| \times |R|$ *stoichiometry matrix* $\mathbf{M}$ such that, for species $S \in \Lambda$ and reaction $\alpha = (\mathbf{r}, \Delta, \mathbf{p}) \in R$, $\mathbf{M}(S, \alpha) = \mathbf{p}(S) - \mathbf{r}(S)$ is the net amount of S produced by α (negative if S is consumed).[4] For example,

---

[3] It is customary to define, for each reaction, a *rate constant* $k \in \mathbb{R}_{>0}$ specifying a constant multiplier on the mass-action rate (i.e., the product of the reactant concentrations), but as we are studying CRNs whose output is independent of the reaction rates, we leave the rate constants out of the definition.

[4] $\mathbf{M}$ does not fully specify $\mathcal{C}$, since catalysts and inhibitors are not modeled: reactions $A + B \xrightarrow{C} A + D$ and $B \to D$ both correspond to the column vector $(0, -1, 0, 1)^\top$.

if we have the reactions $X \to Y$ and $X + A \to 2X + 3Y$, and if the three rows correspond to A, X, and Y, in that order, then

$$M = \begin{pmatrix} 0 & -1 \\ -1 & 1 \\ 1 & 3 \end{pmatrix}$$

Definition 2.1. *Configuration* d *is* straight-line reachable (aka 1-segment reachable) *from configuration* c, *written* $c \to^1 d$, *if* $(\exists u \in \mathbb{R}_{\geq 0}^R)$ $c + Mu = d$ *and* $u(\alpha) > 0$ *only if reaction* α *is applicable at* c. *In this case write* $c \to_u^1 d$.

Intuitively, by a single segment we mean running the reactions applicable at c at a constant (possibly 0) rate to get from c to d. In the definition, $u(\alpha)$ represents the flux of reaction $\alpha \in R$.

Definition 2.2. *Let* $k \in \mathbb{N}$. *Configuration* d *is* k-segment reachable *from configuration* c, *written* $c \rightsquigarrow^k d$, *if* $(\exists b_0, \ldots, b_k)$ $c = b_0 \to^1 b_1 \to^1 b_2 \to^1 \ldots \to^1 b_k$, *with* $b_k = d$.

Definition 2.3. *Configuration* d *is* segment-reachable *(or simply* reachable*) from configuration* c, *written* $c \rightsquigarrow d$, *if* $(\exists k \in \mathbb{N})$ $c \rightsquigarrow^k d$.

Often Definition 2.3 is used implicitly, when we make statements such as, "Run reaction 1 until X is gone, then run reaction 2 until Y is gone", which implicitly defines two straight lines in concentration space. Although we make no attempt to ascribe an "execution time" to any path followed by segments in Definition 2.3, it is sometimes useful to refer to such paths over time. In this case we suppose that each segment takes one unit of time, so that if $x \rightsquigarrow^k y$, we associate this to a *trajectory* $\rho : [0, k] \to \mathbb{R}_{\geq 0}^\Lambda$, where $\rho(t)$ represents the concentrations of species after t units of time have elapsed, i.e., following the first $\lfloor t \rfloor$ segments, then a fraction of the t'th segment if $t \notin \mathbb{N}$ (so that for integer t, $\rho(t)$ is the configuration b_t in Definition 2.2). In this case we write $x \rightsquigarrow_\rho y$.

Given configurations x, y, z such that $x \rightsquigarrow_{\rho_1} y$ and $y \rightsquigarrow_{\rho_2} z$, we denote the *concatenation* of trajectories ρ_1 and ρ_2 to be the trajectory $\rho_1 : \rho_2$ such that $x \rightsquigarrow_{\rho_1 : \rho_2} z$.

We now formalize what it means for an iCRN to "rate-independently" compute a function f. Since our main result is about simulating register machines that process natural numbers, we define stable computation for functions $f : \mathbb{N} \to \mathbb{N}$.[5] An *inhibitory chemical reaction computer (iCRC)* is a tuple $\mathcal{C} = (\Lambda, R, s, X, Y)$, where (Λ, R) is an iCRN, $s \in \mathbb{N}^\Lambda$ is the *initial context* (species other than the input that are initially present with some constant concentration; in our case, $s(A_1) = 1$ for a single species $A_1 \in \Lambda$ and 0 for all other

---

[5] Since iCRNs operate on real-valued concentrations, a very similar definition for functions $f : \mathbb{R}_{\geq 0} \to \mathbb{R}_{\geq 0}$ makes sense (and was formally defined for non-inhibitory CRNs in [3]); Sect. 4 discusses this issue further. We could also extend the definition to take multiple inputs for a function $f : \mathbb{N}^d \to \mathbb{N}$, but since register machines are Turing universal, we could encode multiple input integers via a pairing function into a single integer, so it is no loss of generality to consider single-input functions.

species), $X \in \Lambda$ is the *input species*, and $Y \in \Lambda$ is the *output species*. We say a configuration $\mathbf{o} \in \mathbb{R}_{\geq 0}^{\Lambda}$ is *stable* if, for all $\mathbf{o}'$ such that $\mathbf{o} \rightsquigarrow \mathbf{o}'$, $\mathbf{o}(Y) = \mathbf{o}'(Y)$, i.e., the concentration of Y cannot change once $\mathbf{o}$ has been reached. Let $f : \mathbb{N} \to \mathbb{N}$. We say $\mathcal{C}$ *stably computes* f if, for all $n \in \mathbb{N}$, starting from initial configuration $\mathbf{i} = \mathbf{s} + \{nX\}$ (i.e., starting with initial context, plus the desired input amount of X), for all configurations $\mathbf{c}$ such that $\mathbf{i} \rightsquigarrow \mathbf{c}$, there is $\mathbf{o}$ such that $\mathbf{c} \rightsquigarrow \mathbf{o}$, such that $\mathbf{o}$ is stable and $\mathbf{o}(Y) = f(n)$.

3 Main Results

Our goal is to design an iCRN that simulates the behavior of a register machine, similar to simulations by discrete CRNs [1,7]. The inclusion of inhibitors to our model allows us to enforce deterministic state transitions in chemical reaction networks, but to emulate the sequential power of discrete computation, we need a mechanism to manage control flow. First, we describe a simpler "stably oscillating" iCRN that is, in a sense, the main conceptual contribution of this paper.

3.1 Stable Oscillation

The following definition captures the behavior of a system of chemical reactions that execute sequentially, and eventually repeat their execution. A similar definition for the discrete model of population protocols appears in [4].[6] In particular, we have species $A_1, \ldots, A_k$ that all start at 0. A_1 monotonically goes up to 1, then monotonically down to 0, then A_2 goes up and down similarly, etc. After A_k does this, the whole thing repeats.

Definition 3.1. *Let* $\mathcal{A} = \{A_1, A_2, \ldots, A_k\}$ *be a set of species in an iCRN, and let* ρ *be a trajectory. We say* $\rho([t_1, t_2])$ *is a* wave *of* A_i *if for some* $t_1 < t < t_2$

- $\rho(t_1)(A_i) = \rho(t_2)(A_i) = 0$,
- $\rho(t)(A_i) = 1$,
- $\rho([t_1, t])(A_i)$ *is nondecreasing, and*
- $\rho([t, t_2])(A_i)$ *is nonincreasing.*

$\rho([T_1, T_2])$ *is a* period of oscillation *of* $\mathcal{A}$ *if there exists* $T_1 = t_1, t_2, \ldots, t_k = T_2$ *such that for all* $0 \leq i < k$,

- $\rho([t_i, t_{i+1}])$ *is a wave of* A_i, *and*
- *for all* $j \neq i$ *and all* $t_i \leq t \leq t_{i+1}$, $\rho(t)(A_j) = 0$.

Definition 3.2. *We say an iCRN* $\mathcal{C}$ stably oscillates *on* $\mathcal{A}$ *from configuration* $\mathbf{i}$ *if for all* $\mathbf{c}$ *such that* $\mathbf{i} \rightsquigarrow_{\rho_1} \mathbf{c}$, *we have* $\mathbf{c} \rightsquigarrow_{\rho_2} \mathbf{i}$ *such that letting* $\rho = \rho_1 : \rho_2$, $\rho([0, t])$ *is one or more periods of oscillation of* $\mathcal{A}$.

---

[6] However, Definition 3.2 is distinct from the that of [4], both by being defined in a continuous-state rather than a discrete-state model, and in that we do not require "self-stabilizing" behavior (which dictates that the behavior should occur from any possible initial state).

The next lemma demonstrates an iCRN that stably oscillates. We note that Lemma 3.3 is not used directly in the rest of the paper. Instead, the proof of Lemma 3.3 is intended to serve as a "warmup" to illustrate some of the key ideas used in the more complex iCRN defined in Sect. 3.2.

Lemma 3.3. *Let* $n \geq 3$ *and* $\mathcal{C}$ *be the iCRN with species* $\Lambda = \{X_0, X_1, \ldots, X_{n-1}\}$ *and for each* $0 \leq i < n$, *reaction* $X_i \xrightarrow{X_{i-1}} X_{i+1}$, *where* $i - 1$ *and* $i + 1$ *are both taken modulo* n. *If* $\mathbf{i} = \{1X_0\}$ *is the starting configuration, then* $\mathcal{C}$ *stably oscillates on* $\mathcal{O} = \{X_i \mid 0 \leq i \leq n, i \text{ is odd}\}$.

Proof. For each $0 \leq i < n$, let α_i be the reaction $X_i \xrightarrow{X_{i-1}} X_{i+1}$. First, observe that for any configuration $\mathbf{c}$ in which the species X_i and X_{i+1} are present, the only applicable reaction is α_i, since the reaction $X_{i+1} \xrightarrow{X_i} X_{i+2}$ is inhibited by X_i, and all other reactions have a reactant absent. Thus every sufficiently long path from $\mathbf{c}$ just executes α_i until X_i is absent. Once X_i is absent, α_{i+1} becomes applicable. At this point, we have only X_{i+1} present, so by similar reasoning, only α_{i+1} is applicable and every sufficiently long path runs only α_{i+1} until X_{i+1} is absent.

Iterating this reasoning over all i, for each $0 \leq i < n$, let $\mathbf{u}_i$ denote the flux vector with $\mathbf{u}_i(\alpha_i) = 1$ and $\mathbf{u}_i(\alpha_j) = 0$ for $j \neq i$ (i.e., execute only reaction α_i, for one unit of flux). Then starting from initial configuration $\mathbf{i} = \{1X_0\}$, we see that every path starting from $\mathbf{i}$ is of the form

$$\{1X_0\} \rightarrow^1_{\mathbf{u}_0} \{1X_1\} \rightarrow^1_{\mathbf{u}_1} \{1X_2\} \rightarrow^1_{\mathbf{u}_2} \cdots$$
$$\{1X_{n-1}\} \rightarrow^1_{\mathbf{u}_{n-1}} \{1X_0\} \rightarrow^1_{\mathbf{u}_0} \{1X_1\} \rightarrow^1_{\mathbf{u}_1} \cdots \{aX_i, (1-a)X_{i+1}\},$$

for some $0 \leq a \leq 1$, or, assuming the path does not get to configuration $\{1X_0\}$ above, $\{1X_0\} \rightarrow^1_{\mathbf{u}_0} \{1X_1\} \rightarrow^1_{\mathbf{u}_1} \{1X_2\} \rightarrow^1_{\mathbf{u}_2} \cdots \{aX_i, (1-a)X_{i+1}\}$.

In either case, by continuing to apply α_i with flux a, then unit fluxes of $\alpha_{i+1}, \alpha_{i+2}$, etc. until we reach configuration $\{1X_0\}$, this does some positive integer number of periods of oscillation. Let $\mathbf{i} = \{1X_0\}$, $\mathbf{c} = \{aX_i, (1-a)X_{i+1}\}$, this satisfies the definition of oscillation for the species in $\mathcal{O}$. □

3.2 Construction of iCRN Simulating a Register Machine

In this section we describe how to construct an iCRN $\mathcal{C}$ to simulate an arbitrary register machine $\mathcal{R}$.

Let the set of states (or lines) of $\mathcal{R}$ be $Q = \{1, 2, \ldots, m\}$, supposing it starts in state 1 with initial input register value $n \in \mathbb{N}$. Suppose $\mathcal{R}$'s input register is r_in and its output register is r_out. To simulate $\mathcal{R}$, $\mathcal{C}$ has input species R_{in} and output species R_{out}, and starts with configuration $\{1A_1, nR_{\text{in}}\}$ (i.e., with initial context $\mathbf{s} = \{1A_1\}$).

Consider these reactions, which implement the stable oscillator of Lemma 3.3 with 3 species (where $X_0 = A, X_1 = B, X_2 = C$).

$$A \xrightarrow{C} B$$

$$B \xrightarrow{A} C$$

$$C \xrightarrow{B} A$$

Although we do not use those exact reactions, it is helpful to see that iCRN as an introduction to how we implement the oscillator component of $\mathcal{C}$. $\mathcal{C}$ has m variants of each of those species $\{A_1, B_1, C_1, \ldots, A_m, B_m, C_m\}$, each subscript representing a state of $\mathcal{R}$. We will additionally have a species $R_1, R_2, \ldots$ to represent the various registers of $\mathcal{R}$ as well as designated input and output species $R_{\text{in}}, R_{\text{out}}$. For ease of exposition, we use the convention that $\mathcal{R}$ has exactly one input and output register, but this is easily extendable.

Intuitively, the variants of the last reaction $C \xrightarrow{B} A$ will perform all the logic of the register machine: incrementing, decrementing, and changing states. The other two (variants of) reactions $A \xrightarrow{C} B$ and $B \xrightarrow{A} C$ are simply to make the oscillator work while remembering the current state. However, since the stateful oscillator will change states in the last reaction, and the last reaction's reactant is an inhibitor for the first reaction, we need to be careful in selecting the correct inhibitors for the first reaction to acknowledge the states are different, and that *multiple* stateful variants of C could be inhibitors of a single variant of A.

Formally, for all $1 \le i \le m$, $\mathcal{C}$ has the reaction

$$B_i \xrightarrow{A_i} C_i.$$

For all $1 \le i \le m$, let $\{j_1, j_2, \ldots, j_l\}$ be the set of states that are potential predecessors of state i. This includes $j = i - 1$ if $i > 1$ and state j is not a goto, as well as all j such that a decrement test for 0 can cause a jump from j to i. For all $1 \le i \le m$, $\mathcal{C}$ also has the reaction

$$A_i \xrightarrow[\bot]{C_{j_1}, C_{j_2}, \ldots, C_{j_l}} B_i.$$

Finally, for all $1 \le i \le m$, $\mathcal{C}$ has the following reactions to simulate register machine instructions.

– if state i is inc r_j (increment register j and move from state i to $i + 1$):

$$C_i \xrightarrow{B_i} A_{i+1} + R_j$$

Note the dual role of C_i: it helps the "clock" to oscillate, but its maximum concentration also defines one "unit" of concentration to help us use real-valued concentrations to represent discrete integer counts in registers of $\mathcal{R}$. In other words, the initial amount of A_1 (which sets the maximum concentration achieved by any C_i) is also the amount by which $[R_j]$ increases (and the amount it decreases in a decrement instruction).

- if state i is dec r_j,k (decrement register j and move from state i to $i+1$, unless it is 0, in which case go to state k):

$$C_i + R_j \xrightarrow{\;\;B_i\;\;} A_{i+1}$$

$$C_i \xrightarrow{\;\;B_i, R_j\;\;} A_k$$

As in the case for the discrete iCRN described in Sect. 1, no reactions are associated to C_i if state i is a halt instruction.

3.3   Proof of Correctness

In this section, we prove that the iCRN $\mathcal{C}$ described in Sect. 3.2 correctly simulates the register machine $\mathcal{R}$.

In the definition of $\leadsto$, it is technically allowed for two consecutive segments to "point the same direction", i.e., $\mathbf{x} \rightarrow^1_{\mathbf{u}_1} \mathbf{y} \rightarrow^1_{\mathbf{u}_2} \mathbf{z}$ such that $\mathbf{u}_1$ and $\mathbf{u}_2$ are multiples of each other. The next observation says that we can assume without loss of generality this does not happen, since any two such consecutive segments $\mathbf{u}_1$ and $\mathbf{u}_2$ can always be concatenated into a single segment $\mathbf{u}_1 + \mathbf{u}_2$.

Observation 3.4. *In any iCRN, if $\mathbf{x} \leadsto \mathbf{y}$, we may assume without loss of generality that each pair of consecutive segments are not multiples of each other. In particular, if exactly one reaction is applicable at any time, then any two consecutive segments use different reactions.*

We also note that there is a distinction between the function of species that "oscillate" (i.e. species $A_1, B_1, C_1, \ldots, A_n, B_n, C_n$) and species that represent the value stored in a register ($R_1, R_2 \ldots$). We call the former *oscillator species* and the latter *register species*. Since the control flow of our construction is driven primarily by the so-called oscillator species, it suffices to focus on their behavior when discussing the properties of the iCRN induced by our construction.

We develop machinery to talk about specific configurations of $\mathcal{C}$ that contain oscillator species at concentration 1.

Definition 3.5. *Let $A \in \Lambda$ be an oscillator species. We say configuration $\mathbf{x} \in \mathbb{R}^\Lambda_{\geq 0}$ is a transition point of A if $\mathbf{x}(A) = 1$ and $\mathbf{x}(B) = 0$ for all other oscillator species B.*

Intuitively, a transition point marks the peak of a species' oscillation, representing a configuration where a previously present oscillator species depletes, allowing a new reaction to become applicable. Definition 3.5 implicitly characterizes the configurations in $\mathcal{C}$: a configuration is either a transition point or lies "between" two transition points. Furthermore, if a configuration is not a transition point, then the applicable reaction is exactly that applicable in the last reached transition point.

For example, the 3-species oscillator described at the start of Sect. 3.2 has A, B, and C as oscillator species. Consider the transition point $\{1A\}$. In this configuration, the only applicable reaction is the reaction $\alpha = A \xrightarrow{C} B$, since A is the only species present. Running α with flux $\frac{1}{2}$, we reach the configuration $\{\frac{1}{2}A, \frac{1}{2}B\}$. Notice that even though we have some amount of B present in this reaction, α is *still* the only applicable reaction, since A inhibits the reaction $\beta = B \xrightarrow{A} C$. β only becomes applicable once we reach the configuration $\{1B\}$, but this is a transition point. This behavior can be generalized as follows:

Observation 3.6. *Let* $\mathbf{x}$, $\mathbf{y}$ *be configurations of the iCRN* $\mathcal{C}$ *described in Sect. 3.2. If* $\mathbf{x}$ *is a transition point of* A, $\mathbf{y}$ *is not a transition point, and* $\mathbf{x} \to^1 \mathbf{y}$, *then the reactions applicable in* $\mathbf{y}$ *are exactly the reactions applicable in* $\mathbf{x}$.

This observation indicates that the applicable reactions of $\mathcal{C}$ changes only upon reaching a new transition point. Therefore, instead of reasoning about arbitrary configurations in concentration space, we can just consider the reachability of transition points. Additionally, observation 3.4 implies that we can assume transition points are reached in a single flux 1 line segment, enabling discrete arguments about the behavior of our construction.

Theorem 1. *Suppose that* $\mathcal{R}$ *computes a function* $f : \mathbb{N} \to \mathbb{N}$ *in the sense that, starting with input register having value* n, *it halts with output register having value* $f(n)$. *Then the iCRN* $\mathcal{C}$ *described above stably computes* f *from the initial configuration* $\mathbf{i} = \{1A_1, nR_{\text{in}}\}$.

Proof. A complete example of this construction is given in Sect. 3.4.

Let R_{in} be the input species and R_{out} be the output species. For $\mathcal{C}$ to stably compute f, we need that for any valid initial configuration $\mathbf{i} = \{1A_1, nR_{\text{in}}\}$, and any configuration $\mathbf{c}$ such that $\mathbf{i} \rightsquigarrow \mathbf{c}$, there exists a configuration $\mathbf{o}$ such that $\mathbf{c} \rightsquigarrow \mathbf{o}$, $\mathbf{o}(R_{\text{out}}) = f(n)$ and for all $\mathbf{o}'$ such that $\mathbf{o} \rightsquigarrow \mathbf{o}'$, $\mathbf{o}'(R_{\text{out}}) = \mathbf{o}(R_{\text{out}})$.

It suffices to show that for any integer initial concentration of R_{in}, there exists exactly one trajectory, ending in a static configuration $\mathbf{h}$ such that $\mathbf{h}(R_{\text{out}}) = f(n)$.

We first prove that the following invariants hold at every reachable transition point $\mathbf{x}$.

(a) For every register species R_j, $\mathbf{x}(R_j) \in \mathbb{N}$.
(b) Exactly one reaction is applicable in $\mathbf{x}$ (unless $\mathbf{x}(A_i) = 1$ for a halting state i, in which case no reactions are applicable).

We proceed by induction on the number of flux one-line segments connecting transition points $\mathbf{i}$ and $\mathbf{c}$. (By Observation 3.4 we may assume each segment is not a multiple of the previous.)

For the base case, we show these invariants hold at **i**. Invariant (b) is established for all transition points below, including **i**. By construction, the only register species present in **i** is R_{in}, with concentration $n \in \mathbb{N}$, so invariant (a) is satisfied.

Now, we show the inductive case that if the invariants hold at a transition point **x**, then we can execute the one applicable reaction (guaranteed to exist by invariant (b) unless we have halted) with flux 1, and that this will reach the next transition point **y**, such that the invariants still hold.

First, we claim that at any transition point, **x** with oscillator species O_i having $\mathbf{x}(O_i) = 1$, at most one reaction is possible, exactly 1 if i is a non-halting state, and 0 if i is a halting state and $O_i = A_i$. If O_i is B_i or C_i, this is evident by the fact that each of those is a reactant in exactly one reaction in the network, and at transition points all other oscillator species are absent. In the case $O_i = A_i$, this is again evident if i represents an increment instruction, since the $C_i \xrightarrow{B_i} A_{i+1} + R_j$ reaction is the only one with C_i as a reactant. If i is a decrement, then C_i is a reactant in two reactions $C_i + R_j \xrightarrow{B_i} A_{i+1}$ and $C_i \xrightarrow{B_i, R_j} A_k$, but one has R_j as a reactant, and the other has R_j as an inhibitor, so exactly one of those two reactions is applicable. This establishes that invariant (b) holds at the next transition point reached, when the applicable reaction is executed for one unit of flux. By Observation 3.4 we assume a single segment applies this reaction until it is inapplicable, reaching the next transition point.

It remains to argue that invariant (a) also holds at the next transition point. Let $O_i \in \{A_1, B_1, C_1, \ldots, A_m, B_m, C_m\}$ be an oscillator species and let $\mathbf{x} = \{1O_i, m_1 R_1, m_2 R_2 \ldots m_n R_n\}$, be a transition point that is reached from **i**. Assume the induction hypothesis that invariants (a) and (b) hold at **x**. Then each $m_i \in \mathbb{N}$ by invariant (a). By (b) **x** has exactly one applicable reaction. If **x** is a transition point of C_i, and state i of the register machine $\mathcal{R}$ is `inc r_j`, then the applicable reaction in **x** is $\alpha = C_i \xrightarrow{B_i} A_{i+1} + R_j$. By construction, there is no other reaction with C_i as a reactant, and the reaction $A_{i+1} \xrightarrow[C_{j_1}, \ldots, C_i, \ldots C_{j_l}]{\perp} B_{i+1}$ (where each C_{j_x} is a potential predecessor state of $i+1$) is inhibited by C_i, so every sufficiently long path from **x** just executes α until we reach the transition point $\mathbf{y} = \{1A_{i+1}, m_1 R_1, \ldots, (m_j + 1)R_j, \ldots, m_n R_n\}$. So (a) holds.

If line i of $\mathcal{R}$ is instead `dec r_j,k` then there are reactions

$$\beta_1 = C_i + R_j \xrightarrow{B_i} A_{i+1}$$

$$\beta_2 = C_i \xrightarrow{B_i, R_j} A_k$$

When R_j is present in **x**, the only applicable reaction is β_1. By a similar argument to the previous case, the reaction $A_{i+1} \xrightarrow{C_i} B_{i+1}$ is inhibited, so every sufficiently long path from **i** executes β_1 until we reach $\{1B_{i+1}, m_1 R_1, \ldots,$

$(m_j - 1)R_j, \ldots, m_n R_n\}$. If R_j is not present then the only applicable reaction is now β_2. Then every sufficiently long path from $\mathbf{i}$ reaches the transition point $\{1B_k, m_1 R_1, \ldots m_n R_n\}$. In either case, invariant (a) holds. This establishes the claim that invariants (a) and (b) hold at each reachable transition point.

We now show that the sequence of states for oscillator species aligns with the execution order of lines in $\mathcal{R}$ and results in a correct simulation of $\mathcal{R}$. By construction of $\mathcal{C}$, for each line i of $\mathcal{R}$ of the form $\mathtt{inc\ r\_j}$, $\mathcal{C}$ has corresponding reaction $C_i \xrightarrow{B_i \ \perp} A_{i+1} + R_j$. By invariant (b), this reaction will be applicable when transition point $\mathbf{c}$ has a C_i species present, so the next transition point will contain species A_{i+1}. Thus when $\mathcal{R}$ goes from line i to $i+1$, the present oscillator species in $\mathcal{C}$ simulates this transition in the sense that the subscript i is updated to $i+1$, and the concentration of R_j increases by 1. Similarly, for each line i of $\mathcal{R}$ of the form $\mathtt{dec\ r\_j,k}$, there are reactions $C_i + R_j \xrightarrow{B_i \ \perp} A_{i+1}$ and $C_i \xrightarrow{B_i, R_j \ \perp} A_k$. When R_j is present, species A_{i+1} is 1, and R_j decreases by 1 at the next transition point, and when R_j is not present, A_k is 1. Thus decrement reactions are also properly simulated by $\mathcal{C}$.

Since $\mathcal{R}$ halts with its output register having value $f(n)$, and $\mathcal{C}$ simulates $\mathcal{R}$, by (b) any sufficiently long sequence of reactions will eventually reach some static configuration $\mathbf{h}$ representing $\mathcal{R}$'s halting configuration. Furthermore, by (a) the values of the register species at the halting point are equal to the values of the registers in $\mathcal{R}$ when it halts. Thus the configuration contains the correct concentration of R_{out}. Since this is a static (thus stable) configuration, this shows that $\mathcal{C}$ stably computes f. $\square$

3.4   Example of Construction of iCRN from Register Machine

We demonstrate an example of our construction by translating a register machine $\mathcal{R}$ that computes the function $f(n) = 2n$ to an iCRN $\mathcal{C}$. The machine $\mathcal{R}$ that computes f requires only input and output registers $r_{\text{in}}, r_{\text{out}}$.

Figure 1 shows a plot of this iCRN's trajectory, under the mass-action rate model for reactants, and where each inhibitor I contributes a term $1/(1 + 10^5 \cdot [I])$ to the rate of the reaction, as an approximation of "absolute" inhibition.[7]

---

[7] The long wave seen in the middle is because the reaction $C_1 + R_{\text{in}} \xrightarrow{B_1 \ \perp} A_2$, when R_{in} starts at 1, has a much slower rate of convergence (linear, compared to exponential convergence when R_{in} starts 2 or higher). Consequently, C_1 from time ≈ 300 to time ≈ 800, despite being "close" to 0, is decaying to 0 much more slowly than in previous oscillations. Thus C_1 much more strongly inhibits the reaction $A_2 \xrightarrow{C_1 \ \perp} B_2$ than in previous oscillations. A_2 and B_2 are the two species "swapping" very slowly between time 300 and 900.

Instructions	Reactions
1: dec r_in,5	$A_1 \xrightarrow{C_4} B_1$ $B_1 \xrightarrow{A_1} C_1$ $C_1 + R_{in} \xrightarrow{B_1} A_2$ $C_1 \xrightarrow{B_1, R_{in}} A_5$
2: inc r_out	$A_2 \xrightarrow{C_1} B_2$ $B_2 \xrightarrow{A_2} C_2$ $C_2 \xrightarrow{B_2} A_3 + R_{out}$
3: inc r_out	$A_3 \xrightarrow{C_2} B_3$ $B_3 \xrightarrow{A_3} C_3$ $C_3 \xrightarrow{B_3} A_4 + R_{out}$
4: goto 1	$A_4 \xrightarrow{C_3} B_4$ $B_4 \xrightarrow{A_4} C_4$ $C_4 \xrightarrow{B_4} A_1$
5: halt	no reactions

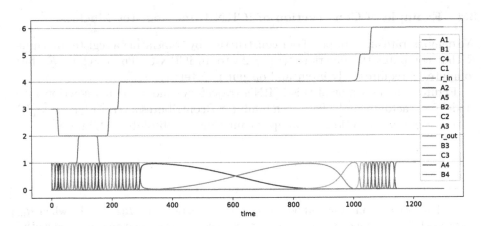

Fig. 1. Plot of iCRN simulating "multiply-by-2" register machine, with input register r_in having initial value 3. Note the species r_in decrements from 3 down to 0, and the species r_out increments from 0 up to 6, while other species oscillate.

4   Conclusion

There are some interesting questions for future research.

Relaxing Absolute Inhibition. The most glaring shortcoming of the inhibitory CRN model is the notion of "absolute" inhibition: any positive concentration of an inhibitor completely disables the reaction. This is clearly unrealistic when taken to extremes: with an enormous amount of reactant R, a tiny amount of I cannot be expected to stop all R from reacting via $R \xrightarrow{I} \dots$. A more realistic model might say that the rate of a reaction is an increasing function of the concentration of its reactants and a decreasing function of the concentration of its inhibitors, for example using a Hill function such as $\frac{[R]}{1+[I]}$ for the rate of the reaction. However, any way of doing this seems to talk about rates, and it is not clear how to meaningfully ask what tasks can be done in a rate-independent way in such a model. One possible way to study this question meaningfully is similar to an approach suggested in the Conclusions of [3] (for studying rate-independence in mass-action CRNs): define a mass-action-like rate law in which a reaction's rate is a decreasing function of its inhibitors' concentrations, and allow the adversary to set constant parameters in the rate law, but not to change the rate law itself.

Characterizing Real-Valued Functions. We have demonstrated that the iCRN model is Turing universal in the sense that it can compute any computable function $f : \mathbb{N} \to \mathbb{N}$. However, the natural data type for continuous iCRNs to process is real numbers. It remains to characterize what functions $f : \mathbb{R}_{\geq 0} \to \mathbb{R}_{\geq 0}$ (or $f : \mathbb{R}_{\geq 0}^d \to \mathbb{R}_{\geq 0}$) can be stably computed by continuous iCRNs. Using a *dual-rail encoding* to encode a value x as the difference of two concentrations $[X^+] - [X^-]$, one can also meaningfully investigate computation of functions $f : \mathbb{R}^d \to \mathbb{R}$ with negative inputs and outputs, similar to the characterization of continuous piecewise linear functions stably computable by continuous (non-inhibitory) CRNs using dual-rail encoding [3].

Acknowledgements. DD and KC were supported by NSF awards 2211793, 1900931, 1844976, and DoE EXPRESS award SC0024467.

References

1. Angluin, D., Aspnes, J., Eisenstat, D.: Fast computation by population protocols with a leader. Distrib. Comput. **21**(3), 183–199 (2008). Preliminary version appeared in DISC 2006
2. Bournez, O., Graça, D.S., Pouly, A.: Polynomial time corresponds to solutions of polynomial ordinary differential equations of polynomial length. J. ACM **64**(6) (2017). https://doi.org/10.1145/3127496
3. Chen, H.L., Doty, D., Reeves, W., Soloveichik, D.: Rate-independent computation in continuous chemical reaction networks. J. ACM **70**(3) (2023). https://doi.org/10.1145/3590776

4. Cooper, C., Lamani, A., Viglietta, G., Yamashita, M., Yamauchi, Y.: Constructing self-stabilizing oscillators in population protocols. Inf. Comput. **255**, 336–351 (2017)
5. Fages, F., Le Guludec, G., Bournez, O., Pouly, A.: Strong turing completeness of continuous chemical reaction networks and compilation of mixed analog-digital programs. In: International Conference on Computational Methods in Systems Biology, pp. 108–127. Springer (2017)
6. Minsky, M.L.: Computation. Prentice-Hall Englewood Cliffs (1967)
7. Soloveichik, D., Cook, M., Winfree, E., Bruck, J.: Computation with finite stochastic chemical reaction networks. Nat. Comput. **7**(4), 615–633 (2008). http://dx.doi.org/10.1007/s11047-008-9067-y
8. Srinivas, N., Parkin, J., Seelig, G., Winfree, E., Soloveichik, D.: Enzyme-free nucleic acid dynamical systems. Science **358**(6369) (2017)

Entropy Transformation Measures
for Computational Capacity

David Griffin$^{(\boxtimes)}$ⓘ and Susan Stepneyⓘ

University of York, York, UK
{david.griffin,susan.stepney}@york.ac.uk

Abstract. Kernel Rank and Generalization Rank are common measures used to characterise reservoir computing systems. However, there are some common issues in literature that make comparisons of these measures difficult, as well as both measures ideally requiring access to the reservoir state. Further, Generalization Rank has an inherent level of arbitrariness in its definition, as well as requiring a separate experiment to compute. This paper introduces the Relative Utilization and Comparative Generalization Measures, as part of the family of Entropy Transformation Measures, which address these issues while capturing similar information.

Keywords: Reservoir Computing · Novelty Search

1 Introduction

Dynamical systems can be exploited in reservoir computing by harnessing the inherent transformations they perform [6]. However, while a dynamical system performs a transformation, it is not known what this transformation may be used to compute. In order to characterise the nature of these computational properties, measures have been proposed which attempt to give insight into aspects of the transformation. Kernel Rank (KR) and Generalisation Rank (GR) [2,3], and Linear Memory Capacity (LMC) [5] are some of the most commonly used measures to characterise reservoir computers.

Due to several parameters that are not specified in the definitions of KR and especially GR, it is difficult to compare the results of different implementations of these measures. Indeed, some implementations [14] measure very different properties under the same name.

A useful property of KR and LMC is that they can be captured in the same experiment [8], which substantially reduces the time required to characterise a system; GR requires a different sequence of inputs [3].

KR and GR have some commonalities in their definition. Here we generalise these to define a new class of measures, the Linear Random Rank (LRR) measures, to which most implementations of KR and GR belong. We examine this class of measures, and show that GR in particular occupies a somewhat arbitrary place within the class. We then introduce a new family of measures, which we call Entropy Transformation, that are defined over arbitrary inputs. Two

D.-J. Cho and J. Kim (Eds.): UCNC 2024, LNCS 14776, pp. 119–133, 2024.
https://doi.org/10.1007/978-3-031-63742-1_9

Algorithm 1. Pseudocode for Kernel Rank (KR) (Dale et al. [3], Vidamour et al. [14])

```
1: S := number of input streams ≥ N
2: T := length of each input stream (timepoints)
3: run reservoir with washout stream
4: for i ∈ 1..S do
5:     u_i(t), t ∈ 1..T := U[-1, 1]
6:     run reservoir with input stream u_i
7:     x_i(T) := reservoir state at final time T
8: end for
9: X := (x_1(T) x_2(T) ... x_S(T))
10: γ := 0.01 for Dale et al. [3], 0.1 for Vidamour et al. [14]
11: return rank(X, threshold=γ)
```

entropy transformation measures are defined; the first, Range Utilisation Measure, captures a specific aspect of KR: namely, whether the transformation of the dynamical system affects the spread of outputs relative the spread of inputs. The second, Comparative Generalisation Measure, provides a more general form of GR which characterises if similar inputs give similar outputs from a dynamical system. Implementations of both of these measures are available as part of the PyCHARC framework [4].

2   Background

Kernel Rank (KR) and Generalisation Rank (GR) were first proposed by Büsing et al. [2]. These measures are intended as lightweight, general purpose measures of the computational properties of a dynamical system. KR is intended as a measure of the complexity of the transformation the system performs on its inputs; GR is a measure of how well a system can filter similar inputs to the same output. It has been argued [3] that, when combined with Linear Memory Capacity (LMC), KR and GR can be used to create a characterisation of a system.

Dale et al. [3] provide an implementation of KR and GR in the CHARC framework (summarised in Algorithms 1 and 2), which is intended to be applied to arbitrary systems. These implementations supply an input signal to the system under analysis, and then compute the rank of the matrix whose rows are a representation of the system over time. For example, for an Echo State Network [6], the representation of the system is typically taken to be the internal state of the network. For a physical system, the representation may be captured from the output. KR is captured by supplying an input signal which follows a uniform random distribution in the range -1 to 1 (here denoted $U(-1, 1)$), and GR is captured with an input in a smaller range, $U(-0.1, 0.1)$. The different ranges allow for different information to be captured: a large range allows KR to characterise the effects of different inputs within that range, and the smaller range allows GR to characterise the effects of similar inputs.

Algorithm 2. Pseudocode for Generalisation Rank (GR) (Dale et al. [3])

1: $S :=$ length of input stream $\geq N$
2: $r :=$ range of input, 1 for KR, 0.1 for GR
3: run reservoir with washout stream
4: **for** $t \in 1..S$ **do**
5:     step reservoir with input $u(t) \in U[-r, r]$
6:     $\mathbf{x}(t) :=$ reservoir state at time t
7: **end for**
8: $\mathbf{X} := (\mathbf{x}(1)\,\mathbf{x}(2)\,\ldots\,\mathbf{x}(S))$
9: **return** rank($\mathbf{X}$, threshold=0.01)

Algorithm 3. Pseudocode for Generalisation Rank (GR) (Vidamour et al. [14])

1: $S :=$ number of input streams $\geq N$
2: $T :=$ length of each input stream (timepoints)
3: $\tau :=$ length of common input stream
4: $tail(t), t \in 1..\tau := U[-1, 1]$
5: run reservoir with washout stream
6: **for** $i \in 1..S$ **do**
7:     $u_i(t), t \in 1..(T - \tau) := U[-1, 1]$
8:     $u_i := u_i + tail$ ▷ append the tail
9:     run reservoir with input stream u_i
10:     $\mathbf{x}_i(T) :=$ reservoir state at final time T
11: **end for**
12: $\mathbf{X} := (\mathbf{x}_1(T)\,\mathbf{x}_2(T)\,\ldots\,\mathbf{x}_S(T))$
13: **return** rank($\mathbf{X}$)

A fully general purpose implementation turns out to be problematic. Büsing et al. [2] state that the definition of what constitutes 'similar' inputs for a system depends on the nature of the system itself, which implies that the specific range used in Dale et al's implementation of GR [3] may not be appropriate in all cases. While this does not mean that Dale's implementation is a poor measure of reservoir functionality, it does mean that the definition of similarity used is somewhat arbitrary. Further, some systems may have non-trivial input or readout. For example, spiking neural networks [9] provide an output represented by a series of spikes of varying magnitude and frequency. While it is possible to map these outputs to numeric values, this mapping may hide useful information about the dynamics of the system.

The description of GR given by Büsing et al. [2] is open to interpretation. There are alternatives to Dale et al.'s [3] interpretation in the literature. For example, Vidamour et al. [14] use a version of GR which transposes the magnitude of variability with the temporal sequence of inputs, measuring the response of the system transition from a random to a known sequence (summarised in Algorithms 1 and 3). While this may seem like a large deviation from the intuition of GR, it is a possible implementation of the description in [2], using a different but valid interpretation of certain terms.

A further issue with the GR and KR measures is the calculation of the matrix rank. Matrix rank is the number of linearly independent rows of a matrix, and gives a measure of the dimensionality of the subspace actually accessed. The rank can be calculated by performing a singular value decomposition (SVD) [13], which provides a matrix with the singular values on the leading diagonal, and zeroes elsewhere. The rank is the number of non-zero singular values.

When dealing with real numbers extracted from a system with random inputs the probability of any two rows being truly linearly dependent is zero, and so the matrix rank will be the maximum value possible. Some singular values may be very small, however, indicating a small contribution to the space being accessed. The approach mostly used in the literature is to use a cutoff threshold to determine which singular values are sufficiently close to zero to be ignored as a contribution to the rank. Choice of threshold affects the maximum possible rank value. Comparing the GR implementations of Dale et al. (Algorithm 2) and Vidamour et al. (Algorithm 3) also illustrates that the choice of threshold values varies substantially. We are unaware of a single publication reporting KR and GR that states the value of the threshold used (including our own [1,14]!). Even quoting a threshold does not fully remove possibilities for different implementations: the threshold can be applied in multiple ways. The simplest is to ignore all singular values less than the threshold. Dale et al. [3] use an alternative dynamic approach that ignores all singular values less than $(1 - t)s_i$, where s_i is the last accepted singular value.

The issue of an arbitrary threshold can be addressed by using the Effective Rank of the matrix ([10], as cited in [8]). Take all the singular values (which are all non-negative), normalise their sum to one, interpret these normalised values as probabilities, and calculate the exponential of the associated Shannon Entropy [11]. If all N singular values are the same, this results in a rank of N, as expected, otherwise it results in a rank $< N$. This way, effective rank provides a version of matrix rank that does not rely on an arbitrarily set threshold, and naturally accounts for different sized singular values. Use of effective rank is not common in the reservoir computing literature, however.

Given all these factors, it is not possible to directly compare KR and GR ranges across publications, as the parameters and methods used to calculate them are not standardised. For KR, a mitigation exists: as the rank of KR is calculated at the final step, if access to experimental data is available the rank can be recalculated with a different threshold. However, this mitigation does not apply to GR, where the degree of similarity is specified as part of the experiment, and multiple definitions of GR exist in the literature [3,14]. Therefore, while access to data enables comparison of KR without requiring additional experiments, the same is not true for GR.

3   Linear Random Rank (LRR)

As defined by Dale et al. [3], KR and GR differ only in the range over which the input sequence is drawn: $U(-1, 1)$ and $U(-0.1, 0.1)$ respectively. Here we

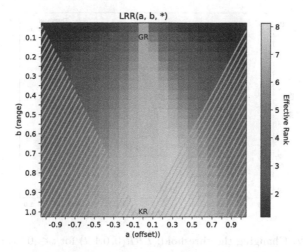

Fig. 1. $LRR(a, b, *)$ of 50-node ESNs. The hatched region represents parameters that fall outside the normalised $[-1, 1]$ input range. The locations of the GR and KR measures are shown.

define a family of measures that encompasses KR and GR, parameterised by that range and the rank threshold. We call this family the Linear Random Rank, $LRR(a, b, t)$, which denotes the rank from the matrix representing the system state when subjected to an input sequence drawn from $U[a - b, a + b]$ with matrix rank threshold t (singular values $< t$ do not contribute to the matrix rank); $LRR(a, b, *)$ denotes use of the effective rank. For example, the measures from Dale et al. [3] are $KR = LRR(0, 1, 0.01)$ and $GR = LRR(0, 0.1, 0.01)$, although as noted earlier, Dale et al. use an alternative interpretation of the threshold value.

Using this definition of LRR, we explore the landscape of LRR measures by varying the parameters, and determine where KR and GR lie within this landscape. Each experiment is carried out by taking the mean LRR measure of 500 randomly connected 50 node non-leaky echo state networks. Parameters are picked to be non-trivial, but reasonable defaults (Table 1).

Table 1. Parameters used for the LRR evaluation of ESNs

Parameter	Value
number of nodes	50
activation function	tanh
weight generation	uniform random
spectral radius	0.8

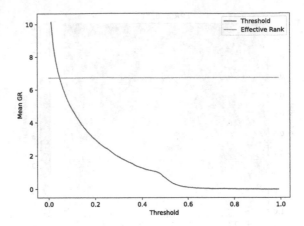

Fig. 2. Changing the threshold: $LRR(0, 0.1, t)$ for $t \in [0.01, 1.0]$

Figure 1 shows the effects of sweeping through the parameters of the LRR family of measures, using the effective rank, with the points corresponding to GR and KR marked. It can be seen that varying the offset from the 0 position results in reducing the rank, in some cases substantially.

The effect of reducing range of inputs (parameter b) is also to reduce the calculated rank. For KR, the position is useful: KR occupies the maximum possible range, $b = 1$, and has the maximum rank. However, GR encounters an issue here: there is no way to define a minimum. $LRR(0, 0, *)$, by the Echo State Property, would cause the state of the ESN to drop to **0**, and therefore the calculated rank would also drop to 0.

To an extent, the issue with GR is expected: GR is intended to measure the ability of an ESN to generalize similar inputs to similar outputs. However, 'similarity' does not have a strict definition, and how similar inputs should be to generate a similar output is task dependant. For example, if classifying an input into one of five different categories, $LRR(0, 0.2, *)$, looking at a fifth of the input range, may be more useful than the more usual $LRR(0, 0.1, *)$.

Further, GR examines only a small proportion of the input range, and as shown in Fig. 1, varying the input offset parameter causes a rapid change in the calculated rank. This means that the method for calculating the effect of similar inputs is not useful for examining similar inputs not centered around 0.

Figure 2 shows the effect of changing the threshold for GR-like parameters. The results are as expected: increasing the threshold decreases the measured rank, as more singular values are discarded. As changing the threshold can alter the value of the rank, it is difficult to compare results from multiple authors if the threshold is not specified.

While GR provides potentially useful information about the generalization behaviour of a reservoir, it has some limitations. Similarity is task dependant, it only characterises similar behaviours around 0, and using a threshold parameter can change the reported result. Combined with the necessity of conducting extra experiments to capture GR, it is worthwhile to investigate other measures that can capture how well a dynamical system can filter information.

4 Entropy Transformation Measures

The two main characteristics for a suitable measure are: (i) it should be fully-specified, as in the measure is unambiguous; (ii) it should be able to be captured at the same time as KR and LMC (to minimise the number of experiments needed to provide the data for the measures). Our approach is to measure how the dynamical system modifies its input. This is analogous to how memory capacity benchmarks work: in the case of a memory capacity benchmark, the goal is to recall as much of the prior input signal as possible; here, our goal is to capture information on the types of transformation available to the system.

While not explicitly used, entropy calculations can be used in KR and GR by the use of the effective rank. The effective rank can be characterised as calculating the Shannon Entropy of a distribution of events whose probabilities are determined by the relative magnitude of the singular values. This establishes that entropy is a useful measure, although in the case of KR and GR the input is specified, meaning this approach cannot be used to reduce the number of experiments.

Shannon Entropy can be calculated for any series of discrete events. A high Shannon Entropy suggests that the distribution of events is uniformly utilised, while a low Shannon Entropy suggests that parts of the distribution are not used as much as others. As such, we propose a novel set of measures that generates events from an experiment, and then uses discretization functions to transform the input and output signal into a series of discrete events, and then compares the entropies of these input and output events to characterise the effects of the reservoir. This differs from existing comparative entropy measurements, such as Kullback-Leibler divergence [7], as it is computationally trivial to calculate.

For the purposes of Entropy Transformation Measures, a reservoir is a discrete time dynamical system. Here we assume the use of single-input/single-output reservoirs. It is possible to extend this approach to multi-input/multi-output reservoirs in a number of ways, such as applying discretisation functions in a piecewise manner to different inputs/outputs. Making the assumption of single-input/single-output reservoirs, and assuming the system is run for T timesteps, we specify the sequences **in** and **out** to represent the inputs and outputs of the reservoir respectively.

KR and GR both seek to characterise how a reservoir responds to changes in input, with the difference between the two being the range of the inputs to the system. For KR, the inputs are drawn from the full range of valid inputs, to characterise the system's response to different sequences of input. For GR, the inputs are drawn from a single narrow range of inputs, with the intent of characterising how similar the outputs are.

Pseudocode for the overall structure of calculating an Entropy Transformation is given in Algorithm 4. First the input and output sequences are sampled

---

Algorithm 4. Pseudocode for Entropy Transformation Measures

1: **in, out** := input and output sequences for experiment
2: ϕ**in**, ϕ**out** := input and output sequences after sampling ▷ Sampling step depends
   on measure
3: D_i, D_o := Discretisation functions for input and output data   ▷ Discretisation
   functions depends on measure and system under analysis
4: **return** $\frac{shannon(\langle D_o(o) \mid o \in \phi \mathbf{out}\rangle)}{shannon(\langle D_i(i) \mid i \in \phi \mathbf{in}\rangle)}$

---

if necessary. Then, a discretisation function is applied to the real-valued sampled sequences to generate a sequence of discrete events, from which we can derive a discrete probability distribution, to calculate the Shannon Entropy of the sequence. Finally, the ratio of output Shannon Entropy and Input Shannon Entropy is returned as the value of the measure. For the purposes of Entropy Transformation Measures, a discretisation function is any function that converts a continuous value into a discrete event. For example, when plotting a histogram, real values are discretized into the various bins used in the histogram. In general, the discretisation functions used for Entropy Transformation Measures is a map $\mathbb{R} \to \mathbb{E}$, where $\mathbb{E}$ is a finite alphabet representing the events.

One potential weakness of Entropy Transformation Measures is that they do not compare input and output directly. This is by design, as it is not known if the input and output of a system are directly comparable. Indeed, this paper presents the Range Utilisation Measure, which highlights when the input and output are not directly comparable. While this limits Entropy Transformation Measures to establishing correlation, not causation, it can be argued that correlation is all the can be established through experimentation. This is especially true with physical systems.

4.1   Range Utilisation Measure (RUM)

The first discretisation function we use derives from the idea of a histogram with equal sized bins. The intuition is that by comparing how the input and output are distributed over their range of values, it is possible to determine how well the reservoir utilises the range of values that it has, leading to the Range Utilisation Measure (RUM). This corresponds to a portion of the Kernel Rank measure: if a reservoir is not utilising the full range of values, then it is not as expressive as it would be otherwise. However, it does not necessarily capture the complexity of the transformation; for example, the Identity function utilises the full range of its output[1].

As RUM is a simple measure to determine the usage of the range of the reservoir, it is not necessary to sample the input and output of the reservoir. Hence, we skip this step and define a uniform discretisation over the range of values for an input, dividing the space into equally sized bins and classifying each input by which bin it belongs to. For example, if the value for an input is

---

[1] A reservoir implementing the identity function would also have a high KR.

in the range $[-1, 1]$, and five bins are used, the bins would be $1 : [-1.0, -0.6]$, $2 : (-0.6, -0.2]$, $3 : (-0.2, 0.2]$, $4 : (0.2, 0.6]$, $5 : (0.6, 1.0]$. We define a function $ud_{mn,mx,k}$ that maps a value to its bin number: $ud_{mn,mx,k} : \mathbb{R} \to \{1, .., k\}$. The set of bin numbers forms the alphabet representing events: $\mathbb{E} = \{1, .., k\}$. The function $ud_{mn,mx,k} : \mathbb{R} \to \{1, .., k\}$, defined on the range $[mn, mx]$ with k bins, is:

$$ud_{mn,mx,k}(x) = max\left(\left\lceil k\frac{x - mn}{mx - mn} \right\rceil, 1\right) \tag{1}$$

It should be noted that as the discretization function is dependant on the properties of the values that it is discretizing, **in** and **out** may require separate discretization functions. Therefore, let udi and udo denote appropriate uniform discretizations for **in** and **out** respectively.

With the ability to discretize the input and outputs of the reservoir, we now move on to calculating the Shannon Entropy for these sequences. To do this, we take all the events returned by the discretisation functions over the **in** and **out** sequences, convert them to probability distributions, and calculate the associated Shannon Entropies. Calculating the entropy for the output sequence gives us information on how the reservoir affects entropy, whereas calculating the entropy for the input gives us information on what the reservoir is performing its calculations on, allowing us to normalize the result. We define the equal-bin range utilisation measure as the ratios of the input to output entropies when discretized into equal sized bins:

$$rum(\mathbf{in}, \mathbf{out}) = \frac{shannon(\langle udi(o) \mid o \in \mathbf{out}\rangle)}{shannon(\langle udo(i) \mid i \in \mathbf{in}\rangle)} \tag{2}$$

where udi and udo are the uniform discretisation functions on the input and output sequences, and $shannon$ is a function that takes a sequence of discrete events, computes the probability distribution of the events, and returns the Shannon Entropy of that distribution.

As designed, a range utilisation of one indicates that the reservoir is using the range of its input and output spaces in a comparable manner. A range utilisation of less than one indicates that some proportion of the output space is underutilised, potentially indicating either improper scaling or a compression of the majority of the input into a smaller range. A range utilisation greater than one indicates that the reservoir is utilising the output space better than the input space, which may indicate improper input scaling or the reservoir injecting noise into the signal.

Range utilisation does not characterise the *computational* properties of the reservoir. For example, the Identity function always has a range utilisation of one if the input and output discretizations are the same. In order to characterise computational properties, it is necessary to perform comparisons of values.

4.2   Comparative Generalisation Measure (CGM)

While the range utilisation measure provides an interesting characterisation of the reservoir, it does not address the challenge of providing a measure of the reservoir's ability to generalise. Generalisation entails that a reservoir produces a similar output for a similar input, which includes two requirements:

1. Defining a sequence of events that enables the comparison of similar values.
2. When events are similar, the measure should to capture information on small differences.

GR meets both of these requirements by restricting the input to only values that are similar to each other. This restriction also means that GR only characterises how inputs within the restricted range behave; inputs outside of this range could be similar, but GR would not characterise how the reservoir responds to them. Therefore, in order to capture information across an arbitrary input, we propose a measure that extracts similar inputs and their outputs from a sequence and compares these, named the Comparative Generalisation Measure (CGM).

To meet the first requirement, we need a way to process the values provided from experiments to find timepoints where the input to the reservoir is similar, and thus the reservoir would ideally produce a similar output. While it would be sufficient to compare every input and output which are sufficiently similar, this grows at a rate of $O(T^2)$, which may produce too much data to reasonably process. Therefore, we introduce a sampling function to sample the data, $s(\mathbf{in}, i)$, which takes the timepoint i for an element to sample and returns the timepoint of a randomly selected similar value. Using this sampling function, we create a sequence of **similar** timepoints:

$$\mathbf{similar} = \langle s(\mathbf{in}, t) \mid t \in \{1, ..., T\} \rangle \tag{3}$$

where each $\mathbf{in}_t$ and $\mathbf{in}_{\mathbf{similar}_t}$ are judged by the sampling function to be similar enough that they should produce a similar output.

For a scalar input, which is the focus of this work, s may be defined as in Eq. 4, which defines similarity as a difference of at most the given parameter ϵ.

$$s_\epsilon(\mathbf{in}, i) = random\_choice(j \in \{1, ...T\} \mid |in_i - in_j| < \epsilon) \tag{4}$$

This definition of s_ϵ looks at values of the input sequence one at a time, with the assumption that replacement by a similar input will immediately produce a similar output. This does not take into account the memory capacity of the reservoir, where outputs can be influenced by a window of previous inputs. For GR, this is achieved by providing already similar inputs (small range), and thus as all prior histories are similar, the effect of memory capacity is minimised. However, CGM does not make this assumption, as it is defined on a broad range of inputs. Therefore, it is necessary to take into account the similarity of recent history as well as the current input. Therefore, we augment the sampling function with a history parameter τ that takes into account similarity for the last τ inputs:

$$smem_{\epsilon,\tau}(\textbf{in}, i) = random\_choice \left(j \in 1, ..., T \,\middle|\, \sum_{k=0}^{\tau} |in_{i-k} - in_{j-k}| < \epsilon \right) \quad (5)$$

Using the sampler function to generate the sequence of **similar** timepoints, we now define sequences of comparative values. These comparative values give the difference between similar inputs and their corresponding outputs. If the reservoir is good a generalisation, then similar inputs should produce similar outputs; therefore, if the difference between similar inputs is small the difference between the outputs should also be small. The sequences of differences in values are defined as follows:

$$\Delta\textbf{in} = \langle ||\textbf{in}_t - \textbf{in}_{\text{similar}_t}|| \mid t \in \{1, ..., T\} \rangle$$
$$\Delta\textbf{out} = \langle ||\textbf{out}_t - \textbf{out}_{\text{similar}_t}|| \mid t \in \{1, ..., T\} \rangle \quad (6)$$

These sequences of differences in values, which we need to discretize for the Shannon entropy, follow a different distribution from the original values. Assuming that the values are relatively similar, uniform discretisation is no longer appropriate, as it would be expected that most, if not all, values would be in the bin containing 0. Therefore, we use an exponential discretisation; bins increase in size exponentially away from zero, allowing more bins to be allocated to the expected smaller values. As the values are now absolute differences, they no have the same range as the original input and output sequences. For example, if the original sequence was distributed in the range $[-1, 1]$, the absolute difference is distributed in the range $[0, 2]$. So, if using five bins, the exponentially distributed bins would be $1 : [0, \frac{1}{8}], 2 : (\frac{1}{8}, \frac{1}{4}], 3 : (\frac{1}{4}, \frac{1}{2}], 4 : (\frac{1}{2}, 1], 5 : (1, 2]$. Note that the first two bins are the same size, as the exponential sequence is truncated on the left. An equation implementing this discretisation is given in Eq. 7 as the function $ed_{mx,k} : \mathbb{R} \to 1, ...k$ where mx is the maximum difference between two values and k is the number of bins.

$$ed_{d,k}(x) = \max \left(\left\lceil log_2 \left(\frac{x}{d} \right) + k \right\rceil, 1 \right) \quad (7)$$

Similarly to the RUM, it is necessary to define a separate exponential discretization function for each of $\Delta\textbf{in}$ and $\Delta\textbf{out}$, so let edi and edo denote the discretization functions for $\Delta\textbf{in}$ and $\Delta\textbf{out}$ respectively. Then CGM can be computed by Eq. 8.

$$cgm(\textbf{in}, \textbf{out}) = \frac{shannon(\langle edo(\textbf{o}) \mid o \in \Delta\textbf{out} \rangle)}{shannon(\langle edi(\textbf{i}) \mid i \in \Delta\textbf{in} \rangle)} \quad (8)$$

where edi and edo are the exponential discretisation functions on the input and output sequences,

Table 2. Evaluation Parameters

Parameter	Value
number of nodes	50
activation function	tanh
weight generation	uniform random
input connectivity	random (0.3, 1.0)
spectral radius	random (0.3, 0.9)

As designed, the Comparative Generalisation Measure compares the degree to which similar inputs produce similar outputs. Unlike GR, CGM is defined for any given sequence of inputs. To account for the memory of the reservoir, the τ parameter must be specified appropriately to take into account the recent history of inputs. Similarity is specified by the ϵ parameter.

A CGM of one indicates that the reservoir produces similar outputs for similar inputs, leading to good generalisation. If the measure is not one, then the greater the distance from one the worse the ability of the reservoir to generalise.

5   Evaluation

To characterise the behaviour of the new measures, testing was conducted using the PyCHARC framework [4] on Echo State Networks. One hundred Echo State Networks were generated using parameters from Table 2. Each of these Echo State Networks was tested using twenty uniform random input sequences in the range $[-1, 1]$; to calculate GR, the input was scaled to the range $[-0.1, 0.1]$. To calculate a single output for the entropy measures, the mean of the internal states was used. While it is possible to define a discretisation function for multiple output sequences, the mean was used to reflect that in physical reservoir computing it is difficult (or impossible) to extract the full set of internal states. For RUM, the discretization function $ud(-1, 1, 100)$ (100 bins across the full range) was used for both input and output. For CGM, the sampling function $s_m em(0.3, 3)$ (a total difference of 0.3 across 3 inputs), and the discretization function $ed(2, 25)$ (25 exponential bins across the full range) were used for both input and output.

The procedures used to capture KR and GR are detailed in Algorithms 1 and 2. In addition, the output from the ESNs used in Algorithm 1 was captured and used to calculate RUM and CGM, demonstrating that it is possible to calculate these measures without performing additional experiments. For comparison, both visual scatter plots and Spearman's Rank Correlation Coefficient [12] were used to evaluate correlation.

Figure 3 shows the distribution of KR with RUM. Due to the use of the mean state as the output, the usage of the output range tends to be low, as the output tends to the mean. However, it can be seen that there is a weak degree of correlation, with Spearman's Rank Correlation Coefficient calculated at 0.37,

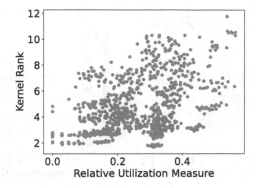

Fig. 3. Kernel Rank vs Relative Utilization Measure, showing a weak correlation

with a p-value of $< 10^{-33}$. The small p-value indicates that the correlation coefficient is significant and unlikely to arise by chance. Therefore, the correlation indicates that RUM captures a portion of the information used to calculate KR, which is expected both by design and the fact that RUM does not have access to the internal state of the reservoir. It should also be noted that a RUM of 0, caused by all outputs being represented by the same event, can be an indicator of low KR, or it can indicate the discretization used does not represent the events in enough detail.

Figure 4 compares GR with CGR. As expected, CGR is more likely to be less than 1, as the input is drawn from a uniform random distribution. However, CGR shows very little correlation with GR, with Spearman's Correlation Coefficient returning a value $< 10^{-2}$ and a p-value of 0.96, indicating at best an insignificant correlation that could be found under the null hypothesis of uncorrelated data. However, this serves to illustrate the problem of GR only sampling a restricted range, where CGR is provided with the full input space.

To illustrate that the difference between GR and CGR is due to the difference in input range, Fig. 5 shows a comparison of GR and CGR, but with CGR having the same restricted input range as GR (adapting the sampling and discretization functions for the new range). Here, we can see that the inputs are correlated, albeit noisily, with a Spearman's Correlation Coefficient of 0.46 and corresponding p-value $< 10^{-52}$ indicating that the effect is significant. As with RUM, exact correlation is not expected as CGR only has the output values, whereas GR is provided with the internal state of the reservoir. However, the degree of correlation is stronger than between RUM and KR. Therefore, one can conclude that CGR does capture similar information to GR, when presented with the same input. However, when provided an input across the full range, CGR captures generalization behaviour across the entire range, including information which GR is not exposed to.

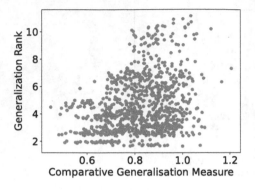
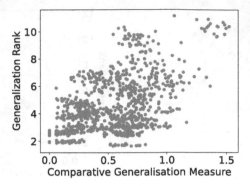

Fig. 4. GR vs CGR, CGR calculated on $[-1, 1]$ No correlation observed

Fig. 5. GR vs CGR, CGR calculated on $[-0.1, 0.1]$ Moderate correlation observed

6   Conclusion

This paper gave a brief overview of the KR and GR measures, and showed that in use in the literature it is difficult, if not impossible, to compare results of these metrics. This is primarily due to a lack of specification of the parameters of the measures, as well as confusion on the implementation of GR. The paper also showed that implementations of GR in particular are somewhat arbitrary.

To counter these issues, this paper proposed two alternative measures, RUM and CGR, which belong to the family of Entropy Transformation Measures. Entropy Transformation Measures work by comparing the effect of the reservoir on the Shannon entropy of the input and output, with respect to a discretization function. These functions are also defined across any sequence of inputs, meaning that they can be collected at the same time as other experiments. By design, these measures require the discretization function to be defined, which makes it difficult for them to be inexactly specified. Finally, the measures do not require any knowledge of the internal state of the reservoir, making them easy to apply to physical systems where the internal state may not be measurable.

When evaluating the new measures, RUM was shown to have a degree of correlation to KR, albeit a very weak correlation due to it only capturing a portion of the information of KR. CGR was more complicated: it only shows correlation to GR when restricted to the same input range. However, this is due to the weakness of GR in characterizing the ability of a reservoir to generalize outside of the input range it examines. As CGR samples across any input presented, it does not have this weakness. Further, as CGR can examine an arbitrary input, it is possible to calculate CGR when calculating other measures.

This paper focuses on single-input single-output systems. While there are a number of straightforward extensions available to multi-input multi-output systems, such as piecewise application of single value discretization functions, further work is required to explore this problem.

Acknowledgments. The authors acknowledge funding from the MARCH project, EPSRC grant numbers EP/V006029/1 and EP/V006339/1. The authors would like to thank Ian Vidamour for providing details on his implementation of Generalisation Rank.

References

1. Allwood, D.A., et al.: A perspective on physical reservoir computing with nano-magnetic devices. Appl. Phys. Lett. **122**(4), 040501 (2023)
2. Büsing, L., Schrauwen, B., Legenstein, R.: Connectivity, dynamics, and memory in reservoir computing with binary and analog neurons. Neural Comput. **22**(5), 1272–1311 (2010)
3. Dale, M., Miller, J.F., Stepney, S., Trefzer, M.A.: A substrate-independent frame-work to characterize reservoir computers. Proc. Roy. Soc. A **475**(2226), 20180723 (2019)
4. Griffin, D.: Pycharc: Python characterisation of reservoir computers framework (2023). https://github.com/dgdguk/pycharc/
5. Jaeger, H.: Short term memory in echo state networks. Technical report 152, GMD (2002)
6. Jaeger, H., Haas, H.: Harnessing nonlinearity: predicting chaotic systems and saving energy in wireless communication. Science **304**(5667), 78–80 (2004)
7. Kullback, S., Leibler, R.A.: On information and sufficiency. Ann. Math. Stat. **22**(1), 79–86 (1951)
8. Love, J., Mulkers, J., Bourianoff, G., Leliaert, J., Everschor-Sitte, K.: Task agnostic metrics for reservoir computing. arXiv:2108.01512v1 [cs.LG] (2021)
9. Maass, W.: Networks of spiking neurons: the third generation of neural network models. Neural Netw. **10**(9), 1659–1671 (1997)
10. Roy, O., Vetterli, M.: The effective rank: a measure of effective dimensionality. In: 15th European Signal Processing Conference, pp. 606–610. IEEE (2007)
11. Shannon, C.E.: A mathematical theory of communication. Bell Syst. Tech. J. **27**(3), 379–423 (1948)
12. Spearman, C.: The proof and measurement of association between two things. Am. J. Psychol. **15**(1), 72–101 (1904). http://www.jstor.org/stable/1412159
13. Stewart, G.W.: On the early history of the singular value decomposition. SIAM Rev. **35**(4), 551–566 (1993)
14. Vidamour, I.T., et al.: Quantifying the computational capability of a nanomagnetic reservoir computing platform with emergent magnetisation dynamics. Nanotechnology **33**(48), 48520 (2022)

Quantum Property Testing Algorithm for the Concatenation of Two Palindromes Language

Kamil Khadiev$^{(\boxtimes)}$ and Danil Serov

Institute of Computational Mathematics and Information Technologies, Kazan Federal University, Kazan, Russia
kamilhadi@gmail.com

Abstract. In this paper, we present a quantum property testing algorithm for recognizing a context-free language that is a concatenation of two palindromes L_{REV}. The query complexity of our algorithm is $O(\frac{1}{\varepsilon}n^{1/3}\log n)$, where n is the length of an input. It is better than the classical complexity that is $\Theta^*(\sqrt{n})$.

At the same time, in the general setting, the picture is different a little. Classical query complexity is $\Theta(n)$, and quantum query complexity is $\Theta^*(\sqrt{n})$. So, we obtain polynomial speed-up for both cases (general and property testing).

Keywords: palindromes · property testing · strings · quantum algorithms · query complexity · context-free languages

1 Introduction

In this paper, we investigate property testing [24,50] that is a relaxation of the standard notion of a decision problem. A property testing algorithm distinguishes between inputs with a certain property and inputs that are far from any input that has the property. By "far" we mean a large Hemming distance. More specifically, for a given property α, a testing algorithm should accept an input that has the property, and reject if the input is ε-far from any input with the property. Here ε-far means that the Hemming distance is at least $\varepsilon \cdot n$, where n is the length of the input. In [23,48], one can find examples of testing algorithms whose query complexity is sublinear or independent of the input size.

Researchers investigate formal languages with respect to the property testing. Alon, Krivelevich, Newman, and Szegedy [5] presented a property testing algorithm for any regular language L with query complexity $O^*(1/\varepsilon)$ that does not depend on the input size. Here O^* hides constant and log factors. Newman [45] extended this result to properties defined by bounded-width branching programs.

At the same time, Alon et al. [5] showed that the situation for context-free languages is completely different. Context-free languages are not testable even

© The Author(s), under exclusive license to Springer Nature Switzerland AG 2024
D.-J. Cho and J. Kim (Eds.): UCNC 2024, LNCS 14776, pp. 134–147, 2024.
https://doi.org/10.1007/978-3-031-63742-1_10

in time square root in the input size. As an example, the context-free language $L_{REV} = \{uu^r vv^r : u, v \in \Sigma^*\}$ that is a concatenation of two palindromes, where Σ is a finite size alphabet (binary as an example), and u^r is a reverse of u. For the language, they proved $\Omega(\sqrt{n})$ lower bound for query complexity, where n is a length of an input. Parnas, Ron, and Rubinfeld presented a property testing algorithm that almost reaches this lower bound. Its query complexity is $O\left(\frac{1}{\varepsilon}\sqrt{n}\log n\right)$.

Buhrman, Fortnow, Newman, and Röhrig [17] introduced quantum property testing. They developed quantum property testing algorithms for some problems that are better than classical counterparts in terms of query complexity. A nice survey on quantum property testing can be found in [44]. At the same time, context-free languages like L_{REV} were not considered. We are interested in developing a quantum property testing algorithm for a context-free language that is better than the classical lower bound.

There are many examples of quantum algorithms [2,6,30,46] that are faster than classical counterparts [27,51] in the general setting (not property testing). Problems for strings are examples of such problems [3,4,28,29,31–38,41–43].

A new interest in recognizing formal languages, including context-free languages, is started from the paper of Aaronson, Grier, and Schaeffer [1]. Dyck language was investigated by different researches [7,8,18,34]. Other formal languages were explored in papers [11,19].

In this paper, we present a quantum property testing algorithm for recognizing L_{REV} language that has $O(\frac{1}{\varepsilon}n^{1/3}\log n)$ query complexity. It shows quantum speed-up and it is better than the classical lower bound $\Omega(\sqrt{n})$. For this result, we use the meet-in-the-middle technique and Grover's search algorithm [14,25].

At the same time, in the general setting (not a property testing algorithm), we show that the problem has $\Theta(n)$ classical query complexity; and $\Theta^*(\sqrt{n})$ quantum query complexity. We present a quantum lower bound $\Omega(\sqrt{n})$, and a quantum algorithm with query complexity $O\left(\sqrt{n}(\log n)^2\right)$. So, we obtain almost quadratic speed-up. We see that in the general setting, the classical lower bound differs from the property testing setting. At the same time, we see quantum speed-up for both cases.

The structure of this paper is the following. Section 2 describes some conventional notions for quantum computation. Section 3 provides quantum and classical algorithms and lower bounds for general setting. The quantum property testing algorithm is given in Subsect. 4. The final Sect. 5 concludes the paper and contains open questions.

2   Preliminaries

For a string $u = (u_1, \ldots, u_M)$, let $|u| = M$ be a length of the string, and let $u^r = (u_M, \ldots, u_1)$ be the reverse of the string u.

Let us formally define the Two Palindromes Concatenation problem.

Suppose Σ is a finite-size alphabet. Let $L_{REV} = \{uu^r vv^r : u, v \in \Sigma^*\}$ be a language of concatenations for two palindromes. We assume that in the definition of L_{REV} u and v are not empty strings. For simplicity, in the paper, we assume that the alphabet is binary, $\Sigma = \{0, 1\}$. At the same time, all results are correct for any finite-size alphabet.

For an integer $n > 0$, let the function $\text{REV}_n : \Sigma^n \to \{0, 1\}$ be such that $\text{REV}_n(x) = 1$ iff $x \in L_{REV}$.

For an integer $n > 0$ and a non-negative $\varepsilon < 1$, let $\text{REV}_{n,\varepsilon}$ be a property testing problem such that for an input $x = (x_0, \ldots, x_{n-1})$ there is a promise that if x is not in L_REV, then x is at least $\varepsilon \cdot n$ far from the closest word from L_{REV}. Formally, if x is not in L_REV, then for any $u \in L_{REV}$ we have $|\{i : x_i \neq u_i\}| \geq \varepsilon \cdot n$.

In the paper, we use a *trie* (prefix tree) data structure [13, 15, 21, 39]. It is a tree that allows us to add a string s and check whether s is in the tree with running time $O(|s|)$. The data structure implements a "set of strings" data structure. Let us have the following operations with a trie T:

- INITTRIE() returns an empty trie. The running time of the operation is $O(1)$.
- ADDTOTRIE(T,S) adds a string s to the trie T. The running time of the operation is $O(|s|)$.
- CONTAINS(T,S) returns 1 if a string s belongs to the trie T, and *False* otherwise. The running time of the operation is $O(|s|)$.

2.1   Quantum Query Model

One of the most popular computation models for quantum algorithms is the query model. We use the standard form of the quantum query model. Let $f : D \to \{0, 1\}, D \subseteq \{0, 1\}^M$ be an M variable function. Our goal is to compute it on an input $x \in D$. We are given oracle access to the input x, i.e. it is implemented by a specific unitary transformation usually defined as $|i\rangle|z\rangle|w\rangle \mapsto |i\rangle|z + x_i \pmod 2\rangle|w\rangle$, where the $|i\rangle$ register indicates the index of the variable we are querying, $|z\rangle$ is the output register, and $|w\rangle$ is some auxiliary workspace. An algorithm in the query model consists of alternating applications of arbitrary unitaries which are independent of the input and the query unitary, and a measurement at the end. The smallest number of queries for an algorithm that outputs $f(x)$ with probability $\geq \frac{2}{3}$ on all x is called the quantum query complexity of the function f and is denoted by $Q(f)$. We refer the readers to [2, 6, 30, 46] for more details on quantum computing.

In this paper, we are interested in the query complexity of the quantum algorithms. We use modifications of Grover's search algorithm [14, 25] as quantum subroutines. For these subroutines, time complexity can be obtained from query complexity by multiplication to a log factor [9, 26].

3   The General Case

In this section, we consider the REV_n problem. Here we show quantum upper and lower bounds that are almost equal up to log factors.

3.1   Quantum and Classical Algorithms

Let us start with the upper bound.

Firstly, let us show one useful property. For the input string $x = (x_0, \ldots, x_{n-1})$, let $\bar{x} = (x_1, \ldots, x_{n-1})$ be the string x without the first symbol. Let $\hat{x} = (x_0, \ldots, x_{n-2})$ be the string x without the last symbol. Let

$$y(x) = \bar{x} \circ \hat{x} = (x_1, \ldots, x_{n-1}, x_0, \ldots, x_{n-2}),$$

where $\circ$ is the concatenation operation. Then, we have the following result

Lemma 1. *A string* $x \in L_{REV}$ *if and only if* $y(x)$ *contains* x^r *as a substring.*

Proof. Assume that $x \in L_{REV}$. It means that we can find two strings u and v such that $x = uu^r vv^r$. Note that $\hat{v^r} = \bar{v}^r$ which means we can either remove the last symbol of a reversed string, or remove the first symbol of the original string and then reverse. Hence, the string $y(x)$ has the following form

$$y(x) = \bar{u}u^r vv^r uu^r v\bar{v}^r$$

We can see that it has $x^r = vv^r uu^r$ as a substring because $y(x) = \bar{u}u^r \circ x^r \circ v\bar{v}^r$.

Assume that x^r is a substring of $y(x)$. Let $n = |x|$, and $k = |y(x)| = 2n - 2$. Assume that x^r starts in $y(x)$ from a position $i \leq n - 1$. It means that $y(x)_i = (x^r)_0$. At the same time, $(x^r)_0 = x_{n-1}$ because x^r is the reverse of x. We also can say, that $y(x)_i = x_{i+1}$. So, we have

$$x_{i+1} = y(x)_i = (x^r)_0 = x_{n-1},$$

$$x_{i+2} = y(x)_{i+1} = (x^r)_1 = x_{n-2},$$

$$x_{i+3} = y(x)_{i+2} = (x^r)_2 = x_{n-3},$$

$$\ldots$$

$$x_{n-1} = y(x)_{n-2} = (x^r)_{n-i-2} = x_{i+1}$$

Therefore, $(x_{i+1}, \ldots, x_{n-1})$ is a palindrome. Let it be vv^r for some string v (See Fig. 1).

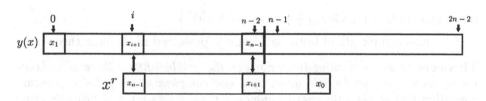

Fig. 1. The string x^r is a substring of $y(x)$ and it starts from position i. We can see that $(x_{i+1}, \ldots, x_{n-1})$ is a palindrome.

Since x^r starts from the i-th symbol of $y(x)$, we have $y(x)_{n-1} = (x^r)_{n-i-1}$. At the same time, $y(x)_{n-1} = x_0$; and $(x^r)_{n-i-1} = x_i$. So, we have

$$x_0 = y(x)_{n-1} = (x^r)_{n-i-1} = x_i,$$

$$x_1 = y(x)_n = (x^r)_{n-i} = x_{i-1},$$

$$x_2 = y(x)_{n+1} = (x^r)_{n-i+1} = x_{i-2},$$

$$\dots$$

$$x_i = y(x)_{n+i-1} = (x^r)_{n-1} = x_0$$

Therefore, $(x_0, \dots, x_i)$ is a palindrome. Let it be uu^r for some string u (See Fig. 2).

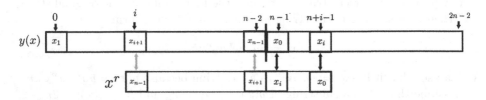

Fig. 2. The string x^r is a substring of $y(x)$ and it starts from position i. We can see that $(x_0, \dots, x_i)$ is a palindrome.

So, we can say that $x = (x_0, \dots, x_i) \circ (x_{i+1}, \dots, x_{n-1}) = uu^r vv^r \in L_{REV}$. $\square$

In fact, we do not construct $y(x)$. To access the symbol $y(x)_i$, we use a function GET(i) that returns x_{i+1} if $i < n - 1$, and returns x_{i-n+1} if $\geq n - 1$. The complexity of this function is $O(1)$ if we use array-like data structures, but not Linked List data structure.

In the classical case, the substring problem can be solved using the Knuth-Morris-Pratt algorithm [20,40]. The complexity of the algorithm is $O(k + n)$, where $n = |x^r|$, and $k = |y(x)| = 2n - 2$. So, the complexity is $O(n)$.

In   the   quantum   case,   we   can
solve the problem using the Ramesh-Vinay algorithm [49]. The complexity of
the algorithm is $O\left(\sqrt{k} \log \sqrt{\frac{k}{n}} \log n + \sqrt{n}(\log n)^2\right)$.

The final complexity of both algorithms is presented in the next theorem.

Theorem 1. *For a positive integer n and the problem REV_n, there is a classical algorithm that works with query and time complexity $O(n)$; and a quantum algorithm that works with query complexity $O\left(\sqrt{n}(\log n)^2\right)$ and two-side error probability strictly less than 0.5.*

Proof. Due to Lemma 1, the problem is equivalent to searching x^r in $y(x)$. Let $k = |y(x)| = 2n - 2$, and $n = |x| = |x^r|$.

In the classical case, time and query complexity of Knuth-Morris-Pratt algorithm [20, 40] is $O(n + k) = O(n + 2n - 2) = O(n)$.

In the quantum case, the query complexity of the Ramesh-Vinay algorithm [49] is

$$O\left(\sqrt{k}\log\sqrt{\frac{k}{n}}\log n + \sqrt{n}(\log n)^2\right)$$

$$= O\left(\sqrt{2n-2}\log\sqrt{\frac{2n-2}{n}}\log n + \sqrt{n}(\log n)^2\right)$$

$$= O\left(\sqrt{n}\log n + \sqrt{n}(\log n)^2\right) = O\left(\sqrt{n}(\log n)^2\right).$$

The error probability is strictly less than 0.5 due to [49].   □

3.2   Lower Bound

Let us present the lower bound for the REV_n problem. In the next theorem, we show that the problem is at least as hard as an unstructured search among n elements.

Theorem 2. *The lower bound for quantum query complexity of REV_n is $\Omega(\sqrt{n})$, and for classical (randomized or deterministic) query complexity is $\Omega(n)$.*

Proof. Assume that $n = 2t + 2$ for some integer t. Let us consider only inputs of two forms:

- $\sigma = (0, \dots, 0)$ is a 0-string. Let $u = (0)$, and $v = (0, \dots, 0)$. Here $|u| = 1$, and $|v| = t$. In that case, $u = u^r$, and $v = v^r$. So, we can say that $\sigma = uu^r vv^r$, and $\text{REV}_n(\sigma) = 1$.
- For $i \in \{0, \dots, n-1\}$, the string $\gamma^i = (0, \dots, 0, 1, 0, \dots 0)$ has 1 on the position i, and 0s on other positions. There is only one position with a 1-value, and it has not a symmetric pair. Therefore, $\text{REV}_n(\gamma^i) = 0$.

Distinguishing between two cases σ and γ^i is equivalent to searching 1 among n elements.

Assume, that we have a quantum algorithm with quantum query complexity $o(\sqrt{n})$ or a classical algorithm with query complexity $o(n)$. Then, we can distinguish between two cases σ and γ^i, and find 1 among n elements with proposed complexity. This claim contradicts the lower bound for unstructured search [12] that is $\Omega(\sqrt{n})$ in the quantum case, and $\Omega(n)$ in the classical case.   □

Finally, we see that the classical complexity for the problem is $\Theta(n)$, and the quantum complexity is $\Theta^*(\sqrt{n})$, where Θ^* hides logarithmic factors. So, we obtain an almost quadratic speed-up for this problem.

4   The Property Testing Case

In this section, we consider the $\mathrm{REV}_{n,\varepsilon}$ problem. Here, we use ideas from [47] paper that provides a randomized algorithm for the problem.

The classical upper bound [47] for the problem is $O\left(\frac{1}{\varepsilon}\sqrt{n}\log n\right)$, and the lower bound [5] is $\Omega(\sqrt{n})$. We can see, that in the property testing case, we have significant improvement. A situation simulation happens for quantum algorithms.

Firstly, let us discuss some observations on properties of a word $x = (x_0, \ldots, x_{n-1}) = uu^r vv^r$ from the language L_{REV}. Let us consider two indexes $i, j \in \{0, \ldots, n-1\}$, and assume that $i < j$ without limiting the generality of the foregoing.

We say that they are in symmetric positions with respect to uu^r if $i, j < 2|u|$, and there is an integer $\delta \leq |u|$ such that $i + \delta = |u| - 1$, and $j - \delta = |u|$. In other words, they are symmetric with respect to the middle of the palindrome uu^r (See Fig. 3).

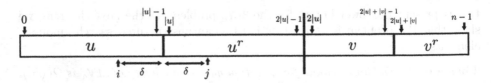

Fig. 3. Indexes i and j are symmetric with respect to the middle of the palindrome uu^r.

We say that indexes i and j are in symmetric positions with respect to vv^r if $i, j \geq 2|u|$, and there is an integer $\delta' \leq |v|$ such that $i + \delta' = 2|u| + |v| - 1$, and $j - \delta' = 2|u| + |v|$. In other words, they are symmetric with respect to the middle of the palindrome vv^r (See Fig. 4).

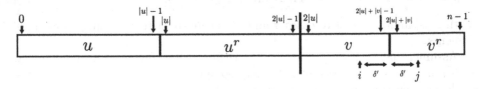

Fig. 4. Indexes i and j are symmetric with respect to the middle of the palindrome vv^r.

Let us consider any two indexes i and j that are in symmetric positions with respect to uu^r or vv^r. In that case, we have the following lemma about these indexes:

Lemma 2. *Indexes i and j are in symmetric positions with respect to uu^r or vv^r if and only if $i + j = 2|u| - 1$ (mod n). Remember that $n = 2|u| + 2|v|$.*

Proof. Without limiting the generality of the foregoing, we can assume that $i < j$. Note that $0 \le i + j \le 2n$ because $i, j \le n$. Therefore, $i + j = 2|u| - 1$ (mod n) means either $i + j = 2|u| - 1$ or $i + j = 2|u| - 1 + n$. We have three cases. Let us consider each of them.

Case 1. Assume that $i, j < 2|u|$. Let i and j be in symmetric positions with respect to uu^r. So, there is δ such that $i + \delta = |u| - 1$ and $j - \delta = |u|$. Hence, $i + j = |u| - 1 - \delta + |u| + \delta = 2|u| - 1 = 2|u| - 1$ (mod n). Let $i + j = 2|u| - 1$ (mod n). Let $\delta = |u| - 1 - i$. Then

$$i = |u| - \delta - 1, \text{ and } j = 2|u| - 1 - i = 2|u| - 1 - |u| + 1 + \delta = |u| + \delta.$$

Due to the definition, i and j are in symmetric positions with respect to uu^r.

Case 2. Assume that $i, j \ge 2|u|$. Let i and j be in symmetric positions with respect to vv^r. So, there is δ' such that $i + \delta' = 2|u| + |v| - 1$ and $2|u| + |v| = j - \delta'$. Hence,

$$i + j = 2|u| + |v| - 1 - \delta' + 2|u| + |v| + \delta' = 2|u| - 1 + (2|u| + 2|v|) \text{ (mod } n).$$

Note that $2|u| + 2|v| = n$. Therefore, $i + j = 2|u| - 1$ (mod n). Let $i + j = 2|u| - 1$ (mod n). Let $\delta' = 2|u| + |v| - 1 - i$. We remember that $n = 2|u| + 2|v|$. Then

$$i = 2|u| + |v| - 1 - \delta', \text{ and } j = 2|u| - 1 - i \text{ (mod } n)$$

$$j = n + 2|u| - 1 - i \text{ (mod } n)$$

$$j = n + 2|u| - 1 - 2|u| - |v| + 1 + \delta' = n - |v| + \delta' = 2|u| + 2|v| - |v| + \delta' \text{ (mod } n)$$

$$j = 2|u| + |v| + \delta' \text{ (mod } n).$$

Note that $2|u| + |v| + \delta' = 2|u| + |v| + 2|u| + |v| - 1 - i \le 2|u| + |v| + 2|u| + |v| - 1 - 2|u| = 2|u| + 2|v| - 1 < n$. Therefore, $j < n$, and we can say that $j = 2|u| + |v| + \delta'$. Due to the definition, i and j are in symmetric positions with respect to vv^r.

Case 3. Assume that $i < 2|u|$, and $j \ge 2|u|$. In that case, i and j are not in symmetric positions with respect to uu^r nor vv^r. Let us show that $i + j \ne 2|u| - 1 \pmod{n}$.
Let $i < n - j - 1$, then $i + j < n - 1$. It means that $(i + j) \bmod n = i + j$. At the same time, $i + j \ge j \ge 2|u| > 2|u| + 1$. Therefore $i + j \ne 2|u| - 1$. Let $i \ge n - j - 1$. It means that $(i + j) \bmod n = i - (n - j) < i - 1 < 2|u| - 1$. Therefore $(i + j) \bmod n \ne 2|u| - 1$.

$\square$

So, we can say that for any i and j such that $i + j = 2|u| - 1 \pmod{n}$, we have $x_i = x_j$.

For an integer $p \in \{0, \ldots, n-1\}$, let us look at two indexes $(i - p) \bmod n$ and $(j + p) \bmod n$ where $i + j = 2|u| - 1 \pmod n$. We have

$$(i - p) + (j + p) = i + j = 2|u| - 1 (\bmod\ n)$$

Therefore, $x_{(i-p) \bmod n} = x_{(j+p) \bmod n}$.

Let us consider the number $2|u| - 1$. Due to the integer division rule and the statement $2|u| - 1 < 2|u| + 2|v| = n$, we can say that

$$2|u| - 1 = \alpha \cdot \lfloor n^{1/3} \rfloor + \beta,$$

where $0 \le \alpha \le \left\lfloor \frac{2|u|-1}{\lfloor n^{1/3} \rfloor} \right\rfloor \le \left\lfloor \frac{n}{\lfloor n^{1/3} \rfloor} \right\rfloor \approx n^{2/3}$ and $0 \le \beta \le \lfloor n^{1/3} \rfloor - 1$.

Let us consider two sets of integers that are

$$\mathcal{I}_n = \{0, \ldots, \lfloor n^{1/3} \rfloor - 1\}$$

and

$$\mathcal{J}_n = \{\alpha \cdot \lfloor n^{1/3} \rfloor, \text{ for } 0 \le \alpha \le \left\lfloor \frac{2|u| - 1}{\lfloor n^{1/3} \rfloor} \right\rfloor\}$$

$$= \{0, \lfloor n^{1/3} \rfloor, 2\lfloor n^{1/3} \rfloor, 3\lfloor n^{1/3} \rfloor, \ldots, \left\lfloor \frac{2|u| - 1}{\lfloor n^{1/3} \rfloor} \right\rfloor \cdot \lfloor n^{1/3} \rfloor\}.$$

Note that $|\mathcal{J}_n| = \left\lfloor \frac{2|u|-1}{\lfloor n^{1/3} \rfloor} \right\rfloor \le \left\lfloor \frac{n}{\lfloor n^{1/3} \rfloor} \right\rfloor \approx n^{2/3}$, and $|\mathcal{I}_n| = \lfloor n^{1/3} \rfloor$.

We are ready to present one more lemma about these indexes.

Lemma 3. *If* $x = (x_0, \ldots, x_{n-1}) \in L_{REV}$, *then there is* $i \in \mathcal{I}_n$ *and* $j \in \mathcal{J}_n$ *such that* $x_{(i-p) \bmod n} = x_{(j+p) \bmod n}$ *for any* $p \in \{0, \ldots, n-1\}$.

Proof. If $x = (x_0, \ldots, x_{n-1}) \in L_{REV}$, then there is u and v from Σ^* such that $x = uu^r vv^r$.

As we discussed before, $2|u| - 1 = \alpha \cdot \lfloor n^{1/3} \rfloor + \beta$, where $0 \le \alpha \le \left\lfloor \frac{2|u|-1}{\lfloor n^{1/3} \rfloor} \right\rfloor$ and $0 \le \beta \le \lfloor n^{1/3} \rfloor - 1$. Let $i = \beta$ and $j = \alpha \cdot \lfloor n^{1/3} \rfloor$.

Therefore, $i + j = 2|u| - 1$ and they are in symmetric positions with respect to uu^r or vv^r due to Lemma 2. Hence, for any $p \in \{0, \ldots, n-1\}$ we have $x_{(i-p) \bmod n} = x_{(j+p) \bmod n}$. $\square$

We are ready to formulate the algorithm.

4.1 Quantum Algorithm

Let us present an algorithm for computing $REV_{n,\varepsilon}(x)$. The algorithm is based on the meet-in-the-middle technique [30] (Section 8) that is widely used in algorithms design and cryptography [22]. The main idea is to split a large set into two small parts, small enough for handling them. Similar ideas were used, for example, in [10,16].

Let us consider the sets $\mathcal{I}_n$ and $\mathcal{J}_n$, and an integer $m = \frac{2}{\varepsilon} \log_2 n$.

Step 1. We choose randomly m numbers $p_1, \ldots, p_m \in_R \{0, \ldots, n-1\}$
Step 2. We add all strings $x^i = (x_{(i-p_1) \bmod n}, \ldots, x_{(i-p_m) \bmod n})$ for $i \in \mathcal{I}_n$
to a *trie* (prefix tree) T.
Step 3. We search $j \in \mathcal{J}_n$ such that $\tilde{x}^j = (x_{(j+p_1) \bmod n}, \ldots, x_{(j+p_m) \bmod n})$
is presented in the *trie* T. We search them using Grover's search algorithm
[14,25]. We define a search function $f : \mathcal{J}_n \to \{0,1\}$ such that $f(j) = 1$ iff $\tilde{x}^j$
is presented in T. The algorithm searches any j_0 such that $f(j_0) = 1$.

If we found an index j_0 on Step 3, then there is $\tilde{x}^j = x^i$ and $i + j = 2|u| - 1$.
Therefore, $\text{REV}_{n,\varepsilon}(x) = 1$.

Assume that we have a $\text{GROVERSEARCH}(\mathcal{D}, f)$ procedure, that implements
Grover's search algorithm for search space $\mathcal{D}$ and a function $f : \mathcal{D} \to \{0,1\}$.
The algorithm finds $j_0 \in \mathcal{D}$ such that $f(j_0) = 1$. The algorithm works with
$O(\sqrt{|\mathcal{D}|} \cdot T(f))$ query complexity, where $T(f)$ is the complexity of computing
the function f. The error probability is at most 0.1. Assume that the procedure
returns *True* in the case of finding the element j_0 and *False* otherwise. In
our algorithm we use $\text{CONTAINS}(T, \tilde{x}^j)$ function as $f(j)$. This function checks
whether $\tilde{x}^j$ belongs to the trie T. The query complexity of the function is $O(m)$
due to properties of the trie data structure that were discussed in Sect. 2. The
main operations with the trie data structure are listed in Sect. 2.

The implementation of the algorithm is presented in Algorithm 1; the complexity is analyzed in Theorem 3.

Algorithm 1. The Quantum Algorithm for $\text{REV}_{n,\varepsilon}$ problem and input $x = (x_0, \ldots, x_{n-1})$.

$m \leftarrow \frac{2}{\varepsilon} \log_2 n$
for $i \in \{1, \ldots, m\}$ **do**
    $p_i \leftarrow_R \{0, \ldots, n-1\}$ ▷ p_i is chosen randomly
end for
$T \leftarrow \text{INITTRIE}()$
for $i \in \{1, \ldots, \lfloor n^{1/3} \rfloor - 1\}$ **do**
    $x^i \leftarrow (x_{(i-p_1) \bmod n}, \ldots, x_{(i-p_m) \bmod n})$
    $\text{ADDTOTRIE}(T, x^j)$
end for
$Result \leftarrow \text{GROVERSEARCH}(\mathcal{J}_n, \text{CONTAINS}(T, \tilde{x}^j))$
return $Result$

Theorem 3. *The provided algorithm computes* $REV_{n,\varepsilon}$ *with* $O\left(\frac{1}{\varepsilon} n^{1/3} \log n\right)$
query complexity and at most $\frac{1}{4}$ *error probability.*

Proof. Let us discuss complexity of the algorithm. Step 2 which is adding all
strings x^i requires $O(|\mathcal{I}_n| \cdot m) = O(n^{1/3} \cdot m)$ query complexity. Grover search
works with $O(|\mathcal{J}_n| \cdot m) = O(\sqrt{n^{2/3}} \cdot m) = O(n^{1/3} \cdot m)$ query complexity. Note

that $m = \frac{2}{\varepsilon}\log n$, that is why the total complexity is

$$O\left(\frac{1}{\varepsilon}n^{1/3}\log n + \frac{1}{\varepsilon}n^{1/3}\log n\right) = O\left(\frac{1}{\varepsilon}n^{1/3}\log n\right)$$

As we discuss in Lemma 3, if $x \in L_{REV}$, then there are $i \in \mathcal{I}_n$ and $j \in \mathcal{J}_n$ such that $x^i = \tilde{x}^j$ for any choice of $(p_1, \ldots, p_m)$. Therefore, the algorithm finds the required i and j and returns the correct answer with an error probability at most 0.1 because of the error probability for Grover's search algorithm.

Assume that x is $\varepsilon \cdot n$ far from any word from the language L_{REV}. In other words, $\text{REV}_{n,\varepsilon}(x) = 0$. Let us show that with high probability we cannot find the i and j indexes.

For fixed j and i, the probability of obtaining a position k of equal symbols, $x_k^i = \tilde{x}_k^j$, is $(1-\varepsilon)$. The total error probability that is the probability of obtaining all m equal positions is

$$(1-\varepsilon)^m = (1-\varepsilon)^{\frac{2}{\varepsilon}\log_2 n} = \left((1-\varepsilon)^{\frac{1}{\varepsilon}}\right)^{2\log_2 n} < \left(\frac{1}{2}\right)^{2\log_2 n} = \left(2^{\log_2 n}\right)^{-2} = n^{-2}.$$

Here $(1-\varepsilon)^{\frac{1}{\varepsilon}} < \frac{1}{2}$ for any ε such that $0 < \varepsilon < 1$.

For all pairs of i and j, the probability of success on all pairs of strings is $(1 - n^{-2})^{n^{1/3} \cdot n^{2/3}} > \frac{3}{4}$ for $n \geq 4$ because $\lim_{n\to\infty}(1 - n^{-2})^n = 1$. So, with probability $\frac{3}{4}$ all elements in the search space of Grover's Search are 0. If the whole input contains only zeroes, then Grover's search algorithm returns 0 with probability 1. So, the Total success probability in that case is at least $\frac{3}{4}$. The error probability is at most $\frac{1}{4}$.   □

5   Conclusion

In this paper, we present a quantum property testing algorithm for recognizing the context-free language L_{REV} that has $O(\frac{1}{\varepsilon}n^{1/3}\log n)$ query complexity. It is better than classical counterparts that have $\Theta^*(\sqrt{n})$ query complexity. At the same time, we do not know a quantum lower bound in the property testing setting. We have a feeling that it is $\Omega(n^{1/3})$.

At the same time, in the general setting, the picture is almost clear. Classical query complexity is $\Theta(n)$, and quantum query complexity is $\Theta^*(\sqrt{n})$. So, we almost obtain quadratic speed-up. The open question is to develop a quantum algorithm that reaches the lower bound without additional log factors.

The third open question is to investigate other context-free languages for quantum property testing.

Acknowledgements. We thank Frédéric Magniez and Yixin Shen for useful discussions.

This paper has been supported by the Kazan Federal University Strategic Academic Leadership Program ("PRIORITY-2030").

References

1. Aaronson, S., Grier, D., Schaeffer, L.: A quantum query complexity trichotomy for regular languages. In: 2019 IEEE 60th Annual Symposium on Foundations of Computer Science (FOCS), pp. 942–965. IEEE (2019)
2. Ablayev, F., Ablayev, M., Huang, J.Z., Khadiev, K., Salikhova, N., Wu, D.: On quantum methods for machine learning problems Part I: quantum tools. Big Data Mining Anal. **3**(1), 41–55 (2019)
3. Ablayev, F., Ablayev, M., Khadiev, K., Salihova, N., Vasiliev, A.: Quantum algorithms for string processing. In: Badriev, I.B., Banderov, V., Lapin, S.A. (eds.) Mesh Methods for Boundary-Value Problems and Applications. LNCSE, vol. 141, pp. 1–14. Springer, Cham (2022). https://doi.org/10.1007/978-3-030-87809-2_1
4. Akmal, S., Jin, C.: Near-optimal quantum algorithms for string problems. In: Proceedings of the 2022 Annual ACM-SIAM Symposium on Discrete Algorithms (SODA), pp. 2791–2832. SIAM (2022)
5. Alon, N., Krivelevich, M., Newman, I., Szegedy, M.: Regular languages are testable with a constant number of queries. SIAM J. Comput. **30**(6), 1842–1862 (2001)
6. Ambainis, A.: Understanding quantum algorithms via query complexity. In: Proceedings of the International Congress of Mathematicians 2018, vol. 4, pp. 3283–3304 (2018)
7. Ambainis, A., et al.: Quantum lower and upper bounds for 2D-grid and Dyck language. In: 45th International Symposium on Mathematical Foundations of Computer Science (MFCS 2020). Leibniz International Proceedings in Informatics (LIPIcs), vol. 170, pp. 8:1–8:14 (2020)
8. Ambainis, A., et al.: Quantum bounds for 2d-grid and Dyck language. Quantum Inf. Process. **22**(5), 194 (2023)
9. Arunachalam, S., de Wolf, R.: Optimizing the number of gates in quantum search. Quantum Inf. Comput. **17**(3&4), 251–261 (2017)
10. Arvind, V., Schuler, R.: The quantum query complexity of 0-1 knapsack and associated claw problems. In: Ibaraki, T., Katoh, N., Ono, H. (eds.) ISAAC 2003. LNCS, vol. 2906, pp. 168–177. Springer, Heidelberg (2003). https://doi.org/10.1007/978-3-540-24587-2_19
11. Barr, K., Fleming, T., Kendon, V.: Simulation methods for quantum walks on graphs applied to formal language recognition. Nat. Comput. **14**(1), 145–156 (2015)
12. Bennett, C.H., Bernstein, E., Brassard, G., Vazirani, U.: Strengths and weaknesses of quantum computing. SIAM J. Comput. **26**(5), 1510–1523 (1997)
13. Black, P.E.: Dictionary of algorithms and data structures— NIST. Technical report (1998)
14. Boyer, M., Brassard, G., Høyer, P., Tapp, A.: Tight bounds on quantum searching. Fortschr. Phys. **46**(4–5), 493–505 (1998)
15. Brass, P.: Advanced Data Structures, vol. 193. Cambridge University Press, Cambridge (2008)
16. Brassard, G., Hoyer, P., Tapp, A.: Quantum algorithm for the collision problem. arXiv preprint quant-ph/9705002 (1997)
17. Buhrman, H., Fortnow, L., Newman, I., Röhrig, H.: Quantum property testing. SIAM J. Comput. **37**(5), 1387–1400 (2008)
18. Buhrman, H., Patro, S., Speelman, F.: A framework of quantum strong exponential-time hypotheses. In: 38th International Symposium on Theoretical Aspects of Computer Science (STACS 2021). Leibniz International Proceedings in Informatics (LIPIcs), vol. 187, pp. 19:1–19:19 (2021)

19. Childs, A.M., Kothari, R., Kovacs-Deak, M., Sundaram, A., Wang, D.: Quantum divide and conquer. arXiv preprint arXiv:2210.06419 (2022)
20. Cormen, T.H., Leiserson, C.E., Rivest, R.L., Stein, C.: Introduction to Algorithms. McGraw-Hill, New York (2001)
21. De La Briandais, R.: File searching using variable length keys. In: Papers presented at the the 3–5 March 1959, Western Joint Computer Conference, pp. 295–298. ACM (1959)
22. Diffie, W., Hellman, M.E.: Special feature exhaustive cryptanalysis of the NBS data encryption standard. Computer $10(6)$, 74–84 (1977)
23. Fischer, E.: The art of uninformed decisions: a primer to property testing. In: Current Trends in Theoretical Computer Science: The Challenge of the New Century Vol 1: Algorithms and Complexity Vol 2: Formal Models and Semantics, pp. 229–263. World Scientific (2004)
24. Goldreich, O., Goldwasser, S., Ron, D.: Property testing and its connection to learning and approximation. J. ACM (JACM) $45(4)$, 653–750 (1998)
25. Grover, L.K.: A fast quantum mechanical algorithm for database search. In: Proceedings of the Twenty-Eighth Annual ACM Symposium on Theory of Computing, pp. 212–219. ACM (1996)
26. Grover, L.K.: Trade-offs in the quantum search algorithm. Phys. Rev. A $66(5)$, 052314 (2002)
27. Jordan, S.: Quantum algorithms zoo (2023). http://quantumalgorithmzoo.org/
28. Kapralov, R., Khadiev, K., Mokut, J., Shen, Y., Yagafarov, M.: Fast classical and quantum algorithms for online k-server problem on trees. In: CEUR Workshop Proceedings, vol. 3072, pp. 287–301 (2022)
29. Khadiev, K., Ilikaev, A.: Quantum algorithms for the most frequently string search, intersection of two string sequences and sorting of strings problems. In: International Conference on Theory and Practice of Natural Computing, pp. 234–245 (2019)
30. Khadiev, K.: Lecture notes on quantum algorithms. arXiv preprint arXiv:2212.14205 (2022)
31. Khadiev, K., Bosch-Machado, C.M., Chen, Z., Wu, J.: Quantum algorithms for the shortest common superstring and text assembling problems. Quantum Inf. Comput. $24(3–4)$, 267–294 (2024)
32. Khadiev, K., Enikeeva, S.: Quantum version of self-balanced binary search tree with strings as keys and applications. In: International Conference on Micro- and Nano-Electronics 2021, vol. 12157, pp. 587–594. International Society for Optics and Photonics, SPIE (2022)
33. Khadiev, K., Ilikaev, A., Vihrovs, J.: Quantum algorithms for some strings problems based on quantum string comparator. Mathematics $10(3)$, 377 (2022)
34. Khadiev, K., Kravchenko, D.: Quantum algorithm for dyck language with multiple types of brackets. In: Unconventional Computation and Natural Computation, pp. 68–83 (2021)
35. Khadiev, K., Machado, C.M.B.: Quantum algorithm for the shortest superstring problem. In: International Conference on Micro- and Nano-Electronics 2021, vol. 12157, pp. 579 – 586. International Society for Optics and Photonics, SPIE (2022)
36. Khadiev, K., Remidovskii, V.: Classical and quantum algorithms for assembling a text from a dictionary. Nonlinear Phenomena Complex Syst. $24(3)$, 207–221 (2021)
37. Khadiev, K., Remidovskii, V.: Classical and quantum algorithms for constructing text from dictionary problem. Nat. Comput. $20(4)$, 713–724 (2021)
38. Khadiev, K., Savelyev, N., Ziatdinov, M., Melnikov, D.: Noisy tree data structures and quantum applications. Mathematics $11(22)$, 4707 (2023)

39. Knuth, D.: Searching and sorting, the art of computer programming, vol. 3 (1973)
40. Knuth, D.E., Morris, J.H., Jr., Pratt, V.R.: Fast pattern matching in strings. SIAM J. Comput. **6**(2), 323–350 (1977)
41. Le Gall, F., Seddighin, S.: Quantum meets fine-grained complexity: sublinear time quantum algorithms for string problems. Algorithmica **85**, 1–36 (2022)
42. Le Gall, F., Seddighin, S.: Quantum meets fine-grained complexity: sublinear time quantum algorithms for string problems. In: 13th Innovations in Theoretical Computer Science Conference (ITCS 2022). Schloss Dagstuhl-Leibniz-Zentrum für Informatik (2022)
43. Montanaro, A.: Quantum pattern matching fast on average. Algorithmica **77**(1), 16–39 (2017)
44. Montanaro, A., de Wolf, R.: A survey of quantum property testing. Theory of Computing, pp. 1–81 (2016)
45. Newman, I.: Testing of function that have small width branching programs. In: Proceedings 41st Annual Symposium on Foundations of Computer Science, pp. 251–258. IEEE (2000)
46. Nielsen, M.A., Chuang, I.L.: Quantum Computation and Quantum Information. Cambridge University Press, Cambridge (2010)
47. Parnas, M., Ron, D., Rubinfeld, R.: Testing membership in parenthesis languages. Random Struct. Algor. **22**(1), 98–138 (2003)
48. Rajasekaran, S.: Handbook of Randomized Computing, vol. 9. Springer, New York (2001)
49. Ramesh, H., Vinay, V.: String matching in $O(\sqrt{n}+\sqrt{m})$ quantum time. J. Discrete Algorithms **1**(1), 103–110 (2003)
50. Rubinfeld, R., Sudan, M.: Robust characterizations of polynomials with applications to program testing. SIAM J. Comput. **25**(2), 252–271 (1996)
51. de Wolf, R.: Quantum Computing and Communication Complexity. University of Amsterdam (2001)

On the Simulation Power of Surface Chemical Reaction Networks

Yi-Xuan Lee and Ho-Lin Chen[✉]

National Taiwan University, Taipei, Taiwan
{r12921065,holinchen}@ntu.edu.tw

Abstract. The Chemical Reaction Network (CRN) is a well-studied model that describes the interaction of molecules in well-mixed solutions. In 2014, Qian and Winfree [21] proposed the abstract surface chemical reaction network model (sCRN), which takes advantage of spatial separation by placing molecules on a structured surface, limiting the interaction between molecules. In this model, molecules can only react with their immediate neighbors. Many follow-up works study the computational and pattern-construction power of sCRNs.

In this work, our goal is to describe the power of sCRN by relating the model to other well-studied models in distributed computation. Our main result is to show that, given the same initial configuration, sCRN, affinity-strengthening tile automata, cellular automata, and amoebot can all simulate each other (up to unavoidable rotation and reflection of the pattern). One of our techniques is coloring on-the-fly, which allows all molecules in sCRN to have a global orientation.

Keywords: Surface chemical reaction networks · Simulation · Tile Automata

1 Introduction

The Chemical Reaction Network (CRN) is a well-studied model that describes the interaction of molecules in well-mixed solutions. The computational power of CRNs has been studied in various settings, including rate-dependent [13,16,23] and rate-independent models [10,11]. In this study, rather than considering molecules in a well-mixed solution, we study the scenarios in which molecules have designated locations and can only react with other molecules in their vicinity.

In 2014, Qian and Winfree [21] proposed the abstract surface chemical reaction network model (sCRN), which takes advantage of spatial separation by placing molecules on a structured surface, limiting the interaction between molecules. In this model, molecules can only react with their immediate neighbors. Qian and Winfree [21] also proposed an implementation of an arbitrary programmable

This work is supported by NSTC (Taiwan) grant number 110-2223-E-002-006-MY3.

sCRN using DNA strand displacement. Furthermore, they demonstrate the computational power of sCRN by building a continuous active logic circuit and cellular automata in a parallel and scalable way.

A follow-up work by Clamons *et al.* [12] discuss the computational and pattern-creation power of sCRNs. They extend the idea of [21] to achieve local synchronicity on a 2-dimensional square lattice, with an initial pattern providing local orientation. This requires tethering the molecules precisely on the surface. On the other hand, they ask whether we can achieve complex spatial arrangements from relatively simple initial conditions, which rely on the ability to control molecular interactions precisely. Some of the open questions are solved in [2], which focused on the complexity of deciding the reachability from a given configuration to another given configuration. Brailovskaya et al. [7] showed that feed-forward circuits can be constructed in sCRN using only swap reactions. In this work, our main goal is to study the computational power of sCRN given a uniform surface with no local orientation.

We seek to describe the power of sCRN by relating the model to other well-studied models in distributed computation, such as abstract tile assembly model (aTAM) [1,15,22,24], cellular automata [6,17,19], and tile automata [3,8,9]. These models have been shown to be Turing universal [8,14,24] and can perform a large variety of tasks, including computation and pattern formation (e.g., [3, 6,20]). We further compare sCRN to the amoebot model, where programmable matter has the ability to move. We use the concept of "simulation" based on the definition given in [18] with some necessary modifications. Intuitively, if two models can simulate each other, they can perform the same tasks in the same way (e.g., create the same pattern in the same ordering).

1.1   Our Results

In this work, our main result is to show that, given the same initial configuration, sCRN, affinity-strengthening tile automata, cellular automata, and amoebot can all simulate each other (up to unavoidable rotation and reflection of the pattern). The results are listed in Table 1, where $\mathcal{M}_S, \mathcal{M}_T$ represent different models. We ask whether $\mathcal{M}_S$ can simulate $\mathcal{M}_T$ (denoted by $\mathcal{M}_S \triangleright \mathcal{M}_T$), and vice versa (denoted by $\mathcal{M}_T \triangleright \mathcal{M}_S$).

The main challenge for this simulation is that sCRN does not have predefined directions. Unlike the tile automata model (and all other models simulated), which has a given direction, the molecules in sCRN do not have the ability to differentiate their neighbors in different directions. We solve this problem by providing a coloring to the surface such that each molecule has four neighbors with different colors. Furthermore, in the simulation of $\mathcal{M}_T$ by $\mathcal{M}_S$, we want to make the behavior of $\mathcal{M}_S$ to be as close to $\mathcal{M}_T$ as possible. When $\mathcal{M}_T$ enters a terminal configuration, $\mathcal{M}_S$ should also enter a terminal configuration without using too much extra space. Therefore, instead of coloring the whole surface, we carefully perform the coloring on the fly. A molecule is colored only when molecules in its vicinity are about to participate in a reaction. This coloring technique can be used in the simulation of all different models, so we describe this coloring technique separately in Sect. 4.

In Sect. 4, we show that unit-seeded sCRN (s-sCRN) can simulate unit-seeded, directed sCRN (s-d-sCRN) up to rotation and reflection, while simulating s-sCRN with s-d-sCRN is trivial. In Sect. 5, we show that s-d-sCRN and unit-seeded tile automata with affinity-strengthening rules (s-as-TA) can simulate each other, and the simulation of aTAM by s-d-sCRN follows. It is easy to show that aTAM cannot simulate sCRN since the reactions are not reversible. In Sect. 6, we show that d-sCRN and asynchronous cellular automata (async-CA) with non-deterministic local function can simulate each other. We also show that clockwise sCRN (c-sCRN) and amoebot can simulate each other. Notice that, when we simulate s-d-sCRN with s-sCRN, we are essentially giving a random global orientation to the surface. When simulating unit-seeded models, the orientation of the seed can be included in the coloring process and thus the terminal configuration of the sCRN is always the same as the system simulated, up to rotation and reflection. On the other hand, cellular automata and amoebots have complicated initial patterns. Therefore, simulating cellular automata and amoebots by s-sCRN (undirected) will inevitably rotate or flip the initial configuration before the simulation starts, unless the direction used in the cellular automata and amoebots is also encoded in the initial configuration of s-sCRN.

Table 1. Cross-Model Simulation Results.

$\mathcal{M}_S$	$\mathcal{M}_T$	$\mathcal{M}_S \triangleright \mathcal{M}_T$	$\mathcal{M}_T \triangleright \mathcal{M}_S$	REF
s-sCRN	s-d-sCRN	✓ (up to rotation and reflection)	✓	Theorem 1
s-d-sCRN	aTAM	✓	✗	Corollary 1
s-d-sCRN	s-as-TA	✓	✓	Theorem 2
d-sCRN	async-CA	✓	✓	Theorem 3, 4
c-sCRN	amoebot	✓	✓	Theorem 5, 6

2   Models

2.1   Surface Chemical Reaction Network

The model of **surface chemical reaction network (sCRN)** was originally proposed by Qian and Winfree [21]. To align the underlying structures of all models and to describe the simulation problem, which is highly relative to the transformation of patterns in each system, we use a slightly different definition given in [2]. In particular, they define the configuration and reachability in sCRN. To make the simulations simpler, we also propose in Sect. 2.1.1 the directed sCRN as a variation of sCRN. We now give a brief description.

A surface chemical reaction network (Q, R) consists of an underlying *surface* L, a finite set of species Q, and a set of *reactions* R. In general, the surface L is an arbitrary planar graph, but we restrict it to the square lattice (viewed as $\mathbb{Z}^2$) and the triangular lattice with nearest neighbor connectivity in this paper. The *cells* are vertices of L, and each cell u is associated with a species $\sigma(u)$ in Q. For the purpose of defining the simulation between computational models in Sect. 3.2, we sometimes call the species "states" of a cell, and Q the set of "states". A *configuration* is a mapping from each cell to a state in Q. Every reaction $r \in R$ has one of the following two forms: $(A, B, C, D \in Q)$

- *Unimolecular reaction* $A \to B$. A cell in state A can change its state to B itself. Or,
- *Bimolecular reaction* $A+B \to C+D$ where A, B, C, D not necessarily distinct, meaning that when two species A and B are adjacent, their states could be replaced with C and D respectively and simultaneously. Note that the orientation of A and B does not matter, but the order cannot be changed (state A must turn into C, and B must turn into D).

In this paper, we consider the sCRN $\Gamma = (Q, S, R)$ with a specified initial configuration S. We further define the **unit-seeded sCRN (s-sCRN)** where the initial configuration S maps every cell to a *blank state* $\mathcal{O} \in Q$ except for a special cell mapped to a *seed state* s. In s-sCRN we don't allow any reactions s.t. $\mathcal{O}$ is the only reactant when considering such unit-seed system. i.e. $\mathcal{O} \to A$ or $\mathcal{O} + \mathcal{O} \to A + B$ is illegal here.

2.1.1 Surface Chemical Reaction Network with Orientation

For the purpose of our simulation, we introduce and investigate two variations of the sCRN model: the **directed sCRN (d-sCRN)** and the **clockwise sCRN (c-sCRN)**. Directed sCRN provides each bimolecular reaction with a global direction $d \in \{\uparrow, \to, \downarrow, \leftarrow\}$. We write (A, B, C, D, d) to indicate that, when $d = \uparrow$ (resp. $\to, \downarrow, \leftarrow$), two adjacent species A and B could turn into species C and D' simultaneously if B is in the North (resp. East, South, West) of A, where "North" means the $(0, 1)$ direction in $\mathbb{Z}^2$. Notice that $\downarrow, \leftarrow$ are actually redundant since the bimolecular reactions are symmetric for all pairs of adjacent species; we use these notations just for convenience when describing protocols in Sect. 4. We use $(A, B, C, D, d)^{-1}$ to represent the reverse reaction (C, D, A, B, d). For a unimolecular reaction such that species A can turn into B, we simply use the notation $(A, B, \odot)$. Clockwise sCRN, defined on the triangular lattice, provides each bimolecular reaction with a local direction $d \in \{0, \cdots, 5\}$ such that (A, B, C, D, d) represents the reaction where B is in the d-th direction in the view of A. The only common knowledge is that for every species, d increases in the clockwise order.

2.1.2   Reachability and Termination We first define the *one-step reach-ability*. For any two configurations α and β, we say that β is reachable from α in one step if there exists a single cell or a pair of adjacent cells such that performing some $r \in R$ on these cells yields β. Write $\alpha \rightarrow^1_\Gamma \beta$.

Let $\rightarrow_\Gamma$ be the reflexive transitive closure of $\rightarrow^1_\Gamma$, a configuration β is *reachable* from another configuration α if $\alpha \rightarrow_\Gamma \beta$. That is, β is reachable from α in one or more steps. A configuration α is *Γ-reachable* (or *reachable* when Γ is clear from the context) if $S \rightarrow_\Gamma \alpha$, and write $\mathcal{A}(\Gamma)$ to denote the set of all Γ-reachable configurations. We say α is *Γ-terminal* if α is Γ-reachable and there exists no configuration $\beta \neq \alpha$ which is Γ-reachable from α. We denote the set of Γ-terminal configurations by $\mathcal{A}_*(\Gamma)$.

2.2   Tile Automata

The tile automata model, combining *2-handed assembly model* with local state-change rules between pairs of adjacent tiles, is a marriage between tile-based self-assembly and asynchronous cellular automata. It was first proposed by Chalk *et al.* [9] and we follow their model definition. Variations like affinity strengthening and unit-seeded system were considered in [8] and [3] respectively. In this paper, we restrict ourselves on the system with both constraints, and slightly modify the description of single tile attachment to align with the one used in aTAM model proposed by Winfree and Rothemund [22]. We include a brief description here to make this paper self-contained.

Similar to how we define a tile in the tile-based self-assembly, here a *tile t* is a unit square located at $\mathbb{Z}^2$, each assigned a *state* $\sigma(t)$ from the finite state set Q. Similar to aTAM, we use null $\in Q$ to represent the lack of any other tile. An *affinity function* $g : Q^2 \times D \rightarrow \mathbb{N}$, where $D = \{\perp, \vdash\}$, represents the *affinity strength* between two states with relative orientation $d \in D$. To describe it explicitly, the affinity strength between two adjacent tiles t_1, t_2 located at

$$(x_1, y_1), (x_2, y_2) \text{ is } \begin{cases} g(\sigma(t_1), \sigma(t_2), \perp), & \text{if } y_1 > y_2 \\ g(\sigma(t_2), \sigma(t_1), \perp), & \text{if } y_1 < y_2 \\ g(\sigma(t_1), \sigma(t_2), \vdash), & \text{if } x_1 < x_2 \\ g(\sigma(t_2), \sigma(t_1), \vdash), & \text{if } x_1 > x_2 \end{cases}.$$

And the affinity strength between a null tile and any other tile is 0.

A *configuration* is a mapping α from $\mathbb{Z}^2$ to Q. Let $Q^\dagger = Q \setminus \{\text{null}\}$. For a configuration α, if the region that mapped to $Q^\dagger$ is connected, we call α an *assembly*. In general, given a *stability threshold* τ, an assembly can break into two pieces along a cut if the total affinity strength on this cut $< \tau$. On the other hand, two assembly could be combined along a border whose total strength sums to at least τ. A special case is the attachment of a single tile attachment. The formal definitions are omitted due to space constraints.

In this paper we only consider the *affinity-strengthening rule* s.t. for each transition rule that takes a state σ^1_x to σ^2_x, it must satisfy that the affinity strength with all other states could only increase. In other words, for every $\sigma \in Q$, $g(\sigma^1_x, \sigma, d) \leq g(\sigma^2_x, \sigma, d) \ \forall d \in D$. Notice that with the affinity-strengthening rule, any tile that has attached to a configuration can not fall off. This implies that the whole assembly is unbreakable after any state transition.

Like asynchronous cellular automata, tile automata has a local state changing rule. The *transition rule* r is a 5-tuple $(\sigma_x^1, \sigma_y^1, \sigma_x^2, \sigma_y^2, d)$ where $\sigma_x^1, \sigma_y^1, \sigma_x^2, \sigma_y^2 \in Q$ and $d \in D$. It means that if states σ_x^1 and σ_y^1 are adjacent with relative orientation d, they can simultaneously turn into state σ_x^2, σ_y^2 respectively. In this paper, we allow the transition rule to be nondeterministic, i.e. there may be two rules $(\sigma_x^1, \sigma_y^1, \sigma_x^2, \sigma_y^2, d)$ and $(\sigma_x^1, \sigma_y^1, \sigma_x^3, \sigma_y^3, d)$ s.t. $(\sigma_x^2, \sigma_y^2) \neq (\sigma_x^3, \sigma_y^3)$.

A **tile automata system (TA)** is a 6-tuple $\Gamma = (Q, S, I, g, R, \tau)$ where Q is a finite set of states, g is an affinity function, S is the initial configuration, R is a set of transition rules, and τ is the stability threshold. We assume that initially, there is a set of tiles whose states belong to the *initial state* $I \subseteq Q$ that could be used in attachment. A configuration β is reachable from α in one step (denoted as $\alpha \rightarrow_\Gamma^1 \beta$) if and only if β is formed by applying some transition rule to α or by an attachment of a tile in I. The *reachability* $\rightarrow_\Gamma$ is defined the same as in Sect. 2.1.2. Also, we follow the definition of terminal set $\mathcal{A}_*(\Gamma)$ in Sect. 2.1.2 with an additional requirement that for any $\alpha \in \mathcal{A}_*(\Gamma)$, α must be τ-stable.

We restrict ourselves to the **unit-seeded TA with affinity-strengthening rule (s-as-TA)** in this paper. The term "unit-seeded" means that there exists a single seed tile s s.t. $S = s_{(0,0)}$ and only single tile attachment is allowed.

3 Simulation

Our simulation definition is adapted from the one used in [4,18]. Let $\mathcal{S}, \mathcal{T} \in$ {sCRN, aTAM, s-as-TA, async-CA, amoebot} be two systems in different models.

3.1 Representation Function

Let $Q_{\mathcal{S}}, Q_{\mathcal{T}}$ be the state sets of $\mathcal{S}, \mathcal{T}$ respectively. A *state representation function* $\mathcal{R}$ from $Q_{\mathcal{S}}$ to $Q_{\mathcal{T}}$ is a function which takes as input a state of $\mathcal{S}$, and returns either information about the state of $\mathcal{T}$ or UND (which implies the image of $\mathcal{R}$ on this state is undefined).

Let $\mathbf{v}$ be the coordinates of a node in the underlying lattice L. Let α be a configuration of $\mathcal{S}$, and let $\alpha(\mathbf{v})$ be the state of α on the node $\mathbf{v}$. A *representation function* $\mathcal{R}^*$ from $\mathcal{S}$ to $\mathcal{T}$ takes as input an entire configuration α of $\mathcal{S}$ and apply $\mathcal{R}$ to every state of α, and returns either a corresponding configuration of $\mathcal{T}$, or UND if there is any state contained in α that mapped to UND.

Note that our definition is more relax than that in [4,18]. In particular we allow UND to be the image of R, which is motivated by the simulation definition in [5]. The relaxation is necessary because when simulating sCRN by non-deterministic async-CA, it is possible that the sCRN perform a bimolecular reaction and hence two adjacent states A, B change simultaneously. While in the non-deterministic async-CA, it can be one cell performing state transition at a time. Suppose A change its state first, so the other cell B must be mapped to different states before and after A performing state transition. Another way of relaxing this definition to fit in with the limitation of non-deterministic async-CA is to let the representation function $\mathcal{R}$ map a neighborhood of CA to a state in sCRN, but this definition is rather non-intuitive in other models and the details are omitted here. Notice that except for the simulation of sCRN by non-deterministic acync-CA and the simulation between sCRN and amoebot system, we don't need this relaxation.

3.2 Simulation Definition

Roughly speaking, if we say that S simulates T, we want the pattern of S to evolve like that in T. Intuitively, for any sequence of configuration changes $\alpha \to \beta$ in T, there must exist a sequence of configuration changes $\alpha' \to \beta'$ s.t. α', β' are mapped to α, β respectively. On the other hand, for any $\alpha' \to \beta'$ in T, it is also required that there is a sequence of configurations that links the images of α', β' under R^*. i.e. $R^*(\alpha') \to R^*(\beta')$.

Definition 1. *We say that S and T have equivalent productions (under $\mathcal{R}$), and we write $S \Leftrightarrow_\mathcal{R} T$ if the following conditions hold:*

1. $\{\mathcal{R}^*(\alpha')|\alpha' \in \mathcal{A}(S)\} = \mathcal{A}(T) \cup \{UND\}$.
2. $\{\mathcal{R}^*(\alpha')|\alpha' \in \mathcal{A}_*(S)\} = \mathcal{A}_*(T)$.

Definition 2. *We say that T follows S (under $\mathcal{R}$) and we write $T \dashv_\mathcal{R} S$ if, $\alpha' \to_S \beta'$ for some $\alpha', \beta' \in \mathcal{A}(S)$ implies that $\mathcal{R}^*(\alpha') \to_T \mathcal{R}^*(\beta')$ or, either $\mathcal{R}^*(\alpha') = UND$ or $\mathcal{R}^*(\beta') = UND$.*

To be more rigorous, we want that for every configuration $\alpha \in T$, there exists a set of reachable configurations in S that are mapped to α (under $\mathcal{R}^*$), and from each of the configurations in the set, we can simulate all possible next configurations of α.

Definition 3. *We say that S models T (under $\mathcal{R}$) and we write $S \models_\mathcal{R} T$, if for every $\alpha \in \mathcal{A}(T)$, there exists $\Pi \subset \mathcal{A}(S)$ where $\Pi \neq \emptyset$ and $\mathcal{R}^*(\alpha') = \alpha \; \forall \alpha' \in \Pi$, such that for every $\beta \in \mathcal{A}(T)$ where $\alpha \to \beta$, the followings hold:*

1. *for every $\alpha' \in \Pi$, there exists $\beta' \in \mathcal{A}(S)$ where $\mathcal{R}^*(\beta') = \beta$ and $\alpha' \to_S \beta'$.*
2. *for every $\alpha'' \in \mathcal{A}(S)$ where $\alpha'' \to_S \beta'$ s.t. $\mathcal{R}^*(\alpha'') = \alpha$ and $\mathcal{R}^*(\beta') = \beta$, there exists $\alpha' \in \Pi$ such that $\alpha' \to_S \alpha''$.*

Definition 4. *We say that S simulates T (under $\mathcal{R}$) if $S \Leftrightarrow_\mathcal{R} T$, $T \dashv_\mathcal{R} S$, and $S \models_\mathcal{R} T$.*

4 Simulation of Unit-Seeded Directed sCRN by Unit-Seeded sCRN (up to Rotation and Reflection)

In this section, we show that an unit-seeded sCRN can simulate an unit-seeded directed sCRN up to rotation and reflection.

Theorem 1. *Given a unit-seeded directed sCRN $\Gamma = (Q, S, R)$, there exists a unit-seeded sCRN $\Gamma' = (Q', S', R')$ which simulates Γ up to rotation and reflection.*

4.1   Simulation Overview

Given a s-d-sCRN $\Gamma = (Q, R, S)$, we want to construct a s-sCRN $\Gamma' = (Q', R', S')$ to simulate Γ. For bimolecular reactions with a specified direction d, it is required that each species has a common knowledge of a global orientation. We achieve this by using a 2-hop coloring. The main idea is to partition the plane into blocks of 9 cells, and color a block with ordering numbers $1, \cdots, 9$ if and only if a reaction is about to happen on it. The simulation consists of the following three parts:

- $\mathtt{Determine\_Global\_Orientation}$: In this protocol, we color the seed and the eight cells around it with $\{1, \cdots, 9\}$.
- $\mathtt{Growing\_Reactions}$: If a reaction is possible on a specific cell, we first color the eight cells around it to make sure the global orientation is clear for that cell, and then perform the reaction.
- $\mathtt{State\_Transitions}$: Simulate any reactions at a cell who has already known the global orientation.

To dive into the details, we first define the *block* of a cell u, $\mathcal{B}(u) = \{v : ||v - u||_\infty \le 1\}$, to be the set of 9 cells around u. And sometimes we use the block of a species ρ, write $\mathcal{B}(\rho)$ (with abuse of notation), to mean the block of the position of ρ. Define $Q^\dagger = Q \setminus \{\mathcal{O}\}$. For any reaction of the form $(A, \mathcal{O}, B, C, d)$ where $A, B, C \in Q^\dagger$, we call it the *growing reaction*, and we denote the set of growing reactions in R by R_g.

We now sketch the idea of our simulation. Let $S' = S$ where S maps every cell to the blank state $\mathcal{O}$ except for a special cell that mapped to a seed state, say s. In the first part $\mathtt{Determine\_Global\_Orientation}$, we color $\mathcal{B}(s)$ with $\{1, \cdots, 9\}$ to give an orientation to the system. And in the second part $\mathtt{Growing\_Reactions}$, we ensure that in the simulation process of any growing reaction $(A, \mathcal{O}, B, C, d)$, the state transition can be performed only if a coloring has been given to $\mathcal{B}(\mathcal{O})$. This provides the information of the determined global orientation for the simulation of future reactions. The last part $\mathtt{State\_Transitions}$ gives the reactions we need for simulating reactions in a complete coloring configuration, which is very straightforward. We construct Γ' by adding states and reactions to Q' and R' successively. The full description of the protocols and more details are provided in the following paragraphs.

$\mathtt{Determine\_Global\_Orientation}$. This protocol aims to color all cells in the block of the seed so that the coloring can be extended to the entire surface and used as the global orientation. Let $S' = S$, and let s be the special seed state of S (and also S'). We color $\mathcal{B}(s)$ with $1, \cdots, 9$ and use $\mathcal{O}^i$ to denote the colored cell, where the superscript $i \in \{1, \cdots, 9\}$ is the color it receives.

Initially, we add the reaction $s + \mathcal{O} \to 0 + 1$ to R'. Then we build the block of 0 by forming X, Y toward each direction of $0, 1$ respectively. When X, Y meet each other, they perform state transition to $(2, 3)$ respectively, meaning that they are parallel and adjacent to $(0, 1)$. From 2, we grow Z toward the remaining two directions. The first to meet X perform $Z + X \to 4 + 5$, and the other, when meeting 5, begins to color the block of 0 in either clockwise or counterclockwise order depending on which side of 5 it is on. Except for s, which is to be turned into s^5, other cells receive $\mathcal{O}^i$ where i depends on their positions. After the coloring is complete, we need to clear off the redundant states Y, Z grown outside $\mathcal{B}(s^5)$. So we also have $\mathcal{O}^8 + Y \to \mathcal{O}^8 + \mathcal{O}$, $\mathcal{O}^6 + Z \to \mathcal{O}^6 + \mathcal{O}$, and $\mathcal{O}^4 + Z \to \mathcal{O}^4 + \mathcal{O}$ in R'. In total we must have the following reactions in R':

1. $s + \mathcal{O} \to 0 + 1$.   ▷ Initiate the coloring.
2. $0 + \mathcal{O} \to 0 + X$, $1 + \mathcal{O} \to 1 + Y$, $X + Y \to 2 + 3$.
3. $2 + \mathcal{O} \to 2 + Z$, $Z + X \to 4 + 5$, $Z + 5 \to \mathcal{O}^1 + \mathcal{O}^2$.
4. $\mathcal{O}^2 + 4 \to \mathcal{O}^2 + \mathcal{O}^3$, $\mathcal{O}^3 + 2 \to \mathcal{O}^3 + \mathcal{O}^6$, $\mathcal{O}^6 + 3 \to \mathcal{O}^6 + \mathcal{O}^9$, $\mathcal{O}^9 + 1 \to \mathcal{O}^9 + \mathcal{O}^8$, $\mathcal{O}^8 + 3 \to \mathcal{O}^8 + \mathcal{O}^7$, $\mathcal{O}^7 + 2 \to \mathcal{O}^7 + \mathcal{O}^4$, $\mathcal{O}^4 + 0 \to \mathcal{O}^4 + s^5$.
                                        ▷ s^5 is the new seed with its block colored.
5. $\mathcal{O}^8 + Y \to \mathcal{O}^8 + \mathcal{O}$, $\mathcal{O}^6 + Z \to \mathcal{O}^6 + \mathcal{O}$, $\mathcal{O}^4 + Z \to \mathcal{O}^4 + \mathcal{O}$.
                                                 ▷ Clear off the rubbish.

Figure 1 shows an evolution when we have this set of reactions.

Notice that the simulation system must be indifferent up to rotation and reflection since any starting reaction $s + \mathcal{O} \to A + B$ looks the same for s in its four directions, and then any reaction can be perform symmetrically around $\overline{AB}$. Therefore, "simulation up to rotation and reflection" is a necessary relaxation.

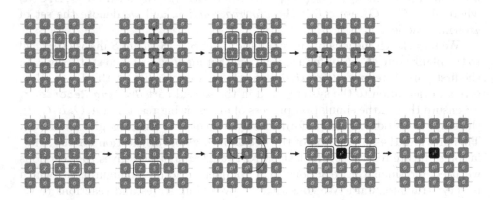

Fig. 1. Coloring the block of the seed by `Determine_Global_Orientation`

Growing_Reactions. For any growing reactions of this form $(A, \mathcal{O}, B, C, d)$, we first give a coloring on $\mathcal{B}(\mathcal{O})$ and then perform the reaction. Before giving the protocol, there are some notations we need to define first. We use ψ^i to represent the colored species, where the superscript i is the color of that species. In the simulation, we have 8 kinds of states in Q', which are introduced in detail later:

$$\{\mathcal{O}\}, \{\mathcal{O}^i : i \in [9]\}, \{\sigma^i : \sigma \in Q^\dagger, i \in [9]\}, \{\chi^i : i \in [9]\}, \{\chi_{ij} : i, j \in [9]\},$$
$$\{\chi_i^j : i, j \in [9]\}, \{\chi_i^j p : i, j \in [9]\}, \{\chi_i^j b_0 b_1 : i, j \in [9], b_0, b_1 \in \{0, 1\}\}.$$

Let Q' be the union of them. Among these states, let

$$\Xi^j = \{\sigma^j, \mathcal{O}^j, \chi^j, \chi_i^j, \chi_i^j p, \chi_i^j b_0 b_1 : \sigma \in Q^\dagger, i \in [9], b_0, b_1 \in \{0,1\}\}$$

be the set of all colored states whose color is j. And let $\Xi = \cup_{j=1}^9 \Xi^j$.

Let $Q_{colored}^\dagger = \{\sigma^i : \sigma \in Q^\dagger, i \in [9]\}$. Through the representation function $\mathcal{R}$, we map the state $\psi^i \in Q_{colored}^\dagger$ to ψ for all $i \in [9]$, and all other states not in $Q_{colored}^\dagger$ are mapped to the blank state $\mathcal{O}$. We say that a configuration $\alpha' \in \Gamma'$ satisfies the *complete coloring property* if for any species $\psi \in Q_{colored}^\dagger$, $\mathcal{B}(\psi)$ are all colored. This protocol is designed to maintain this property.

Suppose now we have a configuration $\alpha' \in \Gamma'$ that satisfies the complete coloring property, and there is some growing reaction $(A, \mathcal{O}, B, C, \rightarrow) \in R$ that can be performed on $\alpha = \mathcal{R}^*(\alpha')$. Take the example in Fig. 2a. We want $A^1, \mathcal{O}^2$ to be able to become (B^1, C^2) while preserving the complete coloring property at the same time. Existing colors $1, 2$ on $A, \mathcal{O}$ help specifying the growing direction. Since $\mathcal{B}(A^1)$ has been colored, we only need to color $W_{A^1}(\mathcal{O}^2) = \mathcal{B}(\mathcal{O}^2) \setminus \mathcal{B}(A^1)$, which are the three vertical cells in Fig. 2b enclosed by the dashed lines. We use the notation $W_\psi(\psi')$ to represent $\mathcal{B}(\psi') \setminus \mathcal{B}(\psi)$ for adjacent species $\psi, \psi' \in Q'$.

Therefore, the first reaction we add to R' is $A^1 + \mathcal{O}^2 \rightarrow A^1 + \chi_1^2$. χ_1^2 serves as the signal to begin the local coloring process. For the remaining part of this section, we'll give several examples of configuration around the block of χ_1^2, and then specify the required reactions according to that situation.

Since $\mathcal{B}(A^1)$ must have been completely colored due to the complete coloring property, we deliver the information of growing direction to the East cell of χ_1^2. Suppose the cell is at position v with state $\psi(v)$. To classify the state possibly encountered by χ_1^2, we need to use the following property of a special kind of species $\{\chi^i, i \in [9]\}$: As soon as some state χ^i ($i \in [9]$) appears, the block of χ^i must have been colored. With this property, we divide the possible states of v into 4 classes:

1. $\psi(v) = \sigma^3$ for some $\sigma \in Q^\dagger \cup \{\chi\}$. It means that $\mathcal{B}(v)$ has been colored, which implies $\mathcal{B}(\chi_1^2) \setminus \mathcal{B}(A^1) \subset \mathcal{B}(v)$ has been colored as well. Then we directly turn χ_1^2 to χ^2, representing that $\mathcal{B}(\chi_1^2)$ has been colored. Therefore we add the following reactions to R':

$$\chi_1^2 + \psi^3 \rightarrow \chi^2 + \psi^3, \text{ for all } \psi \in Q^\dagger \cup \{\chi\}.$$

2. $\psi(v) = \mathcal{O}$ or $\mathcal{O}^3$. We don't know if $\mathcal{B}(v)$ is colored, therefore we add the reaction $\chi_1^2 + \mathcal{O}/\mathcal{O}^3 \rightarrow \chi_1^2 p + \chi_2^3 00$. This announce the starting point of coloring $\mathcal{B}(\chi_2^3 00) \setminus \mathcal{B}(\chi_1^2 p)$. Therefore we add the following reactions to R':

$$\chi_1^2 + \mathcal{O} \rightarrow \chi_1^2 p + \chi_2^3 00.$$
$$\chi_1^2 + \mathcal{O}^3 \rightarrow \chi_1^2 p + \chi_2^3 00.$$

3. $\psi(v) = \chi_6^3$ or χ_9^3. We need to be cautious about the deadlock in Fig. 2b. In this case, we have χ_1^2 continue to color the block of itself. Therefore we add

the following reactions to R':

$$\chi_1^2 + \chi_6^3 \rightarrow \chi_1^2 p + \chi_2^3 00.$$
$$\chi_1^2 + \chi_9^3 \rightarrow \chi_1^2 p + \chi_2^3 00.$$

4. $\psi(v) = \chi_1^3$. It means that some species σ^1 (where $\sigma \in Q^\dagger$) located two cells away from A^1 is also attempting to perform a growing reactions in an opposite direction. i.e. they are growing toward each other. Again by the complete coloring assumption, $\mathcal{B}(\chi_1^2) \backslash \mathcal{B}(A^1) \subset \mathcal{B}(\sigma^1)$ and $\mathcal{B}(\chi_1^3) \backslash \mathcal{B}(\sigma^1) \subset \mathcal{B}(A^1)$. Both χ_1^2, χ_1^3 know their blocks are colored, so they turn into χ^2 and χ^3 simultaneously. Therefore wee add the following reaction to R':

$$\chi_1^2 + \chi_1^3 \rightarrow \chi^2 + \chi^3.$$

For cases 2 and 3, the coloring of $\mathcal{B}(\chi_1^2 p)$ has not been done, $\chi_2^3 00$ is just produced to start coloring the cells to the North and South, call them v_N, v_S respectively. $\chi_2^3 00$ will be turned into $\chi_2^3 b_0 b_1$ for some $b_0, b_1 \in \{0,1\}$ that observes and records whether v_N, v_S has been colored. The detailed reactions are omitted here due to space constraints.

Eventually, $\chi_2^3 00$ will become $\chi_2^3 11$, representing that both v_N, v_S have been colored. Then we use a reaction $\chi_2^3 11 + \chi_1^2 p \rightarrow \mathcal{O}^3 + \chi^2$ to announce the termination of the local coloring process. The state transition can now be simulated by adding reaction $A^1 + \chi^2 \rightarrow B^1 + C^2$ to R'. One thing remains is to eliminate the redundant state χ_{23} produced in the first case. So we need the reaction $\mathcal{O}^3 + \chi_{23} \rightarrow \mathcal{O}^3 + \mathcal{O}$.

The above description shows the simulation process of a special case that apply a growing reaction to a species A colored by 1 toward East. Figure 2c gives a sequence of reactions that could possibly be performed in our simulation process when there is a growing reaction $(A, \mathcal{O}, B, C, \rightarrow)$ in R.

State_Transitions. The simulation of bimolecular reactions that happen on the cells whose blocks have been colored is straight forward. As an example, we simulate $(A, B, C, D, d) \in R \backslash R_g$ on the cells colored $1, 2$ by adding the following reaction to R':

1. $A^1 + B^2 \rightarrow C^1 + D^2$.

For a unimolecular reaction $(A, B, \odot)$, the simulation is simple: For all $i \in [9]$, add the following reactions to R':

1. $A^i \rightarrow B^i$.

We could use the same method to construct the reaction sets needed for the growing reactions and bimolecular reactions on a species colored $i \in [9]$ toward direction $d \in \{\uparrow, \rightarrow, \downarrow, \leftarrow\}$. This is just applying some permutations to all the reactions we constructed so far. The exact permutations are omitted here due to space constraints.

So far we have given the entire simulation for a s-d-sCRN $\Gamma = (Q, S, R)$ using a s-sCRN $\Gamma' = (Q', S', R')$ by combining the above three parts.

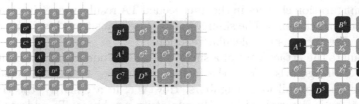

(a) A complete coloring configuration. The wall centered at $\mathcal{O}^3$ are to be colored.

(b) The undesired deadlock.

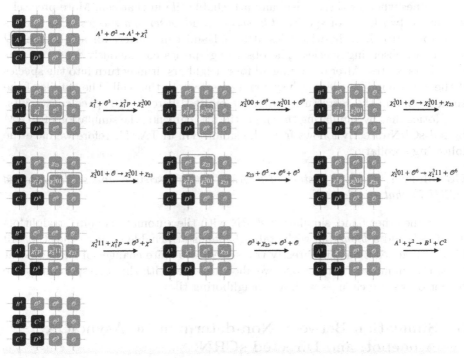

(c) A possible sequence of reactions simulating $(A, \mathcal{O}, B, C, d)$.

Fig. 2. An example of the simulation of a growing reaction.

5   Simulation Between Unit-Seeded TA with Affinity-Strengthening Rule and Unit-Seeded Directed sCRN

In this section, we prove that unit-seeded directed sCRN and unit-seeded TA with affinity-strengthening rule can simulate each other.

Theorem 2. *Given a unit-seeded tile automata system with affinity strengthening rule $\Gamma = (Q, S, I, g, R, \tau)$, there exists a unit-seeded directed sCRN $\Gamma' = (Q', S', R')$ which simulates Γ.*

The configuration changes in the unit-seeded TA result from either state transitions or tile attachments. The simulation of state transitions is straightforward; we simply view them as bimolecular reactions.

To simulate the attachment of a single tile, we encode each tile t by its state. The main challenge arises from the fact that whether a tile is attachable in a position depends on all four neighbors. However, in a d-sCRN, the transition of a cell's state is determined by only one of its neighbors. To address this, we introduce some auxiliary variables to enable a cell to contain a special species capable of "observing" all species around. After observing all four neighbors, it determines whether there exists any attachable tile in that cell. More precisely, we define two kinds of species: *tile species* and *observing species*. Tile species correspond to the cells with tiles attached and can convert all neighboring $\mathcal{O}$ species to observing species. The observing species continuously reads its four neighbors' states. After observing all four neighbors, it may turn into tile species if the corresponding tile in TA system can attach to that cell. The details of the simulation and the correctness proof are omitted here due to space constraints.

Notice that by simulating the single tile attachments, the simulation of aTAM by s-d-sCRN directly follows from the simulation of TA. Therefore we have the following corollary.

Corollary 1. *Given a system of aTAM Γ, there exists a unit-seeded directed sCRN Γ' that simulates Γ.*

On the other hand, simulating sCRN with tile automata is quite straightforward. We add a *blank tile* with state $\mathcal{O}$ that is attachable to any other tile. All bimolecular reactions are directly translated into state changes of two adjacent tiles. For unimolecular reactions, we allow the tiles with the corresponding state to perform state changes with any neighboring tiles.

6   Simulation Between Non-deterministic Async-CA, Amoebot, and Directed sCRN

Simulating cellular automata and amoebot by sCRN is similar to simulating tile automata. One main difference is that amoebots may expand into the size of two cells, and thus a pair of molecules in sCRN must be synchronized to represent one amoebot unit.

Simulating sCRN with cellular automata and amoebot is more complicated. In asynchronous cellular automata and amoebot, only one cell can change its state in each step. Therefore, to simulate a bimolecular reaction, two cells must synchronize and lock each other before making state changes.

Due to space constraints, we state the results here and omit the formal definitions and the simulation protocols.

Theorem 3. *Given a non-deterministic, asynchronous CA Γ, there exists a directed sCRN Γ' which simulates Γ.*

Theorem 4. *Given a directed sCRN Γ, there exists a non-deterministic, asynchronous CA Γ' which simulates Γ.*

Theorem 5. *Given an amoebot system Γ, there exists a clockwise sCRN Γ' which simulates Γ.*

Theorem 6. *Given a clockwise sCRN Γ, there exists an amoebot system Γ' which simulates Γ.*

References

1. Adleman, L., Cheng, Q., Goel, A., Huang, M.D.: Running time and program size for self-assembled squares. In: Proceedings of the Thirty-Third Annual ACM Symposium on Theory of Computing, pp. 740–748 (2001)
2. Alaniz, R.M., et al.: Complexity of reconfiguration in surface chemical reaction networks (2023)
3. Alaniz, R.M., et al.: Building squares with optimal state complexity in restricted active self-assembly. J. Comput. Syst. Sci. **138**, 103462 (2023)
4. Alumbaugh, J.C., Daymude, J.J., Demaine, E.D., Patitz, M.J., Richa, A.W.: Simulation of programmable matter systems using active tile-based self-assembly. In: DNA Computing and Molecular Programming, pp. 140–158 (2019)
5. Angluin, D., Aspnes, J., Fischer, M.J., Jiang, H.: Self-stabilizing population protocols. ACM Trans. Auton. Adapt. Syst. **3**(4) (2008). https://doi.org/10.1145/1452001.1452003
6. Bhattacharjee, K., Naskar, N., Roy, S., Das, S.: A survey of cellular automata: types, dynamics, non-uniformity and applications. Nat. Comput. **19**, 433–461 (2020)
7. Brailovskaya, T., Gowri, G., Yu, S., Winfree, E.: Reversible computation using swap reactions on a surface. In: DNA Computing and Molecular Programming, pp. 174–196 (2019)
8. Caballero, D., Gomez, T., Schweller, R., Wylie, T.: Verification and computation in restricted tile automata. Nat. Comput., 1–19 (2021). https://doi.org/10.1007/s11047-021-09875-x
9. Chalk, C., Luchsinger, A., Martinez, E., Schweller, R., Winslow, A., Wylie, T.: Freezing simulates non-freezing tile automata. In: DNA Computing and Molecular Programming, pp. 155–172 (2018)
10. Chen, H.L., Doty, D., Soloveichik, D.: Deterministic function computation with chemical reaction networks. Nat. Comput. **13**(4), 517–534 (2014)
11. Chen, H.L., Doty, D., Soloveichik, D., Reeves, W.: Rate-independent computation in continuous chemical reaction networks. J. ACM **70**(3), 1–61 (2023)
12. Clamons, S., Qian, L., Winfree, E.: Programming and simulating chemical reaction networks on a surface. J. R. Soc. Interface **17**, 20190790 (2020)
13. Cook, M., Soloveichik, D., Winfree, E., Bruck, J.: Programmability of Chemical Reaction Networks, pp. 543–584. Springer, Heidelberg (2009). https://doi.org/10.1007/978-3-540-88869-7_27
14. Dennunzio, A., Formenti, E., Manzoni, L.: Computing issues of asynchronous CA. Fundam. Inf. **120**(2), 165–180 (2012)
15. Doty, D., Lutz, J.H., Patitz, M.J., Schweller, R.T., Summers, S.M., Woods, D.: The tile assembly model is intrinsically universal. In: IEEE 54th Annual Symposium on Foundations of Computer Science, pp. 302–310 (2012)

16. Fages, F., Le Guludec, G., Bournez, O., Pouly, A.: Strong turing completeness of continuous chemical reaction networks and compilation of mixed analog-digital programs. In: Feret, J., Koeppl, H. (eds.) CMSB 2017. LNCS, vol. 10545, pp. 108–127. Springer, Cham (2017). https://doi.org/10.1007/978-3-319-67471-1_7

17. Fatès, N., Gerin, L.: Examples of fast and slow convergence of 2D asynchronous cellular systems. In: Umeo, H., Morishita, S., Nishinari, K., Komatsuzaki, T., Bandini, S. (eds.) ACRI 2008. LNCS, vol. 5191, pp. 184–191. Springer, Heidelberg (2008). https://doi.org/10.1007/978-3-540-79992-4_24

18. Hader, D., Patitz, M.J.: The impacts of dimensionality, diffusion, and directedness on intrinsic cross-model simulation in tile-based self-assembly. Algorithmica (2023). https://doi.org/10.1007/s00453-024-01219-2

19. von Neumann, J.: Theory of self-reproducing automata (1966). https://cba.mit.edu/events/03.11.ASE/docs/VonNeumann.pdf

20. Patitz, M.J.: An introduction to tile-based self-assembly. In: Durand-Lose, J., Jonoska, N. (eds.) Unconventional Computation and Natural Computation, pp. 34–62 (2012)

21. Qian, L., Winfree, E.: Parallel and scalable computation and spatial dynamics with DNA-based chemical reaction networks on a surface. In: Murata, S., Kobayashi, S. (eds.) DNA 2014. LNCS, vol. 8727, pp. 114–131. Springer, Cham (2014). https://doi.org/10.1007/978-3-319-11295-4_8

22. Rothemund, P., Winfree, E.: The program-size complexity of self-assembled squares. In: Proceedings of the Annual ACM Symposium on Theory of Computing, pp. 459–468 (2000)

23. Soloveichik, D., Cook, M., Winfree, E., Bruck, J.: Computation with finite stochastic chemical reaction networks. Nat. Comput. Int. J. **7**(4), 615–633 (2008). https://doi.org/10.1007/s11047-008-9067-y

24. Winfree, E.: Algorithmic self-assembly of DNA. In: Proceedings of the International Conference on Microtechnologies in Medicine and Biology, p. 4 (2006)

A Representative Framework
for Implementing Quantum Finite
Automata on Real Devices

Aliya Khadieva[1,2,5]($\boxtimes$) (iD), Özlem Salehi[3,4] (iD), and Abuzer Yakaryılmaz[1,4] (iD)

[1] University of Latvia, Rīga, Latvia
aliya.khadi@gmail.com , abuzer.yakaryilmaz@lu.lv
[2] Kazan Federal University, Kazan, Russia
[3] Institute of Theoretical and Applied Informatics, Polish Academy of Sciences,
Gliwice, Poland
[4] QWorld Association, Tallinn, Estonia
[5] Zavoisky Physical-Technical Institute, FRC Kazan Scientific Center of RAS,
Kazan, Russia
https://qworld.net

Abstract. We present a framework for the implementation of quantum finite automata algorithms designed for the language $\mathtt{MOD_p} = \{a^{i \cdot p} \mid i \geq 0\}$ on gate-based quantum computers. First, we compile the known theoretical results from the literature to reduce the number of CNOT gates. Second, we demonstrate techniques for modifying the algorithms based on the basis gates of available quantum hardware in order to reduce circuit depth. Lastly, we explore how the number of CNOT gates may be reduced further if the topology of the qubits is known.

Keywords: quantum finite automaton · quantum automata implementation · circuit decomposition

1 Introduction

Finite automata serves as a well established model for data stream processing. Over the past few decades, the quantum analogue known as quantum finite automaton (QFA) has been widely investigated. Quantum finite automata can be exponentially more memory (state) efficient compared to probabilistic finite automata (PFAs) [6]: For any prime number p, any PFA recognizing the language $\mathtt{MOD_p} = \{a^{i \cdot p} \mid i \geq 0\}$ requires at least p states, while bounded-error QFAs use only $O(\log p)$ states. Notably, concepts like quantum fingerprinting [12] and quantum hashing [5] can be considered as generalizations of the QFA algorithm for the $\mathtt{MOD_p}$ language. Moreover, the idea of comparing hashes for two different objects modulo p, which lies at the core of recognizing the $\mathtt{MOD_p}$ language has applications in branching programs [4,14,17] and online algorithms [15,16].

Although, the QFA design for $\mathtt{MOD_p}$ is straightforward, its implementation on gate-based quantum computers faces certain difficulties, as highlighted in [11,13, 27]. Currently, we are in the noisy intermediate-scale quantum era [24], and one of the main problems with the available hardware (including near-future devices) is the noise introduced by quantum operators and measurements. Note that any quantum program is transpiled into two-qubit and single-qubit gates before its execution on real machines. Compared to single-qubit gates, two-qubit gates are more costly to implement and susceptible to errors. The transpilation process works based on a pre-determined set of basis gates, and this set commonly has CNOT (controlled NOT) gate as the only two-qubit gate. Consequently, one of the key measures when assessing the complexity of QFA implementations is the number of CNOT gates. Moreover, the depth of the circuit is also another factor that effects the decoherence and shorter circuits are preferable. Finally, in each real backend, qubits are organized in a certain topology, which determines the pair of gates on which two-qubit gates like CNOT can be applied. Hence, additional SWAP gates, that are composed of CNOT gates become necessary when transpiling any quantum program.

The basic step in implementing a fingerprinting algorithm involves rotating a target qubit by a set of d distinct angles, a task which can be implemented by applying a uniformly controlled rotation gate [6]. Möttönen et al. propose an efficient implementation of such operator in [21], which uses $O(d)$ CNOT gates and $O(d)$ single-qubit gates. However, this method requires rotation angles to be modified, resulting in remarkably smaller angles. Note that for the current quantum computers, there is also a limit to the precision of implementing such rotations [18]. In response to those challenges, we propose a technique for implementing uniformly controlled rotation that enables us to obtain a trade-off between the number of CNOT gates and the precision of rotation angles. The technique combines Möttönen's approach with a particular decomposition of rotation gates. Namely, for any integer value of parameter t such that $0 < t < \log_2 d - 4$, the CNOT-cost is $2^t + \frac{d}{2} \cdot (192(\log_2 d - t) - 768)$. In this case, the angle precision is $\frac{\alpha}{2^t}$ where α is an original angle. If $t = 0$, then the CNOT-cost is $O(d \log_2 d)$ and the original angle is not changed. For $t = \log_2 d - 4$, the CNOT-cost is $O(d)$ and the angle precision is $\alpha \cdot O(\frac{1}{d})$.

One way to reduce the number of CNOT gates dramatically is to pick $\log_2 d + 1$ rotations instead of the full set d and apply them as shown in [13,29]. Those rotations are implemented through R_y gates in [13], whereas R_z gate is used in many of the real backends [1,2] as it is a virtual gate [19]. To align with this choice, we adapt the original QFA algorithm to utilize gates from the basic gates set $\{CNOT, I, R_z, SX, X\}$, which is also the gate set used by IBM Quantum (IBMQ) backends [2]. We test the new algorithm on a real backend and observe a significant reduction in the depth of the circuit.

Designing efficient programs tailored for linear nearest neighbor (LNN) architecture, where the multi-qubit gates can be applied only on adjacent qubits has been extensively studied [9,23,26,30]. In this paper, we propose an approach to reduce the number of CNOT gates in the circuit for the QFA algorithm when implemented on an LNN architecture. We demonstrate our approach by running the algorithm for MOD$_{37}$ on the *ibmq_manila* backend. Our implementation results in a circuit with a CNOT-cost that is twice as efficient as the original approach after Qiskit transpilation, and this advantage increases with the length of the input, showing the superiority of our method.

2   Preliminaries

In this section, we review QFAs and present the QFA algorithm recognizing $\texttt{MOD}_p$. We refer the reader to [22] for the basics of quantum computing and to [8] for further details on QFAs.

Quantum Finite Automaton. Many different QFA models have been proposed in the literature [8]. The QFA algorithm for $\texttt{MOD}_p$ is presented by using the most restricted QFA model known, which is also called the Moore-Crutchfield QFA [20]; we will refer to this model as QFA throughout the paper. Formally, an n-state QFA is a 5-tuple $M = (\Sigma, Q, \{U_\sigma \mid \sigma \in \Sigma \cup \{\mathrm{\textcent}, \$\}\}, q_I, Q_a)$, where Σ is the input alphabet not containing the left and right end-markers (resp., $\mathrm{\textcent}$ and $\$$), $Q = \{q_1, \ldots, q_n\}$ is the set of states, $U_\sigma \in \mathbb{C}^{n \times n}$ is the unitary transition matrix for symbol σ, $q_I \in Q$ is the initial state, and, $Q_a \subseteq Q$ is the set of accepting state(s).

From the set of all strings Σ^*, let x be the given input with l symbols, i.e., $x = x_1 x_2 \cdots x_l$. The computation of M is traced by an n-dimensional complex-valued vector called the quantum state. At the beginning of the computation, M is in quantum state $|v_0\rangle = |q_I\rangle$, having zeros except I-th entry, which is 1. The input x is processed by M one symbol at a time, by applying sequentially the transition matrix of each scanned symbol including the end-markers. Thus, the final quantum state is $|v_f\rangle = U_\$ U_{x_l} U_{x_{l-1}} \cdots U_{x_1} U_{\mathrm{\textcent}} |v_0\rangle$.

After processing the whole input, a measurement in the computational basis is performed. That is, if the j-th entry of $|v_f\rangle$ is a_j, then the state q_j is observed with probability $|a_j|^2$. Thus, the input x is accepted with the probability of observing an accepting state, i.e., $\sum_{q_j \in Q_a} |a_j|^2$.

A language $L \subseteq \Sigma^*$ is recognized by M with bounded error if and only if there exists an error bound $\epsilon \in [0, 1/2)$ such that (i) for each $x \in L$, M accepts x with probability at least $1 - \epsilon$ and (ii) for each $x \notin L$, M accepts (rejects) x with probability at most ϵ (at least $1 - \epsilon$).

QFA Algorithm for $\texttt{MOD}_p$. In [6], it is proven that there exists a QFA with $O(\log p)$ states recognizing the language $\texttt{MOD}_p$ with bounded error. Before discussing that, we start with a simpler construction. For a fixed $k \in \{1, \ldots, p-1\}$, let M_k be a QFA with 2 states, namely $|q_1\rangle$ and $|q_2\rangle$. The QFA M_k starts its computation in $|q_1\rangle$ and applies the identity matrix when reading $\mathrm{\textcent}$ or $\$$. When reading symbol a, M_k applies a rotation on the (real) plane $|q_1\rangle$-$|q_2\rangle$ with angle $k\frac{2\pi}{p}$. Here, q_1 is the accepting state. The QFA M_k can be implemented by using a single qubit by associating $|q_1\rangle$ and $|q_2\rangle$ with states $|0\rangle$ and $|1\rangle$, respectively. Then, the rotation matrix (parameterized with k) is $R_k = \begin{pmatrix} \cos\left(\frac{2k\pi}{p}\right) & -\sin\left(\frac{2k\pi}{p}\right) \\ \sin\left(\frac{2k\pi}{p}\right) & \cos\left(\frac{2k\pi}{p}\right) \end{pmatrix}$.

Note that any member of $\texttt{MOD}_p$ is accepted with probability 1. On the other hand, the accepting probability for non-members is bounded by $\cos^2\left(\frac{\pi}{p}\right)$ and thus, M_k can not recognize $\texttt{MOD}_p$ with bounded error.

Next, we describe a $2d$-state QFA M_K for the $\texttt{MOD}_p$ language, where $K = \{k_1, \ldots, k_d\}$. We pick d as a power of 2 for simplicity. The QFA M_K executes the QFAs $M_{k_1}, \ldots, M_{k_d}$ in parallel. After reading $\mathcal{c}$, M_K enters into equal superposition of M_{k_j}'s for $j \in \{1, \ldots, d\}$. Each M_{k_j} uses two states, and when reading each a, M_{k_j} applies the rotation matrix R_{k_j}. At the end of the computation, M_K applies the inverse of the transition matrix used for the symbol $\mathcal{c}$. It was shown in [6,7] that there exist $O(\log p)$ k values such that M_K recognizes $\texttt{MOD}_p$ with bounded error. (Thus, $d = \Theta(\log p)$.)

When implementing M_K (on real hardware), we can use Hadamard operators for the end-markers. Consequently, the main cost of the implementation comes from the transition matrix for symbol a, which is defined as $U_a = \begin{pmatrix} R_{k_1} & 0 & \cdots & 0 \\ \hline 0 & R_{k_2} & \cdots & 0 \\ \hline \vdots & \vdots & \ddots & \vdots \\ \hline 0 & 0 & \cdots & R_{k_d} \end{pmatrix}$. The operator U_a is also known as uniformly controlled rotation [21]. Thus, we can use its efficient implementations given in the literature, when implementing M_K (Sects. 3.1 and 3.2).

3   Device Independent Implementations

Here, we compile the known results in the literature and present different generic (i.e., device independent) implementation schema with their costs. We consider three different costs: the number of CNOT gates, the number of single-qubit gates, and the precision of rotation angles. We observe that there may be trade-offs between the CNOT-cost and the precision of rotation angles. In the next section, we discuss how to obtain further improvements if the specification of real hardware is available.

Let $x = a^m$ be the given input. We use $\log d + 1$ qubits to implement M_K (see Fig. 1a). The $\log d$ qubits are used to differentiate d subautomata and the additional qubit is the target qubit. We start in a state $|0\rangle$ for each qubit. We

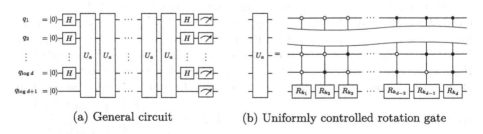

(a) General circuit   (b) Uniformly controlled rotation gate

Fig. 1. QFA construction for $\texttt{MOD}_p$ language.

apply Hadamard on the first $\log d$ qubits, and apply identity operator on the last qubit. Thus, we obtain d sub-QFAs by reserving two states for each of them, and any operator applied to a sub-QFA is controlled by the first $\log d$ qubits. For each symbol of x, we apply U_a. At the end, we again apply Hadamard on the first $\log d$ qubits followed by measurement operators. The input is accepted if and only if all zeros ($|0 \cdots 0\rangle$) is observed. As seen from Fig. 1a, it is enough to find the CNOT-cost of a single U_a, i.e., the number of CNOT gates when U_a is decomposed into a set of single-qubit and CNOT gates. We implement each R_{k_j} of U_a independently as shown in Fig. 1b. The implementation of U_a uses Gray code for decreasing X gates[1]. We have d multi-qubit controlled rotations in our circuit for U_a. Each multi-qubit controlled rotation R_θ by some angle θ can be replaced by two multi-qubit controlled NOT gates and two controlled rotation gates as shown in Fig. 2 due to [10]. The CNOT-cost of multi-qubit controlled NOT gate is bounded by $48(\log d - 3)$ [10] if one ancilla qubit is available. Thus, the CNOT-cost of U_a is bounded by $48 \cdot d(\log d - 3)$.

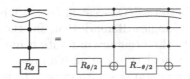

Fig. 2. Multi-qubit controlled rotation operation decomposition.

3.1 Using Möttönen et al. Approach

Möttönen et al. presented an efficient decomposition of the uniformly controlled rotation gate (see Fig. 3a) in [21]. This circuit is based on recursive application of the circuit given in Fig. 3b. They proposed a construction for U_a consisting of d CNOT gates and d rotation gates.

Let $\alpha_i = 2\pi k_i/p$ be the original angle that is used in M_{k_i} for $i \in \{1, \ldots, d\}$. The angles $\{\theta_i\}$ from the efficient decomposition of Möttönen et al. can be obtained from $\{\alpha_i\}$ by using the equation $\left(\theta_1\, \theta_2\, \cdots\, \theta_d\right)^T = B\left(\alpha_1\, \alpha_2\, \cdots\, \alpha_d\right)^T$, where $B_{ij} = \frac{1}{d}(-1)^{(b_j-1)\cdot(g_i-1)}$ and b_m and g_m are binary code and binary reflected Gray code representations of the integer m, respectively. Thus, the

---

[1] As the control operators are fired when a qubit is in state $|1\rangle$, we use several NOT (X) gates between controlled rotations. For example, we apply NOT gates on the first $\log d$ qubits before and after the controlled R_{k_1} operator, and, in this way, we guarantee that R_{k_1} is fired only if the first $\log d$ qubits are in $|0 \cdots 0\rangle$. If we follow the order of indices on the circuit, then there will be several NOT gates. But, if we follow an order based on Gray code, then it will be enough to use only a single NOT gate between the controlled rotations.

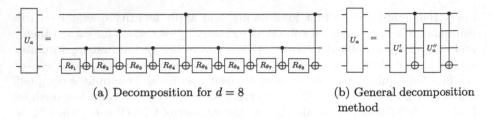

(a) Decomposition for $d = 8$ (b) General decomposition
                                      method

Fig. 3. Efficient decomposition of the uniformly controlled rotation gate [21].

CNOT-cost of U_a is bounded by d, but the angles for the target qubit rotations are transformed, using more sensitive rotation angles, i.e., we use $O(\frac{2\pi}{p\log p})$ instead of $O(\frac{2\pi}{p})$.

3.2   Optimization

We already observed a better CNOT-cost in Sect. 3.1 but at the cost of using more sensitive rotation of angles. Remark that, for the current quantum computers, there is a limit to the accuracy of rotation implementing up to angles $\theta + 0.0001$ [18]. Our main goal is to optimize a given quantum circuit for uniformly controlled rotation operations with respect to not only the CNOT-cost but also the precision of rotation angles.

First, we propose a decomposition of a circuit implementing a pair of multiqubit controlled rotations as given in Fig. 4. This decomposition is based on a known decomposition of a single multi-qubit controlled rotation operation proposed in [10] and shown in Fig. 5a. In our case, we implement consequently two multi-qubit controlled rotations R_{θ_1} and R_{θ_2}, where one of the controller qubits is in orthogonal states for each rotation. That means we apply NOT gate between controlled rotations to this control qubit. For the operation with n control qubits, without loss of generality, we assume that this control qubit is the nth qubit in the register and the target qubit is the $(n+1)^{th}$ qubit.

The CNOT-cost of this implementation is at most $4 \cdot 48(n-4) = 192(n-4)$. The cost is based on the circuit for g-qubit controlled NOT gate presented in [10], where $g > 3$. This operator can be implemented, as long as a single qubit is available to use as ancilla. The CNOT-cost of this g-qubit controlled NOT gate is bounded by $48(g-3)$.

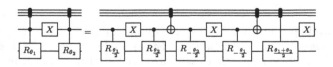

Fig. 4. Proposed decomposition for a pair of rotations.

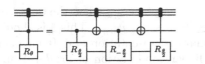

(a) Multi-qubit controlled rotation   (b) Multi-qubit controlled NOT

Fig. 5. Multi-qubit controlled gate decompositions from [10].

On the right circuit in Fig. 4, each one of the two multi-qubit controlled NOT gates is $(n-1)$-qubit controlled. The target $(n+1)^{th}$ qubit is an ancilla qubit for the 2 multi-qubit controlled NOT gates. An $(n-1)$-controlled rotation gate is decomposed into 2 rotation gates and 2 multi-qubit controlled NOT gates as shown in Fig. 2. For their decomposition, we use the nth qubit as an ancilla. Thus, the CNOT-cost of the decomposed circuit (on the right hand side) in Fig. 4 is bounded by $4 \cdot 48(n-4) = 192(n-4)$. The naive implementation of the circuit on the left hand side of Fig. 4 requires 2 decomposition of n-controlled rotation gates. The CNOT-cost of such implementation is bounded by $4 \cdot 48(n-3) = 192(n-3)$.

Then, our optimization approach is to combine the methods presented in Fig. 3b and Fig. 4. To achieve better precision of rotations, we can reduce the number of iterations in the method given in Fig. 3b. For instance, after t iterations of the decomposition, the angles are reduced up to 2^t times. We can stop recursion at this step. Then, the rest 2^t undecomposed uniformly controlled rotations can be split based on the pairs of rotations as in Fig. 4. Compared to the original circuit, the angles are reduced by 2^{t+1} times. For $t < \log_2 d - 4$, the CNOT-cost is $2^t + \frac{d}{2} \cdot (192(\log_2 d - t) - 768)$. Namely, after t iterations, the circuit consists of 2^t CNOT gates and 2^t undecomposed uniformly controlled rotation gates, where each of them consists of $2^{\log_2 d - t - 1}$ pairs of $\log_2 d - t$ - controlled rotations.

The same precision can be achieved if we implement $t + 1$ recursive iterations and use naive circuit (Fig. 1b) for the rest 2^{t+1} undecomposed uniformly controlled rotation gates. In this case, the CNOT-cost is $2^{t+1} + \frac{d}{2} \cdot (192(\log_2 d - t - 1) - 576) = 2 \cdot 2^t + \frac{d}{2}(192(\log_2 d - t) - 768)$, which means that the advantage of the optimized circuit over the naive circuit is 2^t CNOT gates.

Finally, we obtain a bound for CNOT-cost between d and $d \log d$ with rotation angles better than $O(\frac{2\pi}{p \log p})$.

3.3   Pseudo Rotations Approach

The operator U_a is composed of d rotations. One way to reduce the number of CNOT gates dramatically is to pick $\log_2 d + 1$ rotations and apply them as shown in Fig. 6 [13]. Even though the CNOT-cost is $O(\log d)$ in this case, each R_{k_j} will be a linear combination of some rotations, and so the set K is not determined independently, i.e., most choices of K cannot be constructed with this method.

Namely, if the state of control qubits is $|c\rangle = |c_1 c_2 \ldots c_{\log d}\rangle$ then the target qubit is rotated by an angle $\xi = \xi_0 + c_1 \xi_1 + c_2 \xi_2 + \cdots + c_{\log d} \xi_{\log d}$. This ξ is should be equal to $\frac{2k_c \pi}{p}$, where $c_1 c_2 \ldots c_{\log d}$ is a binary representation of c. It means that the set K of size d is constructed by a linear combination of $\log d + 1$ angles. It does not work for all cases. However, numerical experiments given in [29], show that there exists such ξ that produces the required set K which allows to recognize MOD_p with bounded error at most $\frac{1}{3}$.

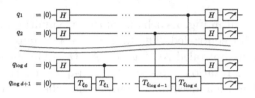

Fig. 6. Pseudo rotations approach.

4   Implementations on Real Hardware

Any program sent for execution on a real quantum computer is transpiled into some sequences of basis gates. Each computer may have a different set of basis gates. Thus, re-writing or modifying the program based on the basis gates can reduce the number of gates in the program, as the automatic transpilation processes are usually generic and so may not guarantee the best solutions. Similar to knowing the basis gates of a real hardware, its qubit topology may also help us to reduce especially the CNOT-costs. For example, a CNOT gate between two qubits that are not neighbour to each other would be implemented by using several CNOT gates.

In this section, we show how we can reduce the number of gates further based on the choice of basis gates and the topology of the real hardware. For the implementation, we use tools and libraries provided by Qiskit framework [25]. For each case, we pick one real hardware of IBM Quantum (IBMQ) [2]. Almost all IBMQ backends use the set of gates $\{CX, I, R_z, SX, X\}$ as basis gates. Here, CX is the CNOT gate, I is the identity gate, X is the NOT gate, and R_z and SX are defined as: $R_z(\theta) = \begin{pmatrix} e^{-i\theta/2} & 0 \\ 0 & e^{i\theta/2} \end{pmatrix}$, $SX = \frac{1}{2} \begin{pmatrix} 1+i & 1-i \\ 1-i & 1+i \end{pmatrix}$.

Re-writing Programs Based on Basis Gates. A single quantum bit is modelled by the Bloch sphere [22]. The rotation operator R_{k_j} is defined between $|0\rangle$ and $|1\rangle$ as a real-valued operator, denoted usually R_y: $R_y(\theta) = \begin{pmatrix} \cos\theta & -\sin\theta \\ \sin\theta & \cos\theta \end{pmatrix}$. On the other hand, almost all IBMQ backends use R_z gate as the basic rotation operator as mentioned before. Hence any R_y gate should be expressed in terms of R_z and other gates in the basis gate set.

To comply with the basis gate set of IBMQ, we will use R_z gates instead of R_y gates in the QFA algorithms for MOD$_p$. For simplicity, we pick $\theta = 2\pi/p$. We start with the following lemma.

Lemma 1. $SX^\dagger R_z(2\pi/p)SX = R_y(2\pi/p)$.

Proof. We can re-write SX as follows:

$$\frac{1}{2}\begin{pmatrix} 1+i & 1-i \\ 1-i & 1+i \end{pmatrix} = \frac{1}{\sqrt{2}}\begin{pmatrix} e^{i\pi/4} & e^{-i\pi/4} \\ e^{-i\pi/4} & e^{i\pi/4} \end{pmatrix} = \frac{1}{\sqrt{2}}e^{-i\pi/4}\begin{pmatrix} e^{i\pi/2} & 1 \\ 1 & e^{i\pi/2} \end{pmatrix}. \quad (1)$$

We calculate $SX^\dagger R_z(2\pi/p)SX$:

$$= \frac{1}{\sqrt{2}}e^{i\pi/4}\begin{pmatrix} e^{-i\pi/2} & 1 \\ 1 & e^{-i\pi/2} \end{pmatrix}\begin{pmatrix} e^{-2\pi i/p} & 0 \\ 0 & e^{2\pi i/p} \end{pmatrix}\frac{1}{\sqrt{2}}e^{-i\pi/4}\begin{pmatrix} e^{i\pi/2} & 1 \\ 1 & e^{i\pi/2} \end{pmatrix}$$

$$= \frac{1}{2}e^0\begin{pmatrix} e^{-i\pi/2} & 1 \\ 1 & e^{-i\pi/2} \end{pmatrix}\begin{pmatrix} e^{i(\pi/2-2\pi/p)} & e^{-i2\pi/p} \\ e^{i2\pi/p} & e^{i(\pi/2+2\pi/p)} \end{pmatrix}$$

$$= \frac{1}{2}\begin{pmatrix} e^{-i2\pi/p} + e^{i2\pi/p} & e^{-i(\pi/2+2\pi/p)} + e^{i(\pi/2+2\pi/p)} \\ e^{i(\pi/2-2\pi/p)} + e^{-i(\pi/2-2\pi/p)} & e^{-i2\pi/p} + e^{i2\pi/p} \end{pmatrix}. \quad (2)$$

We calculate each term of this matrix one by one by using the following trigonometric qualities: (i) $\cos(-\theta) = \cos(\theta)$, (ii) $\sin(-\theta) = -\sin(\theta)$, (iii) $e^{i\theta} + e^{-i\theta} = 2\cos(\theta)$, and (iv) $\cos(\theta + \pi/2) = -\sin(\theta)$.

The top-left and the bottom-right terms are equal to

$$e^{-i2\pi/p} + e^{i2\pi/p} = 2\cos(2\pi/p). \quad (3)$$

The top-right term is equal to

$$e^{-i(\pi/2+2\pi/p)} + e^{i(\pi/2+2\pi/p)} = 2\cos(\pi/2 + 2\pi/p)$$
$$= -2\sin(2\pi/p). \quad (4)$$

The bottom-left term is equal to

$$e^{i(\pi/2-2\pi/p)} + e^{-i(\pi/2-2\pi/p)} = 2\cos(\pi/2 - 2\pi/p)$$
$$= -2\sin(-2\pi/p)$$
$$= 2\sin(2\pi/p). \quad (5)$$

Thus, we obtain that $SX^\dagger R_z(2\pi/p)SX$ is equal to

$$\begin{pmatrix} \cos(2\pi/p) & -\sin(2\pi/p) \\ \sin(2\pi/p) & \cos(2\pi/p) \end{pmatrix} = R_y(2\pi/p).$$

$\square$

We can easily obtain the followings.

Corollary 1. $SX^\dagger R_z(2k\pi/p)SX = R_y(2k\pi/p)$.

Corollary 2. $(R_y(2k\pi/p))^j = (SX^\dagger R_z(2k\pi/p)SX)^j = SX^\dagger R_z^j(2k\pi/p)SX$.

Therefore, for the 2-state QFA, we can apply SX and $SX^\dagger$ on the left and right end-markers instead of Hadamard gate. For each symbol, we apply $R_z(2k\pi/p)$ for some $0 < k < p$. For the $2d$-state QFA (defined in Sect. 2), we make the following modifications. For each R_{k_j} defined with R_y, we define R'_{k_j} defined with R_z, where the rotation angles are identical. When reading a^j, the computation of original algorithm is represented as

$$\underbrace{\left(H^{\otimes \log d} \otimes I\right)}_{U_\$} \underbrace{\begin{pmatrix} R_{k_1} & 0 & \cdots & 0 \\ \hline 0 & R_{k_2} & \cdots & 0 \\ \hline \vdots & \vdots & \ddots & \vdots \\ \hline 0 & 0 & \cdots & R_{k_d} \end{pmatrix}^j}_{U_a^j} \underbrace{\left(H^{\otimes \log d} \otimes I\right)}_{U_\mathbb{C}}.$$

The computation of the modified algorithm is as follows:

$$U_\$ \underbrace{\begin{pmatrix} SX^\dagger & 0 & \cdots & 0 \\ 0 & SX^\dagger & \cdots & 0 \\ \vdots & \vdots & \ddots & \vdots \\ 0 & 0 & \cdots & SX^\dagger \end{pmatrix}}_{U'_\$} \underbrace{\begin{pmatrix} R'_{k_1} & 0 & \cdots & 0 \\ 0 & R'_{k_2} & \cdots & 0 \\ \vdots & \vdots & \ddots & \vdots \\ 0 & 0 & \cdots & R'_{k_d} \end{pmatrix}^j}_{(U'_a)^j} \underbrace{\begin{pmatrix} SX & 0 & \cdots & 0 \\ 0 & SX & \cdots & 0 \\ \vdots & \vdots & \ddots & \vdots \\ 0 & 0 & \cdots & SX \end{pmatrix}}_{U'_\mathbb{C}} U_\mathbb{C}.$$

Taking the pseudo rotations approach discussed in Sect. 3.3, we consider the QFA for the language MOD_{11} whose transition matrices are defined as above. The circuit consists of three qubits. Note that a classical circuit with the same number of qubits can not recognize MOD_p for $p > 8$. For the input a^{11}, the modified algorithm for MOD_{11} produces a shorter circuit. Namely, the modified circuit has 6 SX, 44 CX, 44 R_Z gates, the depth of the circuit is 84, while the original circuit has 70 SX, 44 CX, 74 R_Z gates and the depth of the circuit is 183. Notably, the modification does not reduce the number of CNOT gates, but we can have shorter circuits by using less SX and R_z gates. Here, we run the algorithms in `ibmq_belem` backend [2] and use the default transpilation by Qiskit for both cases. We refer the reader to the technical report [27] for the further details about this subsection.

Re-writing Programs Based on the Qubit Topology. IBM Quantum has several backends with linear topology of qubits. For instance, `ibmq_manila` machine works with 5 linearly connected qubits indexed by 0-1-2-3-4 (see Fig7). When a quantum program is executed on `ibmq_manila`, the program is transpiled based on not only the basis gates but also its topology. Let us note that

Fig. 7. Qubits' topology of `ibmq_manila` machine.

the transpiler provided by Qiskit framework optimizes the circuits to produce less computational error [3,28].

We implemented the QFA algorithm with pseudo rotations given in Sect. 3.3 for MOD_{37} on the simulator of `ibmq_manila` machine using `FakeManilaV2` backend. As in the previous section, we set $p = 37$ so that $p > 2^5$ because a classic computer using 5 bits can recognize MOD_p for any $p \leq 32$ [6]. Based on the topology, we can try to minimize the number of CNOT gates. For this purpose, we move the target qubit to make it closer to the control qubit for CNOT gate implementation. This procedure differs from the one where we move control qubits closer to the target one. Trivially, such moves are made by swapping the target qubit with the neighboring qubits. This approach gives us better results compared to the results reached by the Qiskit transpiler. For comparison, we transpiled the pseudo circuit with optimization level 3.

We implemented both our circuit and the pseudo circuit by picking $K = [3, 6, 19, 2, 8]$ due to [29]. The results are given in Fig. 8, and we can observe that we reduce the number of CNOT gates by more than half. We present our circuit in Fig. 9. Here, we use 5 qubits and set the 4th qubit $q4$ as the target, initially. We may also choose qubit $q2$ as the target qubit initially because the positions of $q2$ and $q4$ correspond to an optimized number of swaps of the target qubit with adjacent qubits while moving the target qubit to control qubit. We note that the number of CNOT gates does not change after using Qiskit transpiler with optimization level 3.

Although QFA reads one symbol at a time by definition, When reading more than one input symbol is allowed, we can further get a small improvement. For the input aa, we give our circuit in Fig. 10. For each input symbol, the circuit

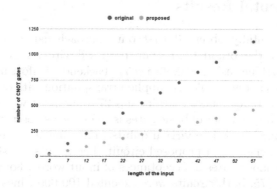

Fig. 8. The number of CNOT gates after transpilation for the pseudo circuit constructed using the original approach and our approach for MOD_{37}.

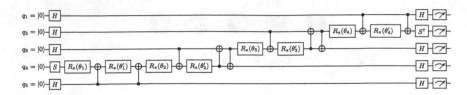

Fig. 9. Proposed circuit for the input a for MOD$_{37}$ language.

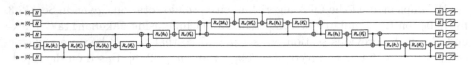

Fig. 10. Proposed circuit for the input aa for MOD$_{37}$ language.

is split into sub-circuits. For the i-th symbol, the last controlled rotation of the corresponding sub-circuit is joined with a rotation of the sub-circuit corresponding to the $(i+1)$-th symbol. This simple maneuver reduces one CNOT gate. We apply this idea for all sub-circuits. But, for the last sub-circuit, we should apply one more controlled rotation with the inverse angle for the correction, and this is implemented while reading the right end-marker.

We calculate the number of CNOT gates of our program executed on a device having linearly connected n qubits. For each input symbol, the first controlled rotation requires 2 CNOT gates. Then, 3 CNOT gates are used for each rotation. The total number of rotations is $n - 3$. While reading the right end-marker, the last rotation uses 2 CNOT gates.

Theorem 1. *For the input string a^j, the circuit proposed in this subsection for recognizing* MOD$_p$ *language uses* $(2 + 3(n - 3))j + 2$ *CNOT gates when executed on an n-qubit device with linear-nearest neighbor topology.*

5   Experimental Results

We also experimentally observed that our approach can give better results. We implemented the original and our proposed circuits on a simulator of ibmq_cairo machine using FakeCairoV2 backend. Unfortunately, 5-qubits ibmq_manila was not available. We applied transpilation with optimization level 3 to both circuits. ibmq_cairo machine has 27 qubits, but we use only 5 qubits in LNN architecture. The set of basic gates is the same as ibmq_manila machine uses. The transpiler maps five virtual qubits to five linearly connected physical qubits while implementing a proposed circuit. The results are shown in Fig. 11, where the y-axis shows rates of acceptances of input words. For each input with length $1, 2, 3, \cdots, 75$, both circuits were executed 100 000 times.

The red and blue lines show the results for the original and optimized circuits, respectively. For the original circuit, the frequency of observing the initial state

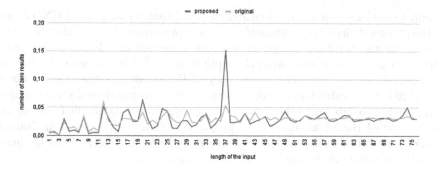

Fig. 11. The experimental results of the original and the proposed pseudo circuits implementations for recognition MOD_{37} language. (Color figure online)

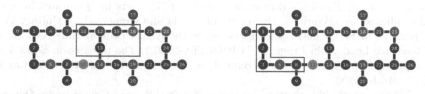

(a) 5 working qubits selected by the tran- (b) 5 working qubits selected by the transpiler for the original circuit implementa- spiler for the proposed circuit implementation.   tion.

Fig. 12. `ibmq_Cairo` machine qubits topology.

is between 0 and 7%. In other words, we have similar statistics for both the member and non-member words. However, for the optimized circuit, the initial state is observed visibly higher (15%) for the input of length 37, which is a member word. Compared to the previous work on QFA implementation on IBM machines, we observed such improvement for the first time.

Our proposed circuit uses LNN architecture of qubits. So, the transpiler selects 5 linearly connected qubits (see bordered qubits in Fig. 12b). While, for the original circuit, the transpiler selects more successfully structured qubits (see Fig. 12a). Despite that, we obtained better results for our proposed circuit.

6   Conclusion

For the current NISQ devices, noise poses a significant challenge both for quantum algorithm developers and physicists, as it can impact the accuracy of the implementation results. In this work, we presented different methods to improve the implementation of the QFA algorithm recognizing the language MOD_p when implemented on real quantum devices. The methods focus on reducing the computational resources, in particular, the number of CNOT gates and depth.

Furthermore, we considered devices with linear nearest neighbour topology and proposed an optimized circuit for the pseudo implementation of the QFA. We executed the circuit on real devices and observed that the number of CNOT gates for the proposed circuit after transpilation is approximately half of the transpilled original circuit. For MOD_{37} language, the new approach enables us to save up to 600 CNOT gates when processing the input string a^{57}. This reduction in the gate count significantly improves the accuracy of the results, as the original circuit with 1126 CNOT gates had a higher probability of computational errors, making it challenging to determine the validity of the results. Moreover, the experimental results showed the advantage of the proposed circuit implementation. Namely, it allows us to distinguish between members and non-members of the language, when the original circuit implementation cannot do it.

Acknowledgments. We sincerely thank our colleagues Kamil Khadiev, Mansur Ziatdinov, Aleksander Vasiliev, and Aida Gainutdinova for useful discussions. Part of this work was done by Khadevia during QCourse570-1 "Projects in Quantum" in Spring 2022 conducted by QWorld & University of Latvia and supported by Unitary Fund. The research in Sect. 3 has been supported by the Kazan Federal University Strategic Academic Leadership Program ("PRIORITY-2030"). The research in Sects. 4 and 5 is supported by Russian Science Foundation Grant 24-21-00406, https://rscf.ru/en/project/24-21-00406/.

Salehi was partially supported by Polish National Science Center under the grant agreement 2019/33/B/ST6/02011.

Yakaryılmaz was partially supported by the Latvian Quantum Initiative under European Union Recovery and Resilience Facility project no. 2.3.1.1.i.0/1 /22/I/CFLA/001, the ERDF project Nr. 1.1.1.5/19/A/005 "Quantum computers with constant memory", and the ERDF project number 1.1.1.5/18/A/020 "Quantum algorithms: from complexity theory to experiment".

References

1. Getting started with native gates. https://ionq.com/docs/getting-started-with-native-gates
2. IBMQ backends. https://quantum-computing.ibm.com/services/resources
3. Transpiler. https://qiskit.org/documentation/apidoc/transpiler.html
4. Ablayev, F., Gainutdinova, A., Khadiev, K., Yakaryılmaz, A.: Very narrow quantum OBDDs and width hierarchies for classical OBDDs. Lobachevskii J. Math. **37**(6), 670–682 (2016)
5. Ablayev, F., Ablayev, M., Vasiliev, A., Ziatdinov, M.: Quantum fingerprinting and quantum hashing. Computational and cryptographical aspects. Balt. J. Mod. Comput. **4**(4), 860 (2016)
6. Ambainis, A., Freivalds, R.: 1-way quantum finite automata: strengths, weaknesses and generalizations. In: FOCS 1998, pp. 332–341. IEEE (1998)
7. Ambainis, A., Nahimovs, N.: Improved constructions of quantum automata. Theoret. Comput. Sci. **410**(20), 1916–1922 (2009)
8. Ambainis, A., Yakaryılmaz, A.: Automata and quantum computing. In: Éric Pin, J. (ed.) Handbook of Automata Theory, vol. 2, chap. 39, pp. 1457–1493 (2021)
9. Bakó, B., Glos, A., Salehi, Ö., Zimborás, Z.: Near-optimal circuit design for variational quantum optimization. arXiv preprint arXiv:2209.03386 (2022)
10. Barenco, A., et al.: Elementary gates for quantum computation. Phys. Rev. A **52**(5), 3457 (1995)

11. Birkan, U., Salehi, Ö., Olejar, V., Nurlu, C., Yakaryılmaz, A.: Implementing quantum finite automata algorithms on noisy devices. In: Paszynski, M., Kranzlmüller, D., Krzhizhanovskaya, V.V., Dongarra, J.J., Sloot, P.M.A. (eds.) ICCS 2021. LNCS, vol. 12747, pp. 3–16. Springer, Cham (2021). https://doi.org/10.1007/978-3-030-77980-1_1
12. Buhrman, H., Cleve, R., Watrous, J., De Wolf, R.: Quantum fingerprinting. Phys. Rev. Lett. **87**(16), 167902 (2001)
13. Kālis, M.: Kvantu Algoritmu Realizācija Fiziskā Kvantu Datorā. Master's thesis, University of Latvia (2018)
14. Khadiev, K., Khadieva, A.: Reordering method and hierarchies for quantum and classical ordered binary decision diagrams. In: Weil, P. (ed.) CSR 2017. LNCS, vol. 10304, pp. 162–175. Springer, Cham (2017). https://doi.org/10.1007/978-3-319-58747-9_16
15. Khadiev, K., Khadieva, A.: Quantum online streaming algorithms with logarithmic memory. Int. J. Theor. Phys. **60**, 608–616 (2021)
16. Khadiev, K., Khadieva, A.: Quantum and classical log-bounded automata for the online disjointness problem. Mathematics **10**(1), 143 (2022)
17. Khadiev, K., Khadieva, A., Knop, A.: Exponential separation between quantum and classical ordered binary decision diagrams, reordering method and hierarchies. Nat. Comput. **22**, 723–736 (2022)
18. Maldonado, T.J., Flick, J., Krastanov, S., Galda, A.: Error rate reduction of single-qubit gates via noise-aware decomposition into native gates. Sci. Rep. **12**(1), 6379 (2022)
19. McKay, D.C., Wood, C.J., Sheldon, S., Chow, J.M., Gambetta, J.M.: Efficient Z gates for quantum computing. Phys. Rev. A **96**(2), 022330 (2017)
20. Moore, C., Crutchfield, J.P.: Quantum automata and quantum grammars. Theoret. Comput. Sci. **237**(1–2), 275–306 (2000)
21. Möttönen, M., Vartiainen, J.J.: Decompositions of general quantum gates. Trends in Quantum Computing Research (2006)
22. Nielsen, M.A., Chuang, I.L.: Quantum Computation and Quantum Information: 10th Anniversary Edition, 10th edn. Cambridge University Press, USA (2011)
23. O'Gorman, B., Huggins, W.J., Rieffel, E.G., Whaley, K.B.: Generalized swap networks for near-term quantum computing. arXiv preprint arXiv:1905.05118 (2019)
24. Preskill, J.: Quantum computing in the NISQ era and beyond. Quantum **2**, 79–590 (2018)
25. Qiskit contributors: Qiskit: an open-source framework for quantum computing (2023). https://doi.org/10.5281/zenodo.2573505
26. Saeedi, M., Wille, R., Drechsler, R.: Synthesis of quantum circuits for linear nearest neighbor architectures. Quantum Inf. Process. **10**, 355–377 (2011)
27. Salehi, Ö., Yakaryılmaz, A.: Cost-efficient QFA algorithm for quantum computers. CoRR **abs/2107.02262** (2021). https://arxiv.org/abs/2107.02262
28. Takita, M., Inoue, K., Lekuch, S., Minev, Z.K., Chow, J.M., Gambetta, J.M.: Exploiting dynamic quantum circuits in a quantum algorithm with superconducting qubits. Phys. Rev. Lett. **127**(10), 100501 (2021)
29. Ziiatdinov, M., Khadieva, A., Yakaryılmaz, A.: Gaps for shallow implementation of quantum finite automata. In: Proceedings of the 16th International Conference on Automata and Formal Languages (AFL 2023). EPTCS, vol. 386, pp. 269–280 (2023)
30. Zinnatullin, I., Khadiev, K., Khadieva, A.: Efficient implementation of amplitude form of quantum hashing using state-of-the-art quantum processors. Russ. Microlectron. **52**(Suppl 1), S390–S394 (2023)

A General Design Method
for Scaffold-Free DNA Wireframe
Nanostructures

Antti Elonen[1], Abdulmelik Mohammed[2], and Pekka Orponen[1(✉)]

[1] Department of Computer Science, Aalto University, Espoo, Finland
{antti.elonen,pekka.orponen}@aalto.fi
[2] Department of Biomedical Engineering, San José State University, San Jose, USA
abdulmelik.mohammed@sjsu.edu

Abstract. In the area of DNA nanotechnology, approaches to composing wireframe nanostructures exclusively from short oligonucleotides, without a coordinating long scaffold strand, have been proposed by Goodman et al. (2004) and Wang et al. (2019). We present a general design method that extends these special cases to arbitrary wireframes, in the sense of graphs linearly embedded in 2D or 3D space. The method works in linear time in the size of the given wireframe model and is already available for use in the online design tool *DNAforge*. We also interpret the method in terms of topological graph embeddings, which opens up further research opportunities in developing this design approach.

Keywords: DNA origami · DNA wireframes · scaffold-free nanostructure design · strong anti-parallel traces · cycle covers · topological graph embeddings

1 Introduction

The research area of DNA nanotechnology [26] uses DNA as a generic, highly programmable building material for creating nanoscale structures and devices. Since almost 20 years now, the technique of *DNA origami*, introduced by Paul Rothemund in 2006 [24] has been the leading approach to DNA nanostructure design. In DNA origami, a long natural *scaffold strand*, typically the ca. 7200 nt (nucleotides) long cyclic genome of the M13 bacteriophage, is guided to fold into the desired shape by a large number of ca. 20–200 nt long *staple strands*. Over the years, this technique has been used to create an amazing collection of nanostructures for a wide variety of interests and purposes [2].

A recent direction of interest have been *wireframe* 2D and 3D DNA nanostructures, where very general design methods based on the origami approach have already been developed [1,23,29], together with fully automated tools [1,8,16,29]. Sparse wireframe structures have the prospective advantage

© The Author(s), under exclusive license to Springer Nature Switzerland AG 2024
D.-J. Cho and J. Kim (Eds.): UCNC 2024, LNCS 14776, pp. 178–189, 2024.
https://doi.org/10.1007/978-3-031-63742-1_13

of being more strand-efficient and more stable in natural low-salt conditions than the commonly used helix-packed designs [3,4].

A critical limitation of the otherwise extremely versatile and robust DNA origami design method is its dependence on the global scaffold strand. For ambitious designs, the ~7200 nt scaffold length provided by the M13 genome variants is quite limited, and while research into longer strands has provided some remarkable demonstrations (e.g. [21,35]), these novel strands are not widely available, and because of little experience with them may also carry unidentified weaknesses such as decreased product yield.

As an alternative route forward, methods for *scaffold-free* nanostructure designs have been proposed [18,22,32–34]. These designs comprise only short single-stranded oligonucleotides, which are interleaved to constitute the target structure. Using the scaffold-free approach, designs 100 times larger than what is achievable using a single M13 scaffold strand have been synthesised [22], although the product yield starts to decrease for really large designs.

For similar reasons as in scaffolded DNA origami, there is emerging interest in *wireframe* scaffold-free nanostructures. The earliest precedent of these kinds of designs is possibly the (pre-origami) DNA tetrahedron by Goodman et al. [12], where the wireframe structure was constituted by routing the four faces of a tetrahedron by one 55-nt oligonucleotide each, in counterclockwise direction. The base sequences in these single-stranded oligos were designed so that for each edge of the tetrahedron, the antiparallel segments of the oligos on both sides of the edge were perfectly matching, in the complementary Watson-Crick pairing sense. (And also so that there were not too long nonspecific pairing domains elsewhere.) This idea was generalised and further developed by Wang et al. [32], who designed a number of convex 3D polyhedral wireframes and 2D wireframe lattices using this approach, and also some 3D cubic lattices by a different approach based on combining 6-arm vertex motifs.

We continue this line of research by presenting in Sect. 2 a simple and efficient design method that works for *any* reasonable 2D or 3D wireframe model, that is, a graph linearly embedded in space. This method is already implemented and available for use in our online design tool *DNAforge* (https://dnaforge.org) [8]. Section 3 then discusses the task of finding good nucleotide sequences for DNA wireframes created using this design method, and Sect. 4 introduces an interesting connection to topological graph embeddings. Section 5 explains the use of the *DNAforge* tool with design examples, and Sect. 6 presents some concluding remarks and suggestions for further work.

2   The Cycle-Cover Design Method

Our general goal is to render a given wireframe model, which we take to be a finite, connected simple graph, with no leaf vertices, that is linearly embedded in 2D or 3D space, as a DNA structure with single-duplex edges. This entails two conditions on the DNA strand arrangement: (i) each edge of the target wirefame must be rendered by two strand segments that traverse the edge in anti-parallel directions (ignoring for the moment any inter-oligo nicks that may be located on the edge), and (ii) the crossover arrangement of the strands meeting at each vertex v must be such that v is *stable*. By this we mean that if one considers two edges e and e' incident to v as *locally connected at v* when there is a strand segment that enters v along e and exits along e' or vice versa, then these local edge connections in the neighbourhood of v form a simple cycle. (The local routing pattern of the strands at a vertex is called a "transition" in [6,10] and the local edge-connectivity graph the "vertex figure" in [9].)

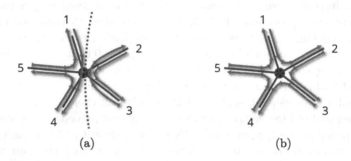

Fig. 1. (a) An unstable vertex that has two disjoint repetition neighbourhoods. (b) A stable vertex whose neighbours constitute a single repetition neighbourhood

An alternative view of condition (ii) is provided by the concept of *repetitions* at a vertex v (Fig. 1) [9]. A *repetition neighbourhood* of a vertex v is a set N of neighbouring vertices, such that every strand segment that enters v from N also exits v to N. A vertex is then stable, if and only if all its neighbours constitute a single repetition neighbourhood. Figure 1 illustrates how an unstable vertex is at risk of becoming detached in a DNA rendering.

The conditions (i) and (ii) were recognised by Fijavž et al. [9] in their notion of a *strong anti-parallel trace*, by which they mean a closed edge walk on the graph that traverses each edge twice, in opposite directions, and so that no vertex has disjoint repetition neighbourhoods. (A complementary perspective on this approach is provided in [5], where the vertex stability condition is called "cyclic compatibility".)

Strong anti-parallel traces give a good characterisation of feasible single-strand designs for DNA wireframes. They, however, exist only in limited cases: more precisely if and only if every component of any co-tree of the target wireframe graph is of even size [9]. (Co-trees are the edge-complements of spanning trees in a graph [14, p. 751].) Many interesting polyhedra lack this characteristic. For instance, a tetrahedron has six edges and four vertices, so any spanning tree of a tetrahedron has three edges and so does its co-tree; which means that every co-tree must have at least one odd-sized component. (In fact all co-trees of a tetrahedron are connected and of size three.) This means that a tetrahedron does not admit a strong anti-parallel trace, and consequently does not have

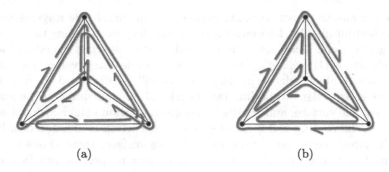

(a)   (b)

Fig. 2. (a) An anti-parallel double trace of a tetrahedron, with an unstable vertex. (b) An s.a.p. cycle cover of a tetrahedron.

a good single-stranded rendering in DNA: any anti-parallel double trace of a tetrahedron contains at least one unstable vertex (Fig. 2(a)).

However, in a scaffold-free setting one does not need to be constrained to a single trace for covering the wireframe. Both of the conditions (i) and (ii) can also be satisfied by covering the graph with multiple oriented edge cycles. This idea gives rise to the concept of a *strong antiparallel cycle cover* (briefly s.a.p. cycle cover). An s.a.p. cycle cover likewise traverses each edge twice, once in both directions, in a way that satisfies the vertex stability requirement, but it consists of multiple cyclic traces. (We are somewhat abusing the term "cycle" here, because our covering cycles may repeat edges, and so are precisely speaking closed walks on the graph.) We note that while the use of antiparallel cycle double covers for the construction of abstract DNA graphs was suggested already by Ellis-Monaghan in [6], the vertex stability condition was addressed there only in terms of antiparallel single-cycle covers that have no repetition neighbourhoods of size 1, which is not sufficient in the case of vertices of degree greater than three.

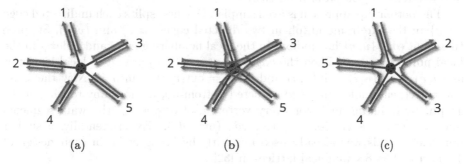

(a)   (b)   (c)

Fig. 3. (a) A vertex with incident edges split into pairs of antiparallel directed edges. (b) A routing around the vertex in numerical order: $1 \rightarrow 2 \rightarrow 3 \rightarrow 4 \rightarrow 5 \rightarrow 1$ (c) A visually more pleasing representation of the routing in subfigure (b).

One can aim to construct s.a.p. cycle covers in two simple ways: either top-down or bottom-up. One first ensures vertex stability by assigning to each vertex v of degree d some local edge-traversal order by numbering the edges incident to v cyclically as $(1, 2, \ldots, d)$. Then, whenever a cycle enters vertex v along edge i, it must exit along edge $(i \bmod d) + 1$. As will be discussed in Sect. 4, this procedure is equivalent to finding facial cycles of an embedding of the graph in some orientable surface, and results in a single repetition neighbourhood at each vertex, i.e., the routing will be strong. The construction is illustrated in Fig. 3.

If the input mesh constitutes an orientable surface, there exists a natural clockwise traversal order on it that has many nice properties, but in principle any family of cyclic permutations of the edges around the vertices induces an embedding of the mesh wireframe in *some* orientable surface (see Sect. 4).

Not all edge permutations may result in physically favourable routings, how-ever, and some care should be taken if the input mesh does not constitute a surface. In that case, a reasonable edge permutation around a vertex v can be determined by finding a shortest Hamiltonian cycle in a metric connectivity graph around v. This graph is constructed by adding one new vertex on each of the edges incident to v at one unit distance away from v, and by fully con-necting all of these new vertices to each other. This procedure minimises the total length of the eventual spacer nucleotide segments between strands, and should also mitigate nucleotide congestion at the vertices. (A refined version of this approach in the setting of scaffold-strand routings is proposed in [7].)

In the top-down approach one then initiates the construction of the first cyclic walk in the cover from some vertex v_0 with degree $d_0 = \deg(v_0)$ along the local edge 1, say. Then one follows the vertices' local routing rules, until one eventually returns to vertex v_0 along edge d_0. (The walk on the graph may of course have revisited the vertex v_0 along other edges already earlier.) After closing this first walk, one checks if there still remains some edge $\{u, v\}$ that has not yet been double-covered. If so, then one chooses either vertex u or v as the new start vertex, depending on which of them has a free exit direction (both will have if the edge $\{u, v\}$ has not yet been traversed in either direction), and initiates a new cyclic walk from there.

The bottom-up approach is even simpler. One first splits each undirected edge $\{u, v\}$ in the wireframe graph in two directed edges (u, v) and (v, u). Suppose then that edge $\{u, v\}$ has index i in the local numbering at u, and index j in the local numbering at v. Then the edges (u, v) and (v, u) are given local identities as $(u, v) = \text{out}(u, i) = \text{in}(v, j)$ and $(v, u) = \text{out}(v, j) = \text{in}(u, i)$. Now the s.a.p. cover cycle ensemble can be constructed bottom-up, without any touring of the graph, by including in it for every vertex u, of degree d_u, the walk segments $[\text{in}(u, i), \text{out}(u, i + 1)]$, for $i = 1, \ldots, d_u \pmod{d_u}$. (Experimentally, a similar approach as this was already used implicitly by Wang et al. in their design of $4 \times 4 \times 4$ and $8 \times 8 \times 4$ cubical lattices in [32].)

With proper data structures and bookkeeping, both approaches can be imple-mented to run in linear time, that is in time $O(|E|)$, where $|E|$ is the number of edges in the wireframe graph. For instance, the top-down method is essentially

Hierholzer's classical (1873) linear-time algorithm for finding an Eulerian cycle in an Eulerian graph [17, Algorithm 2.3.1], adapted to Eulerian digraphs and simplified by not merging the intermediate cycles into a single covering cycle.

3   Sequence Design

When the cycle cover is converted into DNA strands, it will initially consist of a number of long cyclical strands, which are then cut into shorter individual strands without compromising the structural stability of the wireframe. The longer the hybridised area between two overlapping antiparallel strands is, the stronger their chemical bond. However, this length also affects the total length of the strand, which should ideally be as short as possible, since long strands are difficult and expensive to produce.

Given a minimum hybridisation length parameter, N, determining the precise placement of strand gaps, or nicks, becomes a global optimisation problem. Short edges, in particular, present a challenge, as they lack sufficient space for accommodating multiple strand gaps. This means that adding a strand gap to one strand at one particular edge might prevent adding a strand gap to another strand at all.

For instance, an edge shorter than $2N$ nucleotides lacks sufficient space for even a single strand gap, while an edge of length $2N$ can accommodate only one strand gap on only one of the two strands. On the other hand, an edge spanning $5N$ nucleotides provides enough room for at least two strand gaps on each strand.

Once the strand gaps are placed, some strands will traverse at least a portion of two different edges and a possible single-stranded segment of linker/spacer nucleotides in between. These strands tend to be the longest, and minimising their lengths poses the trickiest problem. An edge that spans $5N$ nucleotides allows for these vertex-adjacent strands to be as short as possible on both sides of the edge, facilitating the nicking process for long edges. Short edges, however, remain a challenge, since placing a strand gap at one strand might impede nicking its complementary strand.

Our simple cycle cover nicking algorithm places strand gaps greedily for each edge of length $3N$ or more, i.e., edges that admit one or more nicks at both strands, so that the strands neighbouring the vertices are as short as possible. Next, the algorithm selects all edges of lengths from $2N$ to $3N - 1$ and selects the longer of the two strands and places the strand gap on that one. If any cyclical strands remain, or if any strand is longer than the maximum allowed, the nicking procedure fails and the algorithm needs to be run again with different parameters.

The primary sequence for a cycle cover design is generated with a local search algorithm previously described in [8]. The search algorithm, based on the Focused Metropolis Search method [27], aims to minimise the length of the longest repeated substring to avoid non-specific and unintended pairings, while also adhering to the given constraints of GC-content, forced bases, and prohibited subsequences. Although fully complementary non-specific pairings can exist only if repeated substrings exist, a repeated substring does not necessarily mean that there is potential for a non-specific pairing. Since this distinction is not very restrictive, it was chosen as the optimisation target. Due to computational complexity, the algorithm only considers substrings contained entirely within strands, rather than subsequences or substrings spanning across more than one strand.

The search algorithm works by first assigning each nucleotide a random complementary base and then checking if the constraints are satisfied. If not, a random base corresponding to an unsatisfied constraint is chosen, and it is randomly changed to another. If the number of unsatisfied constraints is decreased, the change is accepted. Otherwise it is reverted with a probability of $1 - \eta$. This process is repeated until all constraints are satisfied. Then, the algorithm uses the same procedure with the repeated substrings: If a repeat of length R exists, a random base associated with such a repeat is changed, and the change is again accepted if no constraints were broken and if the number of repeats decreased. Otherwise, it is reverted with a probability of $1 - \eta$. This search process is iterated for K cycles, or until no repeats of length R exist. Afterwards, if repeats do exist, R is increased by one, and otherwise it is decreased by one. The search algorithm can then be run again with the updated value of R.

This algorithm generally performs well. A strand of length L even without any secondary structure whatsoever must contain repeated substrings of length $\lfloor (log_4 L) \rfloor$, and this algorithm typically yields primary sequences with the longest repeat equal to that number or larger by only one unless the constraints are unusually restrictive.

4   Cycle Covers and Graph Embeddings

The s.a.p. cycle cover design problem can be formulated in terms of graph embeddings in surfaces. We recall that a *(closed) surface* is a compact topological space where every point has a neighbourhood topologically equivalent to the plane and that a surface is *orientable* if it does not contain the Möbius strip. The classification theorem of closed orientable surfaces states that such a surface is either a sphere or a sphere with g handles attached, where g is the genus of the surface [20]. For instance, the surface of the bunny mesh model 4, which is the union of all the points in all the polygons (including their interiors), is topologically equivalent to a sphere.

A *graph embedding* in a surface is an injective mapping of the graph vertices to surface points, along with a mapping of the edges to arcs in the surface, such that a) the interiors of the arcs are disjoint, b) for each edge, the ends of its arc meet the points associated with the end vertices of the edge and c) no vertex is mapped to the interior of an arc. Removing the image of the graph from the surface results in a collection of distinct regions called *faces*, and when these faces are all topological open disks the embedding is said to be a *2-cell embedding*.

In a mesh model such as the bunny in Fig. 4, the surface is given in 3D as the boundary of the solid, and the embedded graph comprises the points and lines of the mesh. However, graphs can also be embedded in abstract representations of surfaces, such as that of the torus as a square where the horizontal and vertical boundaries are appropriately identified to be glued. For a target wireframe like the $3 \times 3 \times 3$ lattice in Fig. 4, no polygonal faces are present, and an embedding of the abstract graph in an abstract surface will be needed for interpreting the s.a.p double covers in terms of graph embeddings in surfaces.

An s.a.p cycle cover of a wireframe is equivalent to a double cover by face-bounding cycles of a 2-cell embedding of the abstract graph in some orientable closed surface. The equivalence of s.a.p cycle covers and facial cycle covers is evident by looking at *pure rotation systems* that capture the combinatorial structure of 2-cell graph embeddings in orientable surfaces [13]. A *pure rotation system* $\Pi(G)$ of a graph G assigns to each vertex v in the graph a cyclic permutation π_v of the edges incident to v. A 2-cell embedding of a graph induces a pure rotation system by fixing the π_v to be the clockwise order of the arcs in the local neighborhood of v. Conversely, a pure rotation system $\Pi(G)$ uniquely determines, up to orientation preserving equivalence, a graph embedding in an orientable surface. The faces of the embedding can be identified using a face tracing algorithm that generates the oriented bounding cycles of the faces [13, p. 115]. For each vertex incident edge pair (v, e), the rotation system induces an *oriented transition* $(e, v, \pi_v(e))$. The face tracing algorithm finds the oriented boundary cycles of the faces by joining the transitions. For example, the two transitions $(e, v, \pi_v(e))$, $(\pi_v(e), w, \pi_w(\pi_v(e))$ can be naturally joined as $(\ldots, e, v, \pi_v(e), w, \pi_w(\pi_v(e), \ldots))$.

There are many ways of selecting a pure rotation system for an abstract graph. If the target wireframe is the edge-skeleton of a given underlying orientable surface mesh, the s.a.p. cycle cover method chooses the pure rotation system that is induced by clockwise cyclic orderings of edges incident to the vertices. If the target wireframe is given without an underlying surface mesh, the s.a.p. cycle cover method extracts a pure rotation system from the geometric proximity of local edges in the real 3-space of the wireframe, as described in Sect. 2.

The set of cycles generated by the method can be seen as the oriented boundary cycles $\mathcal{C} = \{C_1, \ldots, C_k\}$ of the faces by the face tracing algorithm. There are four oriented transitions associated with an edge $e = \{u, v\}$ in the equivalent rotation system: the two transitions $(e, u, \pi_u(e))$, $(\pi_u^{-1}(e), u, e)$ at u and the two transitions $(\pi_v^{-1}(e), v, e)$, $(e, v, \pi_v(e))$ at v. Thus, the cycles in $\mathcal{C}$ that trace e will contain the segments $(\pi_u^{-1}(e), u, e, v, \pi_v(e))$ and $(\pi_v^{-1}(e), v, e, u, \pi_u(e))$, traversing e in antiparallel directions. One can easily show that in this case the repetition neighborhood N of any vertex v induced by $\mathcal{C}$ is the regular neighborhood of v, i.e. the set of all vertices adjacent to v: Let $\pi_v = (e_0, e_1, \ldots, e_{d-1})$ and $e_i = \{v, u_i\}$, for $0 \le i \le d-1$, where d is the degree of v. For any $0 \le i \le d-1$, the vertices u_i, $u_{i+1 \bmod d}$ are in the same repetition neighborhood because of the transition $(e_i, v, e_{i+1 \bmod d})$. Thus all u_i are in the same repetition neighborhood as desired for a stable vertex.

A graph can be cellularly embedded in orientable closed surfaces of different genera. The number of faces in the embedding is related to the genus through the generalised Euler's polyhedron formula $|V| - |E| + |F| = 2 - 2g$, where g is the genus of the surface and $|F|$ denotes the number of faces. The number of circular strands used by the s.a.p. cycle cover method is thus directly connected to the embedded graph, with each face in the embedding corresponding to one strand. Along this line, Jonoska and Saito [15] have used thickened graph models to show that the maximum number of circular strands needed to assemble an abstract connected 3-regular graph is at most $\beta_1 + 1$, where $\beta_1 = |E| - |V| + 1$ is the co-tree size of the graph, also known as its first Betti number.

If the fewest possible circular strands is desirable, a maximum genus embedding should be used. Ideally, a one face embedding would result in a strong antiparallel cover by a single cycle, but as noted earlier this is only possible if and only if each connected component of the co-tree has an even number of edges [9]. Ellis-Monaghan [6] has proved for instance that the minimum number of circular strands needed to assemble the tetrahedral graph is two. Interestingly, the minimum number of circular strands needed for an s.a.p. cycle cover can actually be computed in polynomial time using maximum genus embeddings [11]. If, on the other hand, the number of circular strands should be maximised, a minimum genus embedding can be used. In general, deciding whether a graph can be cellularly embedded into a surface of a given genus g is NP-complete [28] and thus there will not likely be a polynomial time algorithm for determining the maximum number of circular strands for an s.a.p. cover.

5   Design Examples

The s.a.p. cycle cover method is integrated in the *DNAforge* web application, which provides an automated platform for designing nucleic acid nanostructures based on 3D wireframe models. With this method, labelled CC-DNA in the *DNAforge* user interface, users can generate s.a.p. cycle cover routings and nucleotide level models from any target wireframe with a single click. The workflow of the tool is illustrated in Fig. 4, which showcases the examples of a bunny and a $3 \times 3 \times 3$ lattice. Note that while the bunny mesh model is provided with explicit faces and as embedded on a sphere-equivalent surface, the 3×3×3 lattice mesh model contains just the wireframe, because the $3 \times 3 \times 3$ lattice as a 3D linearly embedded graph does not have any natural face structure.

The implementation offers users the flexibility to influence the design by adjusting several parameters such as the scale, minimum hybridisation length, and GC-content of the structures. The user can also optionally reduce strain in the designed structure with a DNA-duplex level physical simulation.

Once the DNA wireframe is designed, it can be exported in various formats, including as a PDB file, a UNF file [19] or as *oxDNA* files [31] for simulation or further editing, or as a CSV file containing the primary sequences. The nucleotide model can also be simulated directly from the interface, provided the *DNAforge* backend together with the *oxDNA* molecular simulation package [25, 30, 31] are locally installed.

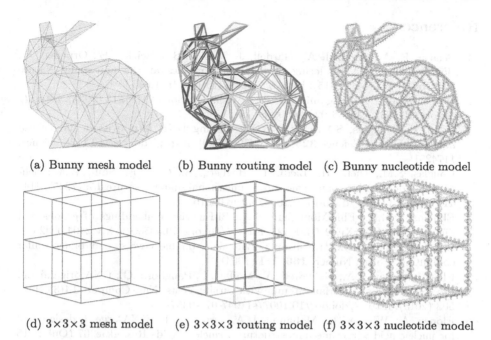

(a) Bunny mesh model   (b) Bunny routing model   (c) Bunny nucleotide model

(d) 3×3×3 mesh model   (e) 3×3×3 routing model   (f) 3×3×3 nucleotide model

Fig. 4. The CC-DNA design workflow in *DNAforge* for a bunny and a 3 × 3 × 3 lattice. The user first uploads a 3D model in the standard OBJ format (a, d). With a click of a button, *DNAforge* constructs an s.a.p. cycle cover routing for the mesh (b, e). The cycle cover is then automatically converted into a nucleotide-level model (c, f).

6   Conclusions and Further Work

We have introduced a general and efficient design method for scaffold-free DNA wireframe nanostructures via strong antiparallel cycle covers. An implementation of the method is available on the online design tool DNAforge, accessible at https://dnaforge.org/.

In some application settings, the user might be interested in the minimum genus embedding of their wireframe model, and this can in principle be determined via the connection of strand count to embedding surface genus. The task is NP-complete, but a combinatorial search might work in many practical scenarios. Also exploring maximum-genus embeddings with the goal of minimising the strand count is of interest, and we are looking forward to experimental validations of the design method.

References

1. Benson, E., Mohammed, A., Gardell, J., Masich, S., Czeizler, E., Orponen, P., Högberg, B.: DNA rendering of polyhedral meshes at the nanoscale. Nature **523**(7561), 441–444 (2015). https://doi.org/10.1038/nature14586

2. Dey, S., et al.: DNA origami. Nat. Rev. Methods Primers **1**(1), 13 (2021). https://doi.org/10.1038/s43586-020-00009-8

3. Dietz, H., Douglas, S.M., Shih, W.M.: Folding DNA into twisted and curved nanoscale shapes. Science **325**(5941), 725 (2009). https://doi.org/10.1126/science.1174251

4. Douglas, S.M., Dietz, H., Liedl, T., Högberg, B., Graf, F., Shih, W.M.: Self-assembly of DNA into nanoscale three-dimensional shapes. Nature **459**(7245), 414–418 (2009). https://doi.org/10.1038/nature08016

5. Ellingham, M.N., Ellis-Monaghan, J.A.: Bi-Eulerian embeddings of graphs and digraphs (2024). arXiv:2404.00325, https://doi.org/10.48550/arXiv.2404.00325

6. Ellis-Monaghan, J.A.: Transition polynomials, double covers, and biomolecular computing. Congr. Numer. **166**, 181 (2004)

7. Ellis-Monaghan, J.A., McDowell, A., Moffatt, I., Pangborn, G.: DNA origami and the complexity of Eulerian circuits with turning costs. Nat. Comput. **14**(3), 491–503 (2015). https://doi.org/10.1007/s11047-014-9457-2

8. Elonen, A., Wimbes, L., Mohammed, A., Orponen, P.: DNAforge: a design tool for nucleic acid wireframe nanostructures. Nucleic Acids Res. gkae367 (Online 15 May 2024). https://doi.org/10.1093/nar/gkae367

9. Fijavž, G., Pisanski, T., Rus, J.: Strong traces model of self-assembly polypeptide structures. MATCH Commun. Math. Comput. Chem. **71**, 199–212 (2014). https://doi.org/10.48550/arXiv.1308.4024

10. Fleischner, H.: Eulerian Graphs and Related Topics. Part 1, vol. 1, Annals of Discrete Mathematics, vol. 45. North-Holland Publishing Co., Amsterdam (1990)

11. Furst, M.L., Gross, J.L., McGeoch, L.A.: Finding a maximum-genus graph imbedding. J. ACM (JACM) **35**(3), 523–534 (1988). https://doi.org/10.1145/44483.44485

12. Goodman, R.P., Berry, R.M., Turberfield, A.J.: The single-step synthesis of a DNA tetrahedron. Chem. Commun. **40**(12), 1372–1373 (2004). https://doi.org/10.1039/B402293A

13. Gross, J.L., Tucker, T.W.: Topological Graph Theory. Courier Corporation (2001)

14. Gross, J.L., Yellen, J., Zhang, P.: Handbook of Graph Theory, 2nd edn. CRC Press, Boca Raton (2014)

15. Jonoska, N., Saito, M.: Boundary components of thickened graphs. In: Jonoska, N., Seeman, N.C. (eds.) DNA Computing, pp. 70–81. Springer, Berlin Heidelberg (2002). https://doi.org/10.1007/3-540-48017-X_7

16. Jun, H., et al.: Rapid prototyping of arbitrary 2D and 3D wireframe DNA origami. Nucleic Acids Res. **49**(18), 10265–10274 (2021). https://doi.org/10.1093/nar/gkab762

17. Jungnickel, D.: Graphs, Networks and Algorithm. Algorithms and Computation in Mathematics. Springer, Berlin, Heidelberg (2013). https://doi.org/10.1007/978-3-642-32278-5

18. Ke, Y., Ong, L.L., Shih, W.M., Yin, P.: Three-dimensional structures self-assembled from DNA bricks. Science **338**(6111), 1177 (2012). https://doi.org/10.1126/science.1227268

19. Kuták, D., Poppleton, E., Miao, H., Šulc, P., Barišić, I.: Unified nanotechnology format: one way to store them all. Molecules **27**(1), 63 (2022). https://doi.org/10.3390/molecules27010063

20. Lee, J.: Introduction to Topological Manifolds, vol. 202. Springer Science & Business Media, Cham (2010). https://doi.org/10.1007/978-1-4419-7940-7

21. Marchi, A.N., Saaem, I., Vogen, B.N., Brown, S., LaBean, T.H.: Toward larger DNA origami. Nano Lett. **14**(10), 5740–5747 (2014). https://doi.org/10.1021/nl502626s

22. Ong, L.L., Hanikel, N., Yaghi, O.K., Grun, C., Strauss, M.T., Bron, P., Lai-Kee-Him, J., Schueder, F., Wang, B., Wang, P., Kishi, J.Y., Myhrvold, C., Zhu, A., Jungmann, R., Bellot, G., Ke, Y., Yin, P.: Programmable self-assembly of three-dimensional nanostructures from 10,000 unique components. Nature **552**(7683), 72–77 (2017). https://doi.org/10.1038/nature24648

23. Orponen, P.: Design methods for 3D wireframe DNA nanostructures. Nat. Comput. **17**(1), 147–160 (2018). https://doi.org/10.1007/s11047-017-9647-9

24. Rothemund, P.W.K.: Folding DNA to create nanoscale shapes and patterns. Nature **440**(7082), 297–302 (2006). https://doi.org/10.1038/nature04586

25. Rovigatti, L., Šulc, P., Reguly, I.Z., Romano, F.: A comparison between parallelization approaches in molecular dynamics simulations on GPUs. J. Comput. Chem. **36**(1), 1–8 (2015). https://doi.org/10.1002/jcc.23763

26. Seeman, N.C., Sleiman, H.F.: DNA nanotechnology. Nat. Rev. Mater. **3**, 17068 (2017). https://doi.org/10.1038/natrevmats.2017.68

27. Seitz, S., Alava, M., Orponen, P.: Focused local search for random 3-satisfiability. J. Stat. Mech. Theory Exp. **2005**(06), P06006 (2005). https://doi.org/10.1088/1742-5468/2005/06/P06006

28. Thomassen, C.: The graph genus problem is NP-complete. J. Algorithms **10**(4), 568–576 (1989). https://doi.org/10.1016/0196-6774(89)90006-0

29. Veneziano, R., et al.: Designer nanoscale DNA assemblies programmed from the top down. Science (2016). https://doi.org/10.1126/science.aaf4388

30. Šulc, P., Romano, F., Ouldridge, T.E., Doye, J.P.K., Louis, A.A.: A nucleotide-level coarse-grained model of RNA. J. Chem. Phys. **140**(23), 235102 (2014). https://doi.org/10.1063/1.4881424

31. Šulc, P., Romano, F., Ouldridge, T.E., Rovigatti, L., Doye, J.P.K., Louis, A.A.: Sequence-dependent thermodynamics of a coarse-grained DNA model. J. Chem. Phys. **137**(13), 135101 (2012). https://doi.org/10.1063/1.4754132

32. Wang, W., et al.: Complex wireframe DNA nanostructures from simple building blocks. Nat. Commun. **10**(1), 1067 (2019). https://doi.org/10.1038/s41467-019-08647-7

33. Wei, B., Dai, M., Yin, P.: Complex shapes self-assembled from single-stranded DNA tiles. Nature **485**(7400), 623–626 (2012). https://doi.org/10.1038/nature11075

34. Yin, P., Hariadi, R.F., Sahu, S., Choi, H.M.T., Park, S.H., LaBean, T.H., Reif, J.H.: Programming DNA tube circumferences. Science **321**(5890), 824–826 (2008). https://doi.org/10.1126/science.1157312

35. Zhang, H., Chao, J., Pan, D., Liu, H., Huang, Q., Fan, C.: Folding super-sized DNA origami with scaffold strands from long-range PCR. Chem. Commun. **48**(51), 6405–6407 (2012). https://doi.org/10.1039/c2cc32204h

Automated Rendering of Multi-stranded DNA Complexes with Pseudoknots

Małgorzata Nowicka[1], Vinay K. Gautam[2], and Pekka Orponen[1(✉)]

[1] Department of Computer Science, Aalto University, Espoo, Finland
{malgorzata.nowicka,pekka.orponen}@aalto.fi
[2] Department of Chemical Engineering, NTNU, Trondheim, Norway
vinay.k.gautam@ntnu.no

Abstract. We present a general method for rendering representations of multi-stranded DNA complexes from textual descriptions into 2D diagrams. The complexes can be arbitrarily pseudoknotted, and if a planar rendering is possible, the method will determine one in time which is essentially linear in the size of the textual description. (That is, except for a final stochastic fine-tuning step.) If a planar rendering is not possible, the method will compute a visually pleasing approximate rendering in quadratic time. Examples of diagrams produced by the method are presented in the paper.

Keywords: DNA strand displacement · DSD systems · multi-strand DNA · pseudoknots · graph drawing · visualisation

1 Background

Multi-stranded DNA complexes are of wide interest in the area of DNA nanotechnology. In the present work, we focus specifically on their use as building blocks in DNA strand displacement (DSD) systems [40], which are a widely-used methodology for embedding computational processes in the interactions of pre-designed short DNA strands.

The design and modelling of DSD systems is typically done at the binding-domain level, where a *domain* is a contiguous and functionally distinct sequence of nucleotides. A DNA *strand* is then a sequence of connected domains. Strands are oriented, starting at the *5'-end* and ending at the *3'-end*. Domains of different strands may bind with each other in antiparallel orientation, forming a DNA complex which is (mathematically speaking) a multiset of strands connected by domain bindings. At the design phase one is however generally not interested in individual strands and complexes, but rather distinct similarity types (equivalence classes) of these. A similarity type of DNA complexes is called a DNA *species*, whereas with some abuse of terminology the term "strand" is retained also for similarity types of strands.

Automated tools for designing and modelling DSD systems commonly follow a four-stage pipeline (Fig. 1) in which we are presently concerned with the final

© The Author(s), under exclusive license to Springer Nature Switzerland AG 2024
D.-J. Cho and J. Kim (Eds.): UCNC 2024, LNCS 14776, pp. 190–202, 2024.
https://doi.org/10.1007/978-3-031-63742-1_14

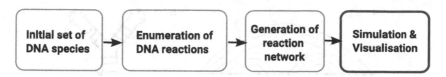

Fig. 1. DSD system design pipeline.

step of visualisation — or more specifically the task of producing 2D diagrams of species generated from an initial set of species. Such diagrams are highly useful to understand the characteristics of species emerging in a given DSD system, validate the system design, and communicate related results to a broader audience.

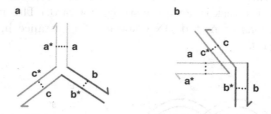

Fig. 2. DNA species diagrams. a: Good drawing. b: Unsatisfactory drawing.

As is customary in the DSD design literature [40], we aim to render multi-strand DNA species as 2D diagrams, where each strand is represented as a sequence of contiguous line or curve segments that depict the domains, and domain pairings are indicated by some connector symbol, for instance a line segment connecting the domain midpoints (Fig. 2). Ideally, a 2D rendering of a given DNA species should satisfy the following conditions: (i) the domain depictions are straight-line segments of equal length; (ii) bound domains are drawn close to each other, ideally at a fixed distance and in antiparallel orientation; (iii) the polylines (or polycurves) representing species do not cross each other in the drawing plane. For structurally complex species, the task of satisfying all these constraints simultaneously and satisfactorily can be quite difficult or even impossible.

The Challenge of Pseudoknots. Many current DNA species rendering algorithms take inspiration from methods used in visualising RNA secondary structures. In RNA, a single strand folds upon itself and forms bindings pairing its nucleotides. In simple "nested" pairing arrangements, this process results in a tree-like secondary structure with contiguous *stem* segments of paired bases constituting the edges and *loops* of unpaired bases forming the leaves (Fig. 3). Visualisation methods for such structures commonly follow this intrinsic tree layout [6, 31].

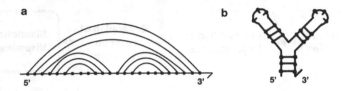

Fig. 3. RNA secondary structure diagrams. a: A 1D arc diagram depicting base pairings. b: Corresponding 2D secondary structure diagram.

This approach extends to DNA visualisations as well, because if the strands constituting a multi-strand DNA species are arranged in some linear order and connected into a single strand, the rendering problem reduces to the corresponding one for RNA secondary structures. Thus, the only additional task is to determine a good ordering for the strands. (Of course for n strands there are $n!$ possible orderings, so the task is not quite straightforward.) This method is widely used in visualisations of nested DNA species, for instance in the DyNAMiC Workbench tool [16].

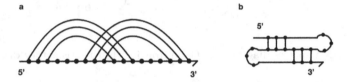

Fig. 4. An H-type RNA pseudoknot. a: Arc diagram. b: Secondary structure diagram.

A problem emerges, however, when base pairings are not nested, but cross each other in the linear strand arrangement, as in Fig. 4a. In this *pseudoknotted* situation, the secondary structure no longer has a tree-like character (Fig. 4b), and many challenges ensue both in diagramming and otherwise analysing the structure [1,25].

A number of RNA visualisers nevertheless support the rendering of pseudoknotted structures using alternative approaches. PseudoViewer3 [7] identifies and draws known types of pseudoknots, and arranges the rest of the structure in relation to them. The tool jViz.Rna 2.0 [36] uses a force-directed algorithm for assembling the nucleotides, whereas jViz.RNA 4.0 [30] and forna [23] identify the pseudoknotting connections and draw them on top of a pruned pseudoknot-free skeleton of the species.

A multi-strand DNA species can be considered pseudoknotted when no linear ordering of its constituent strands results in a nested base-pairing arrangement. Rendering of pseudoknotted species in DSD systems has been little studied, because when there is no tree structure to be identified, exploring the space of $n!$ permutations for a species of n strands becomes challenging. VisualDSD [24], a widely-used tool for designing and modelling DSD systems, takes the approach of rendering a pseudoknot-free skeleton of the species and then just highlighting the pseudoknot-inducing domains, without connecting them visually. While in RNA this approach may be helpful in order to easily identify the type of the pseudoknot, in DNA it is less useful in illustrating the structure. (For examples, see Fig. 7.) A force-directed approach was used in [15] but it covers only relatively simple pseudoknotted structures. Other common DSD system design tools such as NUPACK [39] and DyNAMiC Workbench [16] do not provide options for visualising pseudoknots.

2   A DNA Species Rendering Algorithm

We approach the task of rendering multi-strand DNA species in a Gordian-knot manner: since a key target is to achieve a noncrossing arrangement for the strands, we aim to achieve this directly by a planar graph embedding technique that is guaranteed to find such an arrangement efficiently if one exists. For cases where no planar (noncrossing) representation is possible, we present an efficient and visually appealing approximate method.

Luckily, quite many pseudoknotted (RNA and multi-strand DNA) structures have planar renderings: a simple example is the H-type pseudoknot in Fig. 4, for which a planar drawing is presented in subfigure 4b. In RNA, planar pseudoknots are closely related to the Rivas-Eddy class of secondary structures, which is also one of the largest known algorithmically tractable families of RNA structures [13, 26, 29].

Text Representation. For textual description of multi-strand DNA species we use a 'process calculus' notation based on named-domain pairings and introduced to the DSD context in [27] (see Fig. 5a). Lowercase letters and numbers are used as domain names (e.g. a). A complementary domain has the same name with an additional asterisk appended (e.g. a^*). A domain with a given name can appear repeatedly. A pairing of domains is indicated by an exclamation mark followed by a matching index, appended to the domain names (e.g. $a!1$, $a*!1$). Each pairing must be unique. A strand comprises one or more sequentially connected domains, enclosed in angle brackets: $\langle a\ b \rangle$. A species is a collection of strands, separated by two forward slashes: $\langle a\ b \rangle // \langle c \rangle$. Paired domains must belong to the same species in the description.

Graph Representation and Algorithm Generality. Figure 5a presents an example of a textual description of a species S and Fig. 5b its graph representation G. The vertices in G correspond to the domain boundaries, including the 5'- and 3'-ends, of the strands in S. The domains within the strands (solid lines in Fig. 5b) and the domain pairings connecting the strands (dashed lines in Fig. 5b) constitute the edges in G. To ensure the antiparallel orientation of each domain pairing $\{a, a^*\}$, the 5'-end of a is connected to the 3'-end of a^* and vice versa. We say that a species S is *planar* if G is a planar graph, i.e. can be embedded on a plane

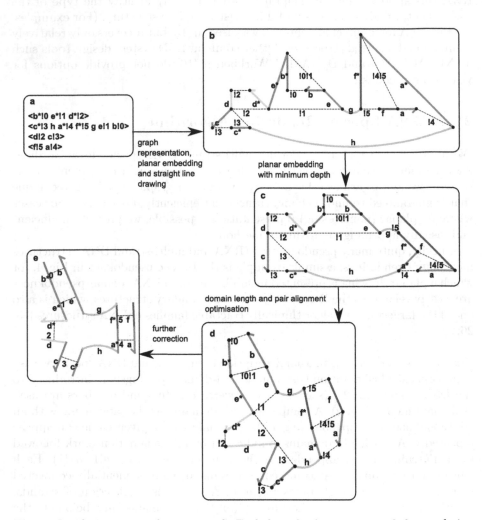

Fig. 5. Rendering steps of a species S. Each box displays a stage of the rendering algorithm. The captions on the arrows indicate the operations taken to achieve the next step. a: Text representation. b: Straight-line drawing. Vertices mark the ends of domains, solid lines represent the domains and dashed lines the pair connections. c: Minimised depth. d: Initial optimisation. e: Final drawing.

without edge crossings. Determining if S is planar can be done in linear time by using any planarity testing algorithm, e.g. the Boyer-Myrvold edge addition method [5].

To characterise the generality of the algorithm we consider the notion of *book thickness* of a graph [2] that is widely used in the context of RNA theory [21]. For a given graph G a *book embedding* comprises a linear ordering of the vertices of G, called the book *spine*, and a partition of its edges. The edges in each class of the partition are drawn as non-crossing arcs on a separate halfplane (a *page*) bordered on the book spine. The book thickness of G is then the minimum number of pages needed to achieve such a book embedding, for some ordering of the vertices along the spine. It is known that the book thickness of a graph G is at most 2 if and only if G is a subgraph of a planar Hamiltonian graph [2].

In RNA the vertices represent nucleotides and the edges their pairings [21]. There is only one possible ordering of the vertices, and in case of linear RNA, connecting the first and the last vertex makes the graph Hamiltonian. Therefore the existence of a planar rendering of an RNA secondary structure is equivalent to the condition that its arc diagram can be embedded on at most 2 pages. This can be tested by e.g. checking the bipartiteness of an inconsistency graph $\theta(V, E)$ [21], where every vertex corresponds to a crossing of the arcs in the arc diagram.

In multi-strand DNA, the ordering of the vertices is not given, which makes the problem of determining if a 2-page embedding exists NP-complete [10,37]. Moreover, there exist maximal planar graphs that are not Hamiltonian, therefore some planar graphs might need more than 2 pages (see Fig. 7c). In fact, any planar graph can be embedded on 4 pages [22,38]. Therefore the notion of planar DNA species as defined in this paper encompasses all 1-page (= nested) species, all 2-page pseudoknots, and some pseudoknots that require more than 2 pages and are planar.

Straight-Line Drawing. It is known that any planar simple graph (= no multi-edges, no self-loops) has a plane embedding with straight-line edges [12,32,35]. By definition, a species graph G as described earlier is always simple, and can thus be drawn with straight lines if it represents a planar species. Rendering G this way satisfies the conditions that the domains are drawn as straight-line segments and the shortest distance between domains within a pair is represented by a straight line.

Given a planar species graph G, a drawing (plane embedding) D of G can be achieved in linear time by an algorithm described in [9] that produces crossing-free, straight-line drawings on an $(n-2) \times (n-2)$ grid for graphs with n vertices. The algorithm comprises four stages:

1. G is augmented by additional edges to achieve the biconnectivity required for the canonical decomposition [20] applied in step 3.
2. A combinatorial embedding of G (clockwise ordering of incident edges at each vertex) is determined e.g. with the Boyer-Myrvold method [5]. The face of G with most vertices is chosen as the external face.

3. The canonical decomposition is computed. This is an ordered partition of the set of vertices of G and determines the order of the vertices in the process of drawing.
4. The graph is drawn on a plane according to the algorithm in [9]. The augmented edges are removed from D.

All stages of the algorithm are of linear time complexity. An example result is presented in Fig. 5b.

The aforementioned algorithm covers only planar graphs, and a different approach needs to be adopted for the non-planar cases. Our non-planar drawing method follows the topology-shape-metrics approach [11, 34] for orthogonal drawings, where the edges may be either straight or bend 90°. It prioritises the minimisation of the number of crossings and adheres to other aesthetic criteria such as minimising the number of edge bends, edge length, and the area of the drawing. These criteria correspond to our criteria of a good DNA species drawing with no crossings and close distances between the paired domains. The algorithm comprises three stages:

1. G is planarised by first finding some maximal planar subgraph of G and then reinserting the remaining edges in a way that minimises the number of crossings [18]. A dummy vertex is created at the location of each crossing. From here, a planar embedding is computed using the same method as in step 2 of the planar drawing.
2. Given the planar embedding, the orthogonalisation stage of the algorithm constructs a network in which the minimum number of bends in G is determined by a min-cost flow method described in [33].
3. Lastly, the compaction stage determines the lengths of the edges and coordinates of the vertices, producing a drawing of minimum possible area. In the final rendering of D, the dummy vertices are removed, edge bending is ignored and the edges are represented with straight lines. This may lead to crossings in D.

The time complexity of this algorithm ranges from $O(n)$ to $O((n + c)^2 \log n)$, where c is the number of crossings, depending on the planarity of the graph and the orthogonalisation and compaction methods [34].

Minimum Depth and Maximum External Face Drawing. The *depth* of a graph is a measure of the topological nesting of its biconnected components (maximal biconnected subgraphs) [28]. In a species graph G, the biconnected components comprise connected domains and domain pairs. When depth is not minimised, some domains are topologically nested inside other pairs, which prevents the outer pair from achieving the desired proximity between its domains.

Consider a planar embedding of a graph of a species with strands $\langle e!1\ f \rangle\ \langle e*!1 \rangle$. Let r be a vertex between domains e and f and !1 be the edge connecting the bound domains. There exist two possible combinatorial embeddings in r (see Fig. 6d) but only the one of minimum depth will result in a drawing that minimises the distance between the paired domains. In Fig. 5b, pairs $aa^*\ bb^*$, and ff^* are topologically nested, and therefore pairs cc^*, dd^*, and ee^* cannot properly align.

In order to minimise the depth, a linear time embedding algorithm [19] that uses an SPQR-tree data structure is applied to the second stage of the planar G drawing. It chooses a planar embedding of maximum external face size among all planar embeddings with minimum depth. Embeddings with maximum external face have shown to improve certain metrics like the length of the edges and the size of the area [17]. The result of the new embedding is presented in Fig. 5c.

Drawing Optimisation. The final step for both planar and non-planar G is to adjust the lengths of the edges without introducing new crossings in D. This consideration imposes an additional requirement on force-directed graph layout methods commonly used for such purposes. In a force-directed layout algorithm, the connected vertices are attracting each other until the distance between them is of desirable length, and the unconnected vertices are repelling each other. An additional node-edge repulsion formula tries to prevent the overlapping of nodes and edges, but due to the discreteness of the movements of the vertices, new crossings may appear. Article [3] introduces the use of zones around every vertex that confine its movement at each iteration of the algorithm and prevent the formation of new crossings (see Fig. 5d).

Further correction in the placement of the domains is required, as the previous step does not achieve the desired lengths for all the edges or the right alignment between domains in a pair. A simulated annealing algorithm [4] is used. Let domains d_1 and d_2 be paired and represented by vectors, such that $d_1 = [d_1^3, d_1^5]$ and $d_2 = [d_2^3, d_2^5]$. A distance to the correct placement of d_1 and d_2 is computed in three steps as follows (see Fig. 6).

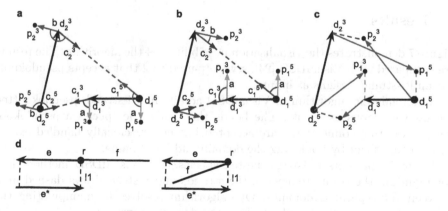

Fig. 6. Computing the correct placement of d_1 and d_2 and choosing the correct embedding for the vertex r.

1. Let a and b be vectors rotated $90°$ counter-clockwise in relation to d_1 and d_2 respectively. Let p_1^3 and p_1^5 be the endpoints of a anchored at both ends of d_1 and p_2^3 and p_2^5 be the endpoints of b anchored at both ends of d_2. Let $c_1^3 = [d_1^3, d_2^5]$, $c_1^5 = [d_1^5, d_2^3]$, $c_2^3 = [d_2^3, d_1^5]$, and $c_2^5 = [d_2^5, d_1^3]$ (Fig. 6a).
2. The correct side for d_1 to bind with d_2 is determined by the inequality:

$$\text{sign}(\cos(a, c_1^3)) + \text{sign}(\cos(a, c_1^5)) + \text{sign}(\cos(b, c_2^3)) + \text{sign}(\cos(b, c_2^5)) \geq 3$$

   where $\text{sign}(x) = 0$ if $x \leq 0$, and 1 otherwise. If the inequality is not satisfied, rotate a and b so that they are in $90°$ clockwise relation to d_1 and d_2 respectively, as shown in Fig. 6b. Note the change of the position of the endpoints of a and b.
3. Compute the distances from d_2^5 to p_1^3, d_2^3 to p_1^5, d_1^5 to p_2^3, and d_1^3 to p_2^5 as in Fig. 6c.

At each step of the algorithm, three factors are being optimised: the distance to the correct placement of domains for all pairs, the deviation from the desired lengths of the edges, the deviation from the desired distance between the ends of loop domains.

Figure 5e presents the final outcome where, to follow standard practice, the double vertices at the domain boundaries have been removed and replaced by single edges connecting the respective paired domains.

Implementation. The planar embeddings of minimum depth and maximum external face for both planar and non-planar species and the graph drawing were achieved with the help of algorithms in the Open Graph Drawing Framework [8]. The visualisation is implemented as a part of the XDSD design tool [14].

3   Results

Figure 7 demonstrates the visualisation possibilities of the algorithm. The results are compared with VisualDSD [24], a widely-used tool that accepts pseudoknotted multi-strand designs as inputs.

The rendering algorithm in VisualDSD admits multi-strand, pseudoknotted species with loops as inputs. The bonds that make the species a pseudoknot (pseudoknotting connections) are accepted but not specifically handled except for denoting them by boldening the domain and bond name.

Figure 7a presents a 1-page, nested species. The VisualDSD method does not maintain the connectedness of the strands and instead draws dashed lines between the separated domains. Our algorithm resolves to manipulating the lengths of the domains in order to keep the domains together.

The species in Fig. 7b is a 2-page pseudoknot. The VisualDSD version breaks the species apart and superposes the pseudoknotting connections after the other parts of the species are rendered. Our method does not distinguish between the regular and pseudoknotting connections and renders all of them.

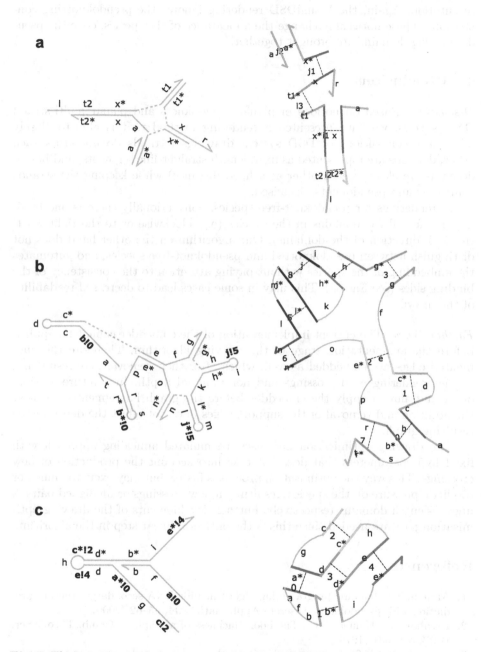

Fig. 7. Three species renderings generated by VisualDSD on the left and our algorithm on the right.

Figure 7c shows another pseudoknot, a 3-page species that has a planar representation. Again, the VisualDSD rendering ignores the pseudoknotting connections. These noticeably change the appearance of the species, once the pseudoknotting domains are brought together.

4 Conclusions

Discussion. Based on notions of planar pseudoknots and planar multi-strand DNA species, we have presented a rendering method that is able to closely follow the conventions of DSD system drawings (strands do not cross each other, domains are represented as fixed length straight-line segments, and bound domains are close to each other at a fixed distance) while keeping the strands connected and pseudoknots visualised.

In renderings for pseudoknot-free species, conventionally there is one binding side for all the domains in the species (e.g. clockwise or to the right w.r.t. the 5'-3' direction of the domains). Our algorithm on the other hand does not distinguish between pseudoknotted and pseudoknot-free species, and automates the embedding of the species without paying attention to the consistency of the binding sides (see Fig. 6a). This may in some cases lead to decreased readability of the drawing.

Further Work. The current implementation of the embedder cannot be applied before the augmentation stage of the drawing algorithm. Therefore the augmented edges are embedded as well, which after their removal may result in a species rendering with crossings and non-minimal depth. In a future version, one could aim to apply the embedder before the graph is augmented, so that the addition and removal of the support edges does not affect the depth of the resulting graph.

The drawing optimisation now uses a simulated annealing approach with fixed hyperparameters that does not take into account the production of new crossings. This way the optimisation process is faster, but may exert too much or too little pressure on the species, resulting in new crossings or unaligned pairs of uneven-length domains respectively. Further developments of the drawing optimisation part are needed since this is the only non-linear step in the algorithm.

References

1. Akutsu, T.: Dynamic programming algorithms for RNA secondary structure prediction with pseudoknots. Discrete Appl. Math. **104**, 45–62 (2000)
2. Bernhart, F., Kainen, P.C.: The book thickness of a graph. J. Comb. Theory Ser. B **27**, 320–331 (1979)
3. Bertault, F.: A force-directed algorithm that preserves edge-crossing properties. Inf. Process. Lett. **74**, 7–13 (2000)
4. Bertsimas, D., Tsitsiklis, J.: Simulated annealing. Stat. Sci. **8**, 10–15 (1993)
5. Boyer, J.M., Myrvold, W.J.: On the cutting edge: simplified O(n) planarity by edge addition. J. Graph Algorithms App. **8**, 241–273 (2004)

6. Bruccoleri, R.E., Heinrich, G.: An improved algorithm for nucleic acid secondary structure display. Comput. Appl. Biosci. **4**, 167–173 (1988)
7. Byun, Y., Han, K.: PseudoViewer3: generating planar drawings of large-scale RNA structures with pseudoknots. Bioinformatics **25**, 1435–1437 (2009)
8. Chimani, M., Gutwenger, C., Jünger, M., Klau, G.W., Klein, K., Mutzel, P.: The Open Graph Drawing Framework (OGDF). In: Handbook of Graph Drawing and Visualization, chap. 17. CRC Press (2014)
9. Chrobak, M., Kant, G.: Convex grid drawings of 3-connected planar graphs. Int. J. Comput. Geom. App. **7**, 211–223 (1997)
10. Chung, F.R.K., Leighton, F.T., Rosenberg, A.L.: Embedding graphs in books: a graph layout problem with applications to VLSI design. SIAM J. Algebr. Discr. Methods **8**, 33–58 (1986)
11. Di Battista, G., Eades, P., Tammasia, R., Tollis, I.G.: Graph Drawing. Prentice Hall, Upper Saddle River (1999)
12. Fáry, I.: On straight-line representation of planar graphs. Acta Sci. Math. **11**, 229–233 (1948)
13. Gao, S., Ding, K.: A graphical criterion of planarity for RNA secondary structures with pseudoknots in Rivas-Eddy class. Theoret. Comput. Sci. **395**, 47–56 (2008)
14. Gautam, V.K., Long, S., Nowicka, M., Orponen, P.: XDSD: A Tool Bridging DSD System Design to Rule-Based Modelling and Simulation. Web server: https://xdsd-web.org
15. Gautam, V.K., Long, S., Orponen, P.: RuleDSD: a rule-based modelling and simulation tool for DNA strand displacement systems. In: Proceedings of the 13th International Joint Conference on Biomedical Engineering Systems and Technologies, pp. 158–167 (2020)
16. Grun, C., Werfel, J., Zhang, D.Y., Yin, P.: DyNAMiC workbench: an integrated development environment for dynamic DNA nanotechnology. J. R. Soc. Interface **12**(111), 20150580 (2015)
17. Gutwenger, C.: Application of SPQR-trees in the planarization approach for drawing graphs. Ph.D. thesis, Technische Universität Dortmund (2010)
18. Gutwenger, C., Mutzel, P.: An experimental study of crossing minimization heuristics. In: Liotta, G. (ed.) GD 2003. LNCS, vol. 2912, pp. 13–24. Springer, Heidelberg (2004). https://doi.org/10.1007/978-3-540-24595-7_2
19. Gutwenger, C., Mutzel, P.: Graph embedding with minimum depth and maximum external face. In: Liotta, G. (ed.) GD 2003. LNCS, vol. 2912, pp. 259–272. Springer, Heidelberg (2004). https://doi.org/10.1007/978-3-540-24595-7_24
20. Harel, D., Meir, S.: An algorithm for straight-line drawing of planar graphs. Algorithmica **20**, 119–135 (2000)
21. Haslinger, C., Stadler, P.F.: RNA structures with pseudo-knots: graph-theoretical, combinatorial, and statistical properties. Bull. Math. Biol. **61**, 437–467 (1999)
22. Kaufmann, M., Bekos, M., Klute, F., Pupyrev, S., Raftopoulou, C., Ueckerdt, T.: Four pages are indeed necessary for planar graphs. J. Comput. Geom. **11**, 332–353 (2020)
23. Kerpedjiev, P., Hammer, S., Hofacker, I.L.: FoRNA (force-directed RNA): simple and effective online RNA secondary structure diagrams. Bioinformatics **31**, 3377–3379 (2015)
24. Lakin, M.R., Youssef, S., Polo, F., Emmott, S., Phillips, A.: Visual DSD: a design and analysis tool for DNA strand displacement systems. Bioinformatics **27**, 3211–3213 (2011)

25. Lyngsø, R.B.: Complexity of pseudoknot prediction in simple models. In: Díaz, J., Karhumäki, J., Lepistö, A., Sannella, D. (eds.) ICALP 2004. LNCS, vol. 3142, pp. 919–931. Springer, Heidelberg (2004). https://doi.org/10.1007/978-3-540-27836-8_77

26. Lyngsø, R.B., Pedersen, C.N.S.: RNA pseudoknot prediction in energy-based models. J. Comput. Biol. **7**, 409–427 (2000)

27. Petersen, R.L., Lakin, M.R., Phillips, A.: A strand graph semantics for DNA-based computation. Theoret. Comput. Sci. **632**, 43–73 (2016)

28. Pizzonia, M., Tamassia, R.: Minimum depth graph embedding. In: Paterson, M.S. (ed.) ESA 2000. LNCS, vol. 1879, pp. 356–367. Springer, Heidelberg (2000). https://doi.org/10.1007/3-540-45253-2_33

29. Rivas, E., Eddy, S.R.: A dynamic programming algorithm for RNA structure prediction including pseudoknots. J. Mol. Biol. **285**, 2053–2068 (1999)

30. Shabash, B., Wiese, K.C.: jViz.RNA 4.0 - visualizing pseudoknots and RNA editing employing compressed tree graphs. PLoS ONE **14**(5), e0210281 (2019)

31. Shapiro, B.A., Maizel, J., Lipkin, L.E., Currey, K., Whitney, C.: Generating non-overlapping displays of nucleic acid secondary structure. Nucleic Acids Res. **12**, 75–88 (1984)

32. Stein, S.K.: Convex maps. Proc. Am. Math. Soc. **2**, 464–466 (1951)

33. Tamassia, R.: On embedding a graph in the grid with the minimum number of bends. SIAM J. Comput. **16**, 421–444 (1987)

34. Tamassia, R., Di Battista, G., Batini, C.: Automatic graph drawing and readability of diagrams. IEEE Trans. Syst. Man Cybern. **18**, 61–79 (1988)

35. Wagner, K.: Bemerkungen zum Vierfarbenproblem. Jahresber. Deutsch. Math.-Verein. **46**, 26–32 (1936)

36. Wiese, K.C., Glen, E., Vasudevan, A.: jViz.Rna - a Java tool for RNA secondary structure visualization. IEEE Trans. NanoBiosci. **4**, 212–218 (2005)

37. Wigderson, A.: The complexity of the Hamiltonian circuit problem for planar graphs. Technical report 298, Princeton University (1982)

38. Yannakakis, M.: Planar graphs that need four pages. J. Combin. Theory Ser. B **145**, 241–263 (2020)

39. Zadeh, J., Steenberg, C., Bois, J., Wolfe, B., Pierce, M., Khan, A., Dirks, R., Pierce, N.: NUPACK: analysis and design of nucleic acid systems. J. Comput. Chem. **32**, 170–3 (2011)

40. Zhang, D.Y., Seelig, G.: Dynamic DNA nanotechnology using strand-displacement reactions. Nat. Chem. **3**, 103–113 (2011)

A Novel Oscillator Ising Machine Coupling Scheme for High-Quality Optimization

Shreesha Sreedhara$^{(\boxtimes)}$ [ID] and Jaijeet Roychowdhury [ID]

EECS Department, University of California at Berkeley, Berkeley, USA
{shreesha,jr}@berkeley.edu

Abstract. Oscillator Ising Machines (OIMs) are networks of coupled nonlinear oscillators that solve the NP-hard Ising problem heuristically. Conventionally, the oscillators in an OIM are coupled using resistors. However, the phase-domain properties of such couplers are unsatisfactory; resistively-coupled OIMs do not realize the optimization performance predicted by simulations of idealized OIMs. This has been a major hurdle impeding the development of high quality analog OIMs on integrated circuits. In this paper, we present a novel coupling scheme, the *sampling coupler*, that addresses this issue theoretically and practically. Essentially, a sampling coupler injects a current that depends on the *phase difference* between interacting oscillators. We prove analytically that using sampling couplers leads to idealized OIMs, abstracting away the waveforms and innate phase sensitivities of the oscillators. We evaluate sampling-coupler OIMs (using simulation) on a practically-important digital wireless communication problem and show that the performance is near-optimal. Sampling couplers therefore open up a way to implement practically feasible, high-performance analog OIMs using virtually any oscillator.

1 Introduction

Ising machines are hardware solvers for the Ising problem, a general mathematical formulation involving an energy-like quantity (the Ising Hamiltonian, a quadratic function of binary problem variables called spins). They have been a focus of research in recent years (*e.g.*, [1,5,11,24,26,27,29]), on account of their ability to solve combinatorial optimization (CO) problems using novel analog mechanisms. Virtually all CO problems can be mapped into Ising form [16], making them amenable to solution using Ising machines, which offer the promise of speed, energy efficiency and miniaturisability.

Oscillator Ising Machines (OIMs), a scheme based on the dynamics of suitably-designed networks of coupled oscillators, have shown particular promise for high-quality optimization [27,28]. Achieving this promise in hardware is currently an important research thrust. So far, OIMs with idealized phase-domain functions ($F_c(\cdot)$, described below) have shown excellent optimization characteristics, in both simulation [23,27,28] and a custom digital IC emulator [22].

© The Author(s), under exclusive license to Springer Nature Switzerland AG 2024
D.-J. Cho and J. Kim (Eds.): UCNC 2024, LNCS 14776, pp. 203–218, 2024.
https://doi.org/10.1007/978-3-031-63742-1_15

However, *integrated circuit realizations of OIMs that employ real analog oscillators to deliver high-quality optimizations on practically-important problems* have not been demonstrated yet. Beyond the intrinsic scientific value of such a demonstration, high-quality analog OIM implementations can offer important practical advantages over simulation and digital emulation, such as significantly lower energy-to-solution.

In this paper, we identify a fundamental difficulty in designing high-quality analog OIMs using prior schemes, and present a new OIM scheme that overcomes it. Existing OIM schemes rely on resistive couplings.[1] An OIM's overall mathematical model (the generalized Kuramoto model, explained below) is obtained by combining the resistive coupling equation with the oscillators' nonlinear phase-sensitivity function (the PPV, see below[2]). This combination results in the generalized-Kuramoto function $F_c(\cdot)$, the precise nature of which crucially determines how well the OIM solves optimization problems. A key problem with resistive coupling is that the resulting $F_c(\cdot)$ function essentially mirrors the oscillator's PPV function—which makes it very difficult, indeed practically impossible, to tailor its shape to improve the OIM's optimization performance. As a result, practical analog OIM hardware designs often do not match results from simulations/emulations, which use idealized $F_c(\cdot)$ functions that result in high-quality optimization performance.

Although it is difficult/impossible to alter oscillator designs to yield a desired $F_c(\cdot)$ shape with resistive coupling, an alternative possibility is to change the coupling mechanism to reach the same goal. We show here that this is not only possible, but easy to achieve in practice using simple circuitry. The new scheme is highly effective in enabling excellent OIM optimization performance using standard analog oscillator designs which do not perform well with resistive coupling.

The essential difference from resistive coupling is that the coupling signal injected into a target oscillator by a source oscillator depends not only on the source oscillator's waveform, but also on the target oscillator's waveform, in a multiplicative manner. In other words, multiplicative feedback from the target oscillator modifies the injection from the source oscillator. Because multiplication captures phase differences, the effect in the phase domain is an *injection that is dependent on the phase difference between the target and source oscillators*—in contrast to resistive coupling, where the injection depends only on the source oscillator's phase.

We present a simple circuit, which we dub the *sampling coupler*, that implements this new coupling scheme using early-late sampling. We prove that the new coupling scheme translates mathematically to a generalized-Kuramoto $F_c(\cdot)$ function that matches idealized ones that achieve excellent optimization quality

---

[1] More precisely: independent of the actual hardware implementation (which can use, *e.g.*, active elements instead of resistors), an oscillator couples to another by injecting a signal proportional to its voltage waveform.

[2] PPV stands for Perturbation Projection Vector; it is a periodic function that completely captures the dynamics of an oscillator's phase response to external inputs, such as those from other oscillators via coupling [7].

in simulation/emulation. We then simulate the generalized-Kuramoto model for the new coupling scheme and show that it performs essentially-perfect optimization, in contrast to resistive coupling, which yields poor results. The problem set we use for validation is a large set of benchmarks for the MU-MIMO[3] detection problem, an important practical problem that arises in modern digital wireless communications [20].

Our invention and validation of the sampling coupler constitutes a key advance for enabling genuinely analog IC realizations of high-performance OIMs in the short term. The concept may also have implications for other types of Ising machines.

The remainder of the paper is organized as follows. We provide background on OIMs and their mathematical models in Sect. 2. This is followed by development of the sampling coupler (Sect. 3). It constitutes the core of this paper. In Sect. 4, we present simulation results evaluating a sampling-coupler based OIM on MU-MIMO detection problems.

2   Background: OIM Mathematical Models

The Ising model is simply a weighted graph, *i.e.*, a collection of nodes/vertices and branches/edges between some pairs of nodes, with each branch having a real-number weight. Each node (termed a "spin" in this context) is allowed to take two values, either 1 or −1. Associated with this graph is an expression, the **Ising Hamiltonian**, which multiplies the weight of each branch by the values of the two spins it connects to, and sums over all branches, *i.e.*,

$$H = -\frac{1}{2} \sum_{\substack{i,j \\ i \neq j}} J_{ij} s_i s_j, \qquad \text{where } s_i \in \{-1, +1\} \tag{1}$$

are the spins. The Ising Hamiltonian is sometimes interpreted as an "energy" associated with a given configuration of the spins, although in many situations they have no connection with energy in physics. The "Ising problem" is to find spin configurations with the minimum possible energy.

In 2016, we proposed using networks of coupled oscillators to solve Ising problems [26]. In our scheme, each of the N spins of an Ising problem is implemented by an oscillator. The information needed to find a solution of the Ising problem is encoded in the phase of each oscillator. This purely classical scheme had a significant advantage over prior Ising machines: OIMs can potentially be implemented entirely on chip in CMOS device technologies, with all the attendant benefits of IC integration—small physical size, low power consumption, easy scalability to many spins and easy mass production at low cost.

A simple model of the phase dynamics of the oscillator network [7,13,26] is the Kuramoto model, which takes the form

$$\frac{1}{f_0} \frac{d}{dt} \Delta\phi_i(t) = -K_c \sum_{\substack{j=1 \\ j \neq i}}^{N} J_{ij} \sin(2\pi(\Delta\phi_i(t) - \Delta\phi_j(t))). \tag{2}$$

---

[3] MU-MIMO stands for Multi-User Multi-Input Multi-Output.

Here, $\Delta\phi_i(t)$ is the phase change of the ith oscillator due to the influences of the other oscillators via coupling, K_c is a positive constant, and f_0 is the nominal oscillation frequency, assumed the same for all the oscillators. Note that (2) is repeated for each oscillator, resulting in a coupled system of nonlinear differential equations describing the dynamics of the network.

This system is (as far as is known) impossible to solve analytically. However, a key result that underpins OIMs has been established analytically [26]. The result is that (2) can be equipped with a Lyapunov function [17], given by

$$E\left(\{\Delta\phi_k\}\right) \triangleq -K_c \sum_{i=1}^{N} \sum_{\substack{j=1 \\ j\neq i}}^{N} J_{ij} \cos(2\pi(\Delta\phi_i - \Delta\phi_j)). \tag{3}$$

The utility of a Lyapunov function is that it is non-increasing (*i.e.*, it always decreases, or remains constant) with time if the phases $\Delta\phi_i(t)$ obey (2). In other words, the Lyapunov function always decreases (eventually settling to a constant) as the oscillator system's dynamics evolve. The minima of the Lyapunov function correspond to stable equilibrium points (DC solutions) of (2), *i.e.*, **the coupled oscillator system's phases settle to values that minimize (locally) the Lyapunov function.**

The Lyapunov function (3) looks very similar to the Ising Hamiltonian (1) if the coupling weights are the same as (or a scaled version of) the Ising problem's J_{ij}. The main difference is that the Ising Hamiltonian contains $s_i s_j$ terms, while the Lyapunov function has a $\cos(2\pi(\Delta\phi_i - \Delta\phi_j))$ term. But if $2\pi\Delta\phi_i$ and $2\pi\Delta\phi_j$ were **restricted to either** 0 or π, with 0 defined as a spin value of 1 and π of -1, $\cos(2\pi(\Delta\phi_i - \Delta\phi_j))$ would equal $s_i s_j$, and the oscillator network's Lyapunov function would simply become a scaled version of the Ising Hamiltonian. In other words, the oscillator network's dynamics would innately solve the Ising problem, at least to the extent that it would find a local minimum of the Lyapunov function, which is a continuized version of the Ising Hamiltonian – if each oscillator's phase could somehow be restricted to be either 0 or π.

In general, there is no guarantee that the oscillator's phases will settle to either 0 or π—indeed, phases settle to steady-state values that range continuously over $[0, 2\pi]$. In such cases, the oscillator network's dynamics do not lead it to solutions that correspond to minima of the Ising Hamiltonian. It is in this context that "binarizing" the oscillator's phases using a phenomenon called SHIL[4] becomes important, since it restricts each oscillator's phase to 0 or π. Modifying the oscillator network with SHIL injection changes the Kuramoto equations to

---

[4] SHIL is an abbreviation of Sub-Harmonic Injection Locking; it is a phenomenon observed in nonlinear oscillators. In SHIL, the oscillator gets forced to oscillate in either one of two stable phases separated by π radians when it is perturbed by an external signal of a frequency that is twice the natural frequency of the oscillator [2].

$$\frac{1}{f_0}\frac{d}{dt}\Delta\phi_i(t) = -K_c\sum_{\substack{j=1\\j\neq i}}^{N} J_{ij}\sin(2\pi(\Delta\phi_i(t) - \Delta\phi_j(t))) - K_s\sin(4\pi\Delta\phi_i(t)). \quad (4)$$

The corresponding Lyapunov function becomes

$$E(\{\Delta\phi_k\}) \triangleq -K_c\sum_{i=1}^{N}\sum_{\substack{j=1\\j\neq i}}^{N} J_{ij}\cos(2\pi(\Delta\phi_i - \Delta\phi_j)) - K_s\sum_{i=1}^{N}\cos(4\pi\Delta\phi_i), \quad (5)$$

i.e., an additional term $\frac{K_s}{2}\sum\cos(4\pi\Delta\phi_i)$ appears, where K_s represents the strength of the input for inducing SHIL (called henceforth as SYNC). Since SHIL forces $2\pi\Delta\phi_i$ to either 0 or π (approximately), this term represents simply an addition of a constant offset to the Ising Hamiltonian, leaving the minima unchanged. Thus, **the coupled oscillator network with the addition of a 2nd harmonic SYNC input to induce SHIL naturally settles to phase solutions that locally minimize the Lyapunov function.**

This result is currently the best-known theoretical basis for oscillator Ising machines.

The above result only guarantees that the oscillator network will find **local** minima. To get the network out of local minima and guide it towards the global minimum, additional steps are needed.[5] An effective way to get the network out of local minima is to relax or remove the SYNC signal (which binarizes each oscillator's phases through SHIL) and restore it again several times. Reducing SYNC allows the oscillators to drift away from $0/\pi$ to continuous values; as SYNC is ramped up again, the system tends to find its way to minima that are lower than previous ones. Adding a moderate amount of noise to the system helps with the Lyapunov minimization process.

The sinusoidal functions in the above equations, originally proposed by Kuramoto [15], do not suffice for practical oscillators, which require the more general form[6]

$$\frac{1}{f_0}\frac{d}{dt}\Delta\phi_i(t) = \sum_{j=1,\,j\neq i}^{n} J_{ij}\,F_c(\Delta\phi_i(t) - \Delta\phi_j(t)) + F_s(2\Delta\phi_i(t)). \quad (6)$$

The key difference from the basic Kuramoto equations (4) is that the $\sin(2\pi(\cdot))$ functions in (4) are replaced by $F_c(\cdot)$ and $F_s(\cdot)$ in (6). These functions can be extracted from, *e.g.*, the detailed circuit description of an oscillator provided to circuit simulators for low-level electronic simulation [2,8]. Extracting $F_c()$

---

[5] This is characteristic of all Ising machines, as well as of optimization algorithms like simulated annealing.

[6] There is a corresponding Lyapunov function [25] that generalizes (5).

and $F_s()$ from low-level circuit differential equations involves first finding an abstraction known as the PPV phase-domain model [7,8] for the oscillator, *i.e.*,

$$\frac{1}{f_0}\frac{d}{dt}\Delta\phi(t) = v^T(f_0 t + \Delta\phi(t)) \cdot b(t). \tag{7}$$

In (7), the quantity $v(t)$, called the PPV, represents a "nonlinear sensitivity" of the oscillator's phase response to input perturbations; it can be extracted from the detailed differential equations of any oscillator using numerical techniques [8]. Furthermore, $b(t)$ represents 'small' perturbations (inputs) to the oscillator, in response to which the oscillator's phase changes by $\Delta\phi(t)$—obtained by solving (7). Note that the waveform of the perturbed oscillator (denoted by $x(t)$) is given by

$$x(t) = x_s(f_0 t + \Delta\phi(t)), \tag{8}$$

where $x_s(\cdot)$ represents the 1-periodic steady-state waveform of the unperturbed oscillator. $\Delta\phi(t)$ thus represents the additional phase shift due to the perturbation.

Once (7) is available, an averaging or "Adlerization" process [2,4] is used to extract $F_c(\cdot)$ and $F_s(\cdot)$. The derivation assumes that couplings between oscillators are resistive—*i.e.*, the injected signal into a target oscillator due to coupling with other oscillators is proportional to the waveform of a source oscillator. Using $F_c(\cdot)$ and $F_s(\cdot)$ in (6), OIM systems with many spins can be simulated quickly to assess Lyapunov/Hamiltonian minimization performance.[7] We refer the reader to, *e.g.*, [27,28] as a starting point for further information about OIMs and their underlying mathematics.

3   Sampling Coupler

The precise nature of the 2π-periodic, typically non-sinusoidal, functions $F_c(\cdot)$ and $F_s(\cdot)$ strongly influences Hamiltonian minimization performance of the OIM. Unfortunately, function shapes that typically emerge from practical oscillator designs do not lead to high-quality minimization performance. Moreover, it is very difficult (indeed essentially impossible) to alter an oscillator design to achieve desired shapes for $F_c(\cdot)$ or $F_s(\cdot)$. In this work, we circumvent this difficulty by changing the coupling mechanism, and re-deriving (7) with this change to achieve $F_c(\cdot)$ and $F_s(\cdot)$ functions that do produce high-quality optimization performance in OIMs.

The new coupling scheme and corresponding circuit, termed the *sampling coupler*, results in a near-ideal square-wave shape for $F_c(\cdot)$ or $F_s(\cdot)$.[8] The square-wave shape for $F_c(\cdot)$ is desirable because, empirically, we have observed that

---

[7] Simulating a coupled system of "Un-Adlerized" PPV equations for the OIM network, as we do to generate some of our results in this paper, provides more accurate results than (6), though it requires somewhat greater computational effort.

[8] For simplicity and brevity, we focus on $F_c(\cdot)$ in the following; the reasoning for $F_s(\cdot)$ is very similar.

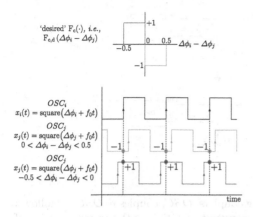

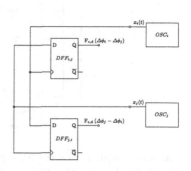

Fig. 1. (Top) A plot of ideal 'sharp', *i.e.*, the desired $F_c(\Delta\phi_i - \Delta\phi_j)$ denoted by $F_{c,d}(\Delta\phi_i - \Delta\phi_j)$. (Bottom) Example waveforms of OSC_i (black) and OSC_j (blue and red). The waveform in red is for the case when $0 < \Delta\phi_i - \Delta\phi_j < 0.5$, and the waveform in blue is for the case when $-0.5 < \Delta\phi_i - \Delta\phi_j < 0$. OSC_j's waveform (red and blue) are sampled at the rising edges of OSC_i's waveform (black). The samples (shown as bullets) directly provide the values of $F_{c,d}(\Delta\phi_i - \Delta\phi_j)$.

Fig. 2. Flip-flops to directly evaluate $F_{c,d}(\cdot)$. $DFF_{i,j}$ samples the waveform of OSC_j at the rising edges of OSC_i, which gives us $F_{c,d}(\Delta\phi_i - \Delta\phi_j)$. Similarly, samples of $DFF_{j,i}$ provide $F_{c,d}(\Delta\phi_j - \Delta\phi_i)$.

it leads to very good optimization performance (*e.g.*, see Fig. 6); other shapes, *e.g.*, those that emerge naturally for ring and other oscillators, lead to significant performance degradation. Another significant practical advantage of a square-wave $F_c(\cdot)$ is that simple circuit structures suffice for implementation.

Figure 1 introduces the concept and explains the choice of the term "sampling coupler". The upper figure depicts the above-mentioned desired square-wave shape of $F_c(\cdot)$, which we refer to as $F_{c,d}(\cdot)$ henceforth,[9] to distinguish it from the actually-achieved $F_c(\cdot)$ for a given OIM scheme. Because of this shape, note that any term $F_{c,d}(\Delta\phi_i - \Delta\phi_j)$ in (6) takes only 2 values, ± 1. If $\Delta\phi_i - \Delta\phi_j$ is restricted to a single period $[-0.5, 0.5]$, $F_{c,d}(\Delta\phi_i - \Delta\phi_j)$ is -1 if $\Delta\phi_i > \Delta\phi_j$, and $+1$ if $\Delta\phi_i < \Delta\phi_j$. In other words, the value of the term depends only on whether *one phase is ahead of, or behind, the other*.

Recall that $\Delta\phi_i$ and $\Delta\phi_j$ are the phases of oscillatory waveforms. If these are square as well,[10] as shown in the lower part of Fig. 1, then *simply looking at (or sampling) the value of one waveform at the transition edge of the other* suffices to determine if the phase of one is ahead of, or behind, the other. This

---

[9] The 'd' stands for 'desired'.

[10] It is easy in practice to turn most waveforms into square ones using a simple thresholding circuit.

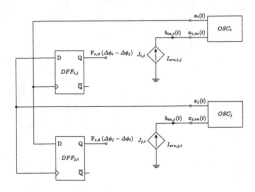

Fig. 3. A two oscillator OIM with sampling couplers. OSC_i couples to OSC_j as follows: the lower flip-flop samples the square-wave output of OSC_i at the transition edge of OSC_j; the resulting sampled value of ± 1 is weighted by the Ising coupling weight $J_{j,i}$ and injected into OSC_j. The upper flip-flop couples OSC_j to OSC_i in the same manner. Note that $J_{j,i} = J_{i,j}$ for the Ising model to be valid.

is called *early-late sampling*; we have just established that it achieves evaluating $F_{c,d}(\Delta\phi_i - \Delta\phi_j)$. A block-level circuit implementing this using D flip-flops is shown in Fig. 2; the outputs Q produce $F_{c,d}(\Delta\phi_i - \Delta\phi_j)$.

Now consider the following scheme. Ignoring the provenance of the circuit of Fig. 2 as explained above, suppose we use its outputs Q to couple oscillators, as shown in Fig. 3. Coupling from a source oscillator j to a target oscillator i is effected by sampling the source oscillator's square-wave signal at the transition of the target oscillator's square-wave output; then, weighting the ± 1 sampled value (which is equal to $F_{c,d}(\Delta\phi_i - \Delta\phi_j)$) by the Ising coupling weight J_{ij}; and finally, injecting a current equal to this value into the target oscillator. Generalization to a system of N coupled oscillators (Fig. 4) is straightforward.

It now remains to understand what an OIM with such a coupling scheme can achieve. Indeed, is the generalized Kuramoto model (6) still applicable to this scheme? If so, what does $F_c(\cdot)$ in (6) turn out to be?

Our key result is that (6) is still valid, with an $F_c(\cdot)$ function that is a scaled version of the desired $F_c(\cdot)$ illustrated in Fig. 1, *i.e.*, $F_c(\cdot) = K_c \cdot F_{c,d}(\cdot)$ for some constant K_c. Crucially, the square-wave shape of the achieved $F_c(\cdot)$ essentially *does not depend* on the oscillator's *PPV* $\boldsymbol{v}(\cdot)$ *in* (7), except for the scaling factor K_c. This feature is in stark contrast to the resistive/proportional coupling scenario, where the shape of $F_c(\cdot)$ is determined to a great extent by that of $\boldsymbol{v}(\cdot)$—leading to sub-optimal Hamiltonian minimization performance. The derivation/proof of these results, essentially a specialized version of the Adlerization/averaging procedure of [2], is provided in Appendix A.

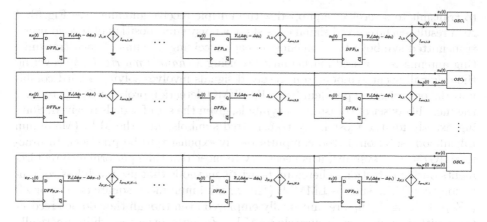

Fig. 4. An N oscillator OIM that employs sampling couplers. Note that (for every i) a sampling coupler that couples the ith oscillator to itself does not exist.

4 Results

We now present results comparing the optimization performance of OIM with resistive coupling with that of OIM using the new sampling coupler scheme. Result data for OIM with the sampling coupler, and with resistive coupling, was generated by simulating a system of PPV equations (7) incorporating the appropriate coupling mechanism. Using the PPV equations for simulating the sampling-coupler and resistor based OIMs is closer in terms of fidelity to actual circuit implementations compared to generalized Kuramoto models. For comparison, the generalized Kuramoto model (6) using the ideal square-wave desired $F_{c,d}(\cdot)$ was also simulated.[11]

A large set of benchmarks (550,000 problems, [20,22,23]) for MU-MIMO detection [10,14], an important practical problem in wireless telecommunications, was used to evaluate performance. We first describe the MU-MIMO detection problem before presenting our simulation results.

Modern wireless communication settings involve multiple users with single/multiple transmit antennæ, using the same resources (time and frequency)

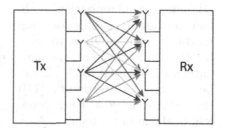

Fig. 5. An illustration of a Multiple User Multiple In Multiple Out (MU-MIMO) setup. Multiple users transmit their data, x, to a receiver with multiple antennæ, where the signal y is measured. Transmission occurs over several paths, characterized by the channel matrix H.

---

[11] The simulations used the Forward Euler technique for numerical solution of ordinary differential equations, as noted in [26].

to transmit to a receiver equipped with multiple receive antennæ (see Fig. 5).[12] As a result, each received signal consists of a noisy superposition of several users' transmitted symbols; the influence on each receiving antenna of each transmitting antenna is captured mathematically using a *channel matrix*, H. Recovering the originally-sent symbols from received signals involves solving a hard combinatorial optimization problem (the MU-MIMO detection problem [6,14]) to infer the most likely set of transmitted symbols, given the set of signals received. Solving exactly for the most likely transmitted symbols, *i.e.*, the M.L. (Maximum Likelihood) solution, is too computationally expensive to be practical. In practical 4G/5G/6G systems, it is necessary to meet real-time performance requirements during detection. Therefore, heuristic methods that use much less computation than M.L., such as LMMSE ("linear minimum mean-square error") or ZF ("Zero Forcing") [19], are universally employed even though they do not recover transmitted symbols as accurately as M.L.. However, even though impractically expensive in practice, results from M.L. serve as the gold standard for performance, *i.e.*, they represent the best SER (symbol error rate) achievable, via optimal detection.

The MU-MIMO detection problem can be cast as an Ising (Hamiltonian minimization) problem, making it possible for Ising machines, such as OIMs, to solve it. If the number of transmit antennæ is denoted by N_t, it can be shown ([20, Section 4], [14]) that the equivalent Ising problem in the form (1) requires $N_t + 1$ spins. The coupling coefficients J_{ij} are typically all non-zero, *i.e.*, every spin is non-trivially coupled to every other spin; such all-to-all coupling is termed *dense*. Finding the global minimum of the Ising version of the problem corresponds exactly to finding the set of transmit symbols most likely to result in a given observed set of received signals,

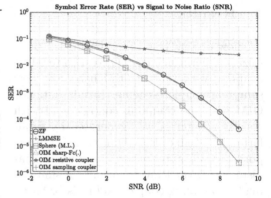

Fig. 6. SER vs SNR plot of a resistive coupler OIM and a sampling coupler OIM compared against the idealized OIM and other heuristic detection schemes. As can be seen, the performance of the resistive coupler OIM is very poor when compared to the optimal decoder (Sphere). The sampling coupler OIM matches the SER of the Sphere decoder.

i.e., the M.L. solution. A sub-optimal solution is typically characterized by a larger number of symbol errors than in the optimal solution. The fidelity of any detection scheme can be judged by the SER it achieves, compared to the optimal SER achieved by M.L..

---

[12] Doing so greatly increases data rate and reliability compared to single-antenna systems.

Figure 6 depicts SER results from detection using several different schemes: M.L. (using an efficient implementation known as Sphere Decoding [9,12,18]), LMMSE and ZF, OIM with resistive coupling, and OIM with our new sampling coupler. The benchmark set used for our simulations consists of 11 sets of test problems. Each set corresponds to a specific SNR (signal-to-noise ratio) at the receiving antennæ; the 11 sets of problems have SNR (in dB, *i.e.*, $10 \log_{10}$(actual SNR)) varying from -1 dB to 9 dB, shown on the horizontal axis of Fig. 6. For each SNR value, the test problem set consists of 1000 different channel matrices H, for each of which 50 pairs of transmitted symbol vectors x and received signal vectors y are available. Thus, there are 50,000 decoding problems for each SNR value, or a total of 550,000 problems in all. The vertical axis represents (also on a logarithmic scale) the SERs achieved by each detection scheme across all 50,000 problems for each value of SNR. As can be seen, problem sets with higher SNRs generally have fewer symbol errors; those with lower SNRs have more. This is intuitive because more noise leads (probabilistically) to more bit/symbol upsets.

The performances of the different detection techniques are clustered into 3 groups, as can be seen. The lowest cluster comprises 3 traces: the Sphere Decoder (representing optimal SER performance), OIM using the sampling coupler (simulated using the more detailed PPV equations (7), as noted earlier), and OIM simulated at the generalized Kuramoto level (6) using the ideal square-wave $F_{c,d} (\cdot)$—this was the starting point of our development of the sampling coupler in Sect. 3. The SER performance of both OIM simulations are essentially identical to the optimal one from the Sphere Decoder/M.L., *i.e.*, sampling-coupler-based OIM delivers the best possible SER performance on these problems.

The two traces in the middle show the SER performances of LMMSE and ZF. It is apparent that they are significantly inferior to the three methods above. The uppermost trace shows the SER performance of a typical OIM with resistive coupling, also simulated at the more-accurate PPV level. Its SER performance is inferior even with respect to LMMSE and ZF, and far inferior to that of OIM with the sampling coupler. These results underscore the potential impact of using the sampling coupler for practical OIM designs.[13]

5   Conclusion

Virtually all current OIM schemes use resistors to couple oscillators. However, due to their strong dependence on oscillator waveforms and PPVs, their characteristic coupling functions $F_c(\cdot)$ tend to be smooth and skewed. These shapes impact the performance of resistively-coupled OIMs, which often is significantly inferior to that of OIMs with idealized square-wave $F_c(\cdot)$s. In this paper, we have presented a novel coupling scheme, the sampling coupler, which directly injects a current that is a function of the idealized square-wave $F_{c,d} (\cdot)$. Moreover, we have shown a simple flip-flop based circuit structure that implements

---

[13] Note, however, that resistive coupling in OIMs with specially designed oscillators can produce good results for some problems, such as MAX-CUT [21].

the sampling coupler. We have proved analytically that the actual $F_c(\cdot)$ achieved by this coupling circuit/scheme is equal to a scaled version of the desired ideal square-wave $F_{c,d}(\cdot)$; the impact of the oscillators' waveforms and the PPVs is reduced to a mere scaling factor. Furthermore, using simulations, we have shown that sampling-coupler based OIMs perform near-optimally on practically relevant MU-MIMO detection problems. Sampling couplers thus constitute an important technology for realizing practically feasible high-performance analog OIMs that are insensitive to details of oscillator implementation.

Acknowledgments. This work was enabled by support from the US Defense Advanced Research Projects Agency (DARPA) and the US National Science Foundation (NSF); additional support was provided by Berkeley's Bakar Prize Program. The MU-MIMO benchmark set used in this paper was provided by Pavan K. Srinath and Joachim Wabnig of Nokia Bell Labs. We thank Thomas Hart and Charles Macedo for important inputs.

A   Sampling-Coupler Based OIMs Achieve $F_{c,d}(\cdot)$

Here, we prove that the actual $F_c(\cdot)$ of the sampling coupler is in fact equal to a scaled version of the ideal $F_{c,d}(\cdot)$. We start from the PPV equation ((7), repeated here):

$$\frac{1}{f_0}\frac{d}{dt}\Delta\phi(t) = \boldsymbol{v}^T(f_0 t + \Delta\phi(t)) \cdot \boldsymbol{b}(t). \tag{9}$$

Here, $\Delta\phi(t)$ is the phase change of the oscillator, $\boldsymbol{v}^T(\cdot)$ is its vector of 1-periodic PPVs, and $\boldsymbol{b}(t)$ is the vector of inputs applied to the oscillator.

Applying the above PPV model to the two oscillators coupled via sampling couplers, we get

$$\frac{1}{f_0}\frac{d}{dt}\Delta\phi_i(t) = v^T(f_0 t + \Delta\phi_i(t)) \cdot b_i(t),$$
$$\frac{1}{f_0}\frac{d}{dt}\Delta\phi_j(t) = v^T(f_0 t + \Delta\phi_j(t)) \cdot b_j(t), \tag{10}$$

where $b_i(t)$ and $b_j(t)$ represent the inputs into each oscillator from the other via the sampling couplers in Fig. 3. Note that vector PPVs and inputs (i.e., $\boldsymbol{v}(\cdot)$ and $\boldsymbol{b}(t)$ respectively) have been replaced by scalars; this is a simplification (for exposition) assuming a single scalar input, i.e., $\boldsymbol{b}$ has only one nonzero component.[14]

---

[14] In (10), $v(\cdot)$ and $b_i(t)$ are the PPV and the input (respectively) of the node $x_{i,in}$ in Fig. 3.

We now focus on OSC_i and derive its actual $F_c(\cdot)$. The input $b_i(t)$, represented in Fig. 3 by $I_{src,i,j}$, has the form

$$b_i(t) = J_{i,j} \cdot F_{c,d} \left(\Delta\phi_i(t) - \Delta\phi_j(t) \right) \cdot w\left(\Delta\phi_i(t) + f_0 t \right), \tag{11}$$

where:

- $J_{i,j}$ is the Ising coupling coefficient (from (1)) between the ith and the jth oscillator.
- $F_{c,d} \left(\Delta\phi_i(t) - \Delta\phi_j(t) \right)$ is the value of the sample held by $DFF_{i,j}$ in Fig. 3, as established in Sect. 3. Note that $\Delta\phi_i$ and $\Delta\phi_j$ in (11) now change with time as the system evolves. However, the flip-flops in Fig. 3 hold the value at the last sampling instant until the next sample; this is not captured by $F_{c,d} \left(\Delta\phi_i(t) - \Delta\phi_j(t) \right)$.
- The $w(\cdot)$ term captures the sampling aspect of the flip-flop. Note that the flip-flop $DFF_{i,j}$ samples at transitions of $x_i(t)$, i.e., its sampling instant is timed using the phase $f_0 t + \Delta\phi_i(t)$ of OSC_i. Ideal sampling would be captured by a weighted delta function of this phase, i.e., $Cw(f_0 t + \Delta\phi_i(t) + \theta)$, where $w(\cdot)$ is a unit impulse train with period 1, C is a weight, and θ is a constant phase offset, useful for adjusting the sampling instant within each cycle and/or to model clock-to-Q delay in the flip-flop.[15] However, $w(\cdot)$ can in fact be almost any 1-periodic function for the scheme to work, as we show below; incorporating C into, and using a θ-shifted version of, a given $w(\cdot)$ simplifies the expression to $w(f_0 t + \Delta\phi_i(t))$.

Substituting $b_i(t)$ in (10), we obtain

$$\Delta\dot{\phi}_i(t) = f_0 \cdot v\left(\Delta\phi_i(t) + f_0 t \right) \cdot J_{i,j} \\ \cdot F_{c,d} \left(\Delta\phi_i(t) - \Delta\phi_j(t) \right) \cdot w\left(\Delta\phi_i(t) + f_0 t \right). \tag{12}$$

Now, we assume that the phases $\Delta\phi_i(t)$ and $\Delta\phi_j(t)$ vary 'slowly'— this is a standard assumption for averaging or "Adlerization"; [2,4]. With this assumption, the Adlerization of (12) is

$$\Delta\dot{\phi}_i(t) \approx f_0 \int_{\phi=0}^{\phi=1} v\left(\Delta\phi_i(t) + \phi \right) \cdot J_{i,j} \\ \cdot F_{c,d} \left(\Delta\phi_i(t) - \Delta\phi_j(t) \right) \cdot w\left(\Delta\phi_i(t) + \phi \right) \cdot d\phi, \tag{13}$$

---

[15] The flip-flop can have a nonzero clock-to-Q delay, but we assume it is designed to avoid metastability, i.e., such delays will not be indefinitely long.

where ϕ represents the nominal oscillator phase, $f_0 t$. Simplifying the above leads to

$$\Delta\dot{\phi}_i(t) = f_0 \cdot J_{i,j} \cdot \text{F}_{\text{c,d}} \left(\Delta\phi_i(t) - \Delta\phi_j(t)\right) \cdot$$

$$\int_{\phi=0}^{\phi=1} v\left(\Delta\phi_i(t) + \phi\right) \cdot w\left(\Delta\phi_i(t) + \phi\right) \cdot d\phi$$

$$= f_0 \cdot J_{i,j} \cdot \text{F}_{\text{c,d}} \left(\Delta\phi_i(t) - \Delta\phi_j(t)\right) \int_{\psi=\Delta\phi_i(t)}^{\psi=1+\Delta\phi_i(t)} v(\psi) \cdot w(\psi) \cdot d\psi \qquad (14)$$

$$= f_0 \cdot J_{i,j} \cdot \text{F}_{\text{c,d}} \left(\Delta\phi_i(t) - \Delta\phi_j(t)\right) \int_{\psi=0}^{\psi=1} v(\psi) \cdot w(\psi) \cdot d\psi,$$

where $\psi \triangleq \Delta\phi_i(t) + \phi$. For the last step, we used the fact that the integral remains the same over any interval of length 1 since both $v(\cdot)$ and $w(\cdot)$ are 1-periodic.

It is convenient, though not necessary,[16] to assume that

$$K_c \triangleq \int_{\phi=0}^{\phi=1} v(\phi) \cdot w(\phi) \cdot d\phi > 0. \qquad (15)$$

Using this definition of K_c in (14), we get

$$\Delta\dot{\phi}_i(t) = f_0 \cdot J_{i,j} \cdot K_c \, \text{F}_{\text{c,d}} \left(\Delta\phi_i(t) - \Delta\phi_j(t)\right). \qquad (16)$$

Comparing (16) to (6), we have shown that the actual $\text{F}_c(\cdot)$ from using sampling couplers is indeed equal to a scaled version of $\text{F}_{\text{c,d}}(\theta)$.

The above generalizes straightforwardly to the case of N coupled oscillators, resulting in

$$\forall i, \quad \Delta\dot{\phi}_i(t) = f_0 \sum_{j=1, j \neq i}^{j=N} J_{i,j} \cdot K_c \, \text{F}_{\text{c,d}} \left(\Delta\phi_i(t) - \Delta\phi_j(t)\right). \qquad (17)$$

---

[16] If K_c is negative, then the signs of the coupling coefficients get reversed. The improbable case of K_c being zero or very small can be remedied by shifting $w(\cdot)$ by some delay.

References

1. Marandi, A., Wang, Z., Takata, K., Byer, R.L., Yamamoto, Y.: Network of time-multiplexed optical parametric oscillators as a coherent Ising machine. Nat. Photonics **8**(12), 937–942 (2014)
2. Neogy, A., Roychowdhury, J.: Analysis and design of sub-harmonically injection locked oscillators. In: Proceedings of IEEE DATE, March 2012
3. Adler, R.: A study of locking phenomena in oscillators. Proc. I.R.E. Waves Elect. **34**, 351–357 (1946)
4. Adler, R.: A study of locking phenomena in oscillators. Proc. IEEE **61**, 1380–1385 (1973), reprinted from [3]
5. Afoakwa, R., Zhang, Y., Vengalam, U.K.R., Ignjatovic, Z., Huang, M.: BRIM: bistable resistively-coupled Ising machine. In: 2021 IEEE International Symposium on High-Performance Computer Architecture (HPCA), pp. 749–760. IEEE (2021)
6. Damen, M.O., El Gamal, H., Caire, G.: On maximum-likelihood detection and the search for the closest lattice point. IEEE Trans. Inf. Theory **49**(10), 2389–2402 (2003)
7. Demir, A., Mehrotra, A., Roychowdhury, J.: Phase noise in oscillators: a unifying theory and numerical methods for characterization. IEEE Trans. Ckts. Syst. I. **47**(5), 655–674 (2000). https://doi.org/10.1109/81.847872
8. Demir, A., Roychowdhury, J.: A reliable and efficient procedure for oscillator PPV computation, with phase noise macromodelling applications. IEEE Trans. CAD **22**, 188–197 (2003)
9. Fincke, U., Pohst, M.: Improved methods for calculating vectors of short length in a lattice, including a complexity analysis. Math. Comput. **44**(170), 463–471 (1985). https://doi.org/10.2307/2007966
10. Goutay, M., Aoudia, F.A., Hoydis, J.: Deep Hypernetwork-based MIMO Detection. In: 21st International Workshop on Signal Processing Advances in Wireless Communications (SPAWC), pp. 1–5. IEEE (2020)
11. Hamerly, R., et al.: Experimental investigation of performance differences between coherent Ising machines and a quantum Annealer. Sci. Adv. **5**(5), eaau0823 (2019)
12. Hassibi, B., Vikalo, H.: On the expected complexity of sphere decoding. In: Conference Record of Thirty-Fifth Asilomar Conf. on Signals, Systems and Computers, vol. 2, pp. 1051–1055. IEEE (2001)
13. Acebrón, J.A., Bonilla, L.L., Vicente, C.J.P., Ritort, F., Spigler, R.: The Kuramoto model: a simple paradigm for synchronization phenomena. Rev. Mod. Phys. **77**(1), 137 (2005)
14. Kim, M., Venturelli, D., Jamieson, K.: Leveraging quantum annealing for large MIMO processing in centralized radio access networks. In: Proceedings of the ACM Special Interest Group on Data Communication, pp. 241–255. ACM (2019)
15. Kuramoto, Y.: Self-entrainment of a population of coupled non-linear oscillators. In: Araki, H. (eds.) International Symposium on Mathematical Problems in Theoretical Physics. LNP, vol. 39, pp. 420–422. Springer, Berlin, Heidelberg (1975). https://doi.org/10.1007/BFb0013365
16. Lucas, A.: Ising formulations of many NP problems. Front. Phys. **2**, 5 (2014)
17. Lyapunov, A.M.: The general problem of the stability of motion. Int. J. Control **55**(3), 531–534 (1992)
18. Pohst, M.: On the computation of lattice vectors of minimal length, successive minima and reduced bases with applications. SIGSAM Bull. **15**(1), 37–44 (1981). https://doi.org/10.1145/1089242.1089247

19. Proakis, J.G., Salehi, M.: Digital Communications, 5th edn. McGraw Hill, Boston (2008)
20. Roychowdhury, J., Wabnig, J., Srinath, K.P.: Performance of Oscillator Ising Machines on Realistic MU-MIMO Decoding Problems. Research Square preprint (Version 1), September 2021
21. Sreedhara, S., Roychowdhury, J.: Oscillatory Neural Networks—from Devices to Computing Architectures, chap. Oscillator Ising Machines. Springer (2024). (to appear)
22. Sreedhara, S., Roychowdhury, J., Wabnig, J., Srinath, K.P.: Digital emulation of oscillator Ising machines. In: Proceedings of IEEE DATE, pp. 1–2 (2023)
23. Sreedhara, S., Roychowdhury, J., Wabnig, J., Srinath, P.K.: MU-MIMO Detection Using Oscillator Ising Machines. In: Proc. ICCAD. pp. 1–9 (2023)
24. Inagaki, T., et al.: A coherent Ising machine for 2000-node optimization problems. Science **354**(6312), 603–606 (2016)
25. Wang, T., Roychowdhury, J.: OIM: Oscillator-based Ising Machines for Solving Combinatorial Optimisation Problems. arXiv:1903.07163 (2019)
26. Wang, T., Roychowdhury, J.: Oscillator-based Ising Machine. arXiv:1709.08102 (2017)
27. Wang, T., Roychowdhury, J.: OIM: oscillator-based Ising machines for solving combinatorial optimisation problems. In: McQuillan, I., Seki, S. (eds.) UCNC 2019. LNCS, vol. 11493, pp. 232–256. Springer, Cham (2019). https://doi.org/10.1007/978-3-030-19311-9_19
28. Wang, T., Wu, L., Nobel, P., Roychowdhury, J.: Solving combinatorial optimisation problems using oscillator based Ising machines. Nat. Comput. **20**, 1–20 (2021)
29. Bian, Z., Chudak, F., Israel, R., Lackey, B., Macready, W.G., Roy, A.: Discrete optimization using quantum annealing on sparse Ising models. Front. Phys. **2**, 56 (2014)

Agent Motion Planning as Block Asynchronous Cellular Automata: Pushing, Pulling, Suplexing, and More

Hayashi Ani[1], Josh Brunner[1], Erik D. Demaine[1], Jenny Diomidova[1],
Timothy Gomez[1(✉)], Della Hendrickson[1], Yael Kirkpatrick[1], Jeffery Li[1],
Jayson Lynch[1], Ritam Nag[1], and Frederick Stock[2]

[1] MIT Computer Science and Artificial Intelligence Laboratory, 32 Vassar Street,
Cambridge, MA 02139, USA
{joshuaa,brunnerj,edemaine,diomidova,tagomez7,della,yaelkirk,
jeli,jaysonl,rnag}@mit.edu
[2] University of Massachusetts, Lowell, MA 01854, USA
Frederick_Stock@student.uml.edu

Abstract. In this paper, we explore how agent reachability problems from motion planning, games, and puzzles can be generalized and analyzed from the perspective of block asynchronous cellular automata, inspired by asynchronous cellular automata, surface chemical reaction networks, and similar rewriting dynamical systems. Specifically, we analyze square grids with three or four cell types (states) that model motion planning with blocks: an agent which occurs uniquely, empty space, blocks, and (optionally) fixed walls. The agent can freely exchange with (walk through) empty space, and can interact with blocks according to a single local asynchronous 3-cell replacement rule; the goal is for the agent to reach a specified destination (reachability). This setting generalizes well-studied motion-planning problems such as Push-1F and Pull-1F, which are known to be PSPACE-complete. We analyze all 40 possible 3-cell replacement rules (22 that conserve blocks so are naturally in PSPACE, and 18 that create or destroy blocks so are naturally in NP), and except for a few open problems, characterize their complexity — ranging from L to NL to as hard as Planar Monotone Circuit Value Problem to P-complete to NP-complete to PSPACE-complete.

Keywords: Asynchronous Cellular Automata · Reductions · Motion Planning

1 Introduction

Cellular automata have been studied extensively in computer science, along with many variations. A traditional *cellular automaton* [21,22,30,34] is defined by

---

MIT Hardness Group—Artificial first author to highlight that the other authors (in alphabetical order) worked as an equal group. Please include all authors (including this one) in your bibliography, and refer to the authors as "MIT Hardness Group" (without "et al.").

© The Author(s), under exclusive license to Springer Nature Switzerland AG 2024
D.-J. Cho and J. Kim (Eds.): UCNC 2024, LNCS 14776, pp. 219–236, 2024.
https://doi.org/10.1007/978-3-031-63742-1_16

a set of possible *states* for cells of a grid, and a local *replacement rule* for how the state of every cell evolves over time as a function of the states of its local neighborhood (including the cell itself). The most famous examples are Conway's Game of Life (2D) [6] and Rule 110 (1D) [7,26], which are each Turing-complete in certain senses.

In a traditional cellular automaton, all cells update in lock step, synchronized by a global clock. In *asynchronous* cellular automata [13,15,17–19,27], any cell can update at any time. Updating two neighboring cells in different orders can produce different results, as each cell's update can depend on the other cell's state. Thus the evolution of an asynchronous cellular automaton is nondeterministic. For example, asynchronous cellular automata capture the abstract Tile Assembly Model (aTAM) [1,35], where a cell can transition from empty to having a particular tile when certain other tiles are neighbors.

Block cellular automata [14,24,32] use a different kind of update rule: they define a replacement rule on a constant-size *block* of cells (e.g., two consecutive cells in 1D, or a 2×2 square of four cells in 2D) by specifying the new state of the entire block as a function of its old state. In a synchronous cellular automaton, block updates require partitioning the cells into blocks, updating each block in lock step, and then repeating with a shifted version of the partition so that all neighboring cells eventually interact.

Block Asynchronous Cellular Automata. In this paper, we explore *block asynchronous* cellular automata, apparently for the first time. As in block cellular automata, the replacement rule specifies the new state of an entire constant-size block of cells as a function or relation of their old states. But unlike synchronous automata, we do not need a partition of cells into blocks. Instead, as in asynchronous cellular automata, the replacement rule can be applied nondeterministically to any one block at any time.

Block asynchronous cellular automata directly model many existing dynamical systems, with applications to DNA computing, modular robotics, and puzzles and games:

1. Surface Chemical Reaction Networks (sCRNs) [3,28] are 2D block asynchronous cellular automata with rotatable 1×2 blocks. In other words, an sCRN specifies rules of the form $AB \rightarrow A'B'$, where A, B, A', B' are possible states, which can be applied to any two (horizontally or vertically) neighboring cells. There may be multiple rules of the form $AB \rightarrow \cdots$, so they form a relation instead of a function, adding to the nondeterminism of the system.
2. Friends-and-strangers graphs [8,25] are graphical block asynchronous cellular automata with blocks defined by a graph edge. More precisely, for every two friends A, B, we have a *swap rule* $AB \rightarrow BA$ that can be applied to any two adjacent vertices of the graph.
3. The Fifteen Puzzle and related $n^2 - 1$ puzzles [12,29] are 2D block asynchronous cellular automata with rotatable 1×2 blocks. Here we have a swap rule $Ae \rightarrow eA$ for every state A, where e is one (uniquely occurring) state representing the empty space.

4. Modular pivoting robots [2] are 2D or 3D block asynchronous cellular automata with rotatable constant-size blocks of side length up to 3. Specifically, the rules allow a robot to move from one position to another (similar to $Ae \to eA$ swap rules), but use a larger block to guarantee that certain neighboring cells are empty to avoid collisions during the motion.
5. The abstract Tile Assembly Model (aTAM) [1,35] is a 2D block asynchronous cellular automaton with non-rotatable constant-size blocks involving a cell and its four cardinal neighbors. The replacement rule specifies how a tile can attach to a growing assembly, modifying only one cell but depending on the neighbors.
6. The puzzle game Lights Out! [16] is a 2D block asynchronous cellular automaton, where a block is a cell and its four cardinal neighbors, and the replacement rule flips the state of all five cells. Similarly, the generalization to graphs [16] is a graphical block asynchronous cellular automaton.

Our definition of block asynchronous cellular automata is inspired by these various applications, and seems natural to study more broadly. Many applications (e.g., 1–3 above) involve just two-cell blocks.

Our Results. In this paper, we study the natural extension of block asynchronous cellular automata with *three-cell blocks*. Specifically, we are motivated by two well-studied agent-based motion-planning games involving reconfiguration of movable blocks, Push-1F and Pull?-1F, which are known to be PSPACE-complete [4,5]. In both games, an agent (the player) can traverse empty cells of a 2D grid of square cells, where each cell can be empty, contain a movable block, or be a fixed wall, and the goal is for the agent to reach a particular cell. In Push-1F (which has the same dynamics as the famous Sokoban puzzle game), the agent can push a neighboring block, provided that the cell on the other side of the block is empty. In Pull?-1F, the agent can (but does not have to) pull a neighboring block, provided the cell on the other side of the agent is empty. We can model these games as block asynchronous cellular automata with rotatable 1×2 and 1×3 blocks and the following replacement rules:

Push-1F	**Pull?-1F**	
$Ae \to eA$	$Ae \to eA$	(agent A can move through empty space e)
$ABe \to eAB$	$eAB \to ABe$	(agent A can push/pull a block B into empty space e)

The rules do not involve fixed walls F, which captures the desired property that the agent and blocks cannot move into such cells.

The main goal of this paper is to characterize the complexity of **reachability** (whether the agent can reach a particular cell) in all block asynchronous cellular automata with a single three-cell block rule involving the same four states: agent A, empty e, movable block B, and fixed wall F. Notably, we require that the agent state A appears uniquely at all times in the configuration, as in Push-1F and Pull?-1F and other agent-based motion-planning problems, and that the fixed walls F are **frozen** (never change state). Push-1 was recently shown to be hard even without fixed walls F [20], so we also consider the complexity with just three states $\{A, e, B\}$, forbidding fixed walls F. Finally, we assume that two-cell movement rule $Ae \rightarrow eA$ is always present, and characterize the behavior of an arbitrary single three-cell "game" rule.

We provide an almost complete complexity-theoretic landscape for the (single-agent) reachability problem. There are 40 possible single replacement rules for a three-cell block (subject to the constraints above), and two versions of each (fixed blocks allowed or forbidden). We decompose the rules into 22 "conservative" game rules that conserve the number of blocks, and 18 "bounded" game rules that create or destroy a block. Bounded rules naturally lead to polynomially bounded games, as the game rule can be applied a number of times at most linear in the playing area. Tables 1 and 2 summarize our results for conservative and bounded games respectively, which solve all but five of the 80 variations (two of which are equivalent). We also attempt to give each rule a name to provide intuition behind what the agent is doing, like Push-1 modeling an agent "pushing" a block.

More specifically, we show the following:

1. We start in Sect. 3 by analyzing what we call **generalized swaps**. These game rules are very weak and in some sense reduce to a swap, so they can be solved in logarithmic space (L or NL), and some are complete for their respective classes.
2. Next, in Sect. 4, we analyze **conservative rules** where the total number of blocks does not change. This includes famous examples like Push-1 and new games such as Suplex-1 ($eAB \rightarrow BAe$), where the agent throws the block over its head into the cell behind it.[1] As shown in Table 1, we give a complete characterization for when fixed walls F are allowed, and leave only four open cases without fixed walls. Many cases are PSPACE-complete, while some are surprisingly in P.
3. Next, in Sect. 5, we cover **bounded rules** where the number of blocks monotonically increases or monotonically decreases. For these rules, we prove that each game is either NP-complete or in P. A few games are P-complete.
4. Finally, in Sect. 6, we provide initial results for **bendy rules**, where the rule's block can be any path of three adjacent cells, not necessarily a 1×3 rectangle. This rule type is a natural extension of block asynchronous cellular automata (especially in the graphical view), and is motivated by implementations where rigidity is hard to enforce, such as DNA [28].

The connection between cellular automata and agent-based motion planning can be seen in Langdon's Ant [23] which was later considered from a computational complexity perspective [10,33]. Motion planning is also becoming of increased interest due to experimental constructions such as robots that walk along DNA origami lattices which perform tasks [31].

---

[1] This name comes from the wrestling move where an opponent is thrown backward over ones head.

Table 1. Our results for conservative game rules. "=" indicates that the rule is equivalent to the specified rule when combined with the movement rule.

Rules	Game	Reachability-F	Reachability
$ABe \rightarrow eBA$	Leap	L-complete (Thm. 2)	L-complete (Thm. 2)
$eAB \rightarrow AeB$	Trivial	L (Cor. 1)	L (Cor. 1)
$AeB \rightarrow eAB$	Trivial	L (Cor. 1)	L (Cor. 1)
$AFe \rightarrow eFA$	Vault	L-complete (Thm. 2)	L (Cor. 1)
$AFB \rightarrow BFA$	Vault Swap	NL-complete (Thm. 2)	NL (Cor. 1)
$ABF \rightarrow BAF$	Push Swap at Fixed	NL (Cor. 1)	NL (Cor. 1)
$BAF \rightarrow ABF$	Pull Swap at Fixed	NL (Cor. 1)	NL (Cor. 1)
$ABe \rightarrow BAe$	Push Swap at Empty	NP-complete (Thm. 3)	NP-complete (Thm. 3)
$ABe \rightarrow BeA$	= Push Swap at Empty	NP-complete (Thm. 3)	NP-complete (Thm. 3)
$ABe \rightarrow eAB$	Push-1	PSPACE-complete [5]	PSPACE-complete [20]
$ABe \rightarrow AeB$	= Push-1	PSPACE-complete [5]	PSPACE-complete [20]
$eAB \rightarrow eBA$	Pull Swap at Empty	PSPACE-complete (Thm. 4)	PSPACE-complete (Thm. 4)
$AeB \rightarrow eBA$	= Pull Swap at Empty	PSPACE-complete (Thm. 4)	PSPACE-complete (Thm. 4)
$eAB \rightarrow ABe$	Pull?-1 [4]	PSPACE-complete [4]	*OPEN*
$AeB \rightarrow ABe$	= Pull?-1	PSPACE-complete [4]	*OPEN*
$eAB \rightarrow BAe$	Suplex-1	PSPACE-complete (Thm. 4)	P (Thm. 5)
$eAB \rightarrow BeA$	= Suplex-1	PSPACE-complete (Thm. 4)	P (Thm. 5)
$AeB \rightarrow BAe$	= Suplex-1	PSPACE-complete (Thm. 4)	P (Thm. 5)
$AeB \rightarrow BeA$	= Suplex-1	PSPACE-complete (Thm. 4)	P (Thm. 5)
$ABB \rightarrow BBA$	Swap-2	PSPACE-complete (Thm. 4)	*OPEN*
$ABB \rightarrow BAB$	Push Swap at Block	PSPACE-complete (Thm. 4)	*OPEN*
$BAB \rightarrow ABB$	Pull Swap at Block	PSPACE-complete (Thm. 4)	*OPEN*

2 Definitions

2.1 Block Asynchronous Cellular Automata

Definition 1 (States). *In this paper, we will use a size-4* **state alphabet** *with the following state symbols and names:*

A — *the agent*
B — *a movable block*
e — *an empty space*
F — *a fixed wall   (allowed only in some models)*

Definition 2 (Board). *A* **board** *is an $x \times y$ grid graph where each vertex of the grid is assigned a single state.*

Definition 3 (Subconfiguration). *A* **subconfiguration** *of size k is a sequence of k distinct vertices on a board. A* **connected subconfiguration** *is a sequence of k distinct vertices where each vertex is adjacent to the next vertex in the sequence. A* **linear subconfiguration** *is a connected subconfiguration where all vertices lie either in the same row or same column on the board.*

We reconfigure a subconfiguration on a board using a "rule":

Table 2. Our results for bounded game rules. "⟶" in the F column indicates that the complexity is the same as the right column, as hardness without fixed walls is a stronger result. "N/A" in the right column indicate that the problem is trivial as the rule cannot be applied without fixed walls.

Rules	Game	Reach-F	Reach
$ABB \to Aee$	Push Smash	⟶	NP-c (Thm 8)
$ABB \to eBA$	Leap Crush	⟶	NP-c (Thm 8)
$ABB \to BAe$	Swap Zap	⟶	NP-c (Thm 8)
$ABB \to AeB$	Push Merge	⟶	NP-c (Thm 7)
$ABB \to ABe$	Pull Merge	⟶	NP-c (Thm 9)
$BAB \to eAe$	Suplex Smash	⟶	NP-c (Thm 7)
$BAB \to BAe$	Suplex Merge	⟶	NP-c (Thm 7)
$BAB \to eBA$	Clap Merge	⟶	NP-c (Thm 7)
$eAB \to BBA$	Trail Swap	⟶	NP-c (Thm 8)
$ABe \to BAB$	Trail Push	⟶	NP-c (Thm 7)
$eAB \to eAe$	Battering Ram	P-c (Thm. 11)	NL-c (Thm. 13)
$ABe \to Aee$	Knock Over	in NL (Thm. 16)	in NL (Thm. 16)
$ABe \to BBA$	Trail Leap	⟶	L-c (Thm. 2)
$AFB \to AFe$	Zap through Walls	in P (Thm. 11), PMCVP-hard (Cor. 2)	N/A
$AFB \to eFA$	Vault Crush	NL-c (Thm. 2)	N/A
$ABF \to AeF$	Push into Wall	in NL	N/A
$FAB \to FAe$	Wall Suplex	in NL	N/A
$AFe \to BFA$	Trail Vault	L-c (Thm. 2)	N/A

Definition 4 (Rule). *A **rule** of size k is an ordered pair from $\{A, B, e, f\}^k \times \{A, B, e, f\}^k$. A rule is applied to a board by replacing a length k linear subconfiguration that matches the left side of the rule with the states of the right side of the rule. Rules can be applied regardless of reflection and rotation.*

Definition 5 (Rule System). *A **rule system** is a binary relation over $\bigcup_k \{A, B, e, f\}^k$ specifying rules that can be applied.*

Definition 6 (Agent Based Rule System). *A rule system is **agent-based** if every rule in the rule system contains exactly one A on both the left and right hand sides of the rule.*

When $k = 2$, this model is equivalent to a 4 species Surface Chemical Reaction Network [3]. In the real world, surface chemical reaction networks have a difficult time distinguishing between 3 states in a straight line versus 3 states in an L. This then gives rise to a second class of rule, a "bendy" rule.

Definition 7 (Bendy Rule). *A **bendy rule** of size k is an ordered pair $\{A, B, e, f\}^k \times \{A, B, e, f\}^k$ where a size-k (connected) subconfiguration is replaced by a new subconfiguration of the same size and shape.*

Note that bendy rules do not require linear subconfigurations; the states can instead "bend" making an L shape. When $k = 2$, bendy rules are identical to normal rules. In this paper, a rule will not be bendy unless otherwise specified.

We study the *Single Agent Reachability Problem*. This is characterized by tracking a special agent state which the rules and starting configuration ensure only one can exist at a time. If a node becomes the state A we say it is occupied by the agent.

Definition 8 (Single Agent Reachability Problem). *Given a board B with a single agent state A, an agent-based rules system R, and a target location t, does there exist a sequence of rules applied to subconfigurations which causes the node at t to be in state A?*

This problem is commonly studied in the context of block pushing puzzles, and therefore we use a naming convention found in block pushing literature. For example, given the rule $ABe \rightarrow eAB$, we call Single Agent Reachability problem Push-1 if we do not allow fixed walls F, Push-1F if we allow fixed walls, and Push-1W if we allow *thin walls*, which can be thought of as removing edges from the board (changing whether we have a full grid, an induced subgraph, or a general subgraph of the grid). We include the name of each rule in the tables. In the future, when we refer to the Single Agent Reachability problem by a rule r we really mean the Single Agent Reachability Problem using the set or rules consisting of r and the *movement rule*, $\{r, Ae \rightarrow eA\}$. For example, in Table 1, the results for the rule $ABe \rightarrow eBA$ are in fact results for the Single Agent Reachability Problem for the set of rules $\{ABe \rightarrow eBA, Ae \rightarrow eA\}$. This is because in typical pushing block puzzles the agent is allowed to move freely unless it comes in contact with a fixed wall or movable block, where in the latter case the agent can then either push or pull the block. Hence, any ruleset that does not include the movement rule is an incomplete representation of these puzzles.

2.2   Gadgets

Almost all of our hardness results reduce from the motion-planning-through-gadgets model [9,11]. This framework was introduced by a series of papers [9,11], and attempts to generalize motion planning problems where an autonomous agent attempts to navigate an environment to get between two distinct points.

A *gadget* consists of a finite set of *states*, a finite set of *locations*, and a finite set of *transitions* of the form $(q, a) \rightarrow (r, b)$, meaning that, when the gadget is in state q, an agent can enter at location a and exit at location b while changing the gadget's state to r. Given a system of such gadgets, with locations connected together by a graph, the *reachability* problem asks whether the agent can start at one specified location and reach another through a sequence of gadget traversals and connections between gadgets.

As pushing-block puzzles are motion-planning problems at their core, we make extensive use of this framework to show the vast majority of our rules are NP-hard or PSPACE-hard.

3   Generalized Swaps

We start by defining a generalized swap and prove that all generalized swaps are in NL and all symmetric generalized swaps are in L. We also prove that many generalized swaps are L-hard and NL-hard. For hardness, we reduce from non-planar graph reachability and thus we need a crossover gadget.

3.1   Rules in L and NL

Definition 9 (Generalized Swap). *Let P denote a subconfiguration that a rule is being applied to. A set of rules is a generalized swap if for each rule:*

1. *The only vertices that change state are the start s and ending location t of an agent, and*
2. *For all other vertices $p \in P \backslash \{s, t\}$ which do not contain a fixed wall F, adding or removing a block B from p does not impact the ability of the agent to move from s to t, though perhaps using different rules from the set.*

*Adding or removing blocks may prevent movement through other positions in P, however. A generalized swap is **symmetric** if the rule with the agent starting at t and moving to s is also a generalized swap.*

Theorem 1. *Single Agent Reachability with a generalized swap is in NL. If the generalized swap is symmetric, it is in L.*

Corollary 1. *The following games are in L under both the non-bendy setting and the bendy setting:*

- *Trivial ($eAB \rightarrow AeB$ and $AeB \rightarrow eAB$)*
- *Leap-F ($ABe \rightarrow eBA$)*
- *Vault-F ($AFe \rightarrow eFA$)*
- *Trail Leap-F ($ABe \rightarrow BBA$)*
- *Trail Vault-F ($AFe \rightarrow BFA$)*

The following games in in NL under both the non-bendy setting and the bendy setting:

- *Vault Swap-F ($AFB \rightarrow BFA$)*
- *Vault Crush-F ($AFB \rightarrow eFA$)*
- *Push into Wall-F ($ABF \rightarrow eAF$)*
- *Wall Suplex-F ($BAF \rightarrow eAF$)*
- *Fixed Wall's Push Swap ($ABF \rightarrow BAF$)*
- *Fixed Wall's Pull Swap ($BAF \rightarrow ABF$)*

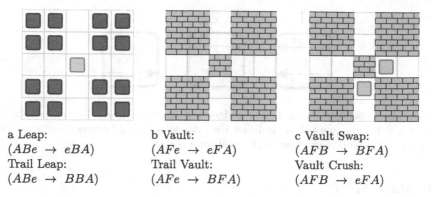

a Leap:
$(ABe \rightarrow eBA)$
Trail Leap:
$(ABe \rightarrow BBA)$

b Vault:
$(AFe \rightarrow eFA)$
Trail Vault:
$(AFe \rightarrow BFA)$

c Vault Swap:
$(AFB \rightarrow BFA)$
Vault Crush:
$(AFB \rightarrow eFA)$

Fig. 1. Undirected crossovers in (a) and (b), and a directed crossover in (c)

3.2 Path Reductions

For L-hardness and NL-hardness we must provide a crossover gadget; whether or not the crossover gadget is directed influences the hardness of the ruleset (Fig. 1).

Theorem 2. *The following games are complete for their corresponding complexity classes:*

- *Leap ($ABe \rightarrow eBA$) is L-complete.*
- *Vault-F ($AFe \rightarrow eFA$) is L-complete.*
- *Trail Leap ($ABe \rightarrow BBA$) is L-complete.*
- *Trail Vault-F ($AFe \rightarrow BFA$) is L-complete.*
- *Vault Crush-F ($AFB \rightarrow eFA$) is NL-complete.*
- *Vault Swap-F ($AFB \rightarrow BFA$) is NL-complete.*

4 Conservative Games

We present the complete set of "conservative" rules on three nodes. A rule is *conservative* if and only if:

1. The number of movable blocks present on the board before the rule is applied is equal to the number of movable blocks after, and
2. The number of fixed walls is the same before and after applying the rule, and fixed walls do not change position.

There are several rules which are "congruent" to other rules. Two rules R_1, R_2 are **congruent** if applying the movement rule to either the left or right hand states of R_1 can produce identical states to R_2. If the movement rule is congruent to a rule R, then R is *trivial*.

Fig. 2. The Locking 2-Toggle (L2T) gadget and its states from the motion planning framework. The numbers above indicate the state and when a traversal happens across the arrows, the gadget changes to the indicated state.

4.1   Rules in NP

Theorem 3. *Single-Agent Reachability for Push Swap at Empty (ABe → BAe) is NP-complete.*

4.2   PSPACE-Complete Rules

Theorem 4. *Single-agent Reachability for the following rules is PSPACE-complete:*

- *Swap-2 (ABB → BBA)*
- *Pull Swap at Empty (eAB → eBA)*
- *Suplex-1F (eAB → BAe)*
- *Pull Swap at Block (BAB → ABB)*
- *Push Swap at Block (ABB → BAB) (Figs. 2, 3 and 4).*

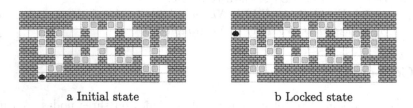

a Initial state   b Locked state

Fig. 3. An L2T gadget for Swap-2 (ABB → BBA) model

4.3   Polynomial Time Rules

Here we show agent reachability Suplex-1 with no fixed walls is in P. Recall that Suplex-1 is the rule $eAB \rightarrow BAe$ (or equivalently, $eAB \rightarrow BeA$). We will work with the version with the rule $eAB \rightarrow BAe$. We call applications of the this rule (which does not move the agent) **suplex moves** to distinguish it from moving the agent with the movement rule. We call empty locations **holes**; because the agent needs a hole behind it in order to move blocks, keeping track of the location of holes will be key to our algorithm. Call a location **reachable** if it is possible for the agent to ever reach that location, and call a move a **turn** if it is in a different direction than the previous move (i.e., horizontal after a vertical or vice versa). We will think of the path the agent takes as a sequence of **segments** and turns, where a segment is the sequence of consecutive moves in the same direction. Most of the time, when following a path, the agent will alternate between using suplex moves to clear the space in front of them, and then moving into the newly cleared space. Using these ideas we show Suplex-1 without fixed blocks in P.

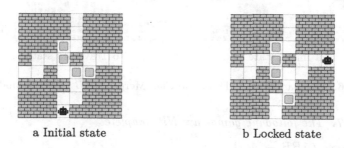

a Initial state   b Locked state

Fig. 4. An L2T gadget for Suplex-1F ($eAB \rightarrow BAe$)

Theorem 5. *Computing the set of reachable locations for an agent is in P so Suplex-1 is in P.*

5 Bounded Games

In this section we study what we call "bounded" games. In a **bounded game**, the total number of movable blocks monotonically increases or decreases with each application of the game rule. We can divide the bounded games into two types: **Zap**, which deletes blocks in each rule application, and **Trail**, which adds blocks. The results are outlined in Table 2. We then prove the remaining bounded games are all easy via a greedy algorithm. Finally we investigate which of these games are P-complete. We start with the proof bounded games are all in NP.

Theorem 6. *All bounded games are in NP.*

5.1 NAND Gadgets

In many of these games we get NP-hardness by building a NAND gadget. This gadget has two tunnels which both start open. Traversing either tunnel closes the other and leaves the first open. We use two variants: anti-parallel and crossing. The first is shown in Fig. 5. For the last reduction we introduce a new version of the NAND called the **Delayed NAND**. This NAND adds an extra initial state where the gadget must be "activated" by a button before solving. It is of note that all of these NP-complete reductions do not use fixed walls (Figs. 6 and 7).

Fig. 5. Antiparallel NAND gadget shown. This gadget is drawn with all transitions directed however some of our gadgets are undirected or mixed, i.e., having both types. In all of these settings the motion planning problem is NP-complete.

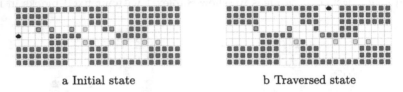

a Initial state   b Traversed state

Fig. 6. Anti-Parallel NAND for the Clap Merge ($BAB \rightarrow eBA$) model

Theorem 7. *The following games are NP-complete:*

- *Push Merge ($ABB \rightarrow AeB$)*
- *Bendy Push Merge-F ($ABB \rightarrow AeB$)*
- *Suplex Smash ($BAB \rightarrow eAe$)*
- *Bendy Suplex Smash-F ($BAB \rightarrow eAe$)*
- *Suplex Merge ($BAB \rightarrow BAe$)*
- *Bendy Suplex Merge-F ($BAB \rightarrow BAe$)*
- *Clap Merge ($BAB \rightarrow eBA$)*
- *Bendy Clap Merge-F ($BAB \rightarrow eBA$)*
- *Trail Push ($ABe \rightarrow BAB$)*

Theorem 8. *The following rules are NP-complete:*

- *Trail Swap ($eAB \rightarrow BBA$)*
- *Swap Zap ($ABB \rightarrow BeA$)*
- *Leap Crush ($ABB \rightarrow eBA$)*
- *Push Smash ($ABB \rightarrow Aee$)*

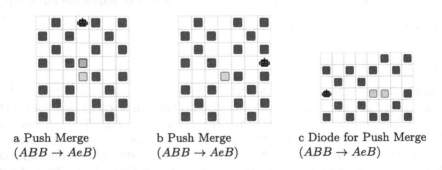

a Push Merge   b Push Merge   c Diode for Push Merge
($ABB \rightarrow AeB$)   ($ABB \rightarrow AeB$)   ($ABB \rightarrow AeB$)

Fig. 7. Initial states of Antiparallel NANDs

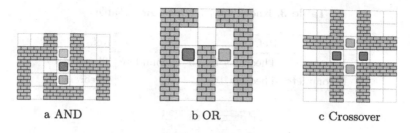

a AND   b OR   c Crossover

Fig. 8. Battering Ram $(eAB \rightarrow eAe)$ P-complete Reduction

Theorem 9. *Pull Merge $(ABB \rightarrow ABe)$ is NP-complete.*

5.2 More Easy Cases

First we will describe a greedy algorithm which gives membership in P for a few games. We only include rules here that aren't covered by log-space algorithms described in Sect. 3.

Theorem 10. *The following games are in P:*

- *Battering Ram-F $(eAB \rightarrow eAe)$*
- *Knock over-F $(ABe \rightarrow Aee)$*
- *Zap Through Walls-F $(AFB \rightarrow AFe)$ (Fig. 8)*

Theorem 11. *The following games are P-complete:*

- *Battering Ram-F $(eAB \rightarrow eAe)$*
- *Zap Through Walls-F $(AFB \rightarrow AFe)$ in 3D*
- *Zap Through Walls-F $(AFB \rightarrow AFe)$ with Multiple Agents*

Zap-Through-Walls

Corollary 2. *Zap-Through-Walls-F $(AFB \rightarrow AFe)$ is PMCVP-hard.*

Theorem 12. *Bendy Zap Through Wall $(AFB \rightarrow AFe)$ is PMCVP-hard in 2D and P-complete in 3D.*

Battering Ram. Here, we give a result for Battering Ram $(eAB \rightarrow eAe)$ with no fixed blocks:

Theorem 13. *Battering Ram is NL-complete.*

Table 3. Knock Over ($ABe \rightarrow Aee$) Table

	−W	Ref.	−F	Ref.
3D	P-complete	Theorems 14, 15	P-complete	Theorem 15
2D	P-complete	Theorem 14	NL	Theorem 16

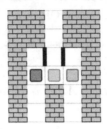

Fig. 9. Knockover-W ($ABe \rightarrow Aee$)

Knock Over. Knock Over ($ABe \rightarrow Aee$) is of interest because the problem is P-complete if we allow thin walls or if the problem is in 3D, but is in NL if we only allow fixed walls. This is the only section we have where -W vs -F makes a distinction so we specify this in our Theorems. Note that Theorem 10 holds for −W (Table 3) (Fig. 9).

Theorem 14. *Knock Over-W ($ABe \rightarrow Aee$) is P-complete.*

Theorem 15. *Knock Over-F ($ABe \rightarrow Aee$) in 3D is P-complete.*

Theorem 16. *Knock Over-F ($ABe \rightarrow Aee$) is in NL.*

6 Bendy Rules

Here, we consider length-3 bendy rules, that have not been considered in earlier sections. Recall that length-3 bendy rules can be applied in an L-shape. For example, for Push-1 ($ABe \rightarrow eAB$), allowing the rule to be bendy allows for an agent to push a block around a corner.

6.1 Other Conservative Bendy Results

Here, we obtain partial results for some conservative bendy rules not mentioned in earlier sections:

Theorem 17. *Bendy Push-1F ($ABe \rightarrow eAB$) is NP-hard (Fig. 10).*

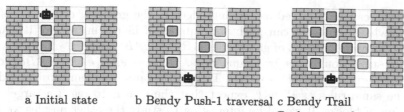

a Initial state   b Bendy Push-1 traversal c Bendy Trail
Push traversal

Fig. 10. An undirected NAND gadget for Bendy Push-1F ($ABe \rightarrow eAB$) and an undirected matched crumblers gadget for Bendy Trail Push ($ABe \rightarrow BAB$).

Theorem 18. *Bendy Push Swap at Block-F (ABB $\rightarrow$ BAB) is NP-hard.*

Theorem 19. *Bendy Pull Swap at Block-F (BAB $\rightarrow$ ABB) is NP-hard.*

Here, we note a particularly surprising easiness result:

Theorem 20. *Bendy Suplex-1F (AeB $\rightarrow$ BAe and congruent) is in L.*

6.2 Other Bounded Bendy Results

Here, we obtain some results (some partial, some full) for bounded bendy rules that are not mentioned in earlier sections:

Theorem 21. *Bendy Trail Push-F (ABe $\rightarrow$ BAB) is NP-complete.*

Theorem 22. *Bendy Push Smash-F (ABB $\rightarrow$ Aee) and Bendy Swaplex-F (ABB $\rightarrow$ BAe) are NP-complete.*

Theorem 23. *Bendy Pull Merge-F (ABB $\rightarrow$ ABe) is NP-complete.*

Theorem 24. *Bendy Trail Swap-F (eAB $\rightarrow$ BBA) is NP-complete.*

Theorem 25. *Bendy Knock-Over-F (ABe $\rightarrow$ Aee) is PMCVP-hard in 2D and P-complete in 3D.*

Theorem 26. *Bendy Battering Ram-F (AeB $\rightarrow$ eAe) is in L.*

7 Future Directions

Many other variants of Push-1F and Pull?-1F have been introduced and studied. Some of them require further extentions to our block asynchronous cellular automata framework. For example, Pull!-1 [4] forces the agent to pull a block when it moves away from a block. We can model this by replacing the $Ae \rightarrow eA$ swap with the more restrictive $eAe \rightarrow Aee$ as the movement rule, in addition to the rule $eAB \rightarrow ABe$ representing the pull. It would be interesting to consider the other games with this movement rule. Pull-1W [4] allows thin 0×1 walls.

Thin walls can be modeled as missing edges in the graph of cells. Games like Push-*, where the agent can push any number of blocks in front of it, can be modeled as an infinite set of game rules $AB^i e \rightarrow eAB^i$ for all $i > 0$. PushPull-1 is a game that would have two game rules, $\{ABe \rightarrow eAB, eAB \rightarrow ABe\}$, or as a single reversible rule $ABe \leftrightarrow eAB$. The puzzle game Sokoban can be modeled with the same rules as Push-1, expect that the goal is to reach a target configuration of blocks. It would be interesting to study the other puzzles we have introduced in these variants as well.

References

1. Adleman, L., et al.: Combinatorial optimization problems in self-assembly. In: Proceedings of the 34th Annual ACM Symposium on Theory of Computing, pp. 23–32 (2002)
2. Akitaya, H.A., et al.: Characterizing universal reconfigurability of modular pivoting robots. In: Proceedings of the 37th International Symposium on Computational Geometry (2021)
3. Alaniz, R.M., et al.: Complexity of reconfiguration in surface chemical reaction networks. In: Chen, H.-L., Evans, C.G. (Eds.) Proceedings of the 29th International Conference on DNA Computing and Molecular Programming (DNA 29), vol. 276. Leibniz International Proceedings in Informatics (LIPIcs), pp. 10:1–10:18, Dagstuhl, Germany (2023). Schloss Dagstuhl – Leibniz-Zentrum für Informatik
4. Ani, H., et al.: PSPACE-completeness of pulling blocks to reach a goal. J. Inf. Process. **28**, 929–941 (2020)
5. Ani, H., Chung, L., Demaine, E.D., Diomidova, J., Hendrickson, D., Lynch, J.: Pushing blocks via checkable gadgets: PSPACE-completeness of Push-1F and Block/Box Dude. In: Proceedings of the 11th International Conference on Fun with Algorithms (FUN 2022) (2022)
6. Berlekamp, E.R., Conway, J.H., Guy, R.K.: What is life? In: Winning Ways for Your Mathematical Plays, vol. 4. A K Peters, 2nd (edn.) (2004)
7. Cook, M.: Universality in elementary cellular automata. Complex Syst. **15**(1), 1–40 (2004)
8. Defant, C., Kravitz, N.: Friends and strangers walking on graphs. Comb. Theory. 1 (2021)
9. Demaine, E.D., Grosof, I., Lynch, J., Rudoy, M.: Computational complexity of motion planning of a robot through simple gadgets. In: Proceedings of the 9th International Conference on Fun with Algorithms (FUN 2018) (2018)
10. Demaine, E.D., Hearn, R.A., Hendrickson, D., Lynch, J.: PSPACE-completeness of reversible deterministic systems. In: Proceedings of the 9th Conference on Machines, Computations and Universality (MCU 2022), pp. 91–108, Debrecen, Hungary, August–September 2022
11. Demaine, E.D., Hendrickson, D.H., Lynch, J.: Toward a general complexity theory of motion planning: characterizing which gadgets make games hard. In: Proceedings of the 11th Innovations in Theoretical Computer Science Conference (ITCS 2020), pp. 62:1–62:42 (2020)
12. Demaine, E.D., Rudoy, M.: A simple proof that the (n^2-1)-puzzle is hard. Theoret. Comput. Sci. **732**, 80–84 (2018)

13. Dennunzio, A., Formenti, E., Manzoni, L., Mauri, G., Porreca, A.E.: Computational complexity of finite asynchronous cellular automata. Theoret. Comput. Sci. **664**, 131–143 (2017)
14. Durand-Lose, J.: Representing reversible cellular automata with reversible block cellular automata. Discrete Mathematics & Theoretical Computer Science Proceedings, AA: Discrete Models: Combinatorics, Computation, and Geometry (DM-CCG 2001), January 2001
15. Fatès, N.: A guided tour of asynchronous cellular automata. In: Kari, J., Kutrib, M., Malcher, A. (eds.) AUTOMATA 2013. LNCS, vol. 8155, pp. 15–30. Springer, Heidelberg (2013). https://doi.org/10.1007/978-3-642-40867-0_2
16. Fleischer, R., Yu, J.: A survey of the game "Lights Out!". In: Brodnik, A., López-Ortiz, A., Raman, V., Viola, A. (eds.) Space-Efficient Data Structures, Streams, and Algorithms. LNCS, vol. 8066, pp. 176–198. Springer, Heidelberg (2013). https://doi.org/10.1007/978-3-642-40273-9_13
17. Gershenfeld, N., et al.: Reconfigurable asynchronous logic automata. ACM SIG-PLAN Not. **45**(1), 1–6 (2010)
18. Goles, E., Maldonado, D., Montealegre, P., Ríos-Wilson, M.: On the complexity of asynchronous freezing cellular automata. Inf. Comput. **281**, 104764 (2021)
19. Goles, E., Ollinger, N., Theyssier, G.: Introducing freezing cellular automata. In: Proceedings of the 21st International Workshop on Cellular Automata and Discrete Complex Systems (AUTOMATA 2015), vol. 24, pp. 65–73 (2015)
20. Group, M.H., et al.: Pushing blocks without fixed blocks via checkable gizmos: Push-1 is PSPACE-complete. Manuscript under submission (2024)
21. Gutowitz, H.: Cellular Automata: Theory and Experiment. MIT Press, Cambridge (1991)
22. Kari, J.: Theory of cellular automata: a survey. Theoret. Comput. Sci. **334**(1), 3–33 (2005)
23. Langton, C.G.: Studying artificial life with cellular automata. Physica D **22**(1–3), 120–149 (1986)
24. Margolus, N.: Physics-like models of computation. Physica D **10**(1), 81–95 (1984)
25. Milojević, A.: Connectivity of old and new models of friends-and-strangers graphs. Adv. Appl. Math. **155**, 102668 (2024)
26. Neary, T., Woods, D.: P-completeness of cellular automaton rule 110. In: Bugliesi, M., Preneel, B., Sassone, V., Wegener, I. (eds.) ICALP 2006. LNCS, vol. 4051, pp. 132–143. Springer, Heidelberg (2006). https://doi.org/10.1007/11786986_13
27. Ollinger, N., Theyssier, G.: Freezing, bounded-change and convergent cellular automata. Discr. Math. Theoret. Comput. Sci. 24(Automata, Logic and Semantics) (2022)
28. Qian, L., Winfree, E.: Parallel and scalable computation and spatial dynamics with DNA-based chemical reaction networks on a surface. In: Murata, S., Kobayashi, S. (eds.) DNA 2014. LNCS, vol. 8727, pp. 114–131. Springer, Cham (2014). https://doi.org/10.1007/978-3-319-11295-4_8
29. Ratner, D., Warmuth, M.: The $(n^2 - 1)$-puzzle and related relocation problems. J. Symb. Comput. **10**, 111–137 (1990)
30. Sutner, K.: On the computational complexity of finite cellular automata. J. Comput. Syst. Sci. **50**(1), 87–97 (1995)
31. Thubagere, A.J., et al.: A cargo-sorting DNA robot. Science. **357**(6356), eaan6558 (2017)
32. Toffoli, T., Margolus, N.: Ii.12: The Margolus neighborhood. In: Cellular Automata Machines: A New Environment for Modeling, pp. 119–138. MIT Press (1987)

236   H. Ani et al.

33. Tsukiji, T., Hagiwara, T.: Recognizing the repeatable configurations of time-reversible generalized Langton's ant is PSPACE-hard. Algorithms **4**(1), 1–15 (2011)
34. von Neumann, J.: Theory of Self-Reproducing Automata. University of Illinois Press (1966)
35. Winfree, E.: Algorithmic self-assembly of DNA. PhD thesis, California Institute of Technology (1998)

Minimizing Cycles in Reaction Systems

Ryan Farrell, Daniela Genova$^{(\boxtimes)}$, and Dylan Strickley

Department of Mathematics and Statistics,
University of North Florida, Jacksonville, FL 32224, USA
d.genova@unf.edu

Abstract. Introduced by Ehrenfeucht and Rozenberg, the formal model
of reaction systems captures the dynamics of biochemical reactions based
on the two main mechanisms of facilitation and inhibition. Functionally
equivalent reaction systems evolve through the same result function and
various types of minimization of reaction systems have been studied. This
paper aims to extend two types of reaction system minimization, rank
and degree, to partially-defined RS functions, with a focus on minimizing cycles within reaction systems. We provide bounds on the rank and
degree of cycles, as well as computational techniques used to determine
when such bounds are strict. Finally, we assign a measure of "complexity" to each family of states via the maximum degree of a cycle over this
family. We show this derived measure of complexity satisfies a useful
monotonicity condition.

Keywords: Natural Computing · Reaction Systems Minimization ·
Cycle minimization · Reaction Systems Rank · Reaction Systems
Degree

1 Introduction

Reaction systems were introduced in [9] as a formal model developed to study the
dynamics of biochemical reactions. They provide rich modeling techniques based
on the complex interaction between the two competing mechanisms of facilitation
and inhibition. The reaction systems paradigm on the one hand models various
biological environments [1,4,8], and on the other, studies information processing
through its underlying mathematical and computational structures, e.g., graphs,
partial orders, functions defined on power sets, transducers [3,12,13] and can be
used as a tool to run computation [2].

The inherent complexity of reaction systems makes them difficult to compare. The question of whether two reaction systems are functionally equivalent was found to be co-NP-complete in [9] and various properties of functional
and enabling equivalences and related partial orders were studied in [12,13,17].
A natural question to investigate is that of finding a minimal reaction system
among equivalent ones. Different types of reaction systems minimality have been
defined and studied. A. Salomaa studied minimal and almost minimal reaction

© The Author(s), under exclusive license to Springer Nature Switzerland AG 2024
D.-J. Cho and J. Kim (Eds.): UCNC 2024, LNCS 14776, pp. 237–252, 2024.
https://doi.org/10.1007/978-3-031-63742-1_17

systems in [21, 22], where each reaction has two or three resources only. Exploring minimality through single-valued or multi-valued Boolean functions lends itself to using Karnaugh maps, McCluskey method, and the Espresso minimization tool to minimize reaction systems in a variety of ways: by minimal number of reactions, as a minimal number of total resources used to generate a certain output, or minimize them when certain states can be ignored [4, 14]. W.C. Teh et al. investigate reaction systems with minimal and strictly minimal number of reactions (rank) in [16, 23, 24].

This paper introduces a novel approach to minimizing reaction systems by the number of resources per reaction, called the degree of the reaction system. The concept of degree is a middle-ground between the minimal reaction systems discussed by [7, 16, 21–25] and $\mathcal{RS}(r, i)$ function classes used in [19]. In our study of minimization, we seek to apply these minimization techniques to cycles. Since RS functions can be conveniently represented by graphs called zero-context graphs, and since each of the components of these graphs ends in a cycle (see [10–12, 14]), cycles are an essential part of RS functions. Cycles have been investigated in the context of minimal reaction systems in [20, 22], which uses recursive constructions to make long terminating sequences/cycles in reaction systems with restricted resources. The existence and length of cycles have also been discussed in an analysis of the computational complexity of several problems associated with reaction systems in [10, 11].

The paper is structured as follows. Section 2 defines the reaction systems model and sets the associated notation and terminology. Two types of minimal reaction systems: those with a minimal number of reactions (minimal rank) and those with a minimal number of resources in each reaction (minimal degree) are defined in Sect. 3. In Sect. 4, we discuss minimization over subset functions, specifically focusing on cycles. We provide bounds on the rank and degree of cycles, as well as computational techniques used to determine when such bounds are strict. In Sect. 5, we assign a measure of "complexity" to each family of states using the maximum degrees of cycles which run over that family. This derived measure of complexity satisfies a monotonicity property which we conjecture is also held by an analogous measure of complexity defined using rank.

2   Reaction Systems and the Result Function

In this section we set the notation and define the terminology associated with reaction systems and their result functions arising from [9].

Given a finite, nonempty *background set* S, a *reaction over* S is a triple $a = (R, I, P)$ of subsets of S. The elements of S are called *entities* - they represent the elements, molecules, or compounds in the environment. The component sets of a reaction are called the *reactants*, *inhibitors*, and *products* of a, and may be denoted by R_a, I_a, and P_a respectively. The set $R_a \cup I_a$ is the set of *resources* of a, sometimes denoted by M_a. If R_a or I_a are empty, we say that a is a *degenerate* reaction. Unless stated otherwise, S will denote an arbitrary but fixed, finite and nonempty set which will be used as our background set. Since the names of entities can be abstracted to integers, we typically let $S = \{1, \ldots, n\}$ be the set containing the first n positive integers, denoted $[n]$.

Let T be a set of entities in S, i.e., $T \subseteq S$. We say a reaction a is *enabled* by T, denoted $\text{en}_a(T)$, if T contains all of the reactants of a and none of its inhibitors. The *result* of a on T, $\text{res}_a(T)$, is defined as $\text{res}_a(T) = P_a$ if $\text{en}_a(T)$ and $\text{res}_a(T) = \varnothing$ otherwise. We call T a *state* of S. States represent the entities currently available in a given environment. Notice the quantity of each entity of T is not provided. This is one way our model of reactions provides abstraction from those present in nature: we assume each element either saturates our environment or is not present.

A reaction system, abbreviated *RS*, is an ordered pair $\mathcal{A} = (S, A)$, where S is a finite, nonempty background set and A is a set of reactions over S. The elements of A are also the *reactions* of $\mathcal{A}$. If $\mathcal{A}$ allows degenerate reactions then it is called a *degenerate reaction system*; otherwise, it is *non-degenerate*. Informally, reaction systems are collections of reactions over a fixed background set S. Just as individual reactions can affect an environment, so too can entire reaction systems. Their effect is cumulative: the result of a reaction system, $\text{res}_\mathcal{A}$, is the result of its set of reactions A, which in turn is the union of its reactions' results. That is, $\text{res}_\mathcal{A}(T) = \text{res}_A(T)$ and $\text{res}_A(T) = \cup_{a \in A} \text{res}_a(T)$. Notice that by this definition, reactions in $\mathcal{A}$ whose reactant sets overlap do not need to compete to be enabled. This is a result of the saturation of resources described earlier, an assumption referred to as the *threshold nature of resources* in [9]. Another result of this definition for $\text{res}_\mathcal{A}(T)$ is the *non-permanency* of entities: if no reactions sustain a particular entity, it will not be maintained by the system. In this way, reaction systems mimic processes in living cells, which require constant upkeep and energy to maintain themselves.

3   RS Functions and Minimization

A reaction system $\mathcal{A}$ can act on states T of S to produce new states via the result function $\text{res}_\mathcal{A}$. To study this behavior, it suffices to focus on those functions defined by a reaction system.

Definition 1 (RS Function). *Given a background set S, a function f is called an RS function over S if $f = \text{res}_\mathcal{A}$ for some reaction system $\mathcal{A} = (S, A)$.*

Denote the set of all subsets of a given set S by $\mathcal{P}(S)$, the power set of S. Note that every function $f : \mathcal{P}(S) \to \mathcal{P}(S)$ is an RS function over S. Indeed, consider the reaction set:

$$A = \{(X, S \setminus X, f(X)) \mid X \subseteq S\}.$$

For the reaction system $\mathcal{A} = (S, A)$, notice that $f = \text{res}_\mathcal{A}$ (see [14]). This is called the *maximally-inhibited reaction system of f* and the reactions in it are called *maximally-inhibited reactions* (see [14,21]). The name emphasizes that each reaction is enabled at exactly one state T of S and adding additional inhibitors will prevent it from being enabled in T. If $f = \text{res}_\mathcal{A}$ for some degenerate reaction system $\mathcal{A}$, we say that f is degenerate, and non-degenerate otherwise. Throughout this paper, we consider degenerate reaction systems and RS functions, though it should be noted that many of the results in this paper can be generalized to non-degenerate reaction systems as well.

In general, the correspondence between reaction systems and RS functions is not unique. Given an RS function f, there may be two distinct reaction systems $\mathcal{A}$ and $\mathcal{B}$ such that $f = \text{res}_\mathcal{A} = \text{res}_\mathcal{B}$. In this case, we say that $\mathcal{A}$ and $\mathcal{B}$ are *functionally equivalent*, denoted $\mathcal{A} \sim \mathcal{B}$. Since there may be many different reaction systems corresponding to the same result function f, one goal is to find a "simplest" reaction system which generates a given RS function. The following are two ways to define minimality.

1. Minimizing the total number of reactions used in the reaction system (rank).
2. Minimizing the number of resources used in each reaction (degree).

These two kinds of minimal reactions systems are defined below. The first was proposed and investigated recently by W. C. Teh et al. (see [23,24]).

Definition 2 (Reaction System Rank). *Suppose $\mathcal{A} = (S, A)$ is a reaction system over S and f is an RS function over S. The* rank *of $\mathcal{A}$, denoted* rs-rank$(\mathcal{A})$, *is defined by* rs-rank$(\mathcal{A}) = |A|$. *The* reaction system rank *of f (or simply* rsrank *of f), denoted* rs-rank(f), *is defined by*

$$\text{rs-rank}(f) = \min\{\text{rs-rank}(\mathcal{A}) \mid \text{res}_\mathcal{A} = f\}$$

The second definition, that of a degree, is a novel notion in reaction systems that we investigate in this paper.

Definition 3 (Reaction System Degree). *Suppose $\mathcal{A} = (S, A)$ is a reaction system over S and f is an RS function over S. The* degree *of $\mathcal{A}$, denoted* rs-deg$(\mathcal{A})$, *is defined by*

$$\text{rs-deg}(\mathcal{A}) = \max\{|R_b \cup I_b| \mid a \in A\}.$$

The reaction system degree *of f, (or simply* rs-deg *of f), denoted* rs-deg(f), *is defined by*

$$\text{rs-deg}(f) = \min\{\text{rs-deg}(\mathcal{A}) \mid \text{res}_\mathcal{A} = f\}.$$

Minimization in terms of number of resources was first studied by Salomaa in [7] where *minimal reactions systems* were defined as non-degenerate reaction systems whose reactions have at most 2 resources. This concept was later generalized by L. Manzoni in [19] who studied the class of reaction systems with at most r reactants and i inhibitors in each reaction, which was denoted $\mathcal{RS}(r, i)$.

Observe that, for an RS function f over a background set S, due to maximally inhibited reactions discussed in [14,21], the maximum number of reactions in any reaction system over S can be at most $|\mathcal{P}(S)|$. On the other hand, the function that maps every state to the empty set requires no reactions and hence,

$0 \leq$ rs-rank$(f) \leq |\mathcal{P}(S)|$. A non-trivial construction employed in [23] shows that this upper bound is tight.

Analogously, the next proposition investigates broad bounds for the degree of functions over a background set S.

Proposition 1. *If f is an RS function over S, then $0 \leq$ rs-deg$(f) \leq |S|$. Furthermore, these bounds are tight.*

Proof. The fewest number of resources in a reaction system is zero and can be achieved either by an empty RS or by an RS consisting of reactions of the form $(\varnothing, \varnothing, P)$. On the other hand, the largest number of resources in a single reaction, and thus the largest degree of an RS, is at most $|S|$, since $R \cap I = \emptyset$ and $R \cup I \subseteq S$ where $R \cup I = S$ is achieved for maximally inhibited reactions.

These bounds are tight for functions since they are achieved by a function that maps every state to the empty set and a function that maps a single state to a nonempty set and every other state to the empty set respectively.   □

Calculating rs-rank and rs-deg can be computationally difficult. It depends on the functional equivalence of reaction systems, which was shown to be co-NP-complete (see [4,9,14]) by its equivalence to deciding Boolean functions in DNF. We introduce the following notions and results in an attempt to simplify such tasks.

Let f and g be RS functions over S, then $f \cup g$ is also an RS function over S defined by $(f \cup g)(X) = f(X) \cup g(X)$. For two reaction systems over S, $\mathcal{A} = (S, A)$ and $\mathcal{B} = (S, B)$, define their union as $\mathcal{A} \cup \mathcal{B} = (S, A \cup B)$, which is also a reaction system over S.

Theorem 1. *Let f and g be RS functions over S, then*

1. rs-rank$(f \cup g) \leq$ rs-rank$(f) +$ rs-rank(g).
2. rs-deg$(f \cup g) \leq \max($rs-deg$(f),$ rs-deg$(g))$.

The first part of Theorem 1 was proven by W. C. Teh et al. in Section 4 of [23] and the second part can be proven using a similar technique. Theorem 1 suggests that we can find an upper bound of the degree of an RS function by decomposing it into functions with known degrees. We now provide a natural decomposition to use in conjunction with these results based on focus functions.

Focus functions aim at studying subsets of reactions that produce a particular entity. They were originally defined in [9] by Ehrenfeucht et al. and later used to characterize resource minimal reaction systems in [7], studied in the context of Boolean functions in [4,14], and as a tool for minimizing rank in [24].

Definition 4 (Focus Function). *Let f be an RS function over S, then for $q \in S$ we can define its q-focus function $f^{(q)}$ by*

$$f^{(q)}(X) = \begin{cases} \{q\}, & \text{if } q \in f(X) \\ \varnothing, & \text{otherwise} \end{cases}$$

Alternatively, we say f is a q-focus function if, for some $q \in S$, we have $f = f^{(q)}$. When q is arbitrary, we simply call $f^{(q)}$ a focus function.

For an arbitrary RS function, let the *support of* f, denoted supp(f), be defined by supp$(f) = \{X \in \mathcal{P}(S) \mid f(X) \neq \varnothing\}$. One convenient property of q-focus functions is that they can be described purely by identifying their support. By our definition of focus function, we can see that the following formula is true for an arbitrary RS function f over S:

$$f(X) = \bigcup_{q \in S} f^{(q)}(X)$$

Using the above equation with Theorem 1, we get the following bounds on the degree of f in terms of its focus functions $f^{(q)}$.

Proposition 2. *If f is an RS function over S, then* rs-deg$(f) = \max_{q \in S}$ rs-deg$(f^{(q)})$.

Proof. Since any RS function f is the union of its focus functions, Theorem 1 tells us that rs-deg$(f) \leq \max_{q \in S}$ rs-deg$(f^{(q)})$. To show the other direction, suppose $\mathcal{A} = (S, A)$ is a reaction system such that res$_A = f$ and each reaction of A has at most rs-deg(f) resources. For an arbitrary $q \in S$, notice we can generate the q-focus function $f^{(q)}$ using the reaction set A_q defined by:

$$A_q = \{(R_a, I_a, \{q\}) \mid a \in A \text{ and } q \in P_a\}$$

If we define the reaction system $\mathcal{A}_q = (S, A_q)$, then res$_{\mathcal{A}_q}(X) = \{q\}$ if and only if $q \in f(X)$, thus $\mathcal{A}_q$ generates $f^{(q)}$. This shows rs-deg$(f^{(q)}) \leq$ rs-deg(f), and since q was an arbitrary entity, $\max_{q \in S}$ rs-deg$(f^{(q)}) \leq$ rs-deg(f). $\qquad\square$

4   Minimization of Subset Functions and Cycles

Functions with restricted domains, *subset functions*, are of a particular interest to reactions systems when certain states can be ignored. When an RS function f is only defined on a subset $\mathcal{C} \subset \mathcal{P}(S)$, we call f a *subset RS function*. Subset functions for reaction systems have been previously studied in a variety of contexts, e.g., in the context of enabling equivalence [17] and in functional equivalence and minimization [14].

In situations when some states can be ignored, we may still be interested in the fewest number of reactions or resources needed to generate a given subset function. As such, we define the rank and degree of a subset function as follows.

Definition 5. *Let f be an RS function over S and $\mathcal{C} \subseteq \mathcal{P}(S)$ be a subset of states over S. The rank of f over $\mathcal{C}$, denoted* rs-rank$(f, \mathcal{C})$, *is defined by*

$$\text{rs-rank}(f, \mathcal{C}) = \min\left\{\text{rs-rank}(g) \mid f\big|_{\mathcal{C}} = g\big|_{\mathcal{C}}\right\}.$$

Similarly, the degree of f over $\mathcal{C}$, denoted rs-deg$(f, \mathcal{C})$, *is defined by*

$$\text{rs-deg}(f, \mathcal{C}) = \min\left\{\text{rs-deg}(g) \mid f\big|_{\mathcal{C}} = g\big|_{\mathcal{C}}\right\}.$$

In this definition, we allow g to be any RS function defined over the states $\mathcal{C}$. If we follow the convention that rs-rank$(f) = $ rs-rank$(f, \mathcal{P}(S))$ and rs-deg$(f) = $ rs-deg$(f, \mathcal{P}(S))$, then this notation agrees with previous definitions. One useful result from this definition is that $\mathcal{C} \subseteq \mathcal{C}' \Rightarrow$ rs-rank$(f, \mathcal{C}) \leq $ rs-rank$(f, \mathcal{C}')$ and rs-deg$(f, \mathcal{C}) \leq $ rs-deg$(f, \mathcal{C}')$ for any RS function defined over $\mathcal{C}'$.

We now focus on a type of subset function present in every RS function: cycles. Due to their frequent occurrence, they have been studied in a variety of contexts including computational complexity [10,11] and long terminating sequences with limited resources [20,22]. There are several equivalent definitions for cycles. For the purposes of this paper, we will use the following.

Definition 6. *Let $\mathcal{C} \subseteq \mathcal{P}(S)$ be a family of p states over S. We say a function $\pi : \mathcal{C} \to \mathcal{C}$ is a p-cycle over $\mathcal{C}$ if π is bijective, and for every $\mathcal{C}' \subset \mathcal{C}$, $\pi|_{\mathcal{C}'}$ is not bijective.*

When the size of $\mathcal{C}$ is arbitrary, we simply refer to π as a cycle. If π is a p-cycle over the states $\{X_1, \ldots, X_p\}$ defined by $\pi(X_i) = X_{i+1}$ for $1 \leq i \leq p-1$ and $\pi(X_p) = X_1$, we may abbreviate π using the tuple notation $(X_1, \ldots, X_p)$. For 3-cycles, this tuple notation may be easily confused for a reaction, but should be interpreted from context.

One goal of this paper is to find good bounds on the rank and degree of cycles. It follows from the definitions that $0 \leq $ rs-deg$(\pi, \mathcal{C}) \leq |S|$ and $0 \leq $ rs-rank$(\pi, \mathcal{C}) \leq 2^{|S|}$ for a cycle π over $\mathcal{C} \subseteq \mathcal{P}(S)$. We can establish stricter bounds on this when considering a fixed p-cycle π.

Theorem 2. *Let π be a p-cycle over states $\mathcal{C} \subseteq \mathcal{P}(S)$ for $p \geq 2$, then*

1. $\lceil \log_2(p) \rceil \leq $ rs-rank$(\pi, \mathcal{C}) \leq p$.
2. $1 \leq $ rs-deg$(\pi, \mathcal{C}) \leq p - 1$.

Proof. It should first be noted that the lower bound $1 \leq $ rs-deg$(\pi, \mathcal{C})$ follows trivially since any reaction system only containing reactions of the form $(\varnothing, \varnothing, P)$ has exactly one state its range and cannot generate a cycle of length at least 2. To prove $\lceil \log_2(p) \rceil \leq $ rs-rank$(\pi, \mathcal{C})$, notice that a reaction system with k reactions can only have 2^k states in its range since each output state is the union of some subset of the k reactions' product sets. Since the reaction system generating π contains at least p output states, it has to have at least $\lceil \log_2(p) \rceil$ reactions, proving the desired result.

Now suppose $\pi = (X_1, \ldots, X_p)$ and let $j, k \in [p]$ be distinct. If $X_j \supseteq X_k$, pick an entity $r_{j,k}$ such that $r_{j,k} \in X_j \setminus X_k$. Otherwise, select an entity $i_{j,k} \in X_k \setminus X_j$. Once such entities have been selected for all distinct pairs $j, k \in [p]$, we construct reactions of the form:

$$c_j = \left(\bigcup_k r_{j,k}, \bigcup_k i_{j,k}, \pi(X_j) \right)$$

By our choices for $r_{j,k}$ and $i_{j,k}$, we have guaranteed that the only states in $\mathcal{C}$ which are enabled by reaction c_j is the state X_j. Defining the reaction system

$\mathcal{A} = (S, \{c_j \mid j \in [p]\})$, we have created a reaction system which generates π. Since $\mathcal{A}$ has only p reactions and each reaction has at most $p-1$ resources, we have proven rs-rank$(\pi, \mathcal{C}) \leq p$ and rs-deg$(\pi, \mathcal{C}) \leq p-1$ respectively.   □

We now provide examples to demonstrate that some of the bounds introduced in Theorem 2 are strict.

Example 1. Consider the background set $S = [p]$, p-cycles $\sigma_p = (\{1\}, \{2\}, \ldots, \{p\})$ over $\mathcal{C}_p$ and $\tau_p = (\{1\}, \{1,2\}, \ldots, \{1,p\})$ over $\mathcal{C}'_p$, then one can see σ_p is generated by the following set of reactions:

$$a_1 = (\{1\}, \varnothing, \{2\})$$
$$a_2 = (\{2\}, \varnothing, \{3\})$$
$$a_3 = (\{3\}, \varnothing, \{4\})$$
$$\vdots$$
$$a_{p-1} = (\{p-1\}, \varnothing, \{p\})$$
$$a_p = (\{p\}, \varnothing, \{1\})$$

This reaction system gives us the upper bounds that rs-rank$(\sigma_p, \mathcal{C}_p) \leq p$ and rs-deg$(\sigma_p, \mathcal{C}_p) \leq 1$. We can further use Theorem 2 to conclude rs-deg$(\sigma_p, \mathcal{C}_p) = 1$. Notice that each entity in S shows up in separate states of σ_p, so at least p reactions are needed to generate σ_p and thus rs-rank$(\sigma_p, \mathcal{C}_p) = p$.

Finally, we claim rs-deg$(\tau_p, \mathcal{C}'_p) = p-1$. Indeed, because $\tau_p(\{1\}) = \{1,2\}$, we may assume τ_p is generated by some reaction system containing reaction $a = (R_a, I_a, \{2\})$. Since $\{1,2\}$ is the only state in τ_p which contains 2, only the state $\{1\}$ in $\mathcal{C}'_p$ can enable a. The only way a can be enabled by $\{1\}$ and not $\{1,k\}$ is if $k \in I_a$ for $2 \leq k \leq p$, but then $|R_a \cup I_a| \geq |I_a| \geq p-1$, so rs-deg$(\tau_p, \mathcal{C}'_p) \geq p-1$ and equality follows from Theorem 2 (Fig. 1).

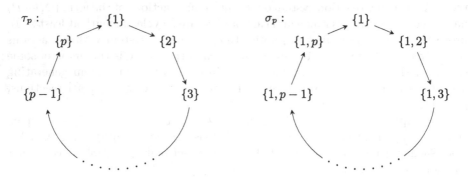

Fig. 1. The cycles τ_p and σ_p from Example 1.

Finding p-cycles for which the rs-rank$(\pi, \mathcal{C}) = \lceil \log_2(p) \rceil$ is achieved is difficult. In fact for particular p, it can be shown that this lower bound is not achievable. To show this, we first prove two lemmas about the structure of reaction systems which generate p-cycles.

For a reaction system $\mathcal{A} = (S, A)$ and $q \in S$, let $A_{(q)}$ be the reactions $a \in A$ for which $q \in P_a$.

Lemma 1. *Let $\mathcal{A} = (S, A)$ be a reaction system which generates a p-cycle and $q \notin R_a \cup I_a$ for all $a \in A$. For any given reaction $a = (R_a, I_a, P_a) \in A$, construct the reaction $a' = (R_a, I_a, P_a \cup \{q\})$, then the reaction system $\mathcal{A}' = (S \cup \{q\}, (A \setminus \{a\}) \cup \{a'\})$ also generates a p-cycle.*

Proof. Pick reaction system $\mathcal{A} = (S, A)$ with p-cycle $\pi = (X_1, \ldots, X_p)$ and $q \in S$ as described above. For ease of notation, let $X_{p+1} = X_1$. Since q is added only to product sets of $\mathcal{A}$ we have that $\mathrm{res}_{\mathcal{A}'}(X_i) = \mathrm{res}_{\mathcal{A}}(X_i \cup \{q\}) \in \{X_{i+1}, X_{i+1} \cup \{q\}\}$ for any of the original states X_i in π. Letting $X'_{i+1} := \mathrm{res}_{\mathcal{A}'}(X_i)$ where $X'_{p+1} = X'_1$, we then claim $\mathcal{A}'$ generates the p-cycle $\pi' = (X'_1, \ldots, X'_p)$. Since $\mathrm{res}_{\mathcal{A}'}(X'_i) = \mathrm{res}_{\mathcal{A}'}(X_i) = X'_{i+1}$ for all i, $\mathrm{res}_{\mathcal{A}'}$ is surjective and hence bijective on its finite domain. The fact that $\mathrm{res}_{\mathcal{A}'}$ is not bijective on any subset of its domain follows from the fact that π was also a cycle. $\qquad\square$

Lemma 2. *If there exists a reaction system $\mathcal{A} = (S, A)$ which generates a p-cycle, then there exists a reaction system $\mathcal{A}' = (S', A')$ generating a p-cycle such that $S' \subseteq S$, $|A'| \leq |A|$ and $A_{(q)} \neq A_{(v)}$ for distinct $q, v \in S'$.*

Proof. Consider a reaction system $\mathcal{A} = (S, A)$ which generates the p-cycle $\pi = (X_1, \ldots, X_p)$ and has two entities $q, v \in S$ such that $A_{(q)} = A_{(v)}$. For a subset of entities $T \subseteq S$, let $T' := (T \cup \{q\}) \setminus \{v\}$ if $v \in T$, and $T' := T$ otherwise. If we define the reaction $a' = (R'_a, I'_a, P'_a)$ for $a \in A$, then we claim the state X_i in π enables a if and only if X'_i enables a'.

Suppose $\mathrm{en}_a(X)$, then $R \subseteq X_i$ and $I \cap X_i = \varnothing$. We can then see $R' \setminus \{q\} = R \setminus \{q, v\} \subseteq X_i \setminus \{q, v\} = X'_i \setminus \{q\}$. If $q \in R'$, then either $q \in R \subseteq X_i \Rightarrow q \in X'_i$ or $v \in R \subseteq X_i \Rightarrow q \in X'_i$. In either case, we see that $R' \subseteq X'_i$. Also notice because all states X_i are in the image of π and $A_q = A_v$, $q \in X_i$ if and only if $v \in X_i$. This means $X'_i \subseteq X_i$, so we have $(I' \setminus \{q\}) \cap X'_i = (I \setminus \{q, v\}) \cap X'_i \subseteq I \cap X_i = \varnothing$. If $q \in I'$, then either $q \in I$ or $v \in I$, both of which imply $q, v \notin X_i$, so $q \notin X'_i$. We can then conclude $I' \cap X'_i = \varnothing$ and X'_i does indeed enable a'.

On the other hand if $\mathrm{en}_{a'}(X'_i)$, then $R' \subseteq X'_i$ and $I' \cap X'_i = \varnothing$. We now see $R \setminus \{q, v\} = R' \setminus \{q\} \subseteq X'_i \setminus \{q\} = X_i \setminus \{q, v\}$. If $q \in R$ or $v \in R$, then $q \in R' \subseteq X'_i \Rightarrow q \in X_i$ or $v \in X_i$. Since $q \in X_i$ if and only if $v \in X_i$, this tells us $\{q, v\} \subseteq X_i$, thus $R \subseteq X_i$. Also notice $(I \cap X_i) \setminus \{q, v\} \subseteq I' \cap X'_i = \varnothing$. If either $q \in I$ or $v \in I$, then $q \in I'$, so $q \notin X'_i \Rightarrow q, v \notin X_i$. This shows $I \cap X_i = \varnothing$ and X_i enables a.

To prove the lemma, we now construct the reaction system $\mathcal{A}' = (S \setminus \{v\}, A')$ where $A' = A \cup \{a'\} \setminus \{a\}$. Since $\mathrm{en}_a(X_i) \Leftrightarrow \mathrm{en}_{a'}(X'_i)$, it quickly follows that $\mathrm{res}_{\mathcal{A}'}(X'_i) = \mathrm{res}_{\mathcal{A}}(X_i)'$ and so $\mathcal{A}'$ generates the p-cycle $(X'_1, \ldots, X'_p)$. Notice that $|(A \cup \{a'\}) \setminus \{a\}| \leq |A|$ removes one such reaction, so repeating this procedure until each $A_{(q)}$ are distinct proves the lemma. $\qquad\square$

It is important to note that Lemmas 1 and 2 naturally act in opposing manners. Lemma 1 allows us to add new entities to a reaction system's product sets, whereas Lemma 2 states we can remove an entity which is present in the same product sets as another entity. Since both preserve cycle length and rank, we can use them to convert reaction systems into a normal form which makes calculations with cycle rank easier.

Theorem 3. *Suppose there exists a reaction system $\mathcal{A} = (S, A)$ that generates a p-cycle. Then there exists a reaction system $\mathcal{A}' = (S', A')$ that also generates a p-cycle such that $|A'| \leq |A|, |S'| = 2^{|A'|} - 1$ and $A'_{(q)} \neq A'_{(v)}$ for distinct $q, v \in S'$.*

Proof. Start with the original reaction system $\mathcal{A} = (S, A)$ and remove any entities from S (and A) which do not occur in the given p-cycle. Then use Lemma 2 to remove any entities which occur in the same product set as other entities. Now each entity q in the reaction system corresponds to some unique subset $A_{(q)} \subseteq A$. Using Lemma 1, we add new entities to the product sets of A until every non-empty subset of reactions $W \subseteq A$ corresponds uniquely to some entity q such that $A_{(q)} = W$. Since both Lemmas 1 and 2 preserve cycle length and do not increase the number of reactions, we have that the new reaction system $\mathcal{A}' = (S', A')$ which also generates a p-cycle and $|A'| \leq |A|$. Lemma 2 guarantees $A_{(q)} \neq A_{(v)}$ for all distinct $q, v \in S'$, and the one-to-one correspondence between S' and non-empty subsets of reactions in A' shows that $|S'| = 2^{|A'|} - 1$.   □

To see how Theorem 3 can be applied, suppose we have a p-cycle of rank 3. By applying Theorem 3 and relabeling entities, we are left with a reaction system $\mathcal{A} = (S, A)$ which generates a p-cycle, where $A = \{a_1, a_2, a_3\}$ and

$$P_{a_1} = \{1, 3, 5, 7\} \qquad P_{a_2} = \{2, 3, 6, 7\} \qquad P_{a_3} = \{4, 5, 6, 7\}$$

Since the states in this p-cycle must be formed from unions of the product sets listed above, we can use a computer to enumerate and check the rank of all possible such p-cycles. This leads to the following corollary.

Corollary 1. *There are no 7-cycles or 8-cycles of rank 3.*

Proof. Assume that there is an 8-cycle of rank 3, then without loss of generality there is an 8-cycle of rank 3 generated by reaction system $\mathcal{A} = (S, A)$ where $A = \{a_1, a_2, a_3\}$ and

$$P_{a_1} = \{1, 3, 5, 7\} \qquad P_{a_2} = \{2, 3, 6, 7\} \qquad P_{a_3} = \{4, 5, 6, 7\}$$

The only family that this 8-cycle can be defined over is $\mathcal{C} = \{\emptyset, P_{a_1}, P_{a_2}, P_{a_3}, P_{a_1} \cup P_{a_2}, P_{a_1} \cup P_{a_3}, P_{a_2} \cup P_{a_3}, P_{a_1} \cup P_{a_2} \cup P_{a_3}\}$. Checking the rank of all 7! possible 8-cycles which can be constructed from this family shows all are rank 4 or higher, thus there exist no 8-cycles of rank 3.

One can similarly show there are no 7-cycles of rank 3 by assuming there is a reaction system $\mathcal{A} = (S, A)$ structured the same as above which generates a 7-cycle. This cycle must be over some family $\mathcal{C}' \subseteq \mathcal{C}$ of size 7. Checking the rank of all 6! cycles from the 8 possible families shows that no cycle has rank 3.   □

Table 1. A table comparing the values between $\ell(p)$ and the $\lceil \log_2(p) \rceil$ for various values of p.

p	1	2	3	4	5	6	7	8	9	10	11	12
$\lceil \log_2(p) \rceil$	0	1	2	2	3	3	3	3	3	4	4	4
$\ell(p)$	0	1	2	2	3	3	4	4	4	4	4	4

In practice, this sort of computation can be sped up by removing families and cycles which differ only by a relabeling of entities - such arguments have been omitted from this paper for simplicity. Let $\ell(p)$ denote the minimum rs-rank of a p-cycle. Using Theorem 3, we have computed values of $\ell(p)$ up to $p = 12$ and put them in Table 1.

While we were able to use Theorem 3 to show the lower bound $\lceil \log_2(p) \rceil$ is not always achievable, it still appears to be a good approximation for the values of p we have computed. The question remains whether this function continues to be a good approximation as cycle length increases. We now provide evidence that $\ell(p)$ should grow at most polylogarithmically with respect to p. Recall the following definition from [25].

Definition 7. *Let f and g be RS functions over S and T respectively, where $S \cap T = \varnothing$. The Cartesian product of f and g, denoted $f \times g$, is the RS function over $S \cup T$ defined by*

$$(f \times g)(X) = f(X \cap S) \cup g(X \cap T)$$

Notice that if we define $\mathcal{A} \times \mathcal{B} = (S \cup T, A \cup B)$ for disjoint reaction systems $\mathcal{A} = (S, A)$ and $\mathcal{B} = (T, B)$, then we have $\mathrm{res}_{\mathcal{A} \times \mathcal{B}} = \mathrm{res}_{\mathcal{A}} \times \mathrm{res}_{\mathcal{B}}$. Using this fact, we now show the following.

Theorem 4. *For $n \in \mathbb{N}$, there exists a cycle of length $\mathrm{lcm}(1, \ldots, n)$ with rank at most $\frac{1}{2}n(n + 1)$.*

Proof. We first notice that if $\mathcal{A}$ and $\mathcal{B}$ are reaction systems over disjoint background sets generating a p-cycle and q-cycle respectively, then $\mathcal{A} \times \mathcal{B}$ will generate a cycle of length $\mathrm{lcm}(p, q)$. To see this, suppose $(X_1, \ldots, X_p)$ and $(Y_1, \ldots, Y_q)$ are generated by $\mathcal{A}$ and $\mathcal{B}$, then by properties of $\mathrm{res}_{\mathcal{A} \times \mathcal{B}}$ we can deduce $\mathrm{res}_{\mathcal{A} \times \mathcal{B}}^{pq}(X_1 \cup Y_1) = \mathrm{res}_{\mathcal{A}}^{pq}(X_1) \cup \mathrm{res}_{\mathcal{B}}^{pq}(Y_1) = X_1 \cup Y_1$. This tells us $X_1 \cup Y_1$ lives on some cycle in $\mathcal{A} \times \mathcal{B}$. Since $\mathrm{lcm}(p, q)$ is the smallest value m for which $\mathrm{res}_{\mathcal{A}}^{m}(X_1) \cup \mathrm{res}_{\mathcal{B}}^{m}(Y_1) = X_1 \cup Y_1$, this cycle must have length $\mathrm{lcm}(p, q)$.

To prove the given statement, fix $n \in \mathbb{N}$ and for $1 \leq i \leq n$, construct reaction systems $\mathcal{A}_i = (S_i, A_i)$ such that each $\mathcal{A}_i$ generates an i-cycle, $|A_i| \leq i$, and $S_i \cap S_j = \varnothing$ for $i \neq j$. Notice we can do this because Theorem 2 tells us any i-cycle has rank at most i. The previous argument can be used inductively to show that $\mathcal{A}_1 \times \cdots \times \mathcal{A}_n$ generates a cycle of length $\mathrm{lcm}(1, \ldots, n)$. By our restriction that $|A_i| \leq i$, we know that the rank of $\mathcal{A}_1 \times \cdots \times \mathcal{A}_n$ is at most $1 + \cdots + n = \frac{1}{2}n(n + 1)$. $\square$

Using Theorem 4 in conjunction with the fact that $\log(\text{lcm}(1,\ldots,n)) \sim n$ [15], we can show that $\ell(p) \notin \omega(\log^2(p))$. If we can further show that $\ell(p)$ is monotonic, that would be enough to prove $\ell(p) \in O(\log^2(p))$. While this is still far from the $\lceil \log_2(p) \rceil$ figure given in Theorem 2, better selection of $\mathcal{A}_i$ in the construction above may lead to tighter bounds (see [6,20]).

One goal in the study of reaction systems and the field of natural computing as a whole is to make the use of biochemical computation a viable strategy for running computations. In this vein, several papers have explored the implementation of traditional computer algorithms through the use of reaction systems. For example, [4] discussed a reaction system algorithm to solve the Tower of Hanoi puzzle using regulatory signals in DNA, and reaction systems were used to model eukaryotic heat shock response in [1].

One important aspect of any algorithm is a halting condition, and a general halting condition for reaction systems uses cycle detection. Cycle detection methods, one of which is the famous tortoise-and-hare method credited to Robert W. Floyd (See Exercise 3.1.6 of [18]), can be implemented using reaction systems through mathematical construction, or the restriction of biochemical reactions via environmental factors such as temperature. In such algorithms, $\ell(p)$ can be used to more precisely describe program efficiency where cycle detection algorithms are used.

5   Cyclic Rank and Degree of Families

One logical inference from the results of Theorem 2 would be that smaller cycles should be less "complex", i.e. have smaller rank or degree. In general, however, this is not true.

Example 2. Let $\mathcal{C} = \{\varnothing, \{1\}, \{2\}, \{1,2\}\}$ and $\mathcal{C}' = \{\{1\}, \{2\}, \{1,2\}\}$, and consider the cycles $\tau = (\varnothing, \{1\}, \{1,2\}, \{2\})$ over $\mathcal{C}$ and $\tau' = (\{1\}, \{1,2\}, \{2\})$ over $\mathcal{C}'$. Notice that τ' is the cycle that results from "cutting out" the state $\varnothing$ from the cycle τ. Because of this, we might assume that τ' should have smaller rank and degree than τ, but this is not true. One can verify that τ is generated by the reaction system $\mathcal{A} = (\{1,2\}, A)$ where

$$A = \big\{(\{1\}, \varnothing, \{2\}), (\varnothing, \{2\}, 1)\big\}$$

This reaction system along with Theorem 2 shows rs-deg$(\tau, \mathcal{C}) = 1$ and rs-rank$(\tau, \mathcal{C}) = 2$. On the other hand, one can show that rs-deg$(\tau', \mathcal{C}') = 2$ and rs-rank$(\tau', \mathcal{C}') = 3$, both of which are larger than their respective measures in τ.

If we cannot use rank or degree to measure how complex a cycle is directly, we may be able to expand our notion of complexity to focus instead on the set of states within a cycle. Definition 8 achieves something to this effect (Fig. 2).

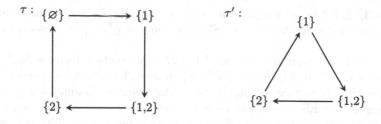

Fig. 2. The cycles τ and τ' from Example 2.

Definition 8. *Let $\mathcal{C}$ be a set of states over S, then we can define the upper and lower cyclic degree of $\mathcal{C}$, denoted $d^+(\mathcal{C})$ and $d^-(\mathcal{C})$ respectively, as follows:*

$$d^+(\mathcal{C}) = \max\{\text{rs-deg}(\pi,\mathcal{C}) \mid \pi \text{ is a cycle over } \mathcal{C}\}$$

$$d^-(\mathcal{C}) = \min\{\text{rs-deg}(\pi,\mathcal{C}) \mid \pi \text{ is a cycle over } \mathcal{C}\}$$

Defining the upper and lower cyclic degree of families in this manner, we can prove d^+ is in fact monotone.

Theorem 5. *If $\mathcal{C} \subseteq \mathcal{C}'$, then $d^+(\mathcal{C}) \leq d^+(\mathcal{C}')$.*

Proof. Let $\mathcal{C} = \{X_1,\ldots,X_n\}$ and $\mathcal{C}' = \mathcal{C} \cup \{E\}$ be families of states over S and let $\pi = (X_1,\ldots,X_n)$ be an arbitrary cycle over $\mathcal{C}$. It suffices to show that rs-deg$(\pi,\mathcal{C})$ is bounded above by the degree of some cycle over $\mathcal{C}'$. Notice by Proposition 2, rs-deg$(\pi,\mathcal{C})$ is at most the degree of its component functions $\pi^{(q)}$, so it further suffices only to bound rs-deg$(\pi^{(q)},\mathcal{C})$ for arbitrary $q \in S$.

We now consider the component function $\pi^{(q)}$. If q is in no state of $\mathcal{C}$ or every state of $\mathcal{C}$, then rs-deg$(\pi^{(q)},\mathcal{C}) = 0$ and is bounded above the degree of any cycle over $\mathcal{C}'$. Otherwise we can assume for some $1 \leq i,j \leq n$, $q \in X_i$ and $q \notin X_j$. For $1 \leq k \leq n$, consider the cycle $\sigma_k = (X_1,\ldots,X_k,E,X_{k+1},\ldots,X_n)$ over $\mathcal{C}'$. If $q \in E$, then we claim supp$(\pi^{(q)}) \cap \mathcal{C} = \text{supp}(\sigma_{i-1}^{(q)}) \cap \mathcal{C}$, so rs-deg$(\pi^{(q)},\mathcal{C}) = $ rs-deg$(\sigma_{i-1}^{(q)},\mathcal{C}) \leq \text{rs-deg}(\sigma_{i-1}^{(q)},\mathcal{C}')$. If instead $q \notin E$, then supp$(\pi^{(q)}) \cap \mathcal{C} = \text{supp}(\sigma_{j-1}^{(q)}) \cap \mathcal{C}$ implies rs-deg$(\pi^{(q)},\mathcal{C}) = \text{rs-deg}(\sigma_{j-1}^{(q)},\mathcal{C}) \leq \text{rs-deg}(\sigma_{j-1}^{(q)},\mathcal{C}')$. In either case, the degree of component function $\pi^{(q)}$ are bounded above by the degrees of cycles over $\mathcal{C}'$, so the result is proven. $\square$

Theorem 5 shows that d^+ agrees with the intuition that smaller families of states should have a lower level of complexity. In comparison, Example 2 demonstrates that the degree function does not satisfy the corresponding notion of monotonicity over cycles. In this manner, d^+ serves as a better measure of complexity than degree.

One immediate question is whether d^- also satisfies this property. The cycles τ and τ' from Example 2 seem to imply d^- does not satisfy this condition for some families, but we can prove an even stronger condition that d^- will not satisfy this property for almost any choice of family. To do this, we must first generalize a result from [22] to work for degenerate reactions.

Lemma 3. *Let f be an RS function over S, then there exists a background set $S' \supseteq S$ and an RS function g over S' such that $f = g^3|_{\mathcal{P}(S)}$ and rs-deg$(g) \leq 2$.*

The proof of Theorem 4 provided in [22] constructs g using a background set of the form $S' = S \cup \bar{S} \cup A \cup \{B, E\}$, where $A = (S, A)$ is a reaction system generating f. In that proof, the same statement as Lemma 3 is proven for a non-degenerate RS functions. To generalize this result for degenerate reaction systems, we use the same reaction system with the additional reaction $(\varnothing, \{B, E\}, \{B\})$. With Lemma 3, we can prove the following claim demonstrating how far d^- is from being monotone.

Theorem 6. *Let $\mathcal{C} \subseteq \mathcal{P}(S)$ be a family of states, then for some $S' \supseteq S$ there exists a family $\mathcal{C}' \subseteq \mathcal{P}(S')$ such that $\mathcal{C} \subseteq \mathcal{C}'$ and $d^-(\mathcal{C}') \leq 2$.*

Proof. If we let f be an RS function which generates a cycle over $\mathcal{C}$, we can use Lemma 3 to create an RS function g over $S' \supseteq S$ such that $g^3 = f$ and rs-deg$(g) \leq 2$. Since f contains a cycle over $\mathcal{C}$, g will contain a cycle over $\mathcal{C}' \supset \mathcal{C}$, where two states have been added between each of the original states in f. By our choice of g, we know $d^-(\mathcal{C}') \leq 2$. $\qquad\square$

Just as d^+ and d^- were defined in terms of the degrees of cycles over a family of states, we may also create analogous functions using rank.

Definition 9. *Let $\mathcal{C}$ be a set of states over S, then we can define the upper and lower cyclic rank of $\mathcal{C}$, denoted $r^+(\mathcal{C})$ and $r^-(\mathcal{C})$ respectively, as follows:*

$$r^+(\mathcal{C}) = \max\{\text{rs-rank}(\pi, \mathcal{C}) \mid \pi \text{ is a cycle over } \mathcal{C}\}$$

$$r^-(\mathcal{C}) = \min\{\text{rs-rank}(\pi, \mathcal{C}) \mid \pi \text{ is a cycle over } \mathcal{C}\}$$

Computations run with Espresso have suggested that a similar inequality to Theorem 5 for r^+ holds, though we have not been able to find a proof. There are two primary difficulties in proving monotonicity of r^+. First, the bounds given in Theorem 1 make decomposition into focus functions insufficient for relating the rank of cycles to those cycles with one less state. Second, experimental calculations of $r^+(\mathcal{C})$ for random families $\mathcal{C}$ tend to be densely packed towards larger values, making the recognition of meaningful patterns in upper cyclic rank difficult. For the time being, we leave it here as a conjecture.

Conjecture 1. If $\mathcal{C} \subseteq \mathcal{C}'$, then $r^+(\mathcal{C}) \leq r^+(\mathcal{C}')$.

One can extend Example 2 to show r^- is not monotone, although the difficulties in analyzing minimal cycle rank in Sect. 4 suggest there is no analogous Theorem 6 which holds for r^-.

6   Conclusion

The results of this paper suggest several prospective avenues for future research. Theorem 3 provides a definitive method for calculating the minimum rank of a general p-cycle in a reaction system, but is computationally-difficult and unrealistic for large values of p. Further work will focus on finding bounds on $\ell(p)$ which require less computation. Additionally, monotonicity of d^+ can be used to construct an independence system over the families of states in S. These objects are a natural generalization from matroids and may be used to study reaction systems through well-established results in combinatorics, e.g., [5].

Many of the results in this paper can be extended to non-degenerate reaction systems. While some of these extensions are straightforward, there are results that require additional conditions to generalize. For example, non-degenerate minimization of subset functions may result in smaller rank when considered over larger background sets.

Finally, we are developing a Rust/Python library for reaction systems which includes features such as exact and heuristic algorithms for minimization of rank and degree of reaction systems and RS functions. Once released, this code will be free and open source.

References

1. Azimi, S., Iancu, B., Petre, I.: Reaction system models for the heat shock response. Fund. Inform. **131**(3–4), 299–312 (2014)
2. Bagossy, A., Vaszil, G.: Simulating reversible computation with reaction systems. J. Membr. Comput. **2**(3), 179–193 (2020)
3. Brijder, R., Ehrenfeucht, A., Main, M., Rozenberg, G.: A tour of reaction systems. Int. J. Found. Comput. Sci. **22**(7), 1499–1517 (2011)
4. Corolli, L., Maj, C., Marini, F., Besozzi, D., Mauri, G.: An excursion in reaction systems: from computer science to biology. Theoret. Comput. Sci. **454**, 95–108 (2012)
5. Dennunzio, A., Formenti, E., Manzoni, L.: Extremal combinatorics of reaction systems. In: Dediu, A.-H., Martín-Vide, C., Sierra-Rodríguez, J.-L., Truthe, B. (eds.) LATA 2014. LNCS, vol. 8370, pp. 297–307. Springer, Cham (2014). https://doi.org/10.1007/978-3-319-04921-2_24
6. Dennunzio, A., Formenti, E., Manzoni, L., Porreca, A.E.: Complexity of the dynamics of reaction systems. Inf. Comput. **267**, 96–109 (2019)
7. Ehrenfeucht, A., Kleijn, J., Koutny, M., Rozenberg, G.: Minimal reaction systems. In: Priami, C., Petre, I., de Vink, E. (eds.) Transactions on Computational Systems Biology XIV. LNCS, vol. 7625, pp. 102–122. Springer, Heidelberg (2012). https://doi.org/10.1007/978-3-642-35524-0_5
8. Ehrenfeucht, A., Kleijn, J., Koutny, M., Rozenberg, G.: Reaction systems: a natural computing approach to the functioning of living cells. In: A Computable Universe: Understanding and Exploring Nature as Computation, pp. 189–208. World Scientific (2013)
9. Ehrenfeucht, A., Rozenberg, G.: Reaction systems. Fund. Inform. **75**(1–4), 263–280 (2007)

10. Formenti, E., Manzoni, L., Porreca, A.E.: Cycles and global attractors of reaction systems. In: Jürgensen, H., Karhumäki, J., Okhotin, A. (eds.) DCFS 2014. LNCS, vol. 8614, pp. 114–125. Springer, Cham (2014). https://doi.org/10.1007/978-3-319-09704-6_11

11. Formenti, E., Manzoni, L., Porreca, A.E.: Fixed points and attractors of reaction systems. In: Beckmann, A., Csuhaj-Varjú, E., Meer, K. (eds.) CiE 2014. LNCS, vol. 8493, pp. 194–203. Springer, Cham (2014). https://doi.org/10.1007/978-3-319-08019-2_20

12. Genova, D., Hoogeboom, H.J., Jonoska, N.: A graph isomorphism condition and equivalence of reaction systems. Theoret. Comput. Sci. **701**, 109–119 (2017)

13. Genova, D., Hoogeboom, H.J., Kleijn, J.: Comparing reactions in reaction systems. Theoret. Comput. Sci. **881**, 83–96 (2021)

14. Genova, D., Hoogeboom, H.J., Prodanoff, Z.: Extracting reaction systems from function behavior. J. Membr. Comput. **2**, 194–206 (2020)

15. Ingham, A.E.: The Distribution of Prime Numbers. Cambridge University Press, Cambridge (1932)

16. Intekhab, H., Lim, J., Teh, W.C.: Ranks of compositionally closed minimal reaction systems. Indian J. Pure Appl. Math. **55**, 1–10 (2023)

17. Kleijn, J., Koutny, M., Mikulski, Ł: Reaction systems and enabling equivalence. Fund. Inform. **171**(1–4), 261–277 (2020)

18. Knuth, D.E.: The Art of Computer Programming: Seminumerical Algorithms, vol. 2. Addison-Wesley Professional, Upper Saddle River (1997)

19. Manzoni, L., Pocas, D., Porreca, A.E.: Simple reaction systems and their classification. Int. J. Found. Comput. Sci. **25**(04), 441–457 (2014)

20. Salomaa, A.: Functions and sequences generated by reaction systems. Theoret. Comput. Sci. **466**, 87–96 (2012)

21. Salomaa, A.: Minimal and almost minimal reaction systems. Nat. Comput. **12**, 369–376 (2013)

22. Salomaa, A.: Minimal reaction systems defining subset functions. In: Calude, C.S., Freivalds, R., Kazuo, I. (eds.) Computing with New Resources. LNCS, vol. 8808, pp. 436–446. Springer, Cham (2014). https://doi.org/10.1007/978-3-319-13350-8_32

23. Teh, W.C., Atanasiu, A.: Irreducible reaction systems and reaction system rank. Theoret. Comput. Sci. **666**, 12–20 (2017)

24. Teh, W.C., Atanasiu, A.: Minimal reaction systems revisited and reaction system rank. Int. J. Found. Comput. Sci. **28**(03), 247–261 (2017)

25. Teh, W.C., Nguyen, K.T., Chen, C.Y.: Ranks of strictly minimal reaction systems induced by permutations. Theoret. Comput. Sci. **872**, 1–14 (2021)

Computing Threshold Circuits with Bimolecular Void Reactions in Step Chemical Reaction Networks

Rachel Anderson[1], Bin Fu[1], Aiden Massie[1], Gourab Mukhopadhyay[1],
Adrian Salinas[1], Robert Schweller[1], Evan Tomai[2], and Tim Wylie[1(✉)]

[1] University of Texas Rio Grande Valley, Edinburg, TX 78539-2999, USA
timothy.wylie@utrgv.edu
[2] University of Texas Dallas, Richardson, TX 75080-3021, USA

Abstract. Step Chemical Reaction Networks (step CRNs) are an augmentation of the Chemical Reaction Network (CRN) model where additional species may be introduced to the system in a sequence of "steps." We study step CRN systems using a weak subset of reaction rules, *void* rules, in which molecular species can only be deleted. We demonstrate that step CRNs with only void rules of size (2,0) can simulate threshold formulas (TFs) under linear resources. These limited systems can also simulate threshold *circuits* (TCs) by modifying the volume of the system to be exponential. We then prove a matching exponential lower bound on the required volume for simulating threshold circuits in a step CRN with (2,0)-size rules under a restricted *gate-wise* simulation, thus showing our construction is optimal for simulating circuits in this way.

1 Introduction

Chemical Reaction Networks (CRNs) are a well-established model of chemistry. In this model, chemical interactions are modeled as molecular species that react to create products according to a set of reaction rules. CRNs have been extensively studied since their standard formulation in the 1960s [6,7]. Several equivalent models were also introduced around the same time with Vector Addition Systems (VASs) [20] and Petri-nets [24]. Further, Population Protocols [3] are a restricted form of the model focused on bimolecular reactions.

Step CRNs. These models all assume a discrete starting number of species or elements and reaction rules that dictate how they can interact. Thus, any change in species numbers is only through these interactions. Motivated by standard laboratory procedures where additional chemical species may be added to an initial container of species after a set of reactions has passed, we utilize an extension to the CRN model known as the Step Chemical Reaction Network model (step CRN) first introduced in [2]. The step CRN model adds a sequence

---

This research was supported in part by National Science Foundation Grant CCF-2329918.

D.-J. Cho and J. Kim (Eds.): UCNC 2024, LNCS 14776, pp. 253–268, 2024.
https://doi.org/10.1007/978-3-031-63742-1_18

Table 1. Results in the paper related to computing circuits with $(2,0)$ void rules in step CRN systems. D is the circuit's depth, G is the number of gates in a circuit, and F_{out} is the maximum fan-out of a gate in the circuit.

Function Computation						
Rules	Species	Steps	Volume	Simulation	Family	Ref
$(2,0)$	$O(G)$	$O(D)$	$O(G)$	Gate-Wise	**TF** Formulas	Theorem 1
$(2,0)$	$O(G)$	$O(D)$	$O(GF_{out}{}^D)$	Gate-Wise	**TC** Circuits	Theorem 2
$(2,0)$	-	-	$2^{\Omega(D)}$	Gate-Wise	**TC** Circuits	Theorem 3

of discrete steps where additional species can be added to the existing CRN configuration after waiting for all possible reaction rules to occur in the system.

Bimolecular Void Rules. In this paper, we use the terms *reaction* and *rule* interchangeably to denote a reaction rule. We focus on step CRN systems that include only *bimolecular void rules* ($(2,0)$ rules) which are CRN rules that have two reactants and no products, and thus can only delete existing species. Void rules of size $(2,0)$ and $(3,0)$ were first studied within the standard CRN model in the context of the reachability problem [1]. While standard CRN rules are powerful thanks to their ability to replace, delete or create new species, (2,0) rules have extremely limited power to compute even simple functions in a standard CRN [2]. In contrast, we show $(2,0)$ void rules become capable of computing Threshold Formulas (TF) and Threshold Circuits (TC) in the step CRN model. Threshold circuits are a computationally universal class of Boolean circuits that have practical application in deep learning, and consist of any Boolean circuit made of AND, OR, NOT, and MAJORITY gates.

Computation in Chemical Reaction Networks. Computation within Chemical Reaction Networks is a well-studied topic. Within stochastic Chemical Reaction Networks with some possibility for error, the systems are Turing-complete [27]. In contrast, error-free stochastic CRNs are capable of computing semilinear functions [5,12]. Further, molecules themselves have long been studied as a method of information storage and Boolean logic computation. In particular, CRNs and similar models have been extensively studied in these areas [8,9,11,13,15,19,21,25,26]. Logic gates such as AND [11,14,22,26,28,30], OR [11,14,26,28], NOT [11], XOR [11,30], NAND [11,13,15,29], NOR [11], Parity [16–18] and Majority [4,10,23] have also been explored.

Our Contributions. Table 1 gives an overview of our results, and the paper is formatted to introduce the general techniques and then expand into the necessary details to prove these results. Section 3.2 shows how a step CRN, using (2,0) void rules, computes individual logic gates. We then show how these gates can be combined to build a general construction of threshold formulas in Sect. 3.4. Theorem 1 shows how a step CRN with only $(2,0)$ rules is capable of computing threshold formulas with $O(G)$ species, $O(D)$ steps, and $O(G)$ volume, where G is the number of gates in a circuit and D is the depth of a circuit.

In Sect. 4, we modify this construction to compute threshold circuits with $O(G)$ species, $O(D)$ steps, and $O(GF_{out}{}^D)$ volume, where F_{out} is the maximum fan-out of the circuit. Finally, in Sect. 5 we show that the volume lower bound for simulating a circuit using *gate-wise* simulation in a step CRN with (2,0) rules is $2^{\Omega(D)}$. This lower bound is of note in that it shows the exponential volume utilized by the positive result is needed for this style of computation, and it shows a provable change in power from the polynomial volume achievable with $(3,0)$ void rules [2].

2   Preliminaries

2.1   Chemical Reaction Networks

Basics. Let $\Lambda = \{\lambda_1, \lambda_2, \ldots, \lambda_{|\Lambda|}\}$ denote some ordered alphabet of *species*. A configuration over Λ is a length-$|\Lambda|$ vector of non-negative integers that denotes the number of copies of each present species. A *rule* or *reaction* has two multisets, the first containing one or more *reactant* (species), used for creating resulting *product* (species) contained in the second multiset. Each rule is represented as an ordered pair of configuration vectors $R = (R_r, R_p)$. R_r contains the minimum counts of each reactant species necessary for reaction R to occur, where reactant species are either *consumed* by the rule in some count or leveraged as *catalysts* (not consumed); in some cases a combination of the two. The product vector R_p has the count of each species *produced* by the *application* of rule R, effectively replacing vector R_r. The species corresponding to the non-zero elements of R_r and R_p are termed *reactants* and *products* of R, respectively.

The *application* vector of R is $R_a = R_p - R_r$, which shows the net change in species counts after applying rule R once. For a configuration C and rule R, we say R is applicable to C if $C[i] \geq R_r[i]$ for all $1 \leq i \leq |\Lambda|$, and we define the *application* of R to C as the configuration $C' = C + R_a$. For a set of rules Γ, a configuration C, and rule $R \in \Gamma$ applicable to C that produces $C' = C + R_a$, we say $C \rightarrow_\Gamma^1 C'$, a relation denoting that C can transition to C' by way of a single rule application from Γ. We further use the notation $C \rightsquigarrow_\Gamma C'$ to signify the transitive closure of $\rightarrow_\Gamma^1$ and say C' is *reachable* from C under Γ, i.e., C' can be reached by applying a sequence of applicable rules from Γ to initial configuration C. Here, we use the following notation to depict a rule $R = (R_r, R_p)$: $\sum_{i=1}^{|\Lambda|} R_r[i]s_i \rightarrow \sum_{i=1}^{|\Lambda|} R_p[i]s_i$.

Using this notation, a rule turning two copies of species H and one copy of species O into one copy of species W would be written as $2H + O \rightarrow W$.

Definition 1 (Discrete Chemical Reaction Network). *A discrete chemical reaction network (CRN) is an ordered pair (Λ, Γ) where Λ is an ordered alphabet of species, and Γ is a set of rules over Λ.*

We denote the set of reachable configurations for a CRN (Λ, Γ) from initial configuration I as $\text{REACH}_{I,\Lambda,\Gamma}$. A configuration is called *terminal* with respect to a CRN (Λ, Γ) if no rule $R \in \Gamma$ can be applied to it. We define the subset

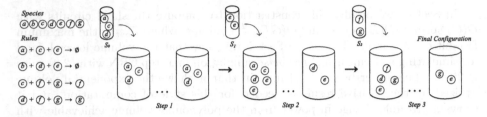

Fig. 1. An example step CRN system. The test tubes show the species added at each step and the system with those elements added. The CRN species and void rule-set are shown on the left.

of reachable configurations that are terminal as $\text{TERM}_{I,\Lambda,\Gamma}$. For an initial configuration I, a CRN (Λ, Γ) is said to be *bounded* if a terminal configuration is guaranteed to be reached within some finite number of rule applications starting from configuration I.

2.2   Void Rules

Definition 2 (Void and Autogenesis Rules). *A rule* $R = (R_r, R_p)$ *is a void rule if* $R_a = R_p - R_r$ *has no positive entries and at least one negative entry. A rule is an* autogenesis *rule if* R_a *has no negative values and at least one positive value. If the reactants and products of a rule are each multisets, a void rule is a rule whose product multiset is a strict submultiset of the reactants, and an autogenesis rule one where the reactants are a strict submultiset of the products. There are two classes of void rules,* catalytic *and* true void. *In catalytic void rules, one or more reactants remain after the rule is applied. In true void rules, such as* $(2,0)$ *and* $(3,0)$ *rules, there are no products remaining.*

Definition 3. *The* size/volume *of a configuration vector* C *is* $\texttt{volume}(C) = \sum C[i]$.

Definition 4 (Size-(i,j) Rules). *A rule* $R = (R_r, R_p)$ *is said to be a size-(i,j) rule if* $(i,j) = (\texttt{volume}(R_r), \texttt{volume}(R_p))$. *A reaction is bimolecular if* $i = 2$.

2.3   Step Chemical Reaction Networks

A step CRN is an augmentation of a basic CRN in which additional copies of some system species are added after each of a sequence of steps. Formally, a step CRN of k steps is a ordered pair $((\Lambda, \Gamma), (s_0, s_1, s_2, \ldots s_{k-1}))$, where the first element of the pair is a normal CRN (Λ, Γ), and the second is a sequence of length-$|\Lambda|$ vectors of non-negative integers denoting how many copies of each species type to add after each step.

Given a step CRN, we define the set of reachable configurations after each sequential step. To start off, let REACH_1 be the set of reachable configurations of (Λ, Γ) with initial configuration s_0, which we refer to as the set of configurations reachable *after step 1*. Let TERM_1 be the subset of configurations in REACH_1 that are terminal. Note that after just a single step we have a normal CRN, i.e., 1-step CRNs are just normal CRNs with initial configuration s_0. For the second step, we consider any configuration in TERM_1 combined with s_1 as a possible starting configuration and define $REACH_2$ to be the union of all reachable configurations from each possible starting configuration attained by adding s_1 to a configuration in $TERM_1$. We then define TERM_2 as the subset of configurations in REACH_2 that are terminal. Similarly, define $REACH_i$ to be the union of all reachable sets attained by using initial configuration c_{i-1} at step s_{i-1} plus any element of $TERM_{i-1}$, and let $TERM_i$ denote the subset of these configurations that are terminal.

The set of reachable configurations for a k-step CRN is the set REACH_k, and the set of terminal configurations is TERM_k. A classical CRN can be represented as a step CRN with $k = 1$ steps and an initial configuration of $I = s_0$.

2.4   Computing Functions in Step CRNs

Here, we define what it means for a step CRN to compute a function $f(x_1, \ldots, x_n) = (y_1, \ldots, y_m)$ that maps n-bit strings to m-bit strings. For each input bit, we denote two separate species types, one representing bit 0, and the other bit 1. An input configuration to represent a desired n-bit input string is constructed by selecting to add copies of *either* the 0 species or the 1 species for each bit in the target bit-string. Similarly, each output bit has two species representatives (for 0 and 1), and we say the step CRN computes function f if for any given n-bit input $x_1, \ldots, x_n$, the system obtained by adding the species for the string $x_1, \ldots, x_n$ to the initial configuration of this system in step 1 results in a final configuration whose output species encode the string $f(x_1, \ldots, x_n)$. Note that for a fixed function f, the species s_i added at each step are fixed to disallow outside computation. We now provide a more detailed formalization of this concept.

Input-Strict Step CRN Computing. Given a Boolean function $f(x_1, \ldots, x_n) = (y_1, \ldots, y_m)$ that maps a string of n bits to a string of m bits, we define the computation of f with a step CRN. An input-strict step CRN computer is a tuple $C_s = (S, X, Y)$ where $S = ((\Lambda, \Gamma), (s_0, s_1, \ldots, s_{k-1}))$ is a step CRN, and $X = ((x_1^F, x_1^T), \ldots, (x_n^F, x_n^T))$ and $Y = ((y_1^F, y_1^T), \ldots, (y_m^F, y_m^T))$ are sequences of ordered-pairs with each $x_i^F, x_i^T, y_j^F, y_j^T \in \Lambda$. Given an n-input bit string $b = b_1, \ldots, b_n$, configuration $X(b)$ is defined as the configuration over Λ obtained by including one copy of x_i^F only if $b_i = 0$ and one copy of x_i^T only if $b_i = 1$ for each bit b_i. We consider this representation of the input to be strict, as opposed to allowing multiple copies of each input bit species. The corresponding step CRN $(\Lambda, \Gamma, (s_0 + X(b), \ldots, s_{k-1}))$ is obtained by adding $X(b)$ to s_0 in the first step, which conceptually represents the system programmed with input b.

An input-strict step CRN computer *computes* function f if, for all n-bit strings b and for all terminal configurations of $(\Lambda, \Gamma, (s_0 + X(b), \ldots, s_{k-1}))$, the terminal configuration contains at least 1 copy of y_j^F and 0 copies of y_j^T if the

j^{th} bit of $f(b)$ is 0, and at least 1 copy of y_j^T and 0 copies of y_j^F if the jth bit of $f(b)$ is 1, for all j from 1 to m.

We use the term *strict* to denote requiring exactly one copy of each bit species. While previous work has focused on strict computation [2], the focus here is a relaxation of this requirement in which multiple copies of each input species are permitted.

Multiple Input Relaxation. In this paper, we focus on a relaxation to strict computing that allows for multiple copies of each input bit species, i.e., we modify the strict definition by allowing some number greater or equal to 1 of each x_i^F or x_i^T species in the initial configuration (but still requiring 0 copies of the alternate choice species). A system that computes a function under this relaxation is said to be *multiple input relaxed.*

Gate-Wise Simulation. In this paper, we utilize a method of simulation we term *gate-wise* simulation, where the output of each gate is represented by a unique species and the gates are computed in the order of their depth level. In other words, multiple gates cannot use the exact same species to represent their output and a gate can only be computed once all gates in the previous depth levels have been computed. We use this method when simulating formulas and circuits with a step CRN in Sects. 3 and 4. A formal definition of gate-wise simulation is provided in Sect. 5.

2.5   Boolean and Threshold Circuits

A Boolean circuit on n variables $x_1, x_2, \ldots, x_n$ is a directed, acyclic multi-graph. The vertices of the graph are referred to as *gates*. The in-degree and out-degree of a gate are called the *fan-in* and *fan-out* of the gate, respectively. The fan-in 0 gates (*source* gates) are labeled from $x_1, x_2, \ldots, x_n$, or from the constants 0 or 1. Each non-source gate is labeled with a function name, such as AND, OR, or NOT. Fan-out 0 gates may or may not be labeled as output gates. Given an assignment of Boolean values to variables $x_1, x_2, \ldots, x_n$, each gate in the circuit can be assigned a value by first assigning all source vertices the value matching the labeled constant or labeled variable value, and subsequently assigning each gate the value computed by its labeled function on the values of its children. Given a fixed ordering on the output gates, the sequence of bits assigned to the output gates denotes the value computed by the circuit on the given input.

The *depth* of a circuit is the longest path from a source vertex to an output vertex. A circuit is a called a *formula* if all non-source vertices have fan-out 1, and there is exactly 1 output gate. Here, we focus on circuits that consist of AND, OR, NOT, and MAJORITY gates with arbitrary fan-in. We refer to circuits that use these gates as *Threshold Circuits* (TC).

Notation. When discussing a Boolean circuit, the following variables are used to denote the properties of the circuit: G denotes the number of gates in the circuit, D the circuit's depth, and F_{out} the maximum fan-out of any gate in the circuit.

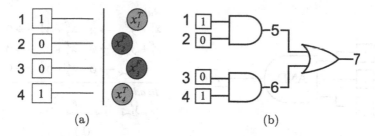

(a)   (b)

Fig. 2. (a) The input bits of a threshold formula and their representation as species.(b) An indexed threshold formula with the input species shown in Fig. 2a.

3 Computation of Threshold Formulas with (2, 0) Rules

Section 3.1 and Sect. 3.2 introduce how a step CRN using only (2,0) rules represents bits and logic gates of a Threshold Formula (TFs), respectively. An example construction of a formula is provided in Sect. 3.3. Section 3.4 then shows the general construction of building TFs, and we prove how the system computes TFs with $O(G)$ species, $O(D)$ steps, and $O(G)$ volume in Theorem 1.

3.1 Bit Representation

Here, we show how the bits of a TF are represented in our model. We first demonstrate a system for indexing the TF's wires before introducing the species used to represent bits.

Indexing. Every wire of the TF has a unique numerical index. The input and output bits that traverse these wires also use the wire's index. If a wire fans out, the fanned-out wires share the same index as the original. This indexing ensures that the bit species only use the rules that compute their respective gates. Note that gates may also be denoted with an index, where its index is that of its output wire.

Bits. Every input bit of a binary gate is represented by the species x_n^b, where $n \in \mathbb{N}$ and $b \in \{T, F\}$. n represents the bit's index and b represents its truth value. An example of these species is shown in Fig. 2a. Every output bit of a binary gate is represented by the species y_n^b or $y_{j \to i}^b$, where j represents the input bit's (x^b) index and i represents the output bit's (y^b) index.

3.2 Logic Gate Computation

We now show how the logic gates of a TF are computed. Let f_i^{in} be the set of all the indexes of the inputs fanning into a gate at index i.

AND Gate. To compute an AND gate such as the one shown in Fig. 3a, a single true output species y_i^T and $|f_i^{in}|$ copies of the false output species $y_{j \to i}^F$ are added in. In one step, the true input and false output species delete each other. Additionally, if at least one false input species exists, it deletes the lone true

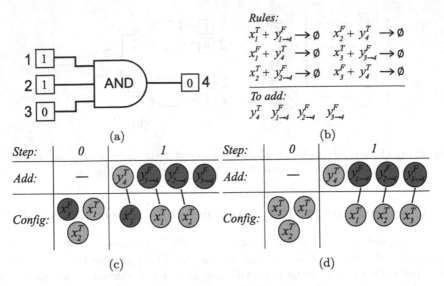

Fig. 3. (a) A threshold formula consisting of a single three-input AND gate. (b) Reaction rules and added species for the step CRN that compute the formula in Fig. 3a. (c) The step CRN computing the formula in Fig. 3a. The black lines connecting species represents a reaction applied to them. (d) The step CRN computing the circuit in Fig. 3a, but with three true inputs.

output species along with itself, guaranteeing a false output as shown in the example steps in Fig. 3c. The only output species remaining after the step are those whose truth value matches the intended output.

AND Gate Example. Consider an AND gate with index 4 and a fan-in of three; the first two inputs are true and the last is false. For computing this gate with our model, the system's initial configuration consists of x_1^T, x_2^T, and x_3^F. We then add y_4^T, representing a true output and $y_{1\to4}^F$, $y_{2\to4}^F$, and $y_{3\to4}^F$, representing false outputs. The rules $x_1^T + y_{1\to4}^F \to \emptyset$, $x_2^T + y_{2\to4}^F \to \emptyset$, and $x_3^F + x_1^T \to \emptyset$ are then applied to the system, removing all reactant species in these rules. The remaining species is $y_{3\to4}^F$, indicating a false output.

OR Gate. To compute an OR gate, a single false output species y_i^F and $|f_i^{in}|$ copies of the true output species $y_{j\to i}^T$ are added in. In one step, the false input and true output species delete each other. Additionally, if at least one true input species exists, it deletes the lone false output species along with itself, guaranteeing a true output. The only output species remaining after the step are those whose truth value matches the intended output.

NOT Gate. To compute a NOT gate, a single copy of the true and false output species are added in. In a single step, the input and output species that share the same truth value b delete each other, leaving the complement of the input species as the remaining output species (Table 2).

Table 2. (2, 0) rules and steps for computing AND, OR, and NOT gates.

Gate Type	Step	Relevant Rules	Description
AND	$Add \ y_i^T$ $\forall j \in f_i^{in} :$ $y_{j \to i}^F$	$x_j^T + y_{j \to i}^F \to \emptyset$ $x_j^F + y_i^T \to \emptyset$	An input species with a certain truth value deletes the complement output species
OR	$Add \ y_i^F$ $\forall j \in f_i^{in} :$ $y_{j \to i}^T$	$x_j^T + y_i^F \to \emptyset$ $x_j^F + y_{j \to i}^T \to \emptyset$	An input species with a certain truth value deletes the complement output species
NOT	$Add \ y_i^T \ y_i^F$	$x_j^T + y_i^T \to \emptyset$ $x_j^F + y_i^F \to \emptyset$	The input and output species that share the same truth value delete each other

Table 3. (2, 0) rules and steps for computing majority gates.

Steps		Relevant Rules	Description
1	$Add \ \ |f_i^{in}| \cdot a_i^T$ $|f_i^{in}| \cdot a_i^F$	$\forall j \in f_i^{in} :$ $x_j^T + a_i^F \to \emptyset$ $x_j^F + a_i^T \to \emptyset$	$\forall j \in f_i^{in}$, convert x_j^b input species into a_i^b species
2	$Add \ \ \lfloor |f_i^{in}|/2 \rfloor \cdot b_i^T$ $\lfloor |f_i^{in}|/2 \rfloor \cdot b_i^F$	$a_i^T + b_i^F \to \emptyset$ $a_i^F + b_i^T \to \emptyset$	Adding $\lfloor |f_i^{in}|/2 \rfloor$ amounts of b_i^T and b_i^F species will delete all of the minority species, leaving some amount of the majority species remaining
3	$Add \ \ y_i^T \ y_i^F$	$a_i^T + y_i^F \to \emptyset$ $a_i^F + y_i^T \to \emptyset$	Convert a_i^b into the proper output species (y_i^b)

Majority Gate. To compute a majority gate, all input species are first converted into a new species a_i^b (Step 1). These species retain the same index and truth value of their original inputs. If the number of bits inputted into a majority gate is even, then an extra *false* input species should be added in. The species b_i^b is then added (Step 2). This species performs the majority operation across all a_i^b species. Any species that represents the minority inputs are deleted. The remaining species are then converted into the matching output species (Step 3) (Table 3).

3.3 Formula Computation Example

We demonstrate a simple example of computing a threshold formula under our constructions. The formula is the same as in Fig. 2b. It has four inputs: x_1, x_2, x_3, and x_4. At the first depth level, x_1 and x_2 fan into an AND gate, as does

x_3 and x_4. Both gate outputs are then fanned into an OR gate, whose output represents the final value of the formula.

The initial configuration consists of bit species that correlate to the input values for the formula. Step 1 converts the species into input species for the first depth level. Step 2 then performs all gate operations at the first depth level. Step 3 converts the output species of the gates into input species for the next and final depth level. Step 4 computes the last gate. Finally, Step 5 coverts the gate;s output into an input species that represents the final output of the formula. A more detailed explanation of computing the formula is in Table 4a.

3.4   Threshold Formula Computation

We now introduce another step with rules that convert the output species of one depth level into input species for the next level, enabling the complete computation of a TF. We then prove the computational complexity of computing TFs within our system.

Depth Traversal. To enable the traversal of every gates' bits at a specific depth level to the next level, every output species is converted into an input species in one step. The same truth value and index is retained between the output and input species. Table 4b shows how to compute depth level traversal for an output bit with index i.

Table 4. (a) (2, 0) rules and steps for computing the formula in Fig. 2b. (b) (2, 0) rules and step for converting outputs to inputs per depth level. Add species for that represent true and false inputs. Delete the species that are the complement of the output. Only the correct input species remains.

Initial Configuration: y_1^T, y_2^F, y_3^F, y_4^T		
	Step	**Relevant Rules**
1	*Add* $x_1^T, x_2^T, x_3^T, x_4^T$ $x_1^F, x_2^F, x_3^F, x_4^F$	$y_1^T + x_1^F \to \emptyset$ $y_2^F + x_2^T \to \emptyset$ $y_3^F + x_3^T \to \emptyset$ $y_4^T + x_4^F \to \emptyset$
2	*Add* $y_5^T, y_{1\to5}^F, y_{2\to5}^F$ $y_6^T, y_{3\to6}^F, y_{4\to6}^F$	$x_1^T + y_{1\to5}^F \to \emptyset$ $x_2^F + y_5^T \to \emptyset$ $x_3^F + y_6^T \to \emptyset$ $x_4^T + y_{4\to6}^F \to \emptyset$
3	*Add* x_5^T, x_6^T x_5^F, x_6^F	$y_{2\to5}^F + x_5^T \to \emptyset$ $y_{3\to6}^F + x_6^T \to \emptyset$
4	*Add* $y_{5\to7}^T, y_{6\to7}^T, y_7^F$	$y_{5\to7}^F + x_5^T \to \emptyset$ $y_{6\to7}^F + x_6^T \to \emptyset$
5	*Add* x_7^T, x_7^F	$y_7^F + x_7^T \to \emptyset$

(a)

Step		**Relevant Rules**
Add	x_i^T x_i^F	$y_i^T + x_i^F \to \emptyset$ $y_i^F + x_i^T \to \emptyset$ $y_{j\to i}^T + x_i^F \to \emptyset$ $y_{j\to i}^F + x_i^T \to \emptyset$

(b)

Theorem 1. *Threshold formulas (TF) can be computed with multiple-input relaxation by a step CRN with only $(2,0)$ rules with upper bounds of $O(G)$ species, $O(D)$ steps, and $O(G)$ volume.*

Proof. Each gate of a TF is represented by a constant number of species, resulting in $O(G)$ unique species. All gates at a given depth level are computed simultaneously in constant steps. Computing a TF therefore requires $O(D)$ steps.

It is possible not all species that are no longer needed after computing a specific gate are deleted. For example, computing an AND gate with three false inputs leaves two of those species in the configuration. While this does not cause computation errors, the volume will increase. Therefore, it is possible for only a fraction of the $O(G)$ species added throughout the simulation to be deleted, resulting in $O(G)$ volume. $\qquad\square$

4   Computation of TCs with Exponential Volume

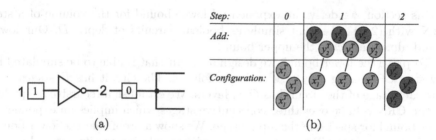

(a)   (b)

Fig. 4. (a) A NOT gate with a fan-out of three. (b) Computing the NOT gate in Fig. 4a in (2, 0) rules.

In this section, we slightly alter the approach presented in Sect. 3 to enable computation of Threshold Circuits (TC). We show in Sect. 4.1 how modifying our volume to be exponentially-sized allows the system to account for unbounded fan-out outside of the first depth level, enabling the computation of TCs. Theorem 2 shows our system computes TCs with $O(G)$ species, $O(D)$ steps, and $O(GF_{out}{}^{D})$ volume.

4.1   Threshold Circuit Computation

Here, we demonstrate how to account for unbounded fan-out when computing TCs, and show the computational complexity of computing TCs with our system.

Bits and Gates. Section 3.1 shows how input bits, output bits, and indexing are represented. Individual gates and depth traversal are computed using the same methods shown in Sects. 3.2 and 3.4, respectively.

Unbounded Fan-Out. To allow the output of a gate at index i to fan-out $k > 1$, such as in the NOT gate shown in Fig. 4a, the count of the species added for all the gates whose output eventually fans into gate i should be multiplied by k. The gate computes all input species concurrently with each other, and result in the gate's output species being equivalent in quantity to the fan-out. Figure 4b shows an example of this process for a NOT gate with a fan-out of three.

Unbounded Fan-Out Example. Consider an AND gate with a fan-in and fan-out of two. Let the two input bits be true and false. To compute the gate with the correct amount of fan-out, our system's initial configuration consists of two copies of each input species (x_1^T, x_1^F, x_2^F, and x_2^F). We then apply the relevant rules to the configuration. Afterwards, we are left with two copies of $y_{2\to1}^F$.

Theorem 2. *Threshold circuits (TC) can be computed with multiple-input relaxation by a step CRN with only (2, 0) rules with upper bounds of $O(G)$ species, $O(D)$ steps, and $O(GF_{out}{}^D)$ volume.*

5   Exponential Volume Lower Bound for Gate-Wise Simulation

In this section, we derive an exponential lower bound for the volume of a step CRN with $(2,0)$ rules that simulates boolean circuits of depth D. Our lower bound almost matches the upper bound.

To prove the lower bound, we design a circuit that is able to be simulated by any step CRN using only $(2,0)$ rules as follows. The circuit has D stages such that each stage of the circuit has $O(1)$ layers. We establish a recursive inequality for the CRN volume over three consecutive stages which implies an exponential lower bound for species in the input stage. We show a proof that the lower bound of volume in a step CRN that uses gate-wise simulation to simulate a boolean circuit with only $(2,0)$ rules is $2^{\Omega(D)}$.

Definition 5. *A step CRN uses* gate-wise simulation *to simulate a circuit $V(\cdot)$ if each gate g is assigned $c_{1,g}$ copies of species 1_g, which represents output 1, and $c_{0,g}$ copies of 0_g, which represents output 0. When gate g computes an output, it will be either $c_{1,g}$ copies of species 1_g for the case 1, or $c_{0,g}$ copies of species 0_g for the case 0. We define $C(g) = c_{1,g} + c_{0,g}$ to be the number of species used for gate g. There is a special case that g is one of the input bits (source gates with fan-in 0) that satisfies $c_{1,g} = 0$ or $c_{0,g} = 0$, as each input bit is either 0 or 1. Let a step CRN have k steps $0, 1, \cdots, k-1$ as defined in Sect. 2.4. It also satisfies the conditions:*

- *Every gate g enters its complete state at exactly one step i, which is denoted by $complete(g) = i$. After step i, the system releases $c_{a,g}$ copies of species a_g and removes all copies of species $(1-a)_g$ to represent gate g having the output a. After step $complete(g)$, the system does not generate any additional copy of 1_g or 0_g (it may keep some existing copies of a_g). The output of gate g determines the simulation according to the logic of circuit.*
- *For two different gates g_1 and g_2, if there is a directed path from g_1 to g_2 (g_1's output may affect g_2's output) in the circuit $V(\cdot)$, then $complete(g_1) < complete(g_2)$.*

If a circuit $V(\cdot)$ computes a function $f(x_1, \cdots, x_n) = y_1, \cdots, y_m$ ($\{0,1\}^n \to \{0,1\}^m$) and $V(\cdot)$ is simulated using gate-wise simulation in a step CRN, define $1_{f(\cdot),i}$ to represent the case y_i to be 1 and $0_{f(\cdot),i}$ to represent the case y_i to be 0.

By Definition 5, when gate g outputs 1, all the $c_{0,g}$ copies of 0_g are removed and it has $c_{1,g}$ copies of 1_g to enter the next layer of a circuit. The step CRN given in Sect. 4 uses gate-wise simulation to simulate threshold circuits. Our lower bound result in this section shows that the exponential volume is required.

Lemma 1. *Assume that a step CRN with $(2,0)$ rules simulates a circuit $V(\cdot)$. Let $b \in \{1_g, 0_g\}$ be the output species. If one copy of a species is removed or added, it results in at most one difference in the number of copies of species b.*

Lemma 2. *Let $f(x_1, \cdots, x_n) = y_1, \cdots, y_m$ be a function $\{0,1\}^n \to \{0,1\}^m$ such that each variable x_i and y_j has a value in $\{0,1\}$. If a step CRN with $(2,0)$ rules computes $f(\cdot)$, and changing variable x_j to $1 - x_j$ will change $y_{i_1}, \cdots, y_{i_t}$ to $1 - y_{i_1}, \cdots, 1 - y_{i_t}$, respectively, then $C(x_j) \geq \sum_{k=1}^{t} C(y_{i_k})$.*

Definition 6. *A list of Boolean circuits $\{H_n(\cdot)\}$ is uniform if there is a Turing machine $M(\cdot)$ such that each $H_n(\cdot)$ can be generated by $M(1^n)$ in a polynomial $p(n)$ steps.*

Theorem 3. *There exist uniform Boolean circuits $\{V_D(x_1, x_2, x_3)\}_{D=1}^{+\infty}$ with each $V_D(x_1, x_2, x_3) : \{0,1\}^3 \to \{0,1\}^3$ s.t. each $V_D(x_1, x_2, x_3)$ has depth $O(D)$, size $O(D)$, 3 output bits, and requires $C(g) = 2^{\Omega(D)}$ for at least one input gate g in a step CRN using gate-wise simulation to simulate $V_D(\cdot)$ with $(2,0)$ rules.*

Proof. We construct a circuit that has $O(D)$ layers. It is built in D stages. Each stage has a circuit of depth $O(1)$ to compute function $s(x_1, x_2, x_3) = y_1 y_2 y_3$. The function $s(\cdot)$ has the properties:

$$s(1,1,1) = 111, \quad (1) \qquad s(0,1,1) = 000, \quad (2) \qquad s(1,0,1) = 011, \quad (3)$$
$$s(1,1,0) = 101, \quad (4) \qquad s(0,0,0) = 110 \quad (5)$$

Define function $s^{(1)}(x_1, x_2, x_3) = s(x_1, x_2, x_3)$ and $s^{(k+1)}(x_1, x_2, x_3) = s(s^{(k)}(x_1, x_2, x_3))$ for all integers $k > 1$. The circuit $V(x_1, x_2, x_3) = s^{(D)}(x_1, x_2, x_3)$. We can also represent the circuit $V(x_1, x_2, x_3) = s^{(D)}(x_1, x_2, x_3) = s_{D-1} \circ s_{D-2} \circ \cdots \circ s_0(x_1, x_2, x_3)$, where $s_i(\cdot)$ represent the function $s(\cdot)$ at stage i. The circuit $V(x_1, x_2, x_3)$, which computes $s^{(D)}(x_1, x_2, x_3)$ links the D circuits $V_s(x_1, x_2, x_3)$ that compute the function $s(x_1, x_2, x_3)$. The three output bits for $s_k(\cdot)$ at stage k become three input bits of $s_{k-1}(\cdot)$ at stage $k - 1$.

Let the output of the circuit be stage 0. The input stage has the largest stage index. Consider the general case. Let $C_k(u)$ be the number of copies of species u in stage k. If u is computed by a gate g, we let $C_k(u) = C(g)$. Let $v_{i,k}$ be the variable v_i at stage k. As we have three output bits $y_{1,0}, y_{2,0}, y_{3,0}$ in the last layer (layer D), each bit $y_{i,0}$ must have a copy of species to represent its $0, 1$-value (see Definition 5). Thus,

$$C_D(y_{1,0}) \geq 1, \ C_D(y_{2,0}) \geq 1, \ C_D(y_{3,0}) \geq 1. \tag{6}$$

When $x_1 x_2 x_3$ is changed from 111 to 011 (by flipping x_1), the output $y_1 y_2 y_3$ is changed from 111 to 000. By Equations (1) and (2) and Lemma 2, we have

$$C_k(x_{1,k}) \geq C_k(y_{1,k}) + C_k(y_{2,k}) + C_k(y_{3,k}). \tag{7}$$

When $x_1 x_2 x_3$ is changed from 111 to 101 (by flipping x_2), the output $y_1 y_2 y_3$ is changed from 111 to 011. By Equations (1) and (3) and Lemma 2, we have Equation 8 below. When $x_1 x_2 x_3$ is changed from 111 to 110 (by flipping x_3), the output $y_1 y_2 y_3$ is changed from 111 to 101. By Equations (1) and (4) and Lemma 2, we have Equation 9 below.

$$C_k(x_{2,k}) \geq C_k(y_{1,k}) \ (8) \qquad\qquad C_k(x_{3,k}) \geq C_k(y_{2,k}) \ (9)$$

When $y_{i,k}$ is equal to $x_{i,k-1}$ as the output of $s_k(\cdot)$ becomes the input of $s_{k-1}(\cdot)$. We have

$$C_k(y_{i,k}) \geq C_{k-1}(x_{i,k-1}) \ \ for \ i = 1, 2, 3. \tag{10}$$

In each stage, the input to the function $s(\cdot)$ can reach all cases $000, 011, 101,$ $110, 111$ by adjusting the 3 input bits of the circuit. When the input is 111, the function $s(\cdot)$ gives the same output 111 at all phases. Through a simple repetition of the above inequalities, we derive a $2^{\Omega(D)}$ volume lower bound.

$$C_k(x_{1,k}) \geq C_{k-1}(x_{1,k-1}) + C_{k-1}(x_{2,k-1}) + C_{k-1}(x_{3,k-1}) (by \ (7), (10)) \ (11)$$
$$\geq C_{k-1}(x_{1,k-1}) + C_{k-1}(y_{1,k-1}) \ \ (by \ inequality \ (8)) \tag{12}$$
$$\geq C_{k-1}(x_{1,k-1}) + C_{k-2}(x_{1,k-2}). \ \ (by \ inequality \ (10)) \tag{13}$$

Let $a_0, a_1, \cdots$ be the Fibonacci series with $a_0 = a_1 = 1$ and recursion $a_k = a_{k-1} + a_{k-2}$ for all $k > 1$. By inequalities (6), (7), and the fact that every input bit affects the output bit in $s(\cdot)$, we have $C_0(x_{1,0}) \geq 1$ and $C_1(x_{1,1}) \geq 1$. This is because when the three input bits are 111, we need bit x_1 to make the output bits 111. By inequality (13), we have $C_k(x_{1,k}) \geq a_k$ for all $k \geq 0$. □

6 Conclusions and Open Problems

In this paper we show how bimolecular void rules, a subset of reaction rules with low power compared to traditional CRNs, become capable of computing threshold formulas and circuits in the step CRN model under gate-wise simulation. We also prove that simulating circuits under this technique requires an exponential lower bound volume that matches the upper bound of our construction methods.

These results naturally lead to some promising future research directions. One approach is constructing another method for simulating threshold circuits under only (2,0) rules. A more general simulation technique could have the benefit of computing circuits without the exponential-sized volume gate-wise simulation requires. Furthermore, our step CRN definition requires the system to reach a terminal configuration before moving to the next step. Relaxing this definition so that a system may reach a step without entering a terminal configuration can make the model more valuable to general CRNs, where reachability to a terminal configuration is not guaranteed.

References

1. Alaniz, R.M., et al.: Reachability in restricted chemical reaction networks. arXiv preprint arXiv:2211.12603 (2022)
2. Anderson, R., et al.: Computing threshold circuits with void reactions in step chemical reaction networks. arXiv preprint arXiv:2402.08220 (2024)
3. Angluin, D., Aspnes, J., Diamadi, Z., Fischer, M.J., Peralta, R.: Computation in networks of passively mobile finite-state sensors. Distrib. Comput. 18(4), 235–253 (2006)
4. Angluin, D., Aspnes, J., Eisenstat, D.: A simple population protocol for fast robust approximate majority. Distrib. Comput. 21, 87–102 (2008)
5. Angluin, D., Aspnes, J., Eisenstat, D., Ruppert, E.: The computational power of population protocols. Distrib. Comput. (2007)
6. Aris, R.: Prolegomena to the rational analysis of systems of chemical reactions. Ration. Mech. Anal. 19(2), 81–99 (1965)
7. Aris, R.: Prolegomena to the rational analysis of systems of chemical reactions II. Some addenda. Ration. Mech. Anal. 27(5), 356–364 (1968)
8. Arkin, A., Ross, J.: Computational functions in biochemical reaction networks. Biophys. J . 67(2), 560–578 (1994)
9. Beiki, Z., Dorabi, Z.Z., Jahanian, A.: Real parallel and constant delay logic circuit design methodology based on the dna model-of-computation. Microprocess. Microsyst. 61, 217–226 (2018)
10. Cardelli, L., Csikász-Nagy, A.: The cell cycle switch computes approximate majority. Sci. Rep. 2(1), 656 (2012)
11. Cardelli, L., Kwiatkowska, M., Whitby, M.: Chemical reaction network designs for asynchronous logic circuits. Nat. Comput. 17, 109–130 (2018)
12. Chen, H.L., Doty, D., Soloveichik, D.: Deterministic function computation with chemical reaction networks. Nat. Comput. 13(4), 517–534 (2014)
13. Cook, M., Soloveichik, D., Winfree, E., Bruck, J.: Programmability of chemical reaction networks. In: Algorithmic Bioprocesses, pp. 543–584 (2009)
14. Dalchau, N., Chandran, H., Gopalkrishnan, N., Phillips, A., Reif, J.: Probabilistic analysis of localized DNA hybridization circuits. ACS Synth. Biol. 4(8), 898–913 (2015)
15. Ellis, S.J., Klinge, T.H., Lathrop, J.I.: Robust chemical circuits. Biosystems 186, 103983 (2019)
16. Eshra, A., El-Sayed, A.: An odd parity checker prototype using dnazyme finite state machine. IEEE/ACM Trans. Comput. Biol. Bioinf. 11(2), 316–324 (2013)
17. Fan, D., Fan, Y., Wang, E., Dong, S.: A simple, label-free, electrochemical DNA parity generator/checker for error detection during data transmission based on "aptamer-nanoclaw"-modulated protein steric hindrance. Chem. Sci. 9(34), 6981–6987 (2018). https://doi.org/10.1039/C8SC02482K

18. Fan, D., Wang, J., Han, J., Wang, E., Dong, S.: Engineering DNA logic systems with non-canonical DNA-nanostructures: basic principles, recent developments and bio-applications. Sci. China Chem. **65**(2), 284–297 (2022)
19. Jiang, H., Riedel, M.D., Parhi, K.K.: Digital logic with molecular reactions. In: International Confernce on Computer-Aided Design (ICCAD) (ICCAD 2013), pp. 721–727 (2013)
20. Karp, R.M., Miller, R.E.: Parallel program schemata. J. Comput. Syst. Sci. **3**(2), 147–195 (1969)
21. Lin, Y.C., Jiang, J.H.R.: Mining biochemical circuits from enzyme databases via Boolean reasoning. In: 39th International Conference on Computer-Aided Design, pp. 1–9 (2020)
22. Magri, D.C.: A fluorescent and logic gate driven by electrons and protons. New J. Chem. **33**(3), 457–461 (2009)
23. Mailloux, S., Guz, N., Zakharchenko, A., Minko, S., Katz, E.: Majority and minority gates realized in enzyme-biocatalyzed systems integrated with logic networks and interfaced with bioelectronic systems. J. Phys. Chem. B **118**(24), 6775–6784 (2014). https://doi.org/10.1021/jp504057u
24. Petri, C.A.: Kommunikation mit Automaten. Ph.D. thesis, Rheinisch-Westfälischen Institutes für Instrumentelle Mathematik an der Universität Bonn (1962)
25. Qian, L., Winfree, E.: Scaling up digital circuit computation with DNA strand displacement cascades. Science **332**(6034), 1196–1201 (2011)
26. Qian, L., Winfree, E.: A simple dna gate motif for synthesizing large-scale circuits. J. R. Soc. Interface **8**(62), 1281–1297 (2011)
27. Soloveichik, D., Cook, M., Winfree, E., Bruck, J.: Computation with finite stochastic chemical reaction networks. Nat. Comput. **7**(4), 615–633 (2008)
28. Thachuk, C., Winfree, E., Soloveichik, D.: Leakless DNA strand displacement systems. In: 21st International Conference on DNA Computing and Molecular Programming (DNA 2015), pp. 133–153. Springer (2015)
29. Winfree, E.: Chemical reaction networks and stochastic local search. In: 25th International Conference on DNA Computing and Molecular Programming (DNA 2019), pp. 1–20 (2019)
30. Xiao, W., Zhang, X., Zhang, Z., Chen, C., Shi, X.: Molecular full adder based on DNA strand displacement. IEEE Access **8**, 189796–189801 (2020)

High Quality Circuit-Based 3-SAT Mappings for Oscillator Ising Machines

Venkata Pavan Sumanth Sikhakollu[1]([⊠])[iD], Shreesha Sreedhara[1][iD],
Rajit Manohar[2][iD], Alan Mishchenko[1], and Jaijeet Roychowdhury[1][iD]

[1] University of California Berkeley, Berkeley, CA 94720, USA
{pavan_sumanth,shreesha_sreedhara,alanmi,jr}@eecs.berkeley.edu
[2] Yale University, New Haven, CT 06520, USA
rajit.manohar@yale.edu

Abstract. 3-SAT is a class of NP-hard combinatorial optimization problems that Ising machines have had difficulty solving successfully. Solution success rate depends not only on the choice of Ising machine, but crucially, also on the mapping from 3-SAT to Ising form. We evaluate the performance of Oscillator Ising Machines (OIMs) on several existing 3-SAT-to-Ising mappings, finding that they yield mediocre or poor results. We propose two novel enhancements to logic-synthesis-based Ising mapping schemes that improve solution success rate significantly (from 0% to about 56% on SATLIB's uf20 problem set). We then propose a new circuit- and clause-based 3-SAT-to-Ising mapping scheme that employs 3-input OR gates. Using this mapping increases OIM's success rate on uf20 to 95.9%—we believe this is by far the best raw performance achieved on any 3-SAT problem class by any Ising machine scheme. We also present a comparison of OIM *vs.* simulated annealing on Ising-mapped 3-SAT problems, revealing that OIM's performance is significantly superior.

Keywords: Ising Machine · Oscillator Ising Machine · 3-SAT · Combinatorial Optimization · Ising Mapping

1 Introduction

In recent years, Ising machines (IMs) have emerged as promising hardware solvers for finding optimal or near-optimal solutions to combinatorial optimization (CO) problems [20]. Several IM schemes have been proposed, each leveraging specialized hardware for addressing CO problems. Notable examples include Quantum Annealers [3,14] that use qubits as spins, Coherent Ising Machines [10,11] that use modulated optical pulses to represent spins, and various other analog-based IMs [5,6]. Among these, Oscillator-based Ising Machines [25] stand out due to their cost-effectiveness, low energy consumption, and the ability to be fabricated on-chip using CMOS technologies. Importantly, they also produce high-quality results on various combinatorial problems [21,22,25].

© The Author(s), under exclusive license to Springer Nature Switzerland AG 2024
D.-J. Cho and J. Kim (Eds.): UCNC 2024, LNCS 14776, pp. 269–285, 2024.
https://doi.org/10.1007/978-3-031-63742-1_19

In practice, CO problems require translation into Ising form to be implementable on Ising hardware. While some problem classes, such as MAX-CUT, have straightforward Ising mappings, mappings of many other problems are complex, requiring additional spins to represent the CO problem [17]. To fully leverage the advantages of analog Ising solvers, the CO problem class should feature an efficient Ising mapping that remains scalable even as problem size increases, while also adhering to hardware-related constraints such as sparsity and coupling resolution. As we demonstrate in this paper, the optimization performance of the IM is highly sensitive to the mapping used, underscoring the importance of selecting an appropriate mapping.

In this paper, we will analyze IMs for solving the *Boolean satisfiability (SAT)* problem. The SAT problem stands as one of the most fundamental and extensively studied problems in computer science. SAT has far-reaching implications in various fields, including formal verification, artificial intelligence, and optimization. In this study, we mainly focus on the translation of 3-SAT problems to Ising form and their solution by OIM, with comparisons against simulated annealing (SA). Applying our proposed techniques to the uf20 benchmark sourced from SATLIB [1], we achieve very good results, surpassing any other IM to the best of our knowledge, while consuming similar hardware and computational resources compared to other mappings.

The main contributions of this paper can be outlined as follows. First, we propose two techniques aimed at improving the performance of OIM on 3-SAT by leveraging logic-synthesis-based Ising mapping methods [13,23]. These enhancements result in a significant increase in the average success rate for uf20 problems, rising from 0% to 55.6%. Secondly, we present a simple yet novel circuit-based mapping approach utilizing 3-input OR Ising gates. As detailed in subsequent sections, this mapping achieves the highest average success rate of 95.9% for uf20 problems among various mapping schemes documented in the literature. Lastly, we conduct a comparative analysis between the performance of OIM and SA, demonstrating the superiority of OIM in solving 3-SAT instances. Note that all the results presented in the paper are based on simulations.

The remainder of the paper is organized as follows. Section 2.1 provides an overview of the Ising model. Section 2.2 outlines the 3-SAT problem. Existing methods for transforming a 3-SAT instance into an Ising network are discussed in Sect. 3. Our novel approaches that yield improved results are presented in Sect. 4. In Sect. 5, we discuss the proposed novel 3OR mapping technique. Finally, Sect. 6 contains a comparative analysis of our results with other mapping techniques.

2 Background

2.1 The Ising Model

The Ising model is a physics-oriented formalism that was first devised for explaining domain formation in ferro-magnets [12]. It comprises a group of discrete variables $\{s_i\}$, referred to as spins, each taking a binary value ± 1, such that an associated "energy function" known as the Ising Hamiltonian is minimized. The Ising Hamiltonian is given by

$$H \triangleq - \sum_{1 \leq i < j \leq n} J_{ij} \cdot s_i \cdot s_j - \sum_{i=1}^{n} h_i \cdot s_i, \qquad (1)$$

where n is the number of spins; $\{J_{ij}\}$ and $\{h_i\}$ are real coefficients. To accommodate the second summation term (known as "magnetic field" or "Zeeman effect" terms) within the first summation term (quadratic in spins), an extra spin can be introduced with its value fixed at "+1". We term this additional spin the REF spin.

Finding the ground state[1] of the Ising model is a classic example of a combinatorial optimization problem. All of Karp's 21 NP-complete CO problems can be mapped to the Ising model by assigning appropriate values to the coefficients [15]. Physical systems that can directly minimize the Ising Hamiltonian are termed Ising machines [3,10,11,14].

Oscillator Ising Machines (OIMs): When an oscillator with a natural frequency f_0 experiences a small periodic external input at a frequency $f_1 \approx f_0$, the oscillator's response can lock on to the input in both frequency and phase [2]. This phenomenon is called injection locking, or more precisely, fundamental harmonic injection locking (FHIL). Sub-harmonic injection locking (SHIL) is a related phenomenon in which an oscillator is perturbed by a periodic input at approximately twice its natural frequency, say $2f_1$. This external signal, known as a synchronization signal (SYNC), causes the oscillator to lock to exactly half the frequency of SYNC, i.e., f_1, and feature bistable phase locks separated by 180° [19]. Consequently, the oscillator functions as a logic latch capable of storing a phase-based binary bit.

It has been shown in [25] that a network of coupled oscillators under SHIL can function as an Ising machine. The dynamics of the network of coupled oscillators with SYNC inputs to each oscillator are described by the generalized Kuramoto equation [24]. However, in a simplified scenario where the oscillations are sinusoidal, and with other approximations, the dynamics can be modeled using the Kuramoto model [24], i.e.,

$$\frac{d}{dt}\phi_i(t) = -K_c \sum_j J_{ij} \cdot \sin(\phi_i(t) - \phi_j(t)) - K_s \cdot \sin(2\phi_i(t)) + K_n \cdot \xi_i(t). \qquad (2)$$

In (2), $\{J_{ij}\}$ are the weights of oscillator couplings; the underlying combinatorial optimization problem is encoded in these weights. The operation of oscillator-based Ising machines modeled by (2) is controlled by several parameters: K_c, a scalar representing the coupling strength; K_s, a scalar modeling the coupling strength from SYNC; and K_n, a scalar representing the magnitude of noise $\xi_i(t)$, which is a Gaussian white noise with zero mean. While K_c, K_s, and K_n can all be

---

[1] The term "ground state" means a state that achieves the minimum Hamiltonian.

time-varying, resulting in various "annealing profiles", our experiments indicate that varying K_s significantly affects the performance of the OIM, whereas the others do not have much impact.

K_s **Parameter Cycling:** A periodic square pulse is assumed for the K_s parameter, alternating between a positive high value and a negative low value over a certain time period. It is important to note that if K_s is static at high positive value, then the oscillator phases will settle to either 0 or π after a few oscillator cycles [25]. Essentially, this means that for each cycle of K_s, we have one set of settled phases. Due to dynamics and noise, the settled phases may not be the same in the next K_s cycle. Therefore, after initializing the OIM, for N K_s cycles, we obtain N samples. These samples are then utilized to evaluate whether the OIM has effectively solved the underlying Ising problem, $i.e.$, settled to the minimum Hamiltonian or possibly a nearby value.

2.2   The Satisfiability Problem: 3-SAT

Given a Boolean formula, the goal of the satisfiability problem is to determine whether there exists an assignment of truth values to variables that evaluates the given Boolean formula to "true". The SAT problem is a classically difficult NP-Hard CO problem [15] with a wide variety of practical applications [18], and it can be transformed into any other NP-complete problem through a polynomial-time transformation [15].

SAT problems are often expressed in Conjunctive Normal Form (CNF), where the Boolean formula is given as a conjunction of multiple clauses, with each clause representing a disjunction of k literals or their negations. This formulation is known as k-SAT, and in the case where $k=3$, it is specifically referred to as 3-SAT. A Boolean function $f()$ expressed in CNF form with 3 literals in each clause takes the form

$$f(x_1, x_2, \cdots, x_n) = C_1 \wedge C_2 \wedge \cdots \wedge C_m,$$
$$\text{with } C_i = x_p \vee x_q \vee x_r; \ p, q, r \in [1, n], 1 \le i \le m, \tag{3}$$

where n is the number of input variables, m is the number of clauses, C_i represents the ith clause, and x_p represents the pth input variable. f is deemed satisfiable if there exists a set of input assignments from $\{0,1\}^n$ such that $f(x_1, x_2, \cdots, x_n)$ evaluates to 1. The 3-SAT problem can be formulated in Ising form using various formulations, as described in the Sect. 3.

3   SAT to Ising Transformation

In this section, we discuss several prior 3SAT-to-Ising formulations. SAT-to-Ising transformations can be broadly categorized into two types: circuit-based transformations and generic transformations. A circuit-based transformation directly maps the structure of the Boolean circuit representing the SAT problem onto an Ising model, preserving the logical relationships and dependencies inherent to the circuit. Unlike generic transformations, which operate at the clause level, circuit-based transformations can map any SAT expression, not just those in CNF form. The MIS-based [8] and Chancellor [7] formulation can be considered generic mappings, while logic-synthesis-based mappings [23] are circuit-based.

3.1 MIS^{3m}-Based Formulation

The maximal independent set (MIS) formulation, also known as the Choi formulation [8], provides a translation of 3-SAT to Ising by assigning one Ising spin for each literal. For a 3-SAT instance with m clauses and n variables, the Choi formulation requires a total of $3m$ spins, excluding the REF spin. In this formulation, the literals within each clause are interconnected in a triangular configuration. Additionally, conflicting edges are established between two literals that represent negated versions of the same variable. The triangular structure aims to satisfy the SAT condition, while the conflicting edges penalize dissimilar assignments for the same variable.

It is worth noting that in the context of the OIM, if different values are assigned to spins copies representing the same variable, conventionally this would be considered illegitimate. However, to achieve more effective results, we relaxed this condition by adopting a majority vote approach among spins to assign the variable value [9].

3.2 The Chancellor^{n+m} Mapping

The Chancellor formulation [7] maps an n-variable m-clause instance using $n+m$ Ising spins, excluding the REF spin. The formulation establishes a 1-1 correspondence between the n SAT variables and the first n Ising spins and introduces one additional Ising spin for each of the m clauses.

3.3 Logic-Synthesis-Based Mapping

A detailed logic-synthesis-based SAT to Ising mapping is described in [13], which is inspired by [23]; a concise summary is provided in this section. Logic-synthesis-based transformation is circuit based and follows the flow shown in Fig. 1. First, the given 3-SAT problem in CNF is converted to a Boolean circuit using logic synthesis. Subsequently, the Boolean circuit is transformed into an Ising network by replacing each Boolean gate in the circuit with its Ising equivalent.

Logic synthesis is the process of converting a high-level (*e.g.*, CNF, RTL) description of a digital circuit into a lower-level representation composed of logic gates, such as AND, OR, and NOT gates, optimizing factors like performance, area, and power consumption. Widely available logic-synthesis tools (such as ABC [4]) utilize a user-specified gate library to synthesize a Boolean circuit for a given CNF. There is ample room for optimization at the synthesis stage, where, depending on the problem, one can control the number of gates, the gate depth, the fan-ins/outs of the gates, *etc.*, in the resulting Boolean network.

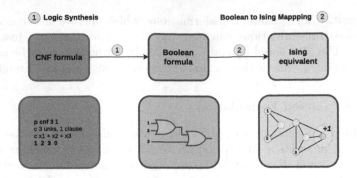

Fig. 1. Converting a CNF instance to an Ising instance.

These optimizations can be useful for hardware feasibility (*e.g.*, fan-ins/outs affect connection sparsity), but at the same time, can significantly impact the performance of the Ising machine.

After synthesis, each logic gate is converted into Ising form using its corresponding *Ising equivalent* network. In this network, the inputs and the output of each logic gate are represented by Ising spins. Coupling weights between the spins are carefully chosen to correspond to the specific type of logic gate in question (*e.g.*, see Fig. 2). The crucial property of these Ising equivalent gates is that if the gate's input-output spins satisfy the corresponding Boolean relationship, then the Hamiltonian of the Ising equivalent network reaches its global minimum. For any other spin combination, the Hamiltonian is strictly above the global minimum. Importantly, this property extends to arbitrary interconnections of these Ising equivalent gates. Thus, the Hamiltonian of the synthesized network achieves its global minimum if, and only if, the logical relationships of all the gates in the network are satisfied.

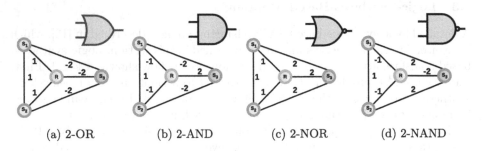

Fig. 2. Ising equivalent networks for 2-input Boolean gates; R is REF/+1 signal.

To enforce the SAT condition, *the output spin in the Ising version of the synthesized network is set to +1* (this is easy to implement in hardware). This constraint ensures that the network's minimum Hamiltonian solutions automatically correspond to SAT solutions. Unlike many other combinatorial optimization problem mappings, for SAT, we already know what the minimum Hamiltonian is—since each individual gate's minimum Hamiltonian is known, and these are simply summed to find the global minimum. We use this information to determine whether the settled spin state is SAT or not. The Ising machine (IM) assumes the problem is SAT and attempts to find the corresponding set of inputs. If the Hamiltonian for the settled spins is not the same as the global minimum, then the IM deems the problem as UNSAT. Therefore, **if the IM indicates that the problem is SAT, then it is indeed SAT. However, if it indicates that the problem is UNSAT, then it may or may not be UNSAT.**

OIM with ABC Mapping: ABC is a widely used open-source tool for logic synthesis and formal verification of digital circuits. It offers a suite of algorithms and techniques for optimizing and verifying designs, making it a valuable resource for hardware designers. ABC can directly process CNF files and synthesize Boolean circuits based on user preferences, such as controlling the depth of the Boolean circuit or limiting fan-in/out. Since we have utilized ABC for logic-synthesis-based mapping, we refer to this mapping as the **ABC mapping**.

The performance of OIM with ABC-mapped 3-SAT problems is good for very small-scale SAT problems. However, it encounters notable challenges with larger instances, such as DIMACS uf-20 problems (see Sect. 6). To enhance performance, the present work introduces two novel ideas, discussed in the following sections.

Success Rate: A metric termed the *success rate* is important for assessing OIM performance on SAT problems. To calculate the success rate of OIM on a problem, we execute OIM on the problem many times with random initial conditions and the fraction of runs resulting in success determines the success rate. For a given Ising-mapped SAT instance, we begin the OIM simulation with random initial conditions for oscillator phases. Following the procedure outlined in Sect. 2.1, we cycle the K_s parameter. Throughout our simulations, we maintain a standard of 100 cycles of K_s, ensuring consistency across all reported experiments in this paper. This yields 100 sets of settled oscillator phase samples per simulation. A simulation is considered successful if at least one of these samples achieves the global minimum Hamiltonian or, equivalently, satisfies the SAT condition.

4   Level-Based Gate Scaling (LGS)

As outlined in the previous section, the objective of an Ising machine is to minimize the system's "energy", or more precisely the Hamiltonian, as defined in (1). In the context of SAT, the problem is deemed satisfiable only if each Ising gate within the Ising equivalent network maintains a logically consistent input-output pairing, which ensures that the Ising Hamiltonian of the Ising equivalent network is the minimum possible.

In cases where the problem remains unsolved, indicating logically inconsistent gates in the overall Ising network, we argue that it is preferable to have these logically inconsistent gates closer to the inputs than to the output. To understand why, consider two scenarios: one where the inconsistent gate is close to the output and another where it is close to the primary inputs. If the gate is closer to the inputs, then the number of primary inputs that affect the input-set of the inconsistent gate is relatively small compared to the other case, *i.e.*, when the gate is far from the inputs. For example, in a "balanced" circuit with 2-input gates, the number of primary inputs affecting the output of a gate that is at a distance of m from the primary inputs is 2^m; so, the smaller the m, the smaller the number of critical primary inputs. Therefore, the Hamming distance (number of positions at which corresponding bits are different) from the actual SAT solution can be expected to be less when the erring gate is closer to the inputs. If the solution given by the OIM is close to the actual solution (smaller Hamming distance), then we can potentially improve the OIM result by using local search algorithms like single bit flip search. Hence, inconsistent gates closer to the primary inputs lead to better solutions. However, *the Hamiltonian achieved by the OIM is the same regardless of where in the circuit the inconsistent gate is located.*

To address this problem, we propose *scaling the Hamiltonian contribution of gates* in the network based on their "proximity" from the primary inputs, or alternatively, their proximity to the output. Higher priorities are assigned to gates closer to the output. While traditionally, the digital design literature measures levels from the primary inputs, we adopt a perspective where levels are measured from the output. The gate attached to the global output is assigned level 0. A gate is assigned level n if its output net serves as an input to a gate of level $(n-1)$. In cases where a gate is connected to multiple gates, priority is given to the one closest to the output. For example, in Fig. 3, gate G_1's output net is connected to a *level-1* gate, hence G_1 is considered a *level-2* gate. Gate G_2's output net is connected to gates at *level-2* and *level-3*; therefore, G_2 is considered a *level-3* gate because *level-2* is closer to the output and receives priority.

We use the term $sizing^2$ to refer to scaling all the edge weights within the Ising equivalent network of a particular gate. In Fig. 4b, a size-K OR gate is depicted. Scaling an Ising equivalent gate by a factor of K implies that the Hamiltonian contribution of that Ising gate is also scaled by K. For example, the minimum Hamiltonian for an unscaled 2-input OR gate is *-3*; if scaled by $K=3$, the minimum Hamiltonian become -9. As discussed in Sect. 2.1, the dynamics of OIM tend to minimize the Hamiltonian of the network. Therefore, OIM will tend to solve the scaled gates correctly, even at the expense of the unscaled ones. This stems from the fact that resolution of scaled gates yields a more significant reduc-

---

[2] Note that sizing in this context does not mean physical scaling.

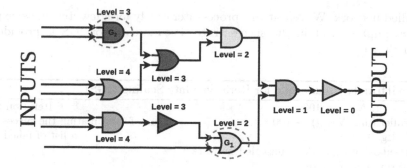

Fig. 3. An example network depicting the concept of gate level.

tion in the Hamiltonian, compared to unscaled/weakly-scaled ones. Therefore, **by applying a scaling function that decreases monotonically with the gate's level**, we encourage OIM to solve gates at the nth level, even if it necessitates not satisfying those at $(n+1)^{th}$ level. As a result, this mechanism facilitates the migration of logically inconsistent gates towards inputs, since gates closer to the inputs have smaller scales, thus leading to solutions closer to SAT in terms of Hamming distance.

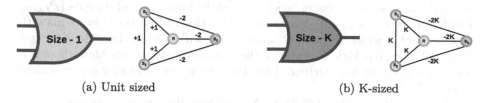

(a) Unit sized   (b) K-sized

Fig. 4. Ising representation of 2-input OR gates; R represents the REF/+1 signal.

4.1 Iterative Gate Scaling (IGS)

The integration of OIM with ABC mapping using the level-based gate scaling (LGS) above suggests an iterative approach for solving SAT problems. As discussed previously, simply scaling a gate to be larger relative to the others effectively drives the scaled gate towards the correct input-output state. If we can identify the gates that are prone to failure, we can up-size these gates to potentially improve the success rate (defined in Sect. 3.3) of OIM on a particular problem. To find gates prone to failure, we simply use OIM and detect which gates are not logically consistent.

We start with an unscaled Ising network and run OIM on this network to identify the failed gates. Then, we up-size these gates and rerun OIM on the modified network. We repeat this process iteratively for a few iterations, expecting an improvement in the success rate. Pseudo-code for IGS is provided in Algorithm 1.

Algorithm 1. Pseudocode for Iterative Gate Scaling (IGS)

$iter \leftarrow 1$, $N_{iter} \leftarrow 100$ ▷ Iteration count
parallel_runs($N_{S,est}$) $\leftarrow 100$ ▷ #runs for estimating the success rate
failed_gates $\leftarrow \{\}$ ▷ list of failed gates
current_Ising_network $\leftarrow$ unscaled_network
while iter $\leq N_{iter}$ **do**
     run OIM on current_Ising_network $N_{S,est}$ times
     failed_gates $\leftarrow$ {collection of all failed gates in this iteration across runs}
     for gate in failed_gates **do**
         gate.scale $\leftarrow$ gate.scale + K · (1 - S) · P$_f$, *gate*
                          ▷ S : success rate; P$_f$: failure rate
     end for
     current_Ising_network $\leftarrow$ network_with_updated_gate_scale
end while

Gate-Scale Update Step: The update step in Algorithm 1 involves two quantities: the success rate of the network (S) and the failure rate of the gate ($P_{f,\text{gate}}$). The failure rate of a gate G is equal to the fraction of runs (used to estimate the success rate) in which the gate G is faulty. We will increase the scale of the gate if the failure rate is high. However, if the success rate is already high, there is no point in scaling the gate further. Therefore, the update quantity is proportional to $(1 - S) \cdot P_{f,\text{gate}}$.

We tested IGS on the *uf20-02* 3-SAT problem; the results are shown in Fig. 5. Initially, in Fig. 5a, all gates in the ABC-mapped network are of unit size. After 80 iterations, as depicted in Fig. 5b, we observe that the sizes of gates closer to the output are larger, which is consistent with the discussion in Sect. 4. Note that, in Fig. 5c, the success rate improves and eventually saturates at close to 90% with iterations.

While IGS appears valuable for increasing the success rate, note that one needs to run the problem several times, updating the weights in between. From a hardware implementation standpoint, the time and overall energy consumption for solving the problem scale with the product of the number of iterations (N_{iter}) and the number of times the problem is executed to estimate success rate ($N_{S,\text{est}}$). Nevertheless, this approach can be a valuable addition to the repertoire of mappings to solve SAT problems.

5 3OR-Based Ising Mapping

In this section, we present $3OR^{n+m}$, a 3SAT-to-Ising transformation technique that requires $n+m$ spins, excluding the REF spin. The number of spins required

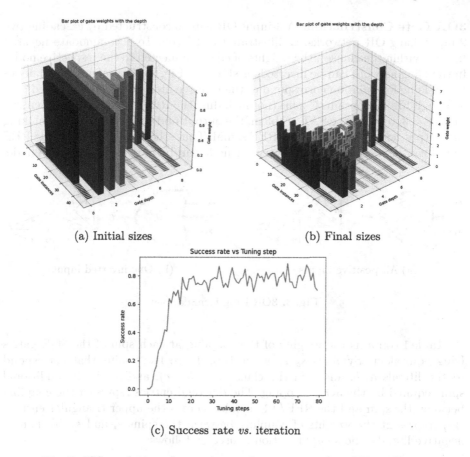

(a) Initial sizes   (b) Final sizes

(c) Success rate *vs.* iteration

Fig. 5. IGS: evolution of gate sizes and success rate for uf-02 problem.

is the same as that for Chancellor^{n+m} mapping. However, the new 3OR mapping yields superior results with OIM (see Sect. 6). For each Boolean variable x_i, $0 \le i \le n - 1$, occurring in the 3-SAT instance, we use one spin to encode its Boolean value. Additionally, we need one more spin for every clause in the 3-SAT instance.

Typically, 3-SAT problems are provided in Conjunctive Normal Form (CNF), where each clause consists of the OR of three literals. These clauses collectively feed into an m-input AND gate, where m represents the total number of clauses. This Boolean circuit structure, utilizing 3-input OR gates, provides a natural mapping for the CNF format. To translate the CNF problem into Ising form, this Boolean circuit representation is directly leveraged. Similar to Choi and Chancellor, the 3OR transformation preserves the notion of clauses even on the hardware.

3OR Gate Construction: A 3-input OR gate is constructed by cascading two 2-input Ising OR networks, as illustrated in Fig. 6a. To accommodate negated literals within the clauses, the weights of edges connected to the respective nodes in the Ising network can be inverted, as shown in Fig. 6b. Consequently, all nodes in the Ising formulation correspond to the positive literals. It must be noted that although Fig. 6a contains 5 spins (not including the REF/+1 signal), as discussed in Sect. 3.3, to solve the SAT problem, the output node is forced to "+1", making the output node the same as the REF signal. Thus, the output spin and the REF signal can be merged. Indeed, every +1 node can be merged into a single node.

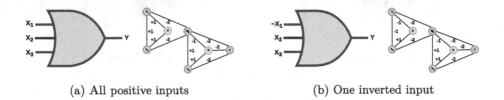

(a) All positive inputs   (b) One inverted input

Fig. 6. 3OR Ising formulations

Table 1 contains the weights of the coupling at each spin of the 3OR gate's Ising equivalent. Symbols s_a, s_b, s_c in Table 1 are Ising spins that correspond to the literals a, b, and c in the clause $(a \vee b \vee c)$, and s_m is the additional spin required by the 3OR mapping. The diagonal entries represent the coupling between the spin and the REF/+1 signal, whereas the upper triangular entries, W_{ij}, represent the weights of coupling between the spins s_i and s_j. To handle negative literals, the *sign()* function is used as follows:

$$\text{sign}(x) = \begin{cases} 1, & \text{if } x \text{ is a positive literal, e.g., } a, \\ -1, & \text{if } x \text{ is a negative literal, e.g., } \bar{a}. \end{cases} \tag{4}$$

For this Ising network, the minimum Hamiltonian is -4, irrespective of the signs of the literals.

Table 1. Coupling weights for different types of clauses $(a \vee b \vee c)$; $H = -4$

	s_a	s_b	s_c	s_m
s_a	sign(a)	sign(a)·sign(b)	0	-2·sign(a)
s_b		sign(b)	0	-2·sign(b)
s_c			$-$sign(c)	sign(c)
s_m				-3

The output node not only serves as the output of the SAT network but also represents the output of the m-input AND gate. Consequently, ensuring the output remains +1 mandates that each input of the AND gate be set to +1. Thus, constraining every clause's output to be +1 is equivalent to implementing an m-input AND gate with the output fixed at +1, making the m-AND implementation redundant.

6 Results

To evaluate the performance of OIM with the various mappings discussed earlier, we used the uf20 dataset of 3-SAT problems from SATLIB [1]. This dataset comprises 1000 randomly generated problems, with each problem referred to as a "3-SAT instance". Each 3-SAT instance consists of 20 variables and contains 91 clauses. We analyze the performance of different mappings using the following criteria.

Spin Count and Connectivity: In the context of solving the problem on hardware, especially IC implementations, an important feature of an efficient mapping is that the mapped Ising problem should use fewer resources, *i.e.*, fewer hardware spins and couplings. In Fig. 7, we show the number of spins and couplings required for uf20 problems with different 3-SAT-Ising mappings. From Fig. 7a, we observe that both Chancellor and 3OR require the minimum number of spins to represent the 3-SAT problem in Ising form. Additionally, Fig. 7b shows that 3OR requires fewer couplings compared to the other mappings. Therefore, of all the mappings, *the 3OR mapping consumes fewer hardware resources to represent the same 3-SAT problem in Ising form.*

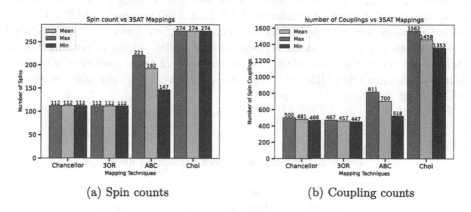

(a) Spin counts   (b) Coupling counts

Fig. 7. Comparison of spins and couplings needed to map uf20 problems into Ising form.

Comparing Mapping Techniques: In this experiment, we assess the effectiveness of various mapping techniques in terms of how easily the OIM can solve a given 3-SAT problem. We primarily consider two criteria to measure the effectiveness of the mappings: the fraction of solved instances and the success rate. To calculate the success rate of an instance, we execute the OIM on the instance 100 times with random initial conditions and record the fraction of runs that result in success, *i.e.*, a SAT solution is found. If the OIM fails to solve the problem in any of these 100 runs, we consider that instance to have failed. In the uf20 dataset, there are 1000 instances. We compute the success rate for all instances and report statistical quantities such as the mean and median for each mapping.

Table 2. Comparison between different mappings.

	Total Instances	Solved Instances	Fraction of Solved Instances	Mean Success Rate	Median Success Rate
ABC (no LGS)	1000	0	0	0	0
ABC (LGS)	1000	999	0.999	0.556	0.58
Choi	1000	990	0.99	0.393	0.29
Chancellor	1000	936	0.936	0.879	1
3OR	1000	**1000**	1	**0.959**	1

From Table 2, it is evident that level-based gate scaling (LGS, Sect. 4) significantly improves the performance of OIM on ABC-mapped 3-SAT instances, with the mean success rate increasing from 0 to 0.556. Overall, 3OR produced the best results, with a mean success rate of 0.959, which is notably higher than other mappings. Considering its requirement of fewer resources and excellent performance with OIM, *the 3OR mapping emerges as the ideal choice for 3SAT-Ising mapping.*

Table 3. Comparison between hardware solvers.

Benchmark	Solver	Total Instances	Solved Instances	Fraction of Solved Instances	Mean Success Rate	Median Success Rate
uf20	SA	1000	**1000**	1	0.587	0.59
uf20	OIM	1000	**1000**	1	**0.959**	1
uf50	SA	1000	920	0.92	0.109	0.07
uf50	OIM	1000	**984**	**0.984**	**0.501**	**0.48**

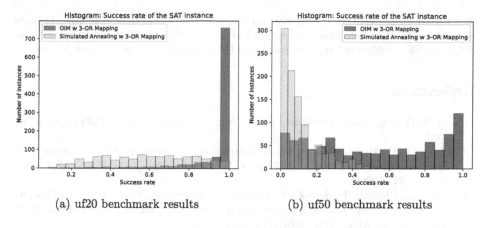

(a) uf20 benchmark results   (b) uf50 benchmark results

Fig. 8. SATLIB benchmark results with 3-OR Ising mapping.

Comparing OIM and SA Using 3OR Mapping: We now compare the effectiveness of the OIM by comparing it to simulated annealing (SA) [16], a well-known method widely used for solving many combinatorial optimization problems. We solve 3OR-mapped uf20 and uf50 SAT problems with both OIM and SA, measure success rates for each problem, and plot a histogram of these in Fig. 8.

From Fig. 8a and 8b, it is evident that the histogram of OIM success rates is heavily weighted towards the right, implying that many uf20/uf50 instances have high success rates. With SA, however, the success rates are very low for most of the problems. As shown in Table 3, OIM achieves much better success rates and was able to solve greater number of instances compared to SA. *This indicates that OIM outperforms SA by a significant margin, highlighting its potential for solving practical and significant combinatorial optimization problems.*

7   Conclusion

In this paper, we introduced two novel techniques to improve the performance of OIM for logic-synthesis-based 3SAT-to-Ising mappings. Additionally, we presented a new circuit-based 3-SAT translation method called 3OR. Despite requiring the same number of spins and a similar number of couplings as the current state-of-the-art Chancellor mapping, we demonstrated that the success rate of OIM is higher with 3OR than with Chancellor. We also showed that OIM outperforms SA when it comes to solving Ising-translated 3-SAT instances.

Why one Ising mapping scheme performs better than another, not only in OIM but in other IM schemes, is poorly understood currently — it is an important direction for further exploration. We hope that empirical results, such as those presented here, will aid in unraveling this central question.

Acknowledgments. We gratefully acknowledge support from the US Defense Advanced Research Projects Agency (DARPA) and the US National Science Foundation (NSF). Additional support was provided by Berkeley's Bakar Prize Award.

References

1. SATLIB benchmark problems. https://www.cs.ubc.ca/~hoos/SATLIB/benchm.html
2. Bhansali, P., Roychowdhury, J.: Gen-Adler: the generalized Adler's equation for injection locking analysis in oscillators. In: Proceedings of the IEEE ASP-DAC, pp. 522–227 (2009)
3. Bian, Z., Chudak, F., Israel, R., Lackey, B., Macready, W.G., Roy, A.: Discrete optimization using quantum annealing on sparse Ising models. Front. Phys. **2**, 56 (2014). https://doi.org/10.3389/fphy.2014.00056
4. Brayton, R., Mishchenko, A.: ABC: an academic industrial-strength verification tool. In: Touili, T., Cook, B., Jackson, P. (eds.) CAV 2010. LNCS, vol. 6174, pp. 24–40. Springer, Heidelberg (2010). https://doi.org/10.1007/978-3-642-14295-6_5
5. Cai, F., et al.: Power-efficient combinatorial optimization using intrinsic noise in memristor Hopfield neural networks. Nature Electron. **3**(7), 409–418 (2020). https://doi.org/10.1038/s41928-020-0436-6
6. Camsari, K.Y., Faria, R., Sutton, B.M., Datta, S.: Stochastic p-bits for invertible logic. Phys. Rev. X **7**, 031014 (2017). https://doi.org/10.1103/PhysRevX.7.031014
7. Chancellor, N., Zohren, S., Warburton, P.A., Benjamin, S.C., Roberts, S.: A direct mapping of max k-SAT and high order parity checks to a chimera graph. Sci. Rep. **6**(1), 37107 (2016)
8. Choi, V.: Adiabatic quantum algorithms for the NP-complete maximum-weight independent set, exact cover and 3SAT problems. arXiv preprint arXiv:1004.2226 (2010)
9. Cılasun, H., et al.: 3SAT on an all-to-all-connected CMOS Ising solver chip. Sci. Rep. **14**, 10757 (2023)
10. Honjo, T., et al.: 100,000-spin coherent Ising machine. Sci. Adv. **7**(40), eabh0952 (2021). https://doi.org/10.1126/sciadv.abh0952
11. Inagaki, T., et al.: A coherent Ising machine for 2000-node optimization problems. Science **354**, 603–606 (2016). https://doi.org/10.1126/science.aah4243
12. Ising, E.: Beitrag zur theorie des ferromagnetismus. Zeitschrift für Physik **31**, 253–258 (1925). https://api.semanticscholar.org/CorpusID:122157319
13. Jagielski, T., Manohar, R., Roychowdhury, J.: FPIM: field-programmable Ising machines for solving SAT. arXiv preprint arXiv:2306.01569 (2023)
14. Johnson, M.W., et al.: Quantum annealing with manufactured spins. Nature **473**(7346), 194–198 (2011). https://doi.org/10.1038/nature10012
15. Karp, R.M.: Reducibility among Combinatorial Problems, pp. 85–103. Springer US, Boston, MA (1972). https://doi.org/10.1007/978-1-4684-2001-2_9
16. Kirkpatrick, S., Gelatt, C.D., Vecchi, M.P.: Optimization by simulated annealing. Science **220**(4598), 671–680 (1983)
17. Lucas, A.: Ising formulations of many NP problems. Front. Phys. **2**, 74887 (2014). https://doi.org/10.3389/fphy.2014.00005
18. Marques-Silva, J.: Practical applications of boolean satisfiability. In: 2008 9th International Workshop on Discrete Event Systems, pp. 74–80 (2008). https://doi.org/10.1109/WODES.2008.4605925

19. Neogy, A., Roychowdhury, J.: Analysis and design of sub-harmonically injection locked oscillators. In: Proceedings of the IEEE DATE (2012)
20. Festa, P., Pardalos, P.M., Resende, M.G.C., Ribeiro, C.C.: Randomized heuristics for the max-cut problem. Optim. Methods Softw. **17**(6), 1033–1058 (2002). https://doi.org/10.1080/1055678021000090033
21. Roychowdhury, J., Wabnig, J., Srinath, K.P.: Performance of Oscillator Ising Machines on Realistic MU-MIMO Decoding Problems. Research Square preprint (Version 1) (2021). Web link to preprint
22. Sreedhara, S., Roychowdhury, J., Wabnig, J., Srinath, P.K.: MU-MIMO Detection Using Oscillator Ising Machines. In: Proceedings of the ICCAD, pp. 1–9 (2023)
23. Su, J., Tu, T., He, L.: A quantum annealing approach for boolean satisfiability problem. In: Proceedings of the IEEE DAC, pp. 1–6 (2016). https://doi.org/10.1145/2897937.2897973
24. Wang, T., Roychowdhury, J.: OIM: oscillator-based Ising machines for solving combinatorial optimisation problems. arXiv:1903.07163 (2019)
25. Wang, T., Roychowdhury, J.: OIM: oscillator-based Ising machines for solving combinatorial optimisation problems. In: Proceedings of the UCNC. LNCS sublibrary: Theoretical Computer Science and General Issues. Springer (2019). https://doi.org/10.1007/978-3-030-19311-9_19

Author Index

D.-J. Cho and J. Kim (Eds.): UCNC 2024, LNCS 14776, pp. 287–288, 2024.
https://doi.org/10.1007/978-3-031-63742-1

Printed in the United States
by Baker & Taylor Publisher Services